Hand of the prince

Manchester University Press

KEY STUDIES IN DIPLOMACY

Series Editors: J. Simon Rofe and Giles Scott-Smith
Emeritus Editor: Lorna Lloyd

The volumes in this series seek to advance the study and understanding of diplomacy in its many forms. Diplomacy remains a vital component of global affairs, and it influences and is influenced by its environment and the context in which it is conducted. It is an activity of great relevance for International Studies, International History, and of course Diplomatic Studies. The series covers historical, conceptual, and practical studies of diplomacy.

To buy or to find out more about the books currently available in this series, please go to: https://manchesteruniversitypress.co.uk/series/key-studies-in-diplomacy/

Hand of the prince

How diplomacy writes subjects, territory, time, and norms

Pablo de Orellana

MANCHESTER UNIVERSITY PRESS

Copyright © Pablo de Orellana 2025

The right of Pablo de Orellana to be identified as the author of this work has been asserted in accordance with the Copyright, Designs and Patents Act 1988.

Published by Manchester University Press
Oxford Road, Manchester, M13 9PL

www.manchesteruniversitypress.co.uk

British Library Cataloguing-in-Publication Data
A catalogue record for this book is available from the British Library

ISBN   978 1 5261 5989 2   hardback

First published 2025

The publisher has no responsibility for the persistence or accuracy of URLs for any external or third-party internet websites referred to in this book, and does not guarantee that any content on such websites is, or will remain, accurate or appropriate.

EU authorised representative for GPSR:
Easy Access System Europe - Mustamäe tee 50, 10621 Tallinn, Estonia
gpsr.requests@easproject.com

Typeset
by Deanta Global Publishing Services, Chennai, India

Talk in song from tongues of lilting grace
Sounds caress my ear
And not a word I heard could I relate
The story was quite clear

Contents

List of figures		*page* viii
Acknowledgements		x
1	Ouverture	1
2	A démarche of meaning: diplomatic practice, identity, and text	29
3	Analysing how diplomatic text describes: a method	57
4	The diplomacy of the First Vietnam War	90
5	The diplomacy of the Western Sahara conflict	147
6	The confessions of the diplomatic text: writing, representation, and the reflection of will	206
7	Epilogue	229
Bibliography		243
Index		270

Figures

1.1 Portrait of (left to right) Duke Cesare Borgia, Cardinal Bandinello Sauli, Segretario della Repubblica di Firenze Niccolò Machiavelli, and Borgia's trusted assassin Michele di Corella, by Sebastiano del Piombo, 1516. Image from Wikimedia Commons. *page* xiv
1.2 A diplomat terribly concerned about accurate diplomatic descriptions. Ernest Satow in 1903, from his book *A Diplomat in Japan*, p. 63. Image from Wikimedia Commons. 10
1.3 The unexpected diplomat on mission. Spanish Navy Captain Adolfo Calles returning to Spain, 1959. Photograph courtesy of the Capitán Adolfo Calles Archive. 13
3.1 Three steps to analyse representation in diplomatic text. Arrows denote where representations (signposted by their topoi) are observed to have crossed over from one text to another. Diagram by Tally de Orellana. 59
3.2 Diagram of step 1 of this method: mapping reporting pathways. Boxes indicate institutions in France, in colonial Indochina, and abroad. Straight lines indicate reporting and instruction pathways. Diagram by Tally de Orellana. 79
3.3 Diagram of step 2 of this method: reading how texts represent subjects and their contexts. Text is from Archive Georges Bidault, AN, author's photographs. Composite diagram by Tally de Orellana. 80
3.4 Diagram of step 3 of this method: tracing the evolution of representations. Photos of documents from AN, MAE, Archive Sainteny, and NARA, author's photographs. Composite diagram by Tally de Orellana. 82

Figures ix

4.1	Diagram of diplomatic knowledge production pathways by institutions studied. Lines denote channels of reporting and instructions. Vertical lines denote hierarchy. Dotted line divides institutions at home, above, from those abroad, below. Diagram by Tally de Orellana.	96
4.2	Map of colonial Indochina showing subdivisions. Image from Wikimedia Commons.	98
4.3	Infographic accompanying an article titled 'Comniform is in sight for Southeastern Asia', *New York Times*, July 1948.	113
4.4	2 September 1945 declaration of Vietnamese independence in Hanoi, photographed by Jean Sainteny. Archive Sainteny.	126
4.5	Diagrammatic summary of the evolution of representations traced from 1948 back to 1945. Diagram by Fey Marin and Tally de Orellana.	129
5.1	Diagram of diplomatic knowledge production pathways by institutions studied. Lines denote channels of reporting and instructions. Vertical lines denote hierarchy. Dotted line divides institutions at home, above, from those abroad, below. Diagram by Tally de Orellana.	153
5.2	Screenshot of map featured in moroccoonthemove.com.	174
5.3	Diagrammatic summary of the evolution of key representations traced from 2010 back to 2003.	188
5.4	8 November 2010: Moroccan police (foreground) and military move to dismantle the protest camp (far background) in al-'Ayun. Note the Moroccan flags and royal portrait. This is one of very few photos of that day's events as the Gendarmerie banned photography, recordings, and journalists. Courtesy of Associazione El Ouali per la libertà del Sahara Occidentale, Italia.	192
6.1	Left: the author about to report to the Segretario di Stato. Right: the offices of the Florentine Republic, including Machiavelli's diplomacy-focused Second Secretariat of State, both at the Palazzo Vecchio. Photographs by Fey Marin, 2023.	207
6.2	Architecture of a representation of Vietminh as analysed in Chapter 4.	211
6.3	Planes of emergence in representations of POLISARIO and Morocco studied in Chapter 5.	212
6.4	Unstable French representations 1945–47.	214
6.5	Stabilisation of French representations from late 1947.	215
6.6	Epistemological constitution of subjectivity in diplomatic text.	218

Acknowledgements

Like diplomats, I am but the most visible part of the work you are holding in your hands. It would not have been possible without the help, assistance, indulgence, and affection of so very many people. Just as diplomacy makes the diplomat visible through the work of hundreds of invisible hands, my name too appears alone on the cover of this book. However, I am only here because so many helped me.

There is no hope of thanking each of you as much as you deserve. Nor am I sure that in my distraction I can truly appreciate what you have done as much as I should. But the kindness given, its importance, and my gratefulness are too great not to try.

Vivienne Jabri, mentor, intellectual pioneer, and inspiration. It is with her that I first began to develop my interest in the very words through which diplomatic knowledge is produced as well as scientific rigour, high expectations about IR theory work, honest hard feedback, and a deep, sincere, and true appreciation of why we do this.

My family. I owe everything to you, and not just in the ways children, siblings, and partners usually do. You have, for decades now, supported me, my ideas, ambitions, intellectual fishing trips, and my love of philosophy. My parents inspired me with authentic intellectual freedom, flair, love of creation, suspicion of intellectual strictures, my mother's exceptional yet kindly drive and thoughtful discipline, and, as my father frequently reflects in his artistic work, the understanding that life itself is at stake in politics. May we all be like you. Tally, my beloved sister, exceptional curator and art thinker, has long indulged my artistic flights of fancy and always ensured my visual explanations made sense. You should be grateful to her too, for she designed the diagrams that help make sense of the analysis in this book. Leoncita, erstwhile partner in mind, body, and ontology: you inspired me every day, fuelled my love of doing this, and, with your endless curiosity, reminded me why it must be done. You were there every day, from first proposal to the day I finished this book and danced all the way home.

Acknowledgements

I have incurred so many intellectual debts that I am certain this word of thanks could only ever be half adequate and, even then, only truly acknowledge far too little of what I owe.

Thanks are due to living intellectual heroes, who at various points gave me advice and encouraged me along the way. My colleagues at the Department of War Studies, King's College London, particularly Mervyn and Lola Frost, Peter Busch, Leonie Ansems de Vries, Flavia Gasbarri, Jack Spence, Didier Bigo, and so many more, including colleagues and partners in intellectual crimes Thomas Bottelier, Claire Yorke, Filippo Costa-Buranelli, and Jill S. Russell, who were the best intellectual environment for an obsessive researcher like myself. A special expression of appreciation and gratefulness is due to Nicholas Michelsen, my partner in researching the history of nationalist ideas, a real intellectual brother and thinker.

I also want to thank quasi-mythical heroes who have made deep impressions on my intellectual life. Michael Shapiro, who a long time ago encouraged me to go all-out on analytically treating political text like literature; Mark Atwood Lawrence, who, never having met me, has always supported my approach to researching diplomacy; Manuele Gragnolati and much-missed Richard Parish, the professors who first introduced me to the magic of language and its analysis. Manuele, I will always hear your voice in my head: 'Focus on the text!'.

Never forgotten, I thank the archivists, assistants, and employees of numerous diplomatic archives that kindly indulged my requests, assisted me in finding documents, and sometimes gave me hints and explanations that were, in hindsight, far more significant than the technicalities of where documents are kept. Likewise, following the paper trail of diplomatic knowledge production while keeping close watch on real-world diplomatic practices was only possible thanks to the many diplomats and foreign policy workers – especially Our Lady of Diplomatic Salvation – that helped me map where reports actually go, understand institutional quirks, and helped me fill in gaps in the documentary record.

Sometimes encouragement and inspiration came from those that will be our future: my history of nationalism class – the Identity Hunters – at King's College, who are unceasingly inspiring, questioning, intellectually challenging, and fill me with hope; my PhD students, especially Felicia Yuwono, who in the last three years reminded me of my passion for analysing diplomatic practices and their impact.

Just as importantly, many artists have contributed to my work, their contributions inspiring and world-changing. My personal imaginary would not exist without the work of painters like my father Gaston Orellana and the visual creativity that fuels understanding of the world. My long-time collaborator and friend Tom de Freston with whom, allied to Mariah Whelan and Christiana Spens, we explore unspeakable traumas in our *Truth Tellers* collective. Dom Bouffard, collaborator in punk endeavour, with whom I explored political memories we inherited but did not live. Their work is not just decoration, but rather millions of little holes patiently carved into the fabric of what we think is reality. Together, they show us how our world is imagined and, consequently, made.

As I drafted this book, thousands of musicians kept me company with countless hours of music. I'd like to highlight my inspiring friends Al Wade and The Modern World, whom I sometimes dragged to university to play for me and my students, and who often send me music and playlists to keep me happy, angry, and writing. The many musicians in my collection, from Pink Floyd and Led Zeppelin to Future Islands and The War on Drugs, not forgetting Buckethead, who helped me stay focused in fierce-mythical guitar riffs. Their music inspired me to remember what is at stake in life, always fuelling hope that 'if you listen very hard / the tune will come to you at last / when all are one and one is all / to be a rock and not to roll'. And it's not just rock: classical composers gave me time, mystery, and never-ending space, particularly Tchaikovsky, whose Manfred symphony inspired the structure of this book. As Nietzsche said: 'without music, life would be a mistake'.

Finally, but decidedly not least since you are holding this book in your hands, I thank the editors at Manchester University Press, who saw the vision of this project, helped me shape it, and were very patient with the many delays to which I subjected them.

To all of you, named and unnamed, I say farewell and sign off as if I were one of the diplomats studied in this book. Not just in diplomatic form, but with sincere gratefulness,

I have the honour to be,
with the highest respect
Madam/Sir,
your most obedient, humble servant

Pablo de Orellana
London 2024

Figure 1.1 Portrait of (left to right) Duke Cesare Borgia, Cardinal Bandinello Sauli, Segretario della Repubblica di Firenze Niccolò Machiavelli, and Borgia's trusted assassin Michele di Corella, by Sebastiano del Piombo, 1516. Image from Wikimedia Commons.

1

Ouverture

An ambassador is honoured by the reports he writes back to those that send him.

Niccolò Machiavelli[1]

Diplomacy is, makes, and trades in knowledge. It is a practice that only exists because of very particular ways of understanding the world. A very special piece of knowledge, that of the state and the delegation of its will in diplomacy, is responsible for the magic that makes diplomacy the fascinating practice we study. This understanding produces sacred diplomatic heralds that are temporarily different from common humans like you and me, keeps them safe on their missions, and makes sense of the material, symbolic, and other practices that constitute diplomacy and enable its conduct.

Crucially, diplomacy also *makes* knowledge about international relations. Producing and communicating knowledge in the form of reports, analysis, policy assumptions, and positions is, in fact, one of its key functions. We can easily picture a diplomat on mission reporting on a conversation, démarche, or observation. Less obviously, but just as importantly, these reports are subsequently analysed, processed, and made useful in diplomatic and policymaking institutions. Some pieces of knowledge might be considered irrelevant, whilst others become prioritised and might come to shape policy.

This book is dedicated to how diplomacy makes, develops, and trades in knowledge. It enquires how diplomatic knowledge-production practices describe what diplomats see; how these descriptions, particularly of other international actors, work, change, develop, are communicated, or disappear; and how we might determine if they were convincing to one's own policymakers or even policymakers of other actors. These descriptions are vital: actors can come to be understood as belonging to categories, like fascism in the 1940s, communism during the Cold War, or Islamic terrorism in the early twenty-first century, that can bring about colossal security, relational, and policy consequences. If US diplomacy identified you as an Islamic terrorist in the 2000s, the United States and its allies would have been likely to act against you or assist your opponents. Diplomacy and policy constitute the world we inhabit based on what policymakers made of descriptions, assessments, and analysis in reports. This is why it is vital to examine how diplomacy produces knowledge.

To research how diplomacy produces and develops knowledge, this book proposes an integrated conceptual, methodological, and analytical approach. In this endeavour, a rigorous empirical and conceptual understanding of diplomatic knowledge production locates bureaucratic text as the key site of its production, communication, and evolution. This informs development of a method to research how diplomatic descriptions work and how they evolve, and to determine whether and how they impact other actors. This method is then applied to two case studies: the diplomacy of the First Vietnam War 1945–48, and that of the Western Sahara conflict 2002–11. These not only demonstrate the utility of the method, but additionally inform theorisation of the key factors that condition, govern, and determine diplomatic knowledge production and its believability.

How does diplomacy report on what it sees? In writing. For diplomacy is principally a linguistic, textual, and representational bureaucratic enterprise. Like any description made in language, it is constrained by the imprecisions and limitations of language, liable to subjectivity and inaccuracy. Language, in turn, is made permanent in text, a piece of written language that performs a function in a given context. One of the founders of modern diplomacy, Florentine Segretario di Stato (Secretary of State) Niccolò Machiavelli, was keenly aware of the issues inherent in diplomatic writing, belying the instrumentalist reputation later given to him by the Catholic Church and the realist appropriation of his legacy.[2] While in office, Segretario Machiavelli repeatedly warned Florentine diplomats of this issue, requesting extensive and accurate reporting as well as analysis, acknowledging that 'to be aware of ongoing proceedings and to estimate their outcome is difficult; for one can only work on the basis of estimates and good judgement'.[3] This is a problem inherent in working with descriptions that are necessarily subjective and, furthermore, can only rely on language (made permanent as text) to be communicated and interpreted.

As Segretario Machiavelli made clear, written description and analysis risk descending into 'punditry'.[4] He attempted to mitigate this issue by having his diplomats report very frequently and write reflective, summary, and analytical reports every two months.[5] Today's diplomatic knowledge production still mitigates risky subjectivities this way by gathering as much reporting as possible and processing it at centralised analysis desks at Ministries of Foreign Affairs (MFA). The stakes are obvious: misidentifying an international situation can have catastrophic policy repercussions.

What if we could trace, assess, and measure the impact and problems of subjective descriptions that might be unhelpful or even dangerous to policymaking?

This is our quest: to enquire *how* diplomatic writing produces, develops, and governs knowledge, specifically focusing on how diplomacy makes and develops knowledge through descriptions of international actors and the contexts that motivate them.

Describing domestic and international political situations has been a key aspect of modern diplomatic practice from its very beginning in the Renaissance. Though constrained by the subjectivity of linguistic communication, knowledge and insight into the politics of given situations, people, countries, and relations among them are essential to achieving the 'grandi cose' – the 'great things' – that diplomacy can enable.[6] As leaked US Embassy cables showed in embarrassing detail, diplomats still report on all aspects of political, social, and economic life in the countries they are sent to, down to the finer detail of Berlusconi's private habits. Kennan's famous 1946 'Long Telegram' was one such report, sent from the US mission in Moscow. Compared to the containment policy it subsequently informed, the Long Telegram demonstrates, firstly, how influential diplomatic descriptions can be in terms of chronological, institutional, linguistic, and policy reach.[7] Secondly, Kennan's disagreement with the containment policy illustrates that diplomats have no control over how their reporting is interpreted. Thirdly, it demonstrates the major role played by drafting and text in bureaucratic knowledge production. As well as within domestic institutions, textual descriptions are a vital site in international diplomacy, where negotiations frequently consist of seeking agreement on specific language to describe a situation.

Diplomatic practices are consistently invested into text. Evidently, human agents carry out most diplomatic practices like speaking, investigating, researching, discussing, raising issues, and, vital for our enquiry, deciding how to describe what they see and learn. The evidence of all these events, materials, agents, and practices, even when orally transmitted, must eventually be committed to text if it is to join processes of knowledge production. This is how the state deals with knowledge: by committing its position or understanding to text. This is for practical reasons: only when submitted to the bureaucratic institution of the Ministry of Foreign Affairs can a diplomat's report or analysis be processed, developed, summarised, passed onto policymakers, and acted upon. This is not to claim that diplomatic writing is more important than other diplomatic practices, structures, and subjectivities – after all, text does nothing on its own and is born of myriad nontextual practices. Rather, what makes diplomatic knowledge production a fundamentally textual endeavour is that, in common with many state bureaucratic practices, the outcomes of all other practices come to be invested into text. A diplomat's information-gathering, social, and investigative practices, for instance, need to be invested into a text or communicated verbally and later transcribed, so that the results might reach the Ministry of Foreign Affairs and be processed. Information is subsequently processed over many texts that analyse it, assess its relevance, summarise its contents, and collate it with other pieces of information which might be added to memoranda for policymakers. Most diplomatic practices result in the consecration of a specific subjectivity to text. Diplomatic text is therefore not an agent in and of itself, but a vital vehicle: the core receptacle and production site of state knowledge about the world.

Diplomatic text presents opportunities for research into diplomatic knowledge. From an analytical perspective, diplomatic text is the immutable witness to how diplomacy represents what it sees, communicates it, and how precisely this knowledge is elaborated. It is both where it happened and where we might find traces of these events. This is because into it are invested the powers, expertise, ideas, and opinions of all its authors, managers, and gatekeepers. The diplomatic authors effectively 'die' after submitting their work, and it is in their texts, as well as their subsequent iterations, that we find their descriptions, interpretations, and points of view. It is here that we can discover how they developed into the descriptions that might have informed a policy decision.

The consequences of diplomatic name-calling are significant. In the 2011 talks preceding US, British, and French imposition of a no-fly zone to support rebels in Libya, we can see how the practices, skill, influence, and competences of diplomatic practitioners were invested into a draft that all participants could sign. Much of the negotiation specifically focused on wording describing the Libyan regime, essentially agreement as to who was whom, the nature, extent, and normative dimension of the conflict.[8] During and after World War II (WWII), calling an actor 'fascist' could unleash difficulties for that actor. After substantial 'fascist' name-calling in the aftermath of WWII, particularly by France, Portugal and Spain found themselves isolated and under sanctions for nearly two decades. As we saw with Segretario Machiavelli's concern five centuries ago, the subjectivity of descriptions and the identities they rely upon is an old problem that can facilitate mistakes – or manipulation. In 1588, King Philip II of Spain's ambassador to France, Bernadino de Mendoza, was able to essentially paralyse France through delicate communication focused on religious identity. By emphasising Catholic identity, he persuaded the hitherto reticent French Catholic League to accept Spanish support in its rebellion against the King, incapacitating France and setting the stage for the attempted invasion of England by Spain.[9] Differentiation between Catholics and Protestants, 'weaponised' by Spanish diplomats, was able to cut across state and social boundaries to support and fund counter-reformation insurgency in both France and England.

Something important happens when a description is made. It classifies actors and the contexts that make sense of them into existing categories that already contain images of and assumptions about subjects and their contexts, as well as methods to address them. The most powerful such discursive categories since the end of WWII are fascism, communism, and Islamic terrorism. When the Chinese Government calls Uyghurs 'terrorists', we see the insertion of anti-regime activity by Uyghurs into the category of international Islamic terrorism, which might bring validation of anti-Uyghur activities and military campaigns by China.[10] Should this name-calling stick, it could insert Uyghur activists, Xinjiang, and the very cause of Uyghur autonomy into the depoliticised realm of the universal enemy: the danger to all existence once provided by fascism and communism. This is not new. In De Mendoza's counter-Reformist machinations in France, Protestantism provided a threatening religious identity that cut across frontiers and governance. In 2011, however, both Bashar Al-Assad and Muammar Gaddafi unsuccessfully attempted to frame enemy insurgents as Islamic extremists. Clearly, name-calling does not always stick.

Diplomacy has long been marked by the power of words that define and classify. As Machiavelli explained to his ambassadors when requesting improved reporting, wording can misrepresent a situation and lead policymakers to make poor choices. Writing 'such as befits prudence and necessity rather than punditry', choosing language to describe to policymakers what diplomats see and learn remains a key concern of diplomatic practitioners.[11] Conversely, many have sought to manipulate this subjectivity to influence how other actors see an international situation, seeking to extract diplomatic advantage. The assumption that the right choice of words can achieve policy outcomes is so widespread that, as of the last few years, numerous businesses have emerged to provide 'national image management'. The rise in such commercial activity, as well as diplomatic and public relations scholarship concerned with 'nation branding', underscore that 'image' is widely considered an enabler of policy objectives.[12] Whether tailored corporate lies, disingenuous misrepresentation, or optimistic writing, these practices raise the urgency of researching what diplomacy does with these attempts to influence it, and how it constructs its own understanding of international actors and the contexts that animate them.

The research puzzle in the diplomatic pouch

Diplomatic practices invest heavily in diplomatic text because it can do so much. The core research puzzle for our enterprise concerns how this text describes, and how these descriptions evolve over time and in response to specific inputs. This section firstly considers this issue in the context of diplomatic dynamics of practice before, secondly, specifying the research questions that focused and drove forward this project.

Firstly, it is vital to treat diplomacy as a practice, not just a symbol. 'Diplomacy' is a loaded word. Its modern use sometimes conflates its meaning with international politics to the extent that the terms 'international relations', the discipline 'International Relations', and 'diplomacy' are often used interchangeably. In this project, I treat diplomacy as a specific state practice defined by its role as the delegation of the presence of the state. This is the practice whose task is contemporarily to represent the state's presence abroad, as well as represent in text what diplomats have learned on mission.

The text diplomats produce is in many ways a standardisation of acquired knowledge. It is written and standardised in its descriptions to facilitate its utility for the MFA.[13] Its descriptions must therefore be analysed not solely in reference to an underlying reality, which they might or might not capture, but particularly in relation to foreign policy discourses already present at the MFA. The power of these descriptions therefore rests on their categorisation of objects, which classifies them into epistemologically comprehensible categories through inscriptions that occur in language.[14] These include categorising understanding about subjects, from small social groups to entire nations, into spatial (including geographical and 'civilisational' frames), temporal ('backward' or 'advanced', for example), and normative ('communist' or 'terrorist') frames that make sense of and explain their interests, goals, relations with other actors, and even their agency (for instance, if an actor is considered a puppet). Though these categories are the result of countless nontextual practices, after they are invested into text, textual features constitute the actual form and dynamics of the knowledge diplomacy produces.

The key feature of diplomatic writing is description. Description is what one finds in text. 'This is a book about diplomatic knowledge' is a description when you read it. When I wrote it, however, I was practising an act of representation that this text has brought all the way to you. Even if I am dead by the time you read this, the description can still be effective, but I would no longer be able to make any more representations. The two appear the same as you read them, but they refer to two separate events: description is the presence of a representation in text, while the act of writing it is the event of 'representing' as a practice. The reason I use both terms is that representation stands in for what Machiavelli called 'the effective reality' of what we know about another actor. Further, to achieve a more precise understanding of what makes them work, I separate descriptions into representations of subjects and of their normative, spatial, and temporal contexts that, together, constitute an understanding of a political identity.

Representation is the bread and butter of diplomacy. In this state practice, it can refer to two vital and closely interrelated functions. The first, and perhaps better known, is the act of representing the presence and will of the state through the delegation of a diplomatic agent: formalised through accredited recognition of diplomats, it allows the diplomat to convey 'His Majesty's warmest greetings' on behalf of the United Kingdom. However, representation also refers to the act of representing what was seen and learned in an account, a testimony of practice, that is ultimately always textualised: 'I have met some readers of this book, and they seem concerned about the finer detail of diplomatic practices'. Writing this sentence was to construct a representation of you; when you read it, it is a description trying to represent you. Crucially, diplomacy is deeply implicated in doing both simultaneously: representing the Self to the Other, and reporting about the Other to the MFA.

Diplomacy's production of knowledge about other actors involves an entire microcosm of practices. These include nontextual practices that gather, analyse, prioritise, triage, and communicate information, which eventually come to be invested into a diplomatic text. It is in this text that we can locate and analyse the framing of ideas about subjects, space, time, and norms. This text is differentiated from all others by the conditions of practice and knowledges enabling the practice of diplomacy. This condition, marked by the claim to be the 'hand of the prince', marks the text of diplomatic communications as a distinctly *diplomatic text*. Policymakers are rarely informed about international matters directly by the many diplomats and other agents that gathered that information. This task is performed by memoranda, reports, analysis, answers to specific enquiries, and direct policy recommendations, not to mention slides and diagrams to make information accessible. This is important to our enquiry for, although these documents are the result of many practices and agents, in the precise instance of informing a policymaker about whom they are dealing with, it is the diplomatic text that is doing the work of representing the situation. For this reason, this project focuses on the descriptive work being done by the text itself.

This is not a question of a single text, but rather of an entire cascade of texts. The work of representing subjects and their contexts takes place over several texts: a description might be first drafted by a diplomat, then analysed and assessed by an analyst who might add to it, pass it up the chain of command, or triage it out of knowledge production processes as irrelevant. The process that makes diplomatic knowledge is more akin to a cascade of texts, juxtaposed and drawing on one another, influenced by other texts such as requests for further reporting or orders that prioritise some items over others. In this intertextual space, representations or aspects thereof are introduced by textual interventions such a new report or assessment. At times, these newly introduced vocabularies and articulations make their way into other pieces of writing (the subsequent texts in the cascade, like summaries, translations, or memoranda) and thrive, coming to dominate the production of a specific set of representations. In other instances, these vocabularies and articulations are lost and discarded. Even in diplomatic name-calling, the devil is in the detail.

This means that research needs to account for what happens across all these texts, the agents that produce each and that govern their evolution and that of the representations they carry. In analysis, this cascade of texts can be reconstructed through references in the texts, which in diplomatic writing always carefully cite one another. When dealing with historical cases, in some countries most documents are available in archives. For contemporary cases, or those involving countries that do not declassify government papers, analysis will need to reconstruct the cascade of texts evidencing diplomatic knowledge production through leaks or convincing an MFA to grant relatively unfettered access to diplomatic data. Regardless of what one might think of this reticence to release diplomatic documents, their secrecy is itself a key condition of diplomatic practice. Part of the problem of studying diplomacy from the inside is, after all, the problem of access.

Whilst it is instinctive that diplomatic actors and agents would highlight the relevance of their reports by speaking to already-stated policy concerns, *how* this takes place in the diplomatic text remains unanswered. Considering this question in the context of the above-discussed diplomatic dynamics raises three specific research questions:

- How does a description committed to diplomatic text work to represent subjects; their spatial, temporal, and normative contexts; and their relations with others?
- Under what conditions can a representation become a feature of an international actor's understanding of the world? In other words, what makes it persuasive to one's diplomatic establishment and policymakers, or even those of another country?
- Following this, under what conditions can a representation replace a previous one and thus impact an actor's view of a situation, actors, or relations?

With these questions in mind, we can now begin discussion of how to go about conceptualising and designing the analytical methods needed to analyse the empirical evidence of diplomatic knowledge production.

Analysing how diplomacy describes

Language describes. Language lies. Language persuades. Text perpetuates these functions, making them transmissible and facilitating their elaboration. That the words of diplomatic communication are important and powerful is an old adage of diplomacy. Communicating on behalf of and reporting back to the prince, even after the death of absolute monarchies, thanks to the fiction of treating a government as a single will, is the main raison d'être of diplomacy. This book takes its title from this traditional diplomatic assumption. Beyond Renaissance-sounding grandiosity, the philosophical commitment behind this title is the role I attribute to the *diploma* of diplomacy. *Diploma* in Classical Greek refers to an official document, reflecting the nature of diplomacy as herald of messages that are, however, not only carried but also written, by the diplomat's own *diplos*, her hand. Though etymological association is suggestive, evidence in the written record of diplomatic practices is more telling and is where we will seek answers.

Our brief romp through diplomacy's troubled relationship with language highlights the power of language, its consecration to text in this sphere of international relations practices, the limitations of its efforts to represent reality in text, and the importance of understanding the influence of descriptions on diplomacy and international relations more broadly. This project starts from the position that diplomacy is chiefly a writing and linguistic enterprise. It means adopting a conceptual, methodological, and empirical commitment to understanding textual knowledge production. This section introduces the basic features of this commitment.

Practitioners and theorists from all walks of diplomatic enquiry agree that the very words of diplomatic text are of enormous importance. For example, the classical canon on diplomatic practice, written by and for diplomatists, has long been obsessed with this functional problem. Machiavelli and François de Callières, perhaps due to their experience as both diplomats and policymakers, highlight the role of diplomatic reporting in deciding policy.[15] Former practitioners Ernest Satow (Figure 1.2) and Harold Nicolson focused on the need for diplomatic writing to avoid the subjectivity that language can engender,[16] and attempt to remain 'faithful' to what they saw.[17] This is a good example of the norms found within the practice itself, the normativity of the habitus and logic of practice in sociological terms, which explicitly seek to treat diplomatic communication as the impersonal tool of the state. This is because in the practice-led canon of diplomatic studies, diplomatic writing is deeply marked by its Janus-like multi-faceted role as official record of positions among international actors, as advisory material to policymakers, and as the official ears and voice of the state.

Figure 1.2 A diplomat terribly concerned about accurate diplomatic descriptions. Ernest Satow in 1903, from his book *A Diplomat in Japan*, p. 63. Image from Wikimedia Commons.

Reflecting in this way on how diplomats themselves understand the role of writing highlights two very practical issues related to diplomatic knowledge production. Firstly, because the practice is based on writing, it is difficult to describe accurately and precisely, an entirely linguistic problem, Callières, Satow, and Nicolson argued, that can lead to text creating unintended representations of situations. Secondly, descriptions, whether disingenuous or mistaken, can lead to major policy impact if found persuasive. In a common example, another state might gain your support by describing their enemy as your enemy. Conversely, as Nicolson commented when discussing British diplomacy in Persia, failing to notice how much the Persian public hated Britain was a key factor in the failure of Lord Curzon's plans in 1921.[18] In other words, description in language can do things beyond the intended and, should it be persuasive, can shape or change the interests of the state. In my view, the issues at stake in these two dynamics bring together the interests of students of diplomacy across the many schools of International Relations (IR) and diplomatic practice.

While schools of international thought do not agree on how far language constitutes reality, they agree that language plays a vast role in diplomacy. The following chapter discusses in detail how various scholarly and practice approaches have addressed these issues. There, and again at the end of this book, I make the case that the empirical analysis of diplomatic descriptions offered in this book can contribute to realist, English School, constructivist, liberal, and critical concerns about diplomacy's language, its rhetoric, and its impact on alliances and other international relationships. This is why, in search of a shared constructive analytical space, this book explores how diplomatic language constitutes perception of international relations, actors, and their motivations.

This project embraces the position that descriptions of subjects and the spaces, temporality, and norms into which they are classified are constituted in the language that represents them. In practical analysis, this means that they are not to be considered solely in reference to an underlying reality, but rather in terms of the linguistic means that constitute their categorisations. The analytical consequence is that understanding of any political identity and its context cannot be independently grounded because, in a description such as we find in diplomatic text, they are not objective truths. Rather, they are the fruit of inscriptions into discursive frames of meaning that only make sense within specific discourses. For example, we must know cold war discourse and understand its categories for a description like 'you are a Commie fellow-traveller' to inspire fear that you are part of a global communist conspiracy. I do not argue that descriptions represented in diplomatic communication are myths with no material reality. Rather, the two – language and material reality – are irremediably linked by the role language plays in making sense of and contextualising what is being described.

Analysing how diplomacy describes necessitates an integrated empirical analytical method. That is the main contribution offered by this book: an integrated method that, drawing on the documentary evidence of diplomatic descriptions, accounts for their constitution, emergence, and evolution, and the extent to which they proved influential. This project fulfils the 1980s promise that discourse analysis could crack open the secrets of the diplomatic pouch,[19] retrieving exactly how diplomacy participates in constituting descriptions of subjects and the temporal, spatial, and normative contexts they inhabit. To facilitate methodological development, I conceptualise diplomacy as a practice of communication and representation of the presence of the state. To link diplomatic knowledge production practices to the empirical evidence found in the archive, this book conceptualises *the diplomatic moment*: the entrance of the textual product (like a report) of an instance of practice into diplomatic knowledge-production processes.

Diplomatic knowledge production leaves a paper trail that lends itself to analysis. Firstly, it makes it possible to analyse how a diplomatic description represents. We are looking at the instance when our diplomat at her desk has just chosen the words with which to describe the subjects she met and the contexts that make sense of them. The moment the cable is sent, it participates in diplomatic knowledge production. For this reason, our analytical lens must commit to text while considering the hands that draft it in order to locate precise instances of representational shift. Secondly, tracing the development of descriptions across the cascade of texts in knowledge production processes, from mission reports up to summaries for policymakers, makes it possible for analysis to locate and examine changes in representation of subjects and their contexts. Thirdly, knowledge-production practices can be further accounted for by mapping pathways channelling information drafted by diplomats on the ground, then summarised by another hand at the ministry, analysed by another, and assessed by yet many others, all the way to the memoranda drafted to inform policymakers. These are the three key ways in which this project exploits the analytical opportunities provided by diplomacy's relationship to textual communication.

Locating the diplomat as the agent of the state needs analytical refinement to yield helpful data selection. Diplomatic knowledge production involves a microcosm of reporting and analytical practices where MFA diplomats are not alone in practising diplomacy. They are complemented and sometimes replaced by unconventional diplomatic agents like leaders, parliamentarians, and other officials.[20] In an interesting and little-known example, in the late 1950s, Spanish Navy Captain Adolfo Calles (Figure 1.3) acted as one of the few active points of contact between fascist Spain and the United States. His attendance at the US Military Mission in Madrid (known as 'Little Korea') was so assiduous that his spouse was trained in English-language American diplomatic and military protocol.[21] In the 1930s, the Chilean Foreign Office took the even more unusual step of sending renowned poets like Pablo Neruda and Gabriela Mistral to key diplomatic postings from Madrid to Rangoon.[22] To conceptually and empirically account for the textual work of such varied agents and its impact on the evolution of the diplomatic text is vital, which is why the approach offered in this book includes the reports of nondiplomatic agents when they submit knowledge into diplomatic knowledge-production processes.

Descriptions, the product carried in the diplomatic text and the focus of this book, are complex and exist only in relation to the known world. You might be nonplussed or confused if I were to accuse you of being a Ghibelline (a description based on a late medieval normative category), but Machiavelli would have found the accusation horrifying. This is not only because you might not know what a Ghibelline is, but also because that political category has long been out of use and real-world political concern, making contextual categorisation as Ghibelline ineffectual and nonsensical. Frequently actors are so little known that sense is made of them entirely through such references, raising the urgency of expanding analysis of identity

Figure 1.3 The unexpected diplomat on mission. Spanish Navy Captain Adolfo Calles returning to Spain, 1959. Photograph courtesy of the Capitán Adolfo Calles Archive.

to representations of subjects and their contexts – a striking example is US support for the Mujahideen in Afghanistan in the 1980s, articulated on the basis that their cause was anti-Soviet. Descriptions can insert subjects into discursive categories that already contain assumptions, histories, modes of acting, and solutions to issues. This identity is not necessarily that of the Other, and, as we shall see, descriptions of like-mindedness are vital. This is why I do not limit my analysis to descriptions of identity and have been referring to representation of human subjects and their contextual representations of temporality ('backward' or 'advanced', for example), spatiality ('Asian'), and normativity ('evil') that make sense of an identity and locate it in the known world.

Delving into diplomatic text, linguistic features carry out a number of tasks, whether 'accidentally' or intentionally.[23] Crucially for our analysis, they represent a situation in such a way that a specific subjectivity emerges.

We could summarise the effects of the 'political classification' tasks undertaken by the diplomatic text as:

- Providing labels to subjects, spaces, time, and conflict;
- Negating, obfuscating, or denying previous statements and positions;
- Associating or approximating subjects and contexts;
- Ordering a set of facts around comprehensible concepts (such as the domino theory) that provide links that make sense of information and context;
- Defining the salience of any item of information or description.

The goods of the text are comparative and mutually constitutive; barbarism, for instance, necessitates a civilised opposite to make alterity possible.

When we look across texts comparing their representations, we find that sometimes specific items, including obvious ones, fall out of knowledge production and are not seen again. On other occasions, new representations, sometimes originating from other international actors, enter knowledge production and are repeated and perpetuated. This leads to remarkable changes in the descriptions that make their way to informing policy. Accounting for what drives these dynamics is a key contribution of this book. Charting the evolution of descriptions reveals the conditions, agents, structures, and events that shaped their change and therefore a shift in how the state saw a situation.

Name-calling doesn't always stick. Russian claims in 2014 and 2022 about Ukrainian 'fascists' attracted no attention from Western states, unlike Vladimir Putin's early 2000s qualification of the Chechen conflict as a war against international Islamic terrorism. The evident difference is that terrorism was a policy concern shared with Western states, but that is not all. Descriptions are not simple labels to slap onto subjects and situations: you name-call an actor and wait for the hounds of hell to get them. What makes a representation convincing is the extent to which it responds to and engages with the articulations of dominant policy concerns as expressed by the interlocutor, without contradictions. This is not to suggest that their interests are either aligned, or instrumentally misrepresented to appear aligned. Both can be the case, and it would be problematic and analytically unhelpful to assume that this is a solely instrumental move. Nor is it my intention to find hypocrisy, truth, or lies in diplomatic communication. What interests me is *how* descriptions produce believable subjects, and the qualities that allow them to persuasively make sense of international subjects and events.

Research strategy

Retrieving how diplomacy produces representation of subjects, space, conflict, and norms requires a series of intellectual moves and methodological developments. This section summarises how this book addresses its analytical challenge, conjugating it as four theoretical, methodological, and analytical moves that, furthermore, inform the structure of this volume.

The first move involves an empirical conceptualisation of diplomacy as a practice that produces knowledge about international actors. Drawing on Constantinou's theorisation of 'the diplomatic' as a simulacrum of the theory of the state, and Neumann's admonishment to pay attention to the practices of knowledge production, the case is made to trace the development of diplomatic text through the functional structures of diplomacy. Consequently, 'the diplomatic' includes those that speak with the claim to represent a sovereign international actor. Leaders, ministers, parliamentarians, military officers, and other agents are only 'diplomatic' at the instances when they speak in representation of the sovereign actor – even 'real' diplomats are only diplomatic at those instances.[24] This is the basis for what I call 'the diplomatic moment', determined by the *submission* of textual output. This first move, discussed in Chapter 2 and resolved in Chapter 3, takes us from the classical instrumental conceptualisation of diplomacy to a functional practice-based definition of what constitutes 'the diplomatic' and an empirical definition of its textual paper trail.

The second involves developing a method to retrieve how diplomacy constitutes representations of subjects and their contexts. The method is designed as a three-step integrated solution. The first step maps the routes taken by the documents of diplomatic knowledge production, revealing the pathways taken by information, rather than just official formal channels. The second analyses how words and phrases, the text itself that is, constitute representation. This step reveals the textual strategies that subjectively frame subjects and additionally identifies textual markers signposting specific representations. The third step in this method follows these textual markers to examine the development of representations across processes and texts of knowledge production, locating and analysing changes in how subjects and their contexts are represented, including when the communications of other actors intervene. Analysis begins at the instance when a specific representation ('communism', for instance) is explicitly linked to a policy decision ('we must contain communists there'), and then traces the development of that representation backwards. That is, representations are considered against previous iterations of themselves, essentially producing a history of their present. This move occurs in Chapter 3, which is devoted to developing this methodological design for an application of discourse analysis for diplomatic text.

The third move identifies case studies to demonstrate the method's utility. Discussed at the end of Chapter 3, the rationale focuses on instances when policy was explicitly based on 'recognising' an identity, but which contained sufficient contradictions to that 'recognition' to reveal how these were dealt with in diplomatic knowledge production. The diplomatic interactions selected relate to two conflicts that meet this rationale: the First Vietnam War, 1945–48, and the Western Sahara conflict, 2001–10. In both cases, representing Vietminh and POLISARIO in association with dominant policy concerns, communism and terrorism, respectively, was crucial in shaping how interlocutors like the United States saw them. The consequences were momentous: France bypassed international restrictions and involved the United States in its reconquest of Vietnam, while Morocco's annexation of Western Sahara became, thanks to US diplomatic and financial support, one of only three successful annexations since WWII. The diplomacy of these case studies is examined in Chapters 4 and 5. Analysis is written against the history of dominant policy concerns, establishing an account of the development of representations, and revealing the interventions from domestic and international actors that shaped this history.

The last move of this project, executed in Chapter 6, draws on the observations and genealogical mapping produced in the empirical chapters to model how changes in representation of subjects, space, time, and norms can change an actor's understanding of other actors and their circumstances. This section advances a conceptualisation that considers representations as dependent on the conjunction of five conditions: articulation, discursive stability, the discursive planes where representations emerge, dominant policy concerns governing knowledge production, and their representation in contextual realms of knowledge such as the press. It is found that, under these conditions, diplomacy can considerably impact how one's policymakers, or even foreign policymakers, see the world. This is diplomacy's power in textual practice.

An old question of diplomacy and IR

How policy is informed by diplomacy is an old question of diplomatic practice and study. Its impact concerns policy choices as to whom to support or attack, and what brings actors together in international relations. It seems obvious that domestic and international actors seek to influence policymakers by appearing to be what they seek. This would make this book a great deal of work for rather little novel insight. While it appears evident that actors do so, what this project has set out to understand is precisely *how* they do so and what makes some descriptions convincing and not others. This section brings our introductory démarche to a close, seeing us off on our mission by raising the practical, intellectual, and analytical contributions stakes of this project.

Diplomatic studies are served most significantly by this contribution. This project adds to the conceptual and methodological tools available for the analysis of diplomatic knowledge production and communication. This is thanks to its elaboration of a specialised, rigorous, and strictly empirical method based on consideration of the practice of diplomacy and its conditions of possibility. This method asks the *how* question, interrogating the empirical evidence of diplomatic communication to ascertain how subjects, spaces, time, and norms are represented in diplomatic knowledge production.

Why does this enterprise matter? Five centuries ago, Machiavelli warned his ambassadors that detailed reporting mattered because it informed policymaking. The identities, situations, and conflicts that inform policymaking are not unproblematically represented in diplomatic communication, for diplomatic practices – and the texts they produce – are implicated in their constitution. The constitution in language of subjects, space, time, and norms has emerged since the 1980s as a key question for the study of political subjectivities that have at their heart the political and social identity of subjects. Among these we can highlight Orientalism and other demarcations of alterity such as those studied by Der Derian (threats to life and society), Neumann (the Russian Other to the European Self), Connolly's pre-colonial and American working-class Others, or Jabri's postcolonial subjects.[25] This project takes this mission to the textual paper trail of diplomatic knowledge production.

Conceptual and practical understanding of diplomacy itself is advanced in three crucial ways. Firstly, through focus on their empirical documentary evidence, this project brings to the fore the practices of writing, rewriting, reading, and assessing information that take place from the diplomatic coalface to the capital's policymakers. This is vital, bridging the practice–discourse divide in critical approaches to diplomacy and contributing a vital empirical link between the production of the 'effective reality' conveyed in descriptions on which policy is based and the practices that collect, collate, and assess this knowledge.[26] This is vital to understanding how diplomacy as a practice actually shapes the world.[27] Secondly, this research allows analysis to locate the very textual instances and practices where the agency of individuals, institutions, and states is invested in particular inscriptions of subjects and their contexts. In so doing, we can assess individual, institutional and government investment into inscriptions. In other words, this makes it possible to link practices to descriptions and policy, uncovering when perception becomes reality by being practiced.[28] Thirdly, this approach helps consider the agency of diplomacy, contributing to intellectual and practical efforts to raise the corpse of diplomacy from a state instrument to an agent that contributes to the constitution of the state. The ultimate consequence is a reconsideration of diplomacy's power to constitute a state's vision and practice of international reality.[29]

The stakes could not be higher. It is through these that I'd like to speak to students of diplomacy of all traditions. The greatest concerns one of the oldest questions of diplomacy and international politics: how international actors see one another. Its empirical focus on large volumes of diplomatic correspondence makes the analytical yield of this project widely applicable, allowing for insights relevant to scholars of many traditions. How actors see one another is a question that has plagued *all* diplomatic and international studies traditions, and we could indeed summarise the history of this concern through the history of parts of international studies, citing early practitioners like Callières and Machiavelli terrified that their diplomats' writing was insufficiently helpful;[30] practitioners concerned with avoiding misrepresentation;[31] realists (and realist practitioners like Kissinger) worried that diplomatic language is instrumentalised;[32] constructivists exploring 'whose identity' is being traded in, its impact, and 'what it might *mean* for identity (or any other factor) to "matter"',[33] as well as those working on how norms are introduced or changed;[34] English Schoolers researching the constitution of international meanings;[35] early criticals enquiring how diplomacy constitutes the international, identity, and the role of language therein;[36] and later criticals like myself studying how international practices like diplomacy do this;[37] not to mention the vast diplomatic history tradition, who have long been studying specific cases, institutions, actors, and histories,[38] and New Diplomatic History's interest in specific diplomatic practices.[39]

More specifically to diplomatic practice, this project contributes an empirical toolkit to engage with the subjective nature of written knowledge. From Segretario Machiavelli exasperatedly demanding that Florentine diplomats write better reports, to those today concerned about policy mistakes informed by poor knowledge production, or policymakers ignoring the nuanced insights collected by diplomats, this method contributes an empirical tool to determine exactly where, when, and under whose orders and direction knowledge takes shape, allowing for these dynamics to be accounted for and utilised.[40] Relatedly, to interest in bureaucratic decision-making à la Graham Allison, this method provides a tool to empirically trace, map, and determine the emergence of what he calls 'groupthink' in worldviews.[41]

For realists concerned with identifying ally or foe, and those that locate diplomacy's power as embedded in its communicative functions,[42] this empirical approach addresses concerns about diplomatic communication being misunderstood, misleading, or instrumentalised, providing an empirical grasp on how reality is or is not captured and acted on.[43] Further, understanding how descriptions inform and contribute to understanding what Walt conceptualises as the alignment of interests and threats and its persuasive power.[44] Not dissimilarly, this book can help materialist approaches to diplomacy to relate, in the unavoidable medium of descriptions that is the currency of diplomacy, how material subjects and objects are made sense of and, furthermore, how logistics and communication media act as key enablers of this and other diplomatic practices.[45] English School analysis would, in turn, find significant substantiation of its concept of polysemy – conflicts over definition of an institution's norms – in this method's treatment of representations competing for supremacy, and possibly far more substantial empirical substantiation of the meaning-producing practices in international institutions.[46] Relatedly, for constructivists, this method can map in empirical detail the emergence of new or reformed norms in institutions, diplomatic or international, and their lifecycle.[47]

For interpretive analyses of international relations, this method lays bare how diplomacy constructs and transmits representations, adding to research on international practices, and the role of discourses of violence therein.[48] The descriptions elaborated in and delivered by diplomacy enable violence by constituting and inscribing the Other: for example, who the enemy and 'fellow travellers' were in Vietnam. Studying the applications of power that govern representations as they evolve reveals the effects of institutional hierarchy, personal performances, social capital, and power relations explored by the practice turn,[49] particularly the effects of 'the bureaucratic mode of knowledge production'.[50] When researching relations among states, analysing self-representation helps understand the constitution of the 'pecking orders' of international diplomacy,[51] as well as revealing the detail of the oft-ignored agency and means of postcolonial diplomacy.[52] Finally, it is worth highlighting that many applications of diplomacy's 'power in practice' are invested into text – an agreed text that stands as the position of signatories, including its representations, which this method can deconstruct and examine.[53]

This volume contributes to diplomatic history, providing a method that can help illuminate old diplomatic mysteries. This is demonstrated in the First Vietnam War 1945–48 case study, which applies this method to the heavily studied case of American involvement in Vietnam to demonstrate its capacity to provide new analytical and scholarly insights to well-known cases. Likewise, the Western Sahara case study provides a powerful contribution to analysis of the US role in that drawn-out, unresolved conflict, demonstrating exactly how Morocco was able to influence US policy on North Africa. This method additionally contributes to decolonising and internationalising diplomatic history approaches. Our case studies provide the understanding of subalternity that postcolonial scholarship seeks to retrieve in the international relations of subaltern and postcolonial actors.[54] This is not the 'hard' power of yesteryear, but the rather unrecognised ways used to gain policy initiative by actors considered subaltern – as demonstrated in our case studies by how France and Morocco, while actively representing themselves as subaltern to the United States, influenced US policymaking on Vietnam and Western Sahara as well as anticommunism and counterterrorism more broadly.

Death, life, torture, protection, or help are at stake in the words of the diplomatic text. This analytical method enlightens, adds detail to, and substantiates how identity contributes to identifying enemies, allies, and the constitution of security communities like NATO or the EU.[55] Crucially, diplomacy's descriptions are one of several inputs into the constitution of identity that enable securitisation and subsequent practices of international security.[56] These acts necessarily draw on previous constructions that demarcate alterity, some of which take place in diplomatic text. By tracing how actors see the world, this method contributes to the study of phenomena that emerge out of diplomacy, including empathy at both the representative and the personal levels,[57] strategic communications choices, the stigmatisation of specific actors, and other relationships that depend on shared representation of a transgressor.[58]

The advances offered in this volume contribute but a grain of sand to a far greater philosophical and ethical endeavour. It is part of the project launched in the Renaissance by those seeking wisdom and critical understanding from past archaeological, philosophical, political, textual, and aesthetic experience. Unlike the work of Da Vinci or Leon Battista Alberti, however, this project does not seek the rescue and rinascita, rebirth, of the logic and works of the past. Its ethos is Machiavelli's, Nietzsche's, and Foucault's: to embrace history in an endeavour to understand the moments that made today and shall make tomorrow.

Our endeavour is to chart the emergence and development in diplomacy of a singularly powerful idea: an understanding of whom we, as an identity and state, are dealing with, their motivations and contexts. In this mission we take Segretario Machiavelli, who will symbolically remind us along the way of what is at stake in this question and represent the concerns of practitioners, as well as the work of many scholars that have long sought answers to the mysteries of diplomacy. In the next chapter, we will first spend some time at the library in Florence to discuss with scholars, analysts, theorists, and practitioners of diplomacy how the secrets of description might be prised open. Then, at the Segretario's office in Chapter 3, we shall forge an analytical machine that can crack open diplomatic writing and force it to reveal its secrets, subjectivities, and the many older texts that informed it. We then leave fair sweet Florence in Chapters 4 and 5, travelling to archives in Paris, Washington (that was difficult to explain to Segretario Machiavelli), Hanoi,

Rabat, London, and Tindouf. But we shall return to discuss what we found, what it means, and why it's worth learning.

Diplomacy, far from an inert instrument, is deeply implicated in constituting this understanding of the world, its actors, what they want, and why. The outcomes can be staggering. Like the Sahrawis studied in this book, a people might be condemned to exile or 'into captivity, because they have no knowledge: and their honourable men are famished, and their multitude dried up with thirst'.[59] After all, these diplomatic histories are the history of diplomacy today. For

Time present and time past
Are both perhaps present in time future,
And time future contained in time past.[60]

Notes

1. This is the beginning of a 1522 letter with instructions to the Florentine ambassador to Spain in Niccolò Machiavelli, *Le opere di Niccolò Machiavelli* (Rome: Tipografia Cenniniana, 1877), 378. The verse in the dedication page ('Talk in song …') is by Robert Plant in Led Zeppelin, 'Kashmir', *Physical Graffitti*, 1975.
2. I call him 'Segretario Machiavelli' both to emphasise that I am referring to his life as a policymaker and diplomat of the Florentine Republic, and in a linguistic effort to dissociate him from the reputation that the Catholic Church, and later realist scholars, gave this exceptional and practised Renaissance theorist, scholar, and diplomat.
3. It is remarkable that all but one paragraph of this letter is dedicated to highlighting the importance of diplomatic reporting and advising on its writing. 'Memoriale a Raffaello Girolami', in Machiavelli, *Le opere di Niccolò Machiavelli*, 375–79. All translations from Machiavelli are my own.
4. Machiavelli, *Le opere di Niccolò Machiavelli*, 379.
5. 'Memoriale', in Machiavelli, *Le opere di Niccolò Machiavelli*, 378.
6. Discourses II, 0–1 in Niccolò Machiavelli, *Tutte Le Opere Storiche, Politiche e Letterarie*, ed. A. Capata (Milan: Newton Compton, 2011), 140–45; 'Memoriale' Machiavelli, *Le opere di Niccolò Machiavelli*, 375–79.
7. 'George Kennan "The Sources of Soviet Conduct" (1946)', accessed 28 July 2012, http://www.historyguide.org/europe/kennan.html
8. See Rebecca Adler-Nissen and Vincent Pouliot, 'Power in Practice: Negotiating the International Intervention in Libya', *European Journal of International Relations* 20 (4), 2014, 889–911.
9. De Lamar Jensen, *Diplomacy and Dogmatism, Bernardino de Mendoza and the French Catholic League* (Cambridge, MA: Harvard University Press, 1964), 73.

10 See declarations by Xinjiang Communist Party chief: 'Zhang Chunxian said some Uyghurs had fled overseas to join Islamic State and some had returned from war in Iraq and Syria to take part in terrorist plots', 'China Week: Xinjiang', *BBC*, 2015, sec. China, accessed 16 March 2015, http://www.bbc.co.uk/news/world-asia-china-31848363; and Sean Roberts, 'Imaginary Terrorism? The Global War on Terror and the Narrative of the Uyghur Terrorist Threat', PONARS EURASIA WORKING PAPER (Washington DC: George Washington University, 2012).

11 Even typeface choice in this book is less innocent than publishing aesthetics might suggest. For 'among the treasures of the [French] National Printing Press are punches cut by Garamond, France's greatest type designer, the pupil Tory taught to use the graver. And for the finest French official printing these types are used today', including for diplomatic treaties, which is why it is used in this book. See William M. Ivins, 'Geoffroy Tory', *Bulletin of the Metropolitan Museum of Art*, 1920, 86.

12 Ying Fan, 'Branding the Nation: Towards a Better Understanding', *Place Branding and Public Diplomacy* 6 (2), 2010, 97–103; Jian Wang, 'Managing National Reputation and International Relations in the Global Era: Public Diplomacy Revisited', *Public Relations Review* 32 (2), 2006, 91–96; Gyorgy Szondi, 'From Image Management to Relationship Building: A Public Relations Approach to Nation Branding', *Place Branding and Public Diplomacy* 6 (4), 2010, 333–43; Gyorgy Szondi, *Public Diplomacy and Nation Branding: Conceptual Similarities and Differences* (The Hague: Netherlands Institute of International Relations 'Clingendael', 2008); Jonathan Fisher, 'Managing Donor Perceptions: Contextualizing Uganda's 2007 Intervention in Somalia', *African Affairs* 111 (444), 2012, 404–23; Jonathan Fisher, '"Some More Reliable Than Others": Image Management, Donor Perceptions and the Global War on Terror in East African Diplomacy', *The Journal of Modern African Studies* 51 (01), 2013, 1–31; Jonathan Fisher, 'Structure, Agency and Africa in the International System: Donor Diplomacy and Regional Security Policy in East Africa since the 1990s', *Conflict, Security & Development* 13 (5), 2013, 537–67.

13 Iver B. Neumann, '"A Speech That the Entire Ministry May Stand For", or: Why Diplomats Never Produce Anything New', *International Political Sociology* 1 (2), 2007, 183–200.

14 'Two Lectures', in M. Foucault, *Power/Knowledge*, ed. C. Gordon (New York: Pantheon Books, 1980), 96.

15 'Memoriale', in Machiavelli, *Le opere di Niccolò Machiavelli*, 375–79; François de Callières, *De la manière de négocier avec les souverains* (Paris: Michel Brunet, 1716).

16 Giovanni Botero, *Relations of the Most Famous Kingdoms and Common-Weales Thorough the World* (London: Iohn Iaggard, 1611); Giovanni Botero, *Della ragion di Stato e delle cause della grandezza della città* (Sala Bolognese: Forni, 1598); Callières, *De la manière de négocier avec les souverains*; Ernest Mason Satow, *A Guide to Diplomatic Practice* (Neully Sur Seine: Ulan

Press, 1917); Harold George Nicolson, *Diplomacy*, Institute for the Study of Diplomacy Ed (Washington, DC: Georgetown University Press, 1998).
17 Satow, *A Guide to Diplomatic Practice*, 71.
18 Harold Nicolson, *Curzon: The Last Phase – 1919–1925: A Study in Post-War Diplomacy*, First Edition (London: Constable, 1934).
19 Richard K. Ashley, 'Living on Border Lines: Man, Poststructuralism, and War', in *International/Intertextual Relations: Postmodern Readings of World Politics*, eds James Der Derian and Michael J. Shapiro (Lexington, MA: Lexington Books, 1989), 259–321; J. Der Derian, *On Diplomacy: A Genealogy of Western Estrangement* (Oxford: Oxford University Press, 1987); J. Der Derian, *Antidiplomacy: Spies, Terror, Speed, and War* (Cambridge, MA: Blackwell, 1992); M. J. Shapiro, 'Textualising Global Politics', in *International/Intertextual Relations*, eds James Der Derian and M. J. Shapiro (Lexington, MA: Lexington Books, 1989).
20 This is a common complaint by diplomats. See Christopher Meyer, *DC Confidential*, New Edition (London: W&N, 2006).
21 Interview with Doña Amparo Calles Zamora, widow of Captain Don Adolfo Calles, interview; also Edwards, *Anglo-American Relations and the Franco Question, 1945–1955*.
22 During his posting in Madrid, Neruda witnessed the Spanish Civil War and wrote the heart-breaking poem 'España en el corazón'.
23 Neumann, '"A Speech That the Entire Ministry May Stand For"'.
24 C. M. Constantinou, *On the Way to Diplomacy* (Minneapolis, MN: University of Minnesota Press, 1996), 116.
25 Edward W. Said, *Orientalism* (London: Penguin, 2003); Der Derian, *Antidiplomacy*; Iver B. Neumann, *Russia and the Idea of Europe: A Study in Identity and International Relations*, vol. 3 (London: Psychology Press, 1996); Iver B. Neumann, *Uses of the Other: 'The East' in European Identity Formation* (Manchester: Manchester University Press, 1999); William E. Connolly, 'Identity and Difference in Global Politics', in *International/Intertextual Relations* (Lexington, MA: Lexington Books, 1989); William E. Connolly, *Identity/Difference: Democratic Negotiations of Political Paradox* (Minneapolis, MN: University of Minnesota Press, 2002); Vivienne Jabri, *The Postcolonial Subject: Claiming Politics/Governing Others in Late Modernity* (Abingdon: Routledge, 2012).
26 I. B. Neumann, 'Returning Practice to the Linguistic Turn: The Case of Diplomacy', *Millenium: Journal of International Studies* 31 (3), 2002, 627; Iver B. Neumann, 'The English School on Diplomacy: Scholarly Promise Unfulfilled', *International Relations* 17 (3), 2003, 341–69; Neumann, '"A Speech That the Entire Ministry May Stand For"'; Iver B. Neumann, *At Home with the Diplomats: Inside a European Foreign Ministry* (Ithaca, NY: Cornell University Press, 2012); Iver B. Neumann, *Diplomatic Sites: A Critical Enquiry* (New York: Columbia University Press, 2013).
27 Ole Jacob Sending, Vincent Pouliot, and I. B. Neumann, eds, *Diplomacy and the Making of World Politics* (Cambridge: Cambridge University Press, 2015);

Tobias Wille, 'Representation and Agency in Diplomacy: How Kosovo Came to Agree to the Rambouillet Accords', *Journal of International Relations and Development* 22 (4), 2019, 808–31.

28 Rebecca Adler-Nissen, 'Diplomatic Agency', in *SAGE Handbook of Diplomacy* (London: SAGE Publications, 2016) 92–103; Rebecca Adler-Nissen and Alena Drieschova, 'Track-Change Diplomacy: Technology, Affordances, and the Practice of International Negotiations', *International Studies Quarterly*, https://doi.org/10.1093/isq/sqz030; Hussein Banai, 'Diplomatic Imaginations: Mediating Estrangement in World Society', *Cambridge Review of International Affairs* 27 (3), 2014, 459–74; Costas M. Constantinou and Sam Okoth Opondo, 'On Biodiplomacy: Negotiating Life and Plural Modes of Existence', *Journal of International Political Theory*, 2019, 1–21; Costas M. Constantinou, 'Between Statecraft and Humanism: Diplomacy and Its Forms of Knowledge', *International Studies Review* 15 (2), 2013, 141–62; Costas M. Constantinou and James Der Derian, 'Sustaining Global Hope: Sovereignty, Power and the Transformation of Diplomacy', 2010, accessed 15 January 2015, http://works.bepress.com/cgi/viewcontent.cgi?article=1003&context=costas_constantinou; Jack Spence, Claire Yorke, and Alastair Masser, 'A New Theory and Practice of Diplomacy', in *New Perspectives on Diplomacy*, eds Claire Yorke and Alastair Masser (London: I. B. Tauris, 2021); Ole Jacob Sending, Vincent Pouliot, and Iver B. Neumann, 'The Future of Diplomacy: Changing Practices, Evolving Relationships', *International Journal* 66 (3), 2011, 527–42.

29 *Making Things International 1*, accessed 11 July 2018, https://www.upress.umn.edu/book-division/books/making-things-international-1

30 G. R. Berridge, 'Machiavelli: Human Nature, Good Faith, and Diplomacy', *Review of International Studies* 27 (04), 2001, 539–56; Vladimiro Arangio Ruiz, ed., *Niccolo Machiavelli, Scritti Scelti* (Verona: Mondadori, 1941); Bruno Figliuolo and Francesco Senatore, 'Per un ritratto del buon ambasciatore: regole di comportamento e profilo dell'inviato negli scritti di Diomede Carafa, Niccolò Machiavelli e Francesco Guicciardini', in *De l'ambassadeur: Les écrits relatifs à l'ambassadeur et à l'art de négocier du Moyen Âge au début du xixe siècle*, eds Stefano Andretta, Stéphane Péquignot, and Jean-Claude Waquet, Collection de l'École française de Rome (Rome: Publications de l'École française de Rome, 2016); Machiavelli, *Tutte Le Opere Storiche, Politiche e Letterarie*; Greg Russell, 'Machiavelli's Science of Statecraft: The Diplomacy and Politics of Disorder', *Diplomacy & Statecraft* 16 (2), 2005, 227–50; Arangio Ruiz, *Niccolo Machiavelli, Scritti Scelti*; Berridge, 'Machiavelli'; Figliuolo and Senatore, 'Per un ritratto del buon ambasciatore'; 'notule agli ambasciatori' in Machiavelli, *Tutte Le Opere Storiche, Politiche e Letterarie*; Russell, 'Machiavelli's Science of Statecraft'; Callières, *De la manière de négocier avec les souverains*.

31 G. Berridge, *Diplomacy: Theory and Practice* (London: Palgrave Macmillan, 2002); Berridge, 'Machiavelli'; G. R. Berridge, Maurice Keens-Soper, and Thomas Otte, *Diplomatic Theory from Machiavelli to Kissinger* (London: Palgrave Macmillan, 2001); Derek Drinkwater, *Sir Harold Nicolson and*

International Relations: The Practitioner as Theorist (Oxford: Oxford University Press, 2005); Nicolson, *Diplomacy*.

32 H. Kissinger, *White House Years* (New York: Simon and Schuster, 1979); H. Kissinger, *Diplomacy* (New York: Simon and Schuster, 1994); Henry A. Kissinger, 'The White Revolutionary: Reflections on Bismarck', *Daedalus* 97 (3), 1968, 888–924.

33 Patrick Thaddeus Jackson, 'Whose Identity?: Rhetorical Commonplaces in "American" Wartime Foreign Policy', in *Identity and Global Politics: Empirical and Theoretical Elaborations*, eds Patricia M. Goff and Kevin C. Dunn, *Culture and Religion in International Relations* (New York: Palgrave Macmillan US, 2004), 169–89; Ronald R. Krebs and Patrick Thaddeus Jackson, 'Twisting Tongues and Twisting Arms: The Power of Political Rhetoric', *European Journal of International Relations* 13 (1), 2007, 35–66.

34 M. Finnemore and K. Sikkink, 'Taking Stock: The Constructivist Research Program in International Relations and Comparative Politics', *Annual Review of Political Science* 4 (1), 2001, 391–416; Martha Finnemore and Kathryn Sikkink, 'International Norm Dynamics and Political Change', *International Organization* 52 (4), 1998, 887–917.

35 Filippo Costa Buranelli, 'Authoritarianism as an Institution? The Case of Central Asia', *International Studies Quarterly* 64 (4), 2020, 1005–16; Filippo Costa-Buranelli, '"Do You Know What I Mean?" "Not Exactly": English School, Global International Society and the Polysemy of Institutions', *Global Discourse* 5 (3), 2015, 499–514.

36 Der Derian, *On Diplomacy*; James Der Derian, 'Great Men, Monumental History, and Not-So-Grand Theory: A Meta-Review of Henry Kissinger's Diplomacy', *Mershon International Studies Review* 39 (1), 1995, 173; Shapiro, 'International/Intertextual Relations'.

37 Rebecca Adler-Nissen, 'The Diplomacy of Opting Out: A Bourdieudian Approach to National Integration Strategies', *JCMS: Journal of Common Market Studies* 46 (3), 2008, 663–84; Adler-Nissen, 'Diplomatic Agency'; Adler-Nissen and Pouliot, 'Power in Practice'; Constantinou, *On the Way to Diplomacy*; Neumann, 'The English School on Diplomacy'; Iver B. Neumann, 'Sublime Diplomacy: Byzantine, Early Modern, Contemporary', *Millennium – Journal of International Studies* 34 (3), 2006, 865–88; Wille, 'Representation and Agency in Diplomacy'.

38 For an excellent example relevant to our case studies, see Frederik Logevall, *Embers of War: The Fall of an Empire and the Making of America's Vietnam* (New York: Random House Incorporated, 2012).

39 Houssine Alloul and Darina Martykánová, 'Introduction: Charting New Ground in the Study of Ottoman Foreign Relations', *The International History Review* 43 (5), 2021, 1018–40.

40 Pablo de Orellana, 'When Diplomacy Identifies Terrorists: Subjects, Identity and Agency in the War on Terror in Mali', in *The Palgrave Handbook of Global Counterterrorism Policy*, eds Scott Romaniuk, Francis Grice, and Stewart Webb (London: Palgrave Macmillan, 2016); Pablo de Orellana, '"You

Can Count on Us": When Malian Diplomacy Stratcommed Uncle Sam and the Role of Identity in Communication', *Defence Strategic Communications* 3 (1), 2017, 99–170.
41 Graham T. Allison and Philip Zelikow, *Essence of Decision: Explaining the Cuban Missile Crisis*, Second Edition (New York: Pearson, 1999).
42 S. M. Walt, 'Alliance Formation and the Balance of World Power', *International Security* 9 (4), 1985, 3–43; S. M. Walt, *The Origins of Alliances* (Ithaca, NY: Cornell University Press, 1987); S. M. Walt, 'Testing Theories of Alliance Formation: The Case of Southwest Asia', *International Organization*, 1988, 275–316; S. M. Walt, 'Why Alliances Endure or Collapse', *Survival* 39 (1), 1997, 156–79.
43 Kissinger, *Diplomacy*; Susanna Erlandsson, *Personal Politics in the Postwar World: Western Diplomacy Behind the Scenes* (London: Bloomsbury Academic, 2022); James P. Farwell, *Persuasion and Power: The Art of Strategic Communication* (Washington, DC: Georgetown University Press, 2012); Pierre Grosser, *Traiter avec le diable ?: Les vrais enjeux de la diplomatie au XXIe siècle* (Paris: Odile Jacob, 2013); Bhagevatula Satyanarayana Murty, *The International Law of Diplomacy: The Diplomatic Instrument and World Public Order* (Leiden: Martinus Nijhoff Publishers, 1989).
44 See particularly Walt, 'Alliance Formation and the Balance of World Power'; *The Origins of Alliances*; 'Why Alliances Endure or Collapse'.
45 Tobias Wille, 'Diplomatic Cable', in *Making Things International 2*, ed. Mark B. Salter (Minneapolis, MN: Minnesota University Press, 2016); Jason Dittmer, *Diplomatic Material: Affect, Assemblage, and Foreign Policy* (Durham, NC: Duke University Press, 2017); Jeffrey Crean, 'War on the Line: Telephone Diplomacy in the Making and Maintenance of the Desert Storm Coalition', *Diplomacy & Statecraft* 26 (1), 2015, 124–38.
46 Costa Buranelli, 'Authoritarianism as an Institution?'; Costa-Buranelli, '"Do You Know What I Mean?"'; Cornelia Navari, 'The Concept of Practice in the English School', *European Journal of International Relations* 17 (4), 2011, 611–30; Barry Buzan and Laust Schouenborg, *Global International Society: A New Framework for Analysis* (Cambridge: Cambridge University Press, 2018); Charlotta Friedner Parrat, 'Change in International Society: How Not to Recreate the "First Debate" of International Relations', *International Studies Review* 22 (4), 2020, 758–78; see also my collaboration using the method expounded in this book in Nicholas Michelsen, Pablo De Orellana, and Filippo Costa Buranelli, 'The Reactionary Internationale: The Rise of the New Right and the Reconstruction of International Society', *International Relations*, 2023, https://doi.org/10.1177/00471178231186392.
47 Moritz Kütt and Jens Steffek, 'Comprehensive Prohibition of Nuclear Weapons: An Emerging International Norm?', *The Nonproliferation Review* 22 (3–4), 2015, 401–20; Finnemore and Sikkink, 'International Norm Dynamics and Political Change'; Finnemore and Sikkink, 'Taking Stock'.

48 Emanuel Adler and Vincent Pouliot, eds., *International Practices* (Cambridge: Cambridge University Press, 2011); Vivienne Jabri, *Discourses on Violence: Conflict Analysis Reconsidered* (Manchester: Manchester University Press, 1996).
49 E. Adler, 'The Spread of Security Communities: Communities of Practice, Self-Restraint, and NATO's Post-Cold War Transformation', *European Journal of International Relations* 14 (2), 2008, 195–230; Vincent Pouliot, 'The Logic of Practicality: A Theory of Practice of Security Communities', *International Organization* 62 (2), 2008, 257–88; Wille, 'Representation and Agency in Diplomacy'; Pouliot, 'The Logic of Practicality'; Vincent Pouliot, *International Security in Practice: The Politics of NATO–Russia Diplomacy* (Cambridge: Cambridge University Press, 2010).
50 Neumann, '"A Speech That the Entire Ministry May Stand For"'.
51 Vincent Pouliot, *International Pecking Orders: The Politics and Practice of Multilateral Diplomacy* (Cambridge: Cambridge University Press, 2016).
52 M. Laffey and J. Weldes, 'Decolonizing the Cuban Missile Crisis', *International Studies Quarterly* 52 (3), 2008, 555–77.
53 Adler-Nissen and Pouliot, 'Power in Practice'.
54 Laffey and Weldes, 'Decolonizing the Cuban Missile Crisis'.
55 Adler, 'The Spread of Security Communities'; Michael C. Williams and Iver B. Neumann, 'From Alliance to Security Community: NATO, Russia, and the Power of Identity', *Millennium – Journal of International Studies* 29 (2), 2000, 357–87; Rebecca Adler-Nissen, *Opting Out of the European Union: Diplomacy, Sovereignty and European Integration* (Cambridge: Cambridge University Press, 2014).
56 Barry Buzan, Ole Wæver, and Jaap De Wilde, *Security: A New Framework for Analysis* (Boulder, CO: Lynne Rienner Publishers, 1998); Barry Buzan and Lene Hansen, *The Evolution of International Security Studies* (Cambridge: Cambridge University Press, 2009); Lene Hansen, 'A Case for Seduction? Evaluating the Poststructuralist Conceptualization of Security', *Cooperation and Conflict* 32 (4), 1997, 369–97; Jef Huysmans, 'The European Union and the Securitization of Migration', *JCMS: Journal of Common Market Studies* 38 (5), 2000, 751–77; Ole Wæver, 'European Security Identities', *JCMS: Journal of Common Market Studies* 34 (1), 1996, 103–32; Michael C. Williams, 'Identity and the Politics of Security', *European Journal of International Relations* 4 (2), 1998, 204–25; Michael C. Williams, 'Words, Images, Enemies: Securitization and International Politics', *International Studies Quarterly* 47 (4), 2003, 511–31.
57 Barbara Keys and Claire Yorke, 'Personal and Political Emotions in the Mind of the Diplomat', *Political Psychology* 40 (6), 2019, 1235–49; Claire Yorke, 'The Significance and Limitations of Empathy in Strategic Communications', *Defence Strategic Communications* 2 (2), 2017, 137–60; Claire Yorke, 'Is Empathy a Strategic Imperative? A Review Essay', *Journal of Strategic Studies* 0 (0), 2022, 1–21.

58 Rebecca Adler-Nissen, 'Stigma Management in International Relations: Transgressive Identities, Norms, and Order in International Society', *International Organization* 68 (01), 2014, 143–76.
59 Isaiah, 5.13, *The Holy Bible: Authorized King James Version* (London: Collins, 2011), 645.
60 T. S. Eliot, 'Burnt Norton', in *Four Quartets* (London: Faber & Faber, 2001).

2

A démarche of meaning: diplomatic practice, identity, and text

> The Russian and Austrian Ambassadors called on [British Foreign Secretary George Canning] on successive days, and stated that they were instructed to read to him despatches from their respective Courts on the subject, but were absolutely prohibited from giving or allowing him to take copies. He therefore requested him to give to whatever they had to say to him the form of a *verbal* communication. He explained to them the difficulty in which he would be placed, when, after listening to the reading of a long despatch, it became his duty to lay before the King, and to convey to his colleagues, a faithful impression of its contents […] He therefore felt bound not to listen to the reading of any despatch without being allowed to retain a copy of it, but was perfectly willing to receive any *verbal* communication which they might wish to make. As soon as they left he noted down his understanding and impression of what they had said and sent his minutes to them respectively for their approbation or correction. These minutes were returned to him – that of Lieven considerably enlarged, Esterhazy's with one alteration.
>
> Ernest Satow, *A Guide to Diplomatic Practice*[1]

As Foreign Secretary Canning insisted, text is the only and best record of diplomatic communication. His determination to have key communications turned into text highlights that the written word is at the heart of how the state processes and works diplomatic messages. As students of diplomacy are fond of pointing out, the philology of the word 'diplomacy' is suggestive. From the Greek *diplos*, the hand, and *diploma*, the writ of accreditation, the name of the practice suggests that writing on behalf of the prince and reporting back have long been at the heart of diplomacy.

After spoiling her guests with Ferrero Rocher, a diplomat will sit down to draft a report to the Foreign Ministry. Her work, like Canning's, is a text that contains descriptions of facts, analysis, impressions, perspectives, and insights, representing what she perceived. After she submits it to the

Ministry, it will be processed, analysed, sometimes sent up for further consideration, sometimes archived. As set out in the overture, this book explores the two lives of diplomatic text: firstly, how any single diplomatic text itself describes, compares, and frames subjects, space, time and their politics, both those of the Self and of other actors; secondly, the subsequent life of that text: how, after being processed, rewritten, or summarised at the Ministry, some of its representations might define an international actor's diplomatic knowledge, sometimes displacing previous ones, or be partially or entirely ignored.

The answer to these questions depends on how diplomacy is understood. Is it an instrument for strategists that simply transmits reality, or a collective of ideas, practices, and agents that constructs as well as conveys meaning? For this reason, a review of how diplomacy is conceptualised is a vital step in our effort to empirically investigate representation.

To focus discussion on how diplomacy produces knowledge, this chapter firstly considers two early guides to diplomatic practice in tandem with a brief discussion on realist and English School conceptualisations of diplomacy. It then explores how the production of meaning can be analysed, from the constructivist 'return of identity' to poststructuralist investigation of how identities are constituted, drawing out what these approaches mean for our endeavour to analyse how diplomacy produces knowledge. At that juncture, this chapter sets the basis to conceptualise how diplomacy produces understanding of political subjects and their contexts, and what this means for our analysis. It is argued that a conceptual and empirical focus on text is vital to researching diplomacy, setting the stage for the next chapter to develop a method to empirically analyse how diplomacy represents subjects and their contexts.

Dispatches from a foreign land

If one sheds appropriation of historical author-practitioners like Machiavelli and Callières, writing about diplomatic practice emerges as far older than the academic discipline of International Relations and animated by practical issues: appearance, status, writing, communication, protocol, dress, and even bribes.[2] Well into the twentieth century, concern with diplomacy as a practice of communication and negotiation remained the preserve of diplomats themselves, who, in writing about the practice, referred to themselves as 'diplomatists'. Celebrated exponents of this tradition Ernest Satow and Sir Harold Nicolson authored guides that are still considered key reading for aspiring diplomats. Satow's, the product of a British Foreign Office request for a practical guide, focuses on specific diplomatic practices: meetings, summits, negotiations, use of language, protocol, and modes of address. It is in the chapter about diplomatic writing that he recounts the above Canning anecdote to emphasise the importance of reporting the exact language of 'diplomatic intercourse'.[3]

Nicolson too considers writing to be the core practice of diplomacy, which is 'a written rather than a verbal art'.[4] Diplomacy is efficient when representation of political positions and negotiation is carried out impersonally and 'loyally'.[5] Nicolson never queries whether the faithfulness of representation and its transcription into a report might be anything other than instrumental. It is conceptualised around the precept – which Nicolson does not entirely embrace – that the limits of diplomacy are dictated by the power available to a state. When considering the writing of diplomatic communications, the diplomat is abstracted: a fax machine passing on information. Nicolson uses the word 'theory', yet it remains a codification of professional diplomacy as a set of techniques, prescriptions, behaviours, and attitudes. His chapter on language, for instance, is a glossary of diplomatic terms. A theory of diplomacy, if one attempts to extrapolate one from this tradition as George Berridge does, fails to address its ontology, the state, and relations among them.[6] What the practice of diplomacy *is* in relation to the state – and therefore its communication – is a key problem to which we shall return later in this chapter.

There is, however, a key lesson to draw from the classical canon by and for practitioners. When a diplomat communicates with representatives of other international actors, she should, as Canning, Satow, and Nicolson prescribe, request approval of a written report of their conversation. This absolves authors of agency in writing when sending it to their superiors. Conversely, reporting on anything except for direct conversations with other diplomats and written démarches does not allow for such abstraction of the diplomat's own role. Furthermore, the process of knowledge production is subject to change by other diplomats as the report is passed on, summarised, analysed, and perhaps included into further knowledge production across many texts – or ignored. Neumann argues that this 'bureaucratic mode of knowledge production' negates the agency of individual diplomats through redrafting, correcting, summarising, and analysing by numerous individuals.[7] This suggests that, as well as a single diplomat's moment of agency in textual production, our project must also consider the superposition of many, potentially contradictory, instances of individual agency, practices, and structures. This points back to the core issue interrogated in this book: what determines whether and how specific representations thrive through the textual process of knowledge production?

Classical realism does not identify this issue of perception. Diplomacy is 'the art of bringing the different elements of national power to bear with maximum effect upon those points in the international situation which concern the national interest'.[8] In his magnum opus, Hans Morgenthau devotes two chapters to diplomacy, conceptualising it as a tool on a par with military force. Communication only informs policymaking through direct representation of what foreign powers are and how they speak. Robert Gilpin, however, discusses diplomacy not merely as a technique to pursue clearly defined interests, but also as a transformative tool conceptualised around the role of mediation.[9] Notably, the extent to which diplomacy defines the means of communicating national interest is obscured, particularly the constitution, articulation, and definition of interests and the subjects, spaces, and conflicts they concern. Henry Kissinger, a scholar-practitioner that led US diplomacy and foreign policy through the Nixon and Ford administrations, is a helpful example of this tradition's take on diplomatic knowledge. He frames policymaking as the preserve of Bismarckian statesmen, himself among them, who identify the national interest and strategise its pursuit.[10] Diplomacy collects and forwards information that the strategist can evaluate on the basis of an underlying reality that lends itself to assessment.[11] Writing diplomatic communication is carefully considered on two levels: it can deceive, mask intentions and interests, and create opportunities;[12] or, alternatively, it can provide strategic opportunities through unspecific wording.[13]

Knowledge about international actors is considered secondary to power balance. Practising this conviction, Kissinger once told Chilean foreign Minister Gabriel Valdés that 'I don't know, and I don't care' about Latin American affairs because the global South had no power and therefore no relevance.[14] Diplomatic communication thus remains strictly instrumental, its agency located only in the grand strategists that direct it.[15] For Stephen Walt too, 'an effective system of diplomatic communication' is a prerequisite 'for balancing behaviour. The ability to communicate enables potential allies to recognise their shared interests and coordinate their responses.'[16] Since diplomacy's recognition of 'shared interests' and understanding of other actors affects the formation of alliances, the question arises as to how they are assessed at the Ministries of Foreign Affairs (MFA). More pointedly, is this assessment the direct representation (or misrepresentation) of the state and its formative context?

This perspective is challenged by focus on diplomatic agency and mediation. Realists like Tony Smith, uncomfortable with attributing agency solely to great power, argued that the Cold War was multipolar, with agency diffused and sometimes enabled by diplomacy.[17] Research carried out in the 1990s on diplomacy, however, retrieved the possibilities of diplomacy at its most dynamic sites: mediation and track-2 practices.[18] It did not challenge realist conceptualisations of diplomacy directly, but rather sought to understand diplomacy in the evidence of its events and policy choices, breaching the inside/outside divide by analysing domestic, regional, and global factors in tandem.[19] Stephen Chan's analysis of Margaret Thatcher's 1980s shift to supporting apartheid South Africa is particularly interesting, as it raises the question of the role played by South African diplomatic representation of itself as anticommunist and free-market in securing UK and US tolerance of apartheid.[20]

The English School too challenged conceptualisations of diplomacy emerging from grounding international relations on the ontology of state power.[21] In the seminal collection *Diplomatic Investigations*, Martin Wight argues that the conceptual and analytical problem lies in 'the intellectual prejudice imposed by the sovereign state'.[22] The challenge is to theorise practices of international relations beyond their instrumentalisation by the state and to decentre the state as their sole conceptual focus. Hedley Bull problematised the state as the container of a homogeneous single-will entity, which led him to challenge treatment of the state as an individual and its assumption as the essential entity of international society.[23] For Bull, diplomacy is the key institution of international society, without which 'there could be no international society, nor any international system'.[24] Considering the extent to which diplomacy constitutes relations among social units destabilises realist conceptualisations of the state, for 'diplomacy fulfils the function of symbolising the existence of the society of states. Diplomatists, even in the pristine form of messengers are the visible expressions of the existence of rules'.[25] Tantalisingly, while Bull suggests that language is key to diplomatic practice, he does not explore the implications since he focuses on how 'diplomatic culture' is 'one of the few visible indications of universal acceptance of the idea of international society'.[26]

Former diplomat Adam Watson allocated diplomacy a greater constitutive role. Diplomacy is co-constitutive of the national interest, which arises from negotiation with other diplomats where consensus-seeking produces tempered the national interest.[27] He does not examine how national interests are negotiated between diplomats and their capital, which is surprising given his insistence that diplomacy no longer represents the king and has to seek democratic consensus.[28] Jönsson and Hall theorise diplomatic practice as an institution of international society, locating it among states, rather than in relation to individual states.[29] They consider language in terms of its instrumental utility and traditions and particularly its capacity for 'constructive ambiguity' in the context of a 'broad range of verbal and non-verbal signalling instruments'.[30]

Paul Sharp follows in Watson's footsteps, raising the stakes to a 'diplomatic understanding' of international relations.[31] Considering international relations through the lens of how diplomacy addresses practical challenges, he argues, reveals the limitations of how nondiplomats think about international affairs and highlights gaps of feasibility in normative theories of international relations.[32] The interrogation of diplomatic practice and theory, contrasting diplomatic limitations against how one would wish to practice foreign affairs, raises two observations to take forward. Firstly, limitations in the constitution and culture of 'diplomatic society' mean that diplomacy is often unable to execute strategic demands, and secondly, the diplomatic roles played by actors beyond the diplomatic corps need serious conceptualisation and examination.

Analysis of diplomatic communication and its constitution of international politics was within reach of the English School, but remains an unfulfilled promise.[33] Though recent English School research has had a tendency to dilute the meaning of diplomacy, sometimes treating it a term for all imbrications among polities,[34] more analytically driven analysis examines how diplomacy makes sense of relations among states and is implicated in constituting the normativity of international groupings and installing new norms as institutions of international society.[35] This is consistent with early English School ambitions, as Bull argued that diplomacy should be conceptualised as constitutive of international society through 'the exchange of messages', which returns us to our question on how diplomacy produces knowledge about subjects and their contexts.[36]

Constructing identity

To constructivists, identity is one of the 'meanings' constructed by social imbrications,[37] along with culture, interests, and security priorities.[38] Collective identity formation among international actors is manifested in the constitution of norms, of which sovereignty and NATO's democratic identity were early examples.[39] Constructivism proposed an ontology based on mutual constitutiveness and signification, the latter arising from the imbrications of the former.[40] Of particular interest in early incarnations of constructivist theory is the conceptual space for agency in identity formation where 'character planning', albeit constrained, is possible.[41] Scope for agency in identity formation was, however, bracketed by Wendt, who based the state on an 'essential identity' that escapes and contradicts the constitutiveness of the constructivist analytical model.[42] This bracketing of identity, an exception from the constructivist ethos, undermines the challenge that constructivism posed to classical IR theories since it essentialises state identities.[43] Bracketing identity makes the constructivist state as anthropomorphic as the neorealist one, since it is 'pre-social relative to other states in the same way that the human body is pre-social'.[44] This takes political agency out of the representation of political identity and, consequently, the conceptual structure that emerges from collective identity formation does not account for its social components to morph and choose the norms that emerge.[45] This 'insensitivity to the multidimensional character of identity formation' does not offer epistemological room for our investigation on how the text frames and constitutes representation of subjects and their contexts.[46]

Diplomacy is posited by constructivists as the international expression of the state rather than as a specific communicative practice. Christian Reus-Smit explores the ramifications of this social aspect of diplomacy through a comparative history informed by interpretative sociological approaches, exploring the 'justificatory frameworks that sanction prevailing forms of political organisation' of which identity is one of the 'substantive values that warrant their status'.[47] Identity is conceptualised as a justification for the existence of the state and, though emerging from social practices, it remains bracketed and unquestioned, not unlike Wendt's.[48] Despite the great validity of constitutive construction of meaning as a basic ontology, bracketing the constitution of state identity evacuates the very social agency that constructivism sought to bring into IR.[49] This is not to say that constructivism has ignored the potential of language to be persuasive, and indeed, understanding its operation has been argued to be a key and necessary development.[50] As with the English School, this raises the question of whether and how agents of state institutions frame the identity of their state, its subjects, territory, norms, and conflicts.

Drawing on Giddens' structuration theory, Jonathan Fisher argues that international actors can intentionally mould 'perception' of their identity,[51] an 'image management' strategy that allows aid-dependent actors to secure some agency in the policymaking of other states.[52] Fisher's analysis of how Uganda and Kenya managed perception by their donors through diplomatic communication additionally suggests the primacy of routine diplomatic communication as the site of identity communication.[53] Fisher examines *what* diplomatic communication says in terms of identity perception, but does not theorise representation beyond perception. If diplomatic communication can unlock agency through representation of identity, it is all the more relevant to ask how it constitutes those representations.[54] A theoretical approach that takes into account the diplomatic formation of knowledge about subjects and the contexts they inhabit is necessary to unlock its 'agencies, properties and possibilities'.[55] The following section addresses this challenge in understanding the power of diplomatic descriptions by proposing a Foucauldian approach to locate the constitution of identity in relation to the construction of meaning in text.

Identity as text

Poststructuralist IR conceptualises power as invested not only in agents but also in institutions and functions which themselves produce subjects and agents and police fields of knowledge.[56] We can think of our diplomats as produced by MFA, and their practices as invested with power. Power is itself not an object that the anyone can hold, but one invested into specific practices, roles, institutions, all of which are in turn sustained by what they say. This philosophical position is based, in the tradition of Nietzsche, Heidegger, Wittgenstein, Derrida, and Foucault, on the insight that language does not unproblematically represent relations between subjects and objects, but constructs, articulates, and inscribes them.[57] Following from this understanding, it is necessary to conceptualise how identity is constructed in political discourse and its relationship to writing representations.

Discourses are part of the construction of truth, a stable entity of signs and semiotic sequences (linguistic relations among signs) that draw on specific ideas and construct the subjects and worlds they describe, classify, and evaluate.[58] Discourses are the medium through which power relations produce speaking subjects. The language, the enunciative articulation, of discourse is the key means of representing subjects and therefore the key site of empirical investigation. On the other side of knowledge production, power is also invested in practices that control discursive inclusion: 'all that appears to our eyes is a truth conceived as a richness, a fecundity, a gentle and insidiously universal force, and in contrast we are unaware of the will to truth, that prodigious machinery designed to exclude'.[59] Within these practices, poststructuralist analytics locate 'the political': the site where, within strict limits, an agent has the agency to make choices that define political realms.[60]

Foucauldian concepts and methods allow political science to understand the mechanisms, history, and origins of what appears transcendental.[61] Genealogy examines the history of an idea by locating instances at which specific forms and pieces of knowledge are changed, classed, or superseded, making it possible to identify applications of power, who produced those classifications, and how. This approach, one of several discourse analysis methodologies, links practices of power to the textual expression of discourses and how these account for the real-world materiality of subjects. The lesson for political science in relating power practices to the constitution of subjectivity is that the resulting concepts are relational and mutually constitutive. The different aspects of representations of subjects and their spatial, temporal, and normative contexts, as well as the inscriptions that these discourses depend on, should therefore be treated as mutually constitutive and as so many aspects of one complete composite product:

representation. Each of these components necessitates examination, which is why this book refers to 'representation of subjects and their contexts' as the multifaceted product of diplomatic knowledge production rather than simply 'identity'.

Each act of articulation and delimitation of identity is an application of power that protects and reproduces the duality of Self and Other. Each of these events is an inscription into a classification of subjects and objects. Genealogy can reach into the detail of this ideational history, revealing how political discourses are built on metaphors, similes, and other textual linkages, rather than sustained logic.[62] In an early and influential example, William Connolly launched his study into identity's inscription into normative discourses with a genealogy of evil, tracing how it is linked via its discursive construction of threats to the 'certainty' of identity. Conversely, the analysis also uncovers efforts to resolve the instability of self-identity by means of further differentiation from the Other. Discourses of identity are inevitably paradoxical, with countless leaks that constantly sabotage differentiation. Paradox must then be transcended by further reassertions of the inscription of difference.[63] The identity of subjects is revealed to be contingent on difference and its construction in time, history, and culture. Some contingencies are 'branded or entrenched' whilst others 'susceptible to reconstruction'.[64] Conceptualisation of 'branded' contingencies accounts for the apparently transcendental aspects of historically constituted identity that are so entrenched that they appear as immanent truths. This is important for IR, since inscription of the foreign often draws on readings of these aspects of identity.

The first move of this discursive approach entails exposing how enunciations of discourse produce meaning. Following from the late-twentieth-century explosion in Foucauldian-inspired critical approaches to literature that analysed textual discourses,[65] Michael Shapiro brought literary theory into political analysis to treat textual production, or equally text*uable* oral expressions, as a politicising practice.[66] This meant importing into IR theory the concept, from Roland Barthes, of 'the text' as literary production, which involves substituting the hermeneutics of representation for those of production. Analysis focuses on how words, grammar, and literary means of location and production such as metaphors, similes, and grammatically posited causal links create meaning, produce relations among meanings, and promote specific interpretations.[67] Barthian theory combined with a Foucauldian approach to the policing of discourse allows analysis to retrieve how text privileges certain subjects, objects, and behaviour, which in turn reveals how 'power resides in the production of discursive entities that become fetishized' and are presented as objective descriptions of reality.[68]

The second move in this poststructuralist approach involves understanding where textual mechanisms inscribe subjects and their contexts. The analytical endeavour of this book does not simply address 'identity' in diplomatic text, but also deconstructs it into representations of subjects and their spatial, temporal, and normative contexts. The advantage of dismantling the constitution of identity in this way is that contextual factors are often the basis upon which the interests of states are speculated on. Geopolitical realist analysis, for instance, regards territory as a key imperative in defining or recognising state interests.[69] Similarly, Kennan's Long Telegram ascribed communist normativity, coupled with the 'eastern mentality' and 'backwardness' of Russian subjects, as key motives for Soviet expansionism.[70] These different inscriptions are mutually dependent and constitutive because they are aspects of the constitution of political subjects that operate by situating subjects in known contexts.

Spatial inscriptions draw on attributes ascribed to particular geographies. 'Global South', for example, generalises the civilisational, economic, and political conditions of less wealthy parts of the world.[71] Temporality is a site where subjects are differentiated by era. The Middle East, for example, is frequently identified as eternally backward in a discourse of history as linear progress.[72] Inscribing subjects in normative discourses relates them in normative terms that locate them as differentiated in terms of the ethics of the Self.[73] Spatial, temporal, and ethical inscriptions are mutually constitutive. As we shall see in the first case study of this book, the Vietnamese were inscribed by French diplomats as 'apolitical' on the basis of their backwardness, which, combined with tropical weather, they argued, had made their race ethically and politically apathetic and decadent.

Political identity is therefore constituted, contingent, inscribed, and re-inscribable into different discourses and frames. Even what Connolly calls 'deep' referents of identity (language and history, for example) are liable to be represented in different ways.[74] That is how loving spaghetti becomes an immanent part of Italian identity and, crucially, how discourses absorb and make sense of the material. This means recognising that identity is unstable and that each inscription is the result of choices that see power invested in promoting specific inscriptions. This approach to reading identity has led to fruitful investigation into how inscriptions of subjects participate in the great tragedy of international relations. Among my personal and methodological favourites, I would highlight Said's dismantling of the constitution of the Orient, Neumann's Russians, Bhabha's Indians, Connolly's Native Americans and welfare scroungers, and Jabri's postcolonial subjects. The insights that postcolonial studies have produced through this approach raise pressing questions about the overlooked agency of smaller actors.[75] This is interesting, for diplomatic communication is potentially a site for postcolonial actors to generate agency for their objectives, one overlooked due to assumptions, like Kissinger's, about great power politics and instrumental diplomacy.[76]

Political identity is a battlefield. Victory in this battle to promote a specific reading of identity can ultimately enable, in the case of diplomatic readings of identities of political actors, legitimation as allies or, conversely, a 'discourse of exclusion implicated in the legitimation of violence'.[77] The next section explores two such analyses of identities in the Bosnian wars, discussing in more detail the concepts and methods involved, before returning to our diplomat writing dispatches at her desk.

Reading identity

David Campbell and Lene Hansen's analyses of identity constructions in the Bosnian War are worth considering in some detail since differences among them reveal conceptual problems and methodological challenges in analysing identity formation. David Campbell conceptualises the Self as radically opposed to the Other, which is framed as imminent security threat to a normatively posited American identity. Foreign policy is thus related to identity/difference, establishing inside/outside boundaries and reifying the state as protector of identity. Its key theoretical underpinning is that representation of the Other as an antithetical, radical, and intractable danger sustains the construction of the state as a space for normative good.[78] His analysis of media, academic, and policy representations of identity in the 1991–95 Bosnian war examined why the conflict was seen as an intractable, indeed unavoidable, result of ancient ethnic hatred.

Campbell's analysis produces impressive insights into the role of narrative *as* history in Western discourse on the conflict, and how it constituted deterministic identities destined to war and genocide. This discourse facilitated representation of identity as radically and timelessly immutable and provided a differentiation that was inscribed as 'primordial'. The temporal inscription is completed by barbarisation of the backward Other, where poverty, former communism and Eastern Europeanness come together to inscribe long-hating ethnic groups.[79] Wide-ranging source selection with little theoretical and methodological delimitation jeopardises Campbell's analysis, however.[80] Analysis is unable to identify individual actors, institutions, and agents invested in specific readings of identity, weakening its capacity to locate its constitution or link them to official discourses. Campbell does not address what other discourses of identity were also present in the war, or how different readings of identity could have affected the conflict, which could have provided a historical counter-narrative disproving the historically deterministic discourse.[81]

Refining the approach to political identity, Hansen makes two significant additions. Firstly, identities are considered dependent on political agency for their epistemological significance, which in practice means that to come into being, they need to be articulated in language by an agent. This is Campbell's missed opportunity: empirically locating the moment of agency shows who invests in specific representations. Secondly, the Other should not be seen as binary and in perpetual radical opposition. Linking and differentiation cannot always be represented in diametrical opposition, meaning that less radical differentiations are also present. There are external constraints too: dominant readings of identity already in place, discourses around materials factors, or the sudden demise of previously dominant normative frames of reference as seen at the end of the Cold War.[82]

Hansen proposes a 'theoretical model of combinability' accounting for discursive instabilities, challenges, contradictions, and how they represent material factors.[83] Hansen's analysis retrieves human agency in discursive choices, yielding critical historical analysis that reveals that what was

> mobilised is not the history *of* the concept but the construction of history *within* the concept; [...] Balkan discourse of the 1990s drew extensively on a construction of the Balkan Other, not as born in the earlier twentieth century, but of 'ancient hatred' going back hundreds of years. Not only did the historical analysis [...] show the youth of the 'ancient' concept, it also brought out two marginalised discourses preceding the concept of Balkanization.[84]

This is achieved with methodology based on the selection of discursive constructions; analysis identifying links, differentiation,s and juxtapositions; and the development of intertextual analysis based on data selection driven by the institutional roles of texts themselves.

The design of Hansen's discourse analysis is shaped around what she calls the 'discursive encounter': contrasting the discourse of the self with counter-constructions by the Other.[85] A key lesson that emerges is that the radical Other is only one of the most extreme discourses of difference, and only parts of foreign policy discourse deploy it.[86] As Cynthia Weber also points out, there are degrees of alterity at play. In the Second Gulf War, Saddam's regime was inscribed as a radical Other, but the Iraqi people were contemporarily inscribed in a lesser degree of alterity.[87] As Ashley suggests, we must look to the 'borderlines' of identity to locate the political.[88] These lessons in methodological design are further discussed in Chapter 3, which develops a method designed specifically for diplomatic text.

What is at stake, therefore, in diplomatic inscriptions of identity? A crucial possible outcome is the securitisation of subjects through inscription as existential threats to society. The securitisation of a subject, particularly the enunciative speech-act that launches the process, is a process that can only occur *after* its identification as a danger by practices such as diplomatic communication, as well as others from espionage to policing, when it is passed on to the technocrats of security in the name of an already-identified and authoritatively enunciated existential threat and exception.[89] Other outcomes are possible, such as support, alliances, an admission that further information is needed, or less radical forms of policing than securitisation. Another possible diplomatic outcome, evidenced by the case studies examined in this book, is protection by other actors from international norms and institutions. Morocco in particular has benefitted from US and French support in ensuring that no enforceable UN resolution has ever been imposed upon it. Diplomatic interventions too can be enabled by the diplomatic name-calling here explored, as these are dependent on ideational constructions, identities, conflict, and norms to constitute consensus around intervention.[90]

Stigmatisation is a more specifically diplomatic outcome. In Rebecca Adler-Nissen's conceptualisation, the process begins with an act of labelling that identifies a normatively deviant international actor. The act is public, seeks to make antinormative deviancy convincing and recognised, and brings nondeviant actors closer. Stigmatisation is not, however, the process in which the Other is discovered and constituted in the eyes of policymakers, but rather the active, public, and intentional imposition of a pre-existing, normatively articulated international subjectivity. Diplomacy's representation of subjects and their contexts is therefore key in creating the united diplomatic front that is a precondition for labelling of an actor as stigmatised.[91]

Producing knowledge about international affairs to inform policymaking is one of the ways in which diplomacy constitutes world politics.[92] Securitisation, interventions, stigmatisation, and other international practices are how the hounds of hell are thrown at you after I persuade the dog handlers to reframe their understanding of you. These are the stakes in diplomatic and policy representations of political identity. We now turn to considering how diplomatic practice might be conceptualised in relation to identity-making.

Towards a poststructuralist theory of diplomacy

Returning to our diplomat at her desk patiently writing dispatches, what is the relationship between her practice and identity-making? The work of three theorists, James Der Derian, Costas Constantinou, and Iver B. Neumann, stands out for their efforts to conceptualise diplomacy as a practice engaged in the mediation and communication of identity and difference.[93] This section interrogates their advances, discussing in detail how their work helps, in theory, approach, and methodology, advance our endeavour to answer how diplomacy produces knowledge about subjects and their contexts.

James Der Derian offers a history of diplomacy's role as constitutive of and mediator between the mutual alterity of international actors. His genealogy of the narratives, rituals, practices, and enabling knowledges of diplomacy, identifies a history – or rather, a contemporary understanding of this history – of constituting and mediating estrangement between particularist forces, such as nationalist ideas of statehood, and universal ones, like Christianity.[94] The basis of contemporary diplomacy, which he terms 'antidiplomacy', involves discursive practices that represent alterity and conflict. Der Derian's genealogy of diplomacy is the first attempt to examine diplomacy through a poststructuralist lens that recognises 'it is increasingly not what is inside or outside the cave that really matters: it is the map of the borders – the textualisation of reality – that has come to matter most'.[95] Diplomacy orders understanding of international relations by signifying boundaries of inside/outside, identity/difference.

Staging the Other in language emerges as the key priority in understanding diplomacy. However, there remain important unresolved conceptual and methodological issues. The first is that Der Derian does not conceptualise diplomatic practice as such, reverting instead to a very mid-century broad understanding of diplomacy as all the international actions of an actor. This is due to lack of conceptual resolution as to what diplomatic practices are. It leads to the methodological choice to analyse an extremely wide array of discursive sources, from news to commentary, military discourse, and practices, whilst diplomatic communication, in the form of cables and other communications between missions and ministry, is not considered at all. This disperses analysis and does not empirically engage with representation of sovereignty, denying conceptual room to examine how they articulate identity. Secondly, agency is not considered in terms of diplomats or the many other agents of antidiplomacy, nor is the encounter of diplomats carrying briefs of Otherness. This means that we cannot locate what agents, ideas, and institutions were invested in the drafting and framing of alterity. Resolving these issues necessitates theorising diplomacy in relation to the state, identity, and practice.

What is, then, the theory of diplomacy? Most efforts to conjugate such a theory have either theorised practical precepts, as Nicholson and Berridge did, or framed diplomacy as everything between international actors. Constantinou, however, focuses on the framing that 'differentiates the diplomatic from the non-diplomatic'.[96] He retrieves the 'framed condition of diplomacy by inverting and deconstructing the way embassy has been conventionally theorized',[97] finding that understanding diplomats as representatives of states is self-referential and locked in a cycle of mutual constitution with the state it purports to represent. That is, diplomacy's condition of possibility is not representation of the state, but rather mutual constitution with the theory of the state achieved through the performance of the state's presence and existence. Diplomatic theory is therefore but theoria, the pre-Aristotelian θεωρία, *contemplation* as opposed to *theory*, a simulacrum that allows diplomacy to 'make credible representations'.[98] This reveals the role of language and rituals of practice in writing and performing diplomacy as related to statecraft to the exclusion of previous meanings, including the *written* condition of diplomacy. Representation of the sovereign is revealed to be a mythological exercise, a performance staging diplomacy to perform the state theories upon which it depends. Likewise, common spaces, dinners, and summits constitute the 'diplomatic community' as a performative space that confuses a community of practice with a single institution, which helps understand common views of diplomacy as a single international institution.

Diplomacy, including the diplomatic community, is the performance of embassy as the representation of the theory of the sovereign: the embassy of theory. This reifies the sovereign because it is there to represent it physically – the delegation of presence. Diplomacy is therefore the representation and reification of the theory of the state itself, which requires that the practice be conceptualised, written, and performed by its practitioners in the same theoretical terms that sustain the existence of the state. No surprise, then, that most diplomatic theory appears Westphalian (and realist), for essentialisation of the state as a unitary single-will sovereign is key to its sending of representatives.[99] If Der Derian saw diplomacy as constitutive of the state itself, Constantinou demonstrates that the theory of diplomacy is a performative re-stating of the theory of the state: it is *both* theory and practice – the practice of the theory of the state.

Theorising diplomacy as a performance of sovereign theory has consequences for research on the agents, communications, texts, gestures, and sites of diplomacy. The diplomatic agent can be conceptualised beyond the formal institution of the foreign ministry, for theory *is* practice: '[i]n her official capacity the diplomat exists only as representing the will of the sovereign and never her own'.[100] This is the key to an analytical understanding that brings theory and practice of diplomatic writing together: if diplomats are the agents that perform and reify the presence of the state, we can conceptualise diplomatic text and methodologically define its analysis around these practices. This involves considering utterances and text from non-MFA agents such as politicians, an Admiral on diplomatic duties, or even a parliamentary delegation. They are diplomatic agents only for short moments, but in those instances they are made diplomatic by their practice, which is conversely also true of those we consider permanently diplomatic, for they too are *only* truly 'diplomatic' when acting in 'official capacities'. Constantinou's reconceptualisation of diplomacy resolves key issues in defining diplomatic practice, returning us to the question of how the all-too-human hands of diplomats write representations of subjects and their contexts.

Iver B. Neumann is a scholar torn between the language and practice turns. His first two monographs apply poststructuralist analysis of identity formation to the mutually constitutive relationship between Europe's Eastern Others: Russia, Turkey, and Eastern Europe,[101] convincingly establishing that identities are mutually dependent, and should therefore not be studied in isolation, but intersubjectively.[102] Locating identity discourses in terms of policy outcomes, he posits that identity is key to the formation of alliances, arguing that mutual identification and recognition of like identities was crucial to the survival of post-Cold War NATO as a security community of democracies.[103] Neumann, however, criticises poststructuralist methodologies, particularly 'emphasis on the unique, context-bound instantiation of identity, which is perhaps its main strength, is also its most crippling weakness because it does not leave much room for an analysis of the social process of identification' as it tends to read 'intentionality out of its analysis'.[104]

Agency in poststructuralist analyses of identity such as his own or even Said's do indeed appear 'conceptualised as an affair between a subject and an order'.[105] The apparent loss of the agent that writes, the institutions that publish, and the audiences that read arises from lack of analytical focus on specific practices, which obscures individual and institutional agency.[106] Most discourse analysis does not set out to locate these instances, but rather to understand how identity discourses operate across a multiplicity of sites. As a result, conceptualisation of the practice and the resulting evidence selection rationale become extremely broad to try and capture how entire societies perceive an identity, as seen with Der Derian's antidiplomats or Campbell's news sources. Their textual selection is not circumscribed by strict conceptualisation of practice, without which analytical insights about a given practice are necessarily limited. To resolve this, Neumann makes a plea for the return of practice to the linguistic turn, arguing that seminal theorists Wittgenstein and Foucault considered focus on text as part of a turn to practices of power,[107] and that the linguistic turn should be complimented with a turn to practices.

A démarche of meaning 45

Neumann put this into practice in an ethnographic study of the Norwegian Foreign Ministry that raises important considerations about diplomatic knowledge production and its research.[108] Tensions and disagreements in the 'bureaucratic mode of knowledge production', such as stress between generalists and specialists, are resolved through homogenising processes that produce texts 'that the entire ministry may stand behind'.[109] Tendency to homogenisation in knowledge production is an old question of diplomatic studies, traditionally answered through simplistic assertions of diplomats as instruments that convey reality when working efficiently.[110] A famous example of such assumptions, and of what happens when reality is subjective and its description comes into question, concerns late 1940s State Department China specialists. The 'China hands' were accused of communist sympathies on the basis that their reporting was pro-communist because it underestimated the potential for a communist takeover. The 'communist-ification' of diplomatic reporting, Senator McCarthy argued, affected the entire State Department because it had institutionally accepted this reporting.[111] The resulting witch-hunt at one point targeted the entire diplomatic reporting system, highlighting how disagreements are institutionally smoothed over and homogenised away from public view, concealing disagreements, differences, and agency. This occurs not only because of ideological or policy pressures, but also because of bureaucratic knowledge production practices at instances of redrafting, correction, redrafting, and reframing, practiced by many individuals.[112]

The homogenisation of MFA textual output raises three vital questions. Firstly, accounting for how diplomatic knowledge production constitutes representation of subjects and their contexts in descriptions necessitates analysis of the entire process of knowledge production.[113] This means accounting for how representations develop from initial diplomatic reports and are changed, homogenised, and developed on the way to the memoranda handed to ministers; what survives and what is flattened in this process; and what determines the success or failure of a specific description. Secondly, any attempt to establish or change how subjects and their contexts are seen would need to overcome bureaucratic homogenisation. Such shifts do occur, as exemplified by the two case studies in this book, which raises the important question of what makes such changes in diplomatic knowledge production possible. Thirdly, Neumann's research on the occasional diplomatic functions of local politicians between Russia and Norway indicates that 'disaggregation in state practices' must account for the diplomatic work of such nondiplomats, which raises the need to conceptualise diplomatic practice beyond the classical focus on the MFA. This is carried out in the following chapter on methodology, which employs Constantinou's conceptualisation of diplomacy to better define diplomatic practice and its evidence for analytical purposes. In the meantime, the next section works towards conceptualising the diplomatic text in relation to its role in diplomatic practice.

Conceptualising the diplomatic text

Diplomacy is, of course, far more than text. Research drawing on critical perspectives based on anthropology, sociology, and Actor–Network theory have highlighted that its practices depend on material assemblages, technology, bureaucratic structures and norms, personal performances, and social capital.[114] In diplomacy, the capacity to influence representatives of other actors as well as one's own superiors emerges from deployment of personal resources, skills, and competences generated by particular practices, drawing on diplomatic goods produced by routine, existing competences, knowledge, and hierarchies.[115] There are influence-enabling practices that construct and maintain diplomatic 'pecking orders' embedded in specific diplomatic organisations, fora, or even dinner tables that are veritable diplomatic sites.[116] The competences of individual diplomats, their spouses, private networks, and positioning choices are deployed at these sites to influence policymakers at home and abroad.[117] Many of these resources and imperatives are the result of inarticulate but effective know-how embedded and self-evident in the practice of diplomacy.[118]

The practice turn takes us back to the diplomatic text, however, by demonstrating how diplomatic practices are consistently invested in writing. Nonrepresentative and nontextual practices, competences, strategies, limitations, and resources from communities of practice are deployed into channels where they are necessarily invested into a démarche, vote, resolution, or declaration. In bilateral and multilateral negotiations such as those that led to UN Security Council Resolution 1970, which in 2011 censured Gadhafi's regime and permitted intervention, diplomats invest their competences into influencing the drafting of a text.[119] Likewise, materialist approaches focusing on the material enablers, logistics, mediums, and locations of diplomacy also suggest that text is almost entirely unavoidable in diplomatic communication technology.[120] All information is eventually transcribed so it can be transmitted as email, telegraphed, typed, dictated, handwritten, or even semaphored. Similarly, conversations are usually textualised into a memorandum. Such instances of agreement, persuasion, or disagreement are committed to text because states and diplomacy's representational link to the state thrive and depend on bureaucratic knowledge, which can only exist in text. This means that, while diplomatic practice is not reducible to text, considering the state's dependence on textualised bureaucratic knowledge means that text stands as the most useful and consistently produced evidence of diplomatic practices.

If diplomatic practices are invested into the production of text, they are also therefore invested into representations of subjects and their contexts. Negotiations such as those around UN Resolutions 1970 and 1973, which unleashed the 2011 French, British, and American intervention in Libya, revolved *entirely* around the description of a subject, in this case Gadhafi's regime, and its spatial, temporal, and normative contexts, which established why threat should be assumed and action required. Such are the stakes of writing who we and the Other are.

How do we locate agency in diplomatic writing practices? A moment of choice, a moment of agency that then defines subsequent politics, the poststructuralist concept of the political is important in understanding diplomacy in relation to agency. Ernesto Laclau called this the moment at which 'the undecidable nature of the alternatives and their resolution through power relations becomes fully visible'.[121] Retrieving the political in the study of diplomacy involves a methodological rather than purely conceptual challenge. I locate the political at the instance when the diplomat drafts her cable and can make multiple choices in writing, drafting, referencing, and advising in her communication to and from the Ministry. This agent can choose language from the options she believes in, has read, or have been suggested by an endless array of agents (of which diplomats of other states are of particular interest here), institutional knowledge, ideology, existing policy, or even an encounter at an opium den. At that instance, the diplomatic agent can participate in the constitution of the representations that inform policymaking. She lives in that moment 'of undecidability', the single instance of drafting, of phrasing, of wording, that might influence policy or, conversely, never be heard of again. The diplomat writing dispatches has, however, but the smallest instance of agency, an instance of the political heavily circumscribed by the delimitation of the sensible and the acceptable permitted by training, practice, hierarchy, and homogenising supervision.

The greatest limitation on the diplomat's writing agency is the fate of her dispatch. The moment of agency ends the moment the cable is submitted, her name forgotten, masked by her superior's loftier rank.[122] As Barthes would say, the author is effectively dead at this point. In its journey through the microcosm of diplomatic writing practices, the text accumulates all the instances of 'the political' invested into it by its many authors as it is rewritten, summarised, analysed, translated, distilled into bullet points, archived, or ignored altogether. Each of these moments of practice is equally brief, single-instance, and circumscribed in terms of individual agency. The words, articulations, and frames of reference authored by a diplomat can, however, survive and thrive in the process of diplomatic knowledge production, perhaps significantly impacting discursive trends and policies, as occurred to Kennan's Long Telegram. The diplomatic text itself can therefore develop great agency. Unlike its authors, it is potentially immortal in time and boundless in dissemination and audiences. It has a life of its own, sometimes contributing to shaping world politics by constituting how international actors are seen and understood.

This journey reflects difficult yet vital philosophical choices. It is not solely because I am the child of an artist that I am so willing to believe that images, texts, and narratives have untold power to persuade. I believe that any work's purely aesthetic choices – as opposed to what that aesthetic might be said to represent – have communicative capacity of their own.[123] After the painting is signed, its capacities are no longer related to the author: they stem from its own aesthetic form and content.[124] This capacity needs to be empirically embraced and understood in investigating diplomacy. We are dealing with myriad instances of agency, instances of 'the political', that participate in representing subjects and their contexts. Consequently, research must focus, firstly, on how a single instance of the diplomatic text, its words and language, constructs subjects and their contexts, and, secondly, how these develop as the text joins the cascade of texts that together constitute diplomatic knowledge.

Researching how diplomatic text inscribes political identity

This chapter has thus far discussed the questions raised in scholarship on diplomacy and identity-making and has discussed approaches to researching how diplomatic knowledge represents subjects and their contexts. Though Der Derian, Neumann, and Constantinou brought poststructuralism to the study of diplomacy, their methods are not applicable to analysing the empirical evidence of diplomatic communication. Between Der Derian's location of diplomacy as an identity-inscribing practice, poststructuralist investigation of textual inscriptions of identity, Neumann's call to focus on specific practices, and Constantinou's conceptualisation of what is diplomatic, the journey towards a poststructuralist analytics of diplomacy is incomplete.

Our core concern is an approach determining how the diplomacy of an international actor recognises who other actors are and the contexts that animate them, how it is recognised by other actors, and interactions between these processes. The need to account for this specific aspect of diplomatic knowledge production helps refocus our work back to the main concern of this book: how diplomacy constitutes and represents knowledge about other actors. This is extremely relevant, for 'recognition' of interlocutors in particular and international actors in general explicitly and implicitly bears upon policymaking. In the light of the questions, conceptualisations, and methods analysed in this chapter, it is now possible to narrow the research puzzle of this project in order to guide the theoretical, methodological, and analytical advances offered in the next chapter.

Over this chapter, this question has been added to, complicated, and refined, allowing us to posit more specific enquiries to lead our analytical efforts. The first concerns how a diplomatic text, at the level of a single letter and at the level of relations among texts, constitutes approximation and differentiation among subjects, spatiality, temporality, and conflict. To understand how words and textual devices posit subjectivity through their literary production of meaning, it will be necessary to analyse a sample of diplomatic texts representative of the language and chief contentions of each case study. The second is to account for how specific representations of subjects and their contexts develop within the discursive economy of an international actor's diplomatic text. This requires analysis of texts across the cascade of diplomatic texts to locate how and in what circumstances new representations enter and change how diplomatic text represents specific subjects and their contexts. The third, and relatedly, is to account for whether and how a representation might replace previous ones. This is a question that reveals the agency of one or several diplomatic texts to transform the diplomatic knowledge production of one's own MFA or that of another actor.

This challenge calls for what might be called a microcosmic application of discourse analysis. This involves firstly bringing practice to the fore when considering the practices of writing, transmitting, analysing, translating, and summarising texts and transmitting those again. Secondly, recognising and embracing the power of words means that diplomatic text needs to be treated as literary production, analysing how its language links or differentiates. The locus of the microcosm of diplomatic knowledge production is the juxtaposition of texts that constitute the diplomatic text, each of which is the archaeological evidence of an instance of practice. This means considering each diplomat's textual contribution to the cascade not as a new iteration (which, as discussed above, risks exaggerating diplomats' agency) but rather as interventions into the textual cascade of knowledge production. Mapping the adventures of specific representations determines which interventions impact subsequent representations and which do not, helping account for the role of diplomatic knowledge production in major policy shifts.

Examining how James O'Sullivan, who was US consul to Hanoi in 1945, might have visited opium smoking establishments is more than quaint curiosity. It highlights that we are exploring texts that emerge from a multitude of small instances of the political, from an unexpected visit to the opium den to the words chosen to explain who the Vietnamese rebels were. When O'Sullivan filed his report, it entered the process of diplomatic knowledge production. The diplomatic agent might never again have the opportunity or agency to influence that text. That investment in agency might thrive in subsequent texts, perhaps even persuading one's own bosses, or even foreign diplomats and their policymakers. Sadly, as we shall see in Chapter 4, few heeded O'Sullivan's insights about Vietnam.

What makes this a distinctly *post*structuralist approach is recognising that diplomatic text is both politically productive and the result of specific practices. Produced by an entire microcosm of practices, diplomatic text does not innocently represent subjects and their contexts. It is implicated in the constitution of representations that classify and order subjects and their contexts into realms of meaning. With these insights in mind, and having specified the conceptual and methodological challenges that are involved in answering how diplomacy represents subjects and their contexts, we are now ready for the next chapter to devise concepts and methods that can turn this theoretical position into the tools necessary for systematic empirical analysis.

Notes

1 Satow, *A Guide to Diplomatic Practice*, 71.
2 See for instance Machiavelli's 'Notule' [notes for ambassadors], in *Tutte Le Opere Storiche, Politiche e Letterarie*; and Louis XIV's ambassador Callières, *De la manière de négocier avec les souverains*.
3 Satow, *A Guide to Diplomatic Practice*, 70.
4 Nicolson, *Diplomacy*, 60.
5 Nicolson, *Diplomacy*, 6.
6 Berridge, Keens-Soper, and Otte, *Diplomatic Theory from Machiavelli to Kissinger*.
7 Neumann, *At Home with the Diplomats*, 74. From Neumann I take the term 'diplomatic knowledge production'.
8 Hans Morgenthau, *Politics among Nations: The Struggle for Power and Peace* (New York: Knopf, 1966), 540.
9 Robert Gilpin, *War and Change in World Politics* (Cambridge: Cambridge University Press, 1983), 45.
10 Kissinger, *Diplomacy*, 28.
11 Kissinger, *White House Years*, 60.
12 Kissinger, *Diplomacy*, 312.
13 Kissinger, *Diplomacy*, 497.
14 William Minter, *King Solomon's Mines Revisited: Western Interests and the Burdened History of Southern Africa* (New York: Basic Books, 1988), 221.

15 This is ironic considering that Bismarck derived so much success from unleashing the ideational power of German nationalism, grounded on an articulation of identity, space, history, and normativity. For a more extensive critique, see Der Derian, 'Great Men, Monumental History, and Not-So-Grand Theory'.
16 Walt, *The Origins of Alliances*, 30.
17 Tony Smith, 'New Bottles for New Wine: A Pericentric Framework for the Study of the Cold War', *Diplomatic History* 24 (4), 2000, 567–91.
18 Vivienne Jabri, *Mediating Conflict: Decision-Making and Western Intervention in Namibia* (Manchester: Manchester University Press, 1990).
19 Vivienne Jabri and S. Chan, 'European Involvement in the Western Contact Group: The Stress and Convenience of Coalition Mediation', *Mediation in Southern Africa* (London: Macmillan, 1993).
20 Lloyd John Chingambo and Stephen Chan, 'Sanctions and South Africa: Strategies, Strangleholds, and Self-Consciousness', *Global Society: Journal of Interdisciplinary International Relations* 2 (2), 1988, 112–32; Stephen Chan, *Exporting Apartheid* (London: Macmillan Education, 1990).
21 Neumann, 'The English School on Diplomacy', 364.
22 Martin Wight, 'Why Is There No International Relations Theory?', in *International Theory: Critical Investigations*, ed. James Der Derian (London: Macmillan, 1995), 20; see also Christian Reus-Smit's analysis of the relationship between Renaissance diplomacy and normative Renaissance constructions, which is impressive in its focus on Lorenzo de' Medici's diplomatic practice in *The Moral Purpose of the State: Culture, Social Identity, and Institutional Rationality in International Relations* (Princeton, NJ: Princeton University Press, 2009), 63–84.
23 Hedley Bull, 'Society and Anarchy in International Relations', in *Diplomatic Investigations: Essays in the Theory of International Politics*, (London: George Allen & Unwin, 1966), 50.
24 Hedley Bull, *The Anarchical Society: A Study of Order in World Politics* (New York: Columbia University Press, 2002), 164.
25 Bull, *The Anarchical Society*, 166.
26 Bull, *The Anarchical Society*, 176.
27 Adam Watson, *Diplomacy: The Dialogue Between States* (London: Routledge, 1984), 148.
28 Watson, *Diplomacy*, 149.
29 C. Jönsson and M. Hall, *Essence of Diplomacy* (London: Palgrave Macmillan, 2005), 25.
30 Jönsson and Hall, *Essence of Diplomacy*, 66.
31 Paul Sharp, *Diplomatic Theory of International Relations* (Cambridge: Cambridge University Press, 2009), 12.
32 Sharp, *Diplomatic Theory of International Relations*, 307.
33 Neumann, 'The English School on Diplomacy'.
34 For instance, Banai, 'Diplomatic Imaginations'.
35 Costa Buranelli, 'Authoritarianism as an Institution?'.
36 Bull, *The Anarchical Society*, 172.

37 Yosef Lapid and Friedrich Kratochwil, *The Return of Culture and Identity in International Relations Theory* (London: Lynne Rienner, 1996).
38 Alexander Wendt, 'Collective Identity Formation and the International State', *The American Political Science Review* 88 (2), 1994, 385.
39 Wendt, 'Collective Identity Formation and the International State', 385.
40 Peter Joachim Katzenstein, *The Culture of National Security: Norms and Identity in World Politics* (New York: Columbia University Press, 1996); Peter Joachim Katzenstein, 'Alternative Perspectives on National Security', in *The Culture of National Security: Norms and Identity in World Politics* (New York: Columbia University Press, 1996).
41 Alexander Wendt, 'Anarchy Is What States Make of It: The Social Construction of Power Politics', *International Organization* 46 (02), 1992, 419.
42 Alexander Wendt, *Social Theory of International Politics* (Cambridge, UK; New York: Cambridge University Press, 1999), act 225; Hidemi Suganami, 'On Wendt's Philosophy: A Critique', *Review of International Studies* 28 (01), 2002, 23–37.
43 Charlotte Epstein, 'Who Speaks? Discourse, the Subject and the Study of Identity in International Politics', *European Journal of International Relations* 17 (2), 2011, 327–50.
44 Wendt, *Social Theory of International Politics*, 198.
45 Epstein, 'Who Speaks?', 338.
46 Neumann, *Uses of the Other*, 35.
47 Reus-Smit, *The Moral Purpose of the State*, 10, 30.
48 This issue has remained in constructivist work, see V. Kubálková, Nicholas Greenwood, and Onuf Paul Kowert, *International Relations in a Constructed World* (Armonk, NY: M. E. Sharpe, 1998), 102.
49 See also Maja Zehfuss, 'Constructivism and Identity: A Dangerous Liaison', *European Journal of International Relations* 7 (3), 2001, 315–48; Bahar Rumelili, 'Constructing Identity and Relating to Difference: Understanding the EU's Mode of Differentiation', *Review of International Studies* 30 (01), 2004, 27–47.
50 See especially Krebs and Jackson, 'Twisting Tongues and Twisting Arms'.
51 Jonathan Fisher, 'International Perceptions and African Agency: Uganda and Its Donors 1986–2010', D. Phil, University of Oxford, 2011, accessed 3 October 2014, http://ora.ox.ac.uk/objects/uuid:92fb2d83-7c05-4d64-a147-23f40c3a5df4; 'Managing Donor Perceptions'.
52 Fisher, 'Structure, Agency and Africa in the International System'.
53 Fisher, '"Some More Reliable Than Others"'.
54 For a more detailed critique of sender–receiver communicative models deriving from K. W. Deutsch, see C. M. Constantinou, O. P. Richmond, and A. Watson, *Cultures and Politics of Global Communication: Volume 34, Review of International Studies* (Cambridge: Cambridge University Press, 2008); Karl Wolfgang Deutsch and Karl W. Deutsch, *The Nerves of Government: Models of Political Communication and Control* (New York: Free Press of Glencoe, 1963); Karl Wolfgang Deutsch, *Nationalism and Social Communication: An*

Inquiry into the Foundations of Nationality (Cambridge, MA: MIT Press 1953); Karl W. Deutsch, 'On Communication Models in the Social Sciences', *Public Opinion Quarterly* 16 (3), 1952, 356–80.
55 Constantinou, Richmond, and Watson, *Cultures and Politics of Global Communication*, 34.
56 Michel Foucault, 'The Order of Discourse', in *Language and Politics*, ed. Michael Shapiro (Oxford: Blackwell, 1984).
57 Following from Wittgenstein and Nietzsche in particular, a fecund philosophy of language, speech, and enunciation emerged in parallel to Foucault but based in scholarly traditions of literary, linguistic, and expression analysis. Stanley E. Fish, 'How to Do Things with Austin and Searle: Speech Act Theory and Literary Criticism', *MLN (Modern Language Notes)* 91 (5), 1976, 983–1025; John R. Searle, 'Meaning and Speech Acts', *The Philosophical Review* 71 (4), 1962, 423–32; John R. Searle, *Speech Acts: An Essay in the Philosophy of Language* (Cambridge: Cambridge University Press, 1969); John R. Searle, *Expression and Meaning: Studies in the Theory of Speech Acts* (Cambridge: Cambridge University Press, 1985); J. L. Austin and Gilles Lane, *Quand Dire, C'est Faire*, 1970; John Langshaw Austin, *How to Do Things with Words* (Oxford: Clarendon Press, 1975). The drive to analyse the link between expression, normativity, emotion, and aesthetics as language is more developed in literary and art philosophy. See for instance the art theory treatment of the emergence of emotion in art in Freeman, *Art's Emotions*.
58 Michel Foucault, *Archaeology of Knowledge* (London: Routledge, 2002), 38.
59 Foucault, 'The Order of Discourse', 114.
60 Jenny Edkins, *Poststructuralism & International Relations: Bringing the Political Back In* (Boulder, CO: Lynne Rienner Publishers, 1999).
61 See the discussion in William E. Connolly, 'The Politics of Discourse', in *Language and Politics*, ed. Michael Shapiro (Oxford: Blackwell, 1984), 157.
62 Connolly, 'The Politics of Discourse', 158.
63 Connolly, *Identity, Difference*, x, 65.
64 Connolly, *Identity, Difference*, 176.
65 See, for example, Edward W. Said, 'The Problem of Textuality: Two Exemplary Positions', *Critical Inquiry*, 1978, 673–714.
66 Michael J. Shapiro, 'Literary Production as a Politicizing Practice', *Political Theory*, 1984, 387–422.
67 See Chapter 4 in Julia Kristeva, *Desire in Language: A Semiotic Approach to Literature and Art*, eds Leon S. Roudiez and Alice Jardine, trans. Thomas Gora (New York: Columbia University Press, 1980), 124.
68 Michael J. Shapiro, 'Literary Production as a Politicizing Practice', in *Language and Politics* (Oxford: Blackwell, 1984), 222; M. J. Shapiro, *The Politics of Representation: Writing Practices in Biography, Photography, and Policy Analysis* (Madison, WI: University of Wisconsin Press, 1988), acts 88–120.
69 Jonathan Haslam, *No Virtue Like Necessity* (New Haven, CT: Yale University Press, 2002), 162.

70 See, for instance, Ranke's influential analysis in *The Theory and Practice of History: Edited with an Introduction by Georg G. Iggers*, ed. Georg G. Iggers, First Edition (London: Routledge, 2010); and 'George Kennan "The Sources of Soviet Conduct" (1946)'.
71 See 'On Geography', in Foucault, *Power/Knowledge*, 1980.
72 Said, *Orientalism*; Ashley, 'Living on Border Lines', 89.
73 Connolly, *Identity, Difference*, 206.
74 Connolly, *Identity, Difference*, 176.
75 See, for example, Laffey and Weldes, 'Decolonizing the Cuban Missile Crisis'.
76 This potential is very evident in Fisher, '"Some More Reliable than Others"'.
77 Jabri, *Discourses on Violence*, 130.
78 David Campbell, *Writing Security: United States Foreign Policy and the Politics of Identity*, Second Revised Edition (Manchester: Manchester University Press, 1998), 56.
79 David Campbell, *National Deconstruction: Violence, Identity and Justice in Bosnia* (Minneapolis, MN: University of Minnesota Press, 1998), 86–99.
80 Campbell, *National Deconstruction*, 245.
81 Campbell, *National Deconstruction*, 94–98.
82 L. Hansen, *Security as Practice: Discourse Analysis and the Bosnian War* (London: Routledge, 2006), 23–37.
83 Hansen, *Security as Practice*, 28.
84 Hansen, *Security as Practice*, 212.
85 Hansen, *Security as Practice*, 76.
86 Hansen, *Security as Practice*, 37.
87 C. Weber, *Simulating Sovereignty: Intervention, the State, and Symbolic Exchange* (Cambridge: Cambridge University Press, 1995), 37.
88 Ashley, 'Living on Border Lines'.
89 Buzan, Wæver, and De Wilde, *Security*.
90 K. M. Fierke, *Diplomatic Interventions: Conflict and Change in a Globalizing World* (Basingstoke: Palgrave, 2005).
91 Adler-Nissen, 'Stigma Management in International Relations', 71; Adler-Nissen, *Opting Out of the European Union*, 91. Stigmatisation is a particularly interesting framework to understand US efforts to form international consensus against Vietminh from 1949, following from the diplomatic events studied in Chapter 4.
92 Sending, Pouliot, and Neumann, *Diplomacy and the Making of World Politics*, 55, 284.
93 Der Derian, *Antidiplomacy*, 3.
94 Der Derian, *On Diplomacy*, 134.
95 Der Derian, *Antidiplomacy*, 2.
96 Constantinou, *On the Way to Diplomacy*, 17.
97 Constantinou, *On the Way to Diplomacy*, 148; see also the vital theory and approach to deconstruction it is based on in Jacques Derrida, Peter Caws, and Mary Ann Caws, 'Sending: On Representation', *Social Research*, 1982, 294–326; J. Derrida, *The Post Card: From Socrates to Freud and Beyond* (Chicago,

IL: University of Chicago Press, 1987); J. Derrida, *Writing and Difference* (London: Routledge, 2001).
98 See Andrea Wilson Nightingale, *Spectacles of Truth in Classical Greek Philosophy: Theoria in Its Cultural Context* (Cambridge: Cambridge University Press, 2004).
99 Constantinou, *On the Way to Diplomacy*, 120–51.
100 Constantinou, *On the Way to Diplomacy*, 116.
101 Neumann, *Russia and the Idea of Europe*; *Uses of the Other*; 'The Other in European Self-Definition: An Addendum to the Literature on International Society', *Review of International Studies* 17 (4), 1991, 327–48.
102 Iver B. Neumann, 'Self and Other in International Relations', *European Journal of International Relations* 2 (2), 1996, 139–74.
103 Williams and Neumann, 'From Alliance to Security Community'.
104 Neumann, *Uses of the Other*, 208.
105 Neumann, *Uses of the Other*, 208–13.
106 I would like to thank Athanasios Gkoutzioulis for many fruitful conversations on this subject. See Athanasios Gkoutzioulis, 'With Great Power Comes Great Responsibility: On Foucault's Notions of Power, Subjectivity, Freedom and Their (Mis)Understanding in IR', *Global Society* 32 (1), 2018, 88–110.
107 Neumann, 'Returning Practice to the Linguistic Turn'.
108 Neumann, *Diplomatic Sites*; *At Home with the Diplomats*.
109 Neumann, *At Home with the Diplomats*, 69–85.
110 Murty, *The International Law of Diplomacy*; Berridge, Keens-Soper, and Otte, *Diplomatic Theory from Machiavelli to Kissinger*.
111 Hannah Gurman, '"Learn to Write Well": The China Hands and the Communist-ification of Diplomatic Reporting', *Journal of Contemporary History* 45 (2), 2010, 452.
112 Neumann, *At Home with the Diplomats*, 67.
113 Neumann, *At Home with the Diplomats*, 89.
114 Dittmer, *Diplomatic Material*; Wille, 'Diplomatic Cable'; Wille, 'Representation and Agency in Diplomacy'; Pouliot, *International Pecking Orders*.
115 Adler-Nissen and Pouliot, 'Power in Practice'.
116 Vincent Pouliot, 'Diplomats as Permanent Representatives: The Practical Logics of the Multilateral Pecking Order', *International Journal* 66 (3), 2011, 543–61; Pouliot, *International Pecking Orders*; Neumann, *Diplomatic Sites*.
117 Cynthia Enloe, *Bananas, Beaches and Bases: Making Feminist Sense of International Politics* (Berkeley, CA: University of California Press, 2014); Iver B. Neumann, 'The Body of the Diplomat', *European Journal of International Relations* 14 (4), 2008, 671–95.
118 Pouliot, 'Diplomats as Permanent Representatives'.
119 Adler-Nissen and Pouliot, 'Power in Practice'.
120 Jason Dittmer and Fiona McConnell, eds, *Diplomatic Cultures and International Politics: Translations, Spaces and Alternatives*, First Edition (London: Routledge, 2015); Dittmer, *Diplomatic Material*; Wille, 'Diplomatic Cable'; Crean, 'War on the Line'.

121 Ernesto Laclau, *New Reflections on the Revolution of Our Time* (London: Verso, 1997), 35.
122 Though this varies mission by mission and is certainly standard in UK DipTels (Diplomatic Telegram Reports), the vast majority of the diplomatic communication analysed for this book bears the name of the head of mission (say the ambassador) and only occasionally (if it is controversial or indeed if it deserves particular praise) bears the name of its original author – the political officer, for instance.
123 In art theory, this is commonly referred to as 'formalism'. See, for example, Judith A. Cizek, 'The "Définition Du Néo-Traditionnisme" of Maurice Denis: Contributing Factors Leading to Its Content, Its Premises, and Later Influences', 1975, accessed 12 August 2022, https://commons.lib.niu.edu/handle/10843/19699.
124 By 'formalism', I mean the communicative capacity of the work's own purely aesthetic choices – as opposed to what those aesthetics attempt to represent. This is the only missing link in Shapiro's analysis of photography's representation-making capacity. Indeed, the only critique I would level at Shapiro's artistic analysis is the underestimation of the distinctly formalist aspect of aesthetic communication. See Shapiro, *The Politics of Representation*.

3

Analysing how diplomatic text describes: a method

> The maker of language was not modest enough to think that he only gave designations to things, he believed rather that with his words he expressed the widest knowledge of the things; in reality language is the first step in the endeavour after science. Here also it is belief in ascertained truth, from which the mightiest sources of strength have flowed. Much later – only now – it is dawning upon men that they have propagated a tremendous error in their belief in language.
> Friedrich Wilhelm Nietzsche, *Human, All Too Human*[1]

Language's hidden reality-making machinery is our core analytical site.[2] The previous chapter concluded that poststructuralist approaches to diplomacy's constitution of identity necessitate development to enable large-scale empirical analysis. In response, I approach diplomatic communication as a textual site governed by the claim to represent the praxis and theory of the state. That is why I write about a distinctly *diplomatic* text. The methodological consequence impels us to treat records of oral, written, and broadcast diplomatic communication as a textual site to explore how it frames representation of subjects and their contexts. As the previous chapter foregrounded, there are two significant conceptual challenges in applying discursive analysis to diplomatic communication that stem from the particularities of the praxis of diplomatic knowledge production.

The first challenge is conceptualising diplomatic practice more specifically than all nonmilitary relations among states. Loose definition conceptually obfuscates the real work of diplomats in discrete knowledge-production practices. The methodological consequences concern the selection of primary evidence for discourse analysis, and how to account for diplomatic practice and institutions in researching its textual knowledge production. Building on Constantinou's conceptualisation of 'the diplomatic', this chapter proposes an understanding of diplomacy that bridges the practice/theory divide and bequeaths us a rigorous praxis-based rationale to inform primary data selection and map knowledge production pathways. The second challenge emerges from the nature of diplomatic textual knowledge production. The production of knowledge is the sum of many individual texts, a veritable cascade of texts, posing methodological questions in accounting for, firstly, a single text's construction of subjects and their contexts and, secondly, the further evolutions of those representations within the Ministry of Foreign Affairs (MFA) and beyond across numerous rewrites of the original. To account for and explore the intertextual nature of the cascade of texts, this chapter advances a rigorous method to trace how representations evolve.

In response to these challenges, I propose three distinct interlinked methodological steps. The first maps reporting and instruction pathways – who reports to whom in other words – allowing analysis to account for where and how information moves up and instructions flow back down the chain of reporting within and beyond the MFA. The second step analyses individual texts in detail, showing how diplomatic knowledge production frames representations of subjects and their contexts in a single text. To achieve this, this approach imports into IR literary analysis methods to analyse text and identify textual markers called topoi. The third step accounts for the evolution of representations of subjects and their contexts across texts and time by following topoi textual markers. The logic of this three-step method is illustrated in Figure 3.1.

On the left is the first step, the mapping of the reporting and instruction pathways. It reveals not only what agents and groups of agents were involved at any one point in knowledge production, but also what texts they produced, defining the cascade of texts to analyse, and informing understanding of links between them. In the centre, the second step involves analysing the constitution of representations, how words are deployed, contexts invoked, differences and similarities inscribed, as well as identifying the topoi textual markers that signpost the presence of each. On the right is the third, which involves an intertextual study that traces the history of representations as they evolve across time and texts, the presence, absence, evolution, and crossovers from the cascade of text of one actor to that of another (crossovers marked with arrows).

This chapter addresses the above challenges to then presents a complete analytical method and research design. This method can be applied to any case of diplomatic knowledge production to determine how it came to represent subjects and their contexts in specific ways. To demonstrate the method's analytical utility and illustrate its applicability, the first section of this chapter identifies two post-World War II (WWII) case studies, from the 1940s to the present, where policy decisions were explicitly determined by specific representations. Analysis of these cases, onto which the method is applied in Chapters 4 and 5, allows us to illustrate the analytics

Analysing how diplomatic text describes

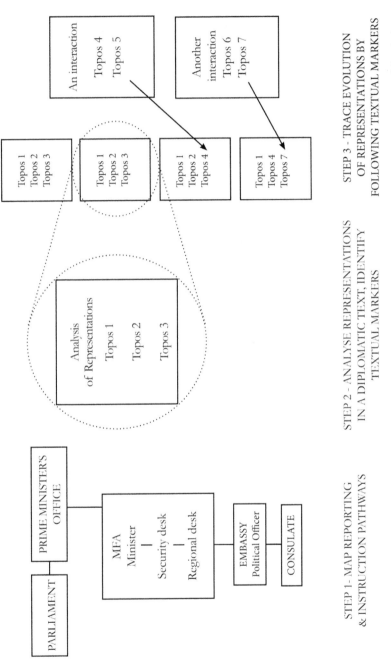

Figure 3.1 Three steps to analyse representation in diplomatic text. Arrows denote where representations (signposted by their topoi) are observed to have crossed over from one text to another. Diagram by Tally de Orellana.

involved and appreciate the detail, evolution, dynamics, and impact of how diplomatic knowledge production deals with representing subjects and their contexts. The second section defines the diplomatic text conceptually and what this means for data selection and mapping reporting pathways. Third, this chapter discusses the approach needed to analyse individual diplomatic texts before, in the fourth section, how to identify topoi textual markers. Fifth, the chapter discusses how to follow these markers to trace the development of representations in the cascade of diplomatic texts, while the sixth section explains how the method is executed.

On the marches of diplomatic knowledge production: selecting case studies

This method can be applied to a variety of cases. Since developing it in 2015, I have applied it to analysis of the diplomacy leading up to the 2011 US–British–French intervention in Libya, US–Malian relations in the 2000s, US–Moroccan diplomacy concerning Western Sahara 1975–2011, the role of French diplomacy in obtaining US assistance against anticolonial Vietnamese rebels in the 1940s, and the emerging international alliance between ethnonationalist governments in the 2020s.[3] While I hope my reader can already imagine further applications, this book relies on two case studies to demonstrate how the method works, its potential, and its historical and contemporary applicability, as well as its relevance to thinking about diplomacy analytically, as practice, policy, and scholarship. Their selection bears some explanation as, besides demonstrating the applicability of this method, it supports conceptual reflection on the dynamics of diplomatic knowledge production at the end of this book.

Effectively demonstrating this method requires us to explore the wild side of diplomacy – that is, cases of diplomacy at the borderlands of knowledge production, where representations change, allowing us glimpses into how representation works and changes and what makes these changes possible.[4] In diplomacy, the most visible examples concern instances when previously little-known actors enter diplomatic attention, uncategorised or with limited categorisations and frames of reference, which means other actors seek to understand their nature and position in global politics. These are the instances when, because categorisation is due, beginning, or on-going, diplomacy invests in representations of newly relevant subjects and the contexts that motivate them, particularly when policy depends upon identifying what kind of actor they are.

To methodically retrieve the nuance for which Hansen criticised Campbell's analysis of Yugoslav identities, our cases involve transition from a major policy concern to another, like antifascism to anticommunism or anticommunism to anti-Islamic terror.[5] These provide the greatest contradictions (it is difficult to represent an actor as both communist *and* Islamist) and instability (the moment of change from one representation to another). They provide opportunities to examine the nuances of these representations, how contradictions are obscured, what made specific representations possible, how other actors intervened, how it was possible to change how an actor sees another, and what was at stake. They include an already well-researched case, which demonstrates that the method can add analytical value to well-parsed scholarship, as well as a little-known one that can show how this method is useful to resolve understanding of ongoing issues. Historically, they cover from the aftermath of WWII until the early twenty-first century, to account for contemporary dynamics and practices.

Two diplomatic cases lend themselves to this demonstration. The first, the diplomacy surrounding the beginning of the 1945–54 Indochina War, exhibits representations of anticolonial rebel alliance Vietminh by French diplomacy that evolved from fascist Japanese puppets to Stalinist stooges. The second, the diplomacy of the Western Sahara conflict, 1975–present, saw Moroccan representation of Sahrawi independence group POLISARIO shift from communist to enabler of Islamist terrorism.[6] Both conflicts, scholarship thus far agrees, were played out in diplomatic communication.[7] Both France in 1948 and Morocco in 1980 and again in 2010 obtained substantial military and diplomatic assistance on the basis that their foes were also threats to the United States due to communism and terrorism, demonstrating the huge policy influence at stake in diplomatic descriptions.[8]

These cases help generalise applicability of this method geographically, historically, and archivally. They place colonial/postcolonial relations at the heart of diplomatic analysis while analysing the diplomatic communications of a range of actors from across both sides of the colonial divide including France, Britain, America, Vietnam 1945–48 and America, Morocco, Western Sahara, France 1990s–2011. This is vital, for in both cases, as with many modern international politics, coloniality and postcoloniality were key issues. Historically, the case studies cover the current late modern era of diplomacy that emerged in the aftermath of WWII. This makes the method valuable in terms of its capacity to produce insights for both historical and contemporary diplomacy. Empirically, the case of Vietnam is ideal in terms of demonstrating the validity of this method, as the last classified documents were finally released in 2016, making it possible to analyse it in depth and detail not available when using a limited range of sources as is usually the case with contemporary events. Likewise, Western Sahara provides a rare glimpse into contemporary diplomacy thanks to the US Wikileaks Embassy Cables leaks.

This book examines these two cases to provide a representative application of the method that does not shy away from diplomatic practice, historical complexity, the contradictions at the heart of all political subjectivity, and the detail where the devil lies. Why select contradictory borderline cases rather than those featuring simpler radical Others emerging from the netherworld like ISIS? Irreconcilable contradictions in representations afford the opportunity to understand how certain representations fail. Uncontradictory representations would reveal how representations work, but not their limit conditions of possibility. For instance, France's failed attempt to frame Vietminh as fascist in 1945, or Morocco's successful late 2000s quest to cast POLISARIO as enablers of terrorism, feature contradictions that reveal the detail of how representations do or do not convince. Our empirical subject lies amid the conflict between representations borne in diplomacy. In the case studies selected, this means looking at three strands of the diplomatic text, each strand the diplomatic knowledge-production machinery of one international actor. For the First Indochina War, these are the United States, France, and Vietminh; for the Western Sahara case, the United States, Morocco, and POLISARIO.

Beyond this book, the only case-selection rationale applicable to all researchers is competence in each historical or contemporary field and locale. This entails access to data in archives and other sources, as well as the means to access cultural, historical, and even literary understanding. The author you are so patiently indulging, for example, is sufficiently competent in these cultural and historical contexts but not others that he would like to explore, such as Chinese diplomacy with Vietnam in 1975–79.[9] This method demands the historical, linguistic, cultural, and cultural resources necessary to understand references and context, as well as how diplomatic communications use language. For example, to research Western Sahara, it is vital to understand why a 'summer in peace' is such a deeply moving and political subject for any Sahrawi, like it is vital to the First Vietnam War that 'Gaullism' is a very particular form of French nationalism. This is because discourse analysis not only needs contextual knowledge; illuminating the many roles, subjectivities, and discourses of a text requires an understanding of its uses and its history. Having chosen our case studies, we can now move on to how to select documents from the vastness of the diplomatic archive.

Selecting and mapping data in the diplomatic pouch: the diplomatic moment

After a speech in the European Parliament attacking Britain's 2005 EU presidency in which MEP Nigel Farage claimed to represent British interests,

Tony Blair responded, 'You sit with our country's flag. You do not represent our country's interest'.[10] Who does, then? As highlighted in the previous chapter, Farage is not alone in being uncertain about diplomatic representation. What is 'the diplomatic'? Consequently, what constitutes diplomatic text?

These questions determine the chronological, documentary, institutional, and authorial limits of data selection. We are particularly concerned with conceptually delimiting who, and at what instances of practice, represents the state – a question that cannot be left to documentary convenience or institutional affiliation. Due to its traditional focus on State Department data, the American Diplomatic History tradition seldom takes into account instances when individuals and institutions outside the Ministry participate in diplomatic knowledge production.[11] Problems delimiting data selection plagued Der Derian and Campbell too and might explain why Neumann never investigated identity formation in diplomatic communication. Hansen proposes three data selection models that 'identify the location of different discourses in relation to official discourse and other sites', resulting in source selection based on collective authorship (institutions, 'sites') and register (audience).[12] Adoption in our method would entail following one based only on the letters of ambassadors, for instance, or an institution. This is inadequate as it cannot capture the work of nondiplomats performing diplomatic tasks but would include nondiplomatic work by diplomats such as the embassy's bills. Neumann, however, points to the solution: focus on diplomatic practice as one of collective authorship.[13]

A model is needed that accounts for functional rather than institutional authorship. Empirical definition of diplomatic authorship can be resolved through a concept I call the *diplomatic moment*. This conceptualisation resolves who is a diplomat (and therefore authors' diplomatic text) by drawing on Constantinou's definition of 'the diplomatic', bridging the theory/praxis divide so apparent in researching diplomacy and offering an opportunity to resolve the crippling indiscipline hitherto found in diplomatic data selection. Bourdieu's critique that social and political theory sometimes fail to 'pay the price of a veritable conversion to the requirements of empirical research' is important.[14] If we were Bourdieusian, we would be looking at the 'field' of diplomatic representation, an important field of research that in our case, however, does not focus on the role of text, sovereignty, representation, and history in diplomacy's rarefied condition as heralds.[15] This book pays the methodological price when considering the empirical textual evidence of diplomatic communication, whence its search for a theory *and* praxis model determining when an instance of practice is diplomatic.

As discussed in the previous chapter, Constantinou's 'embassy of theory' conceptualises diplomatic performance of sovereign state theory as a delegation of presence.[16] Performing the sovereign underpins diplomatic practice in a constitutive loop where practising diplomacy reifies the theory of the state, while the latter enables the practice of representation.[17] Practice is *only* diplomatic when performing the delegation of the state's presence,[18] discounting institutionally 'diplomatic' written practices that do not involve delegation of the state's presence, from leases to laundry and telegraph bills. At those instances, diplomats are only 'diplomatic' because of institutional affiliation, for 'the diplomat exists only as representing the will of the sovereign and never her own'.[19] Conversely, individuals who upon occasion perform representation of the state, such as politicians or military officers like the Spanish Navy Captain in Chapter 1, also become diplomats for the purpose of this analysis: their textual production is, at that instance, diplomatic.

The embassy of the state's theory can be written, spoken, even signalled in unusual ways (think of Khrushchev's shoe), and can take place at various sites, from the embassy to Stalin's private quarters. But this instance of diplomatic practice must be reported into the structure of diplomatic knowledge production if it is to be implemented and mean anything. A crucial conceptual link, an instance of paper-moving praxis, is missing between Constantinou's theory-as-praxis and Neumann's diplomatic knowledge production: how does the result of writing praxis enter diplomatic knowledge? It is a simple move of enormous significance. For the instance of practice to gain significance within the diplomatic machine, somebody must *submit* a text. Click 'send'; the author dies; the text is now diplomatic.

I call this missing step *the diplomatic moment*. In Stalin and Churchill's first meeting in 1942, initial hostility and disagreements were resolved during an epic drinking session in Stalin's private rooms.[20] Before an alliance could emerge, both Stalin and Churchill had to be debriefed, issue instructions, and make notes for their diplomats to implement the agreements. Had they been too hungover to remember (Churchill was terribly unwell the next day), the agreement might have suffered or disappeared. This is just as true for routine diplomacy, which is why countless reports make it explicit: 'I have investigated and found …' 'I have carried out démarche and report that …'. This is the entrance of Constantinou's diplomatic practice into Neumann's 'bureaucratic mode of knowledge production'. Communication *into* diplomatic knowledge production of the instance of praxis can be oral, telephonic, emailed, telegraphic, mailed, or even signalled, but it must occur. Most of these forms of reporting are eventually textualised, which is why text is so important to state bureaucracy, as it makes the ephemeral instance of practice permanent by institutionalising its results.[21] After Stalin and Churchill were debriefed on their agreement, Anthony Eden, Vyacheslav Molotov, and their diplomats could proceed with forming the alliance.

Analysing how diplomatic text describes 65

We are following the paper trail left behind by the diplomatic moments. If the diplomatic moment involves spoiling foreign dignitaries with Ferrero Rocher and sending information back, then the reports to the MFA, and textual evidence of what MFA officers did with it, are our data. The diplomatic moment's textualisation of praxis allows analysis to explore the evidence of that instance. This is the diplomatic text. Moving from methodological concepts to archival research, the consequence is a firm and clear rationale for data selection determined by the entrance of accounts of diplomatic practice into diplomatic knowledge, which are, usually, consistently filed in diplomatic archives.

This method includes the following main categories of textual documentary evidence, ordered by functional authorship delimited with reference to the diplomatic moment. For the two case studies in this book, this has meant collecting over eight thousand documents of these types from archives and beyond. Specific sources are discussed in each empirical chapter.

MFA diplomats	Cables, summaries of cables, reports, analysis, scene-setters, and recommendations drafted based on reporting and other sources. Triangulation and cross-referencing with other reporting and derived texts is helpful because reporting is but the beginning of diplomacy's knowledge production. Data triangulation furthermore evidences how a text relates to and draws on existing concerns and priorities.
Political figures	*Only* when they perform diplomatic duties or missions representing government. Farage's membership of the European Parliament is not such an instance, but a 2014 visit to Hong Kong by a British parliamentary committee was.[22] In the Vietnam case, we shall meet Pham Ngoc Thach, a young surgeon who frequently represented the Vietnamese government.[23] This highlights the usefulness of the diplomatic moment concept, as it can account for the old diplomatic concern with accreditation and bridge it for the purpose of data selection.
Nondiplomatic state institutions	This category is the most liable to overextend into irrelevance. It includes the textual production of non-MFA government bodies, agencies, and quasi-governmental organisations. On one end of this spectrum, we find the CIA providing reports to State Department officials or the Moroccan Ministry of Saharan affairs (CORCAS), which represents 'Moroccan Sahara'. On the other end, we include research by affiliate bodies and charities, but only when their texts are employed in diplomatic communication.

(*Continued*)

(Continued)

Private firms	Commercial bodies tasked with representation of the policy of a state, such as British strategic communications consultancy Portland Communications. Their diplomatic links are not evident, but their textual production sometimes conforms to the data selection rationale. An example used in this book is the Moroccan-American Center for Policy (MACP), a NGO US-registered 'agent of the Moroccan Government', which promotes Moroccan policy in Washington.[24]

Let us not, however, be naïve about archives. The greatest challenge to studying diplomacy from the inside is access. Most diplomatic archives are entirely inaccessible and fiercely guarded, a challenge for this data-hungry method. Even where laws commit governments to declassify, MFAs and governments can keep information inaccessible to research for decades, an average of forty years in the United States and Britain and closer to sixty years in France – seventy-five years if it concerns colonial wars, probably forever in the case of Algeria. This has implications for the applicability of the analytical toolkit here presented. It means that ideal application of the method, which requires access to vast volumes of internal and external diplomatic communications, is usually only possible for historical cases. This is why the fullest and most ideal application of this method has been an extensive account of how French diplomacy between 1945 and 1948 persuaded the United States to support their colonial war in Vietnam. Even that account could have been archivally incomplete, as Vietnamese diplomatic archives are classified. What saved that project was communication triangulation. That is, if I send you an email, it is likely that both of us will have a copy, and, if we are lucky, even copies of preceding ones, allowing research to find them in the correspondent's archive.

Analysis of contemporary cases, however, relies heavily on leaks, unless one is lucky enough to collaborate with an MFA, and in those cases research dissemination is very restricted. Reconstructing the data of the cascade of diplomatic knowledge production through leaks is possible if the leaks are substantial and comprehensive enough. The *Pentagon Papers*, for example, do not cover the entire hierarchy of the cascade and are too sparse to analytically relate to one another. Conversely, the Wikileaks State Department documents, the Moroccan Wikileaks du Makhzen, and the hack of Hillary Clinton's entire email server are very useful because they are comprehensive and include messages from across the diplomatic and policy hierarchy, from diplomats on the ground to replies by the White House and the National Security Council.[25]

Analysing how diplomatic text describes 67

There is controversy about the use of diplomatic leaks in scholarship, with discomfort expressed at their analytical use usually focusing on the *need* for secrecy in diplomacy and unintended tragic consequences, of which Wikileaks had a lot.[26] I would advance, however, that this concern is more relevant to the leak itself than to its scholarly analysis. The broader question of diplomatic secrecy is ultimately an ontological one that ethically and analytically sends us back to think about the 'symbiotic relationship between diplomatic knowledge and practice' and the very real issue of who statecraft is for and its accountability, which concerns the 'contested character of contemporary diplomacy and ultimately its potential for change'.[27]

In chronological delimitation of data selection, the text itself reveals when to stop. This is achieved by applying Nietzsche's own approach to the history of an idea, genealogy, which runs backwards in time from the consecration of a myth, tracing its evolution to reveal its history. The conceptualisation behind this is discussed below in the section dedicated to tracing the history of representations in diplomatic text, but it is worth explaining in terms of archival practice: if a representation is present in a text, the imperative is to research in reverse chronological order how it got there and where it came from, eventually reaching its initial appearances, revealing the agents and contextual epistemological environment that permitted that representation to appear and thrive but not others. In this way, the presence or absence of certain representations in the text determines the chronological extent of data collection, making the rationale for source selection, chronology, and archival research methodologically transparent.

The final démarche involves mapping the cascade of diplomatic knowledge production. This involves ascertaining the validity of the diplomatic paper trail by deferring to practice in addition to official hierarchies. This is because, though formally diplomats are supposed to report through official channels, these pathways are sometimes shortened for institutional or policy convenience or take unexpected paths. The lower institutional end of the textual cascade poses less problems as documents explicitly refer to one another, making it possible to find them. Following orders to diplomats is also possible since they are widely disseminated and are explicitly referenced in reporting. The difficulty lies in following the textual trail up to policymakers to gauge how diplomacy informs them, for the documented textual trail stops at that bureaucratic caesura. This is not essential for our project as we do not examine executive decision-making, but it is vital to understand how diplomatic text contributes to informing policymakers.[28]

A small set of interviews with diplomats and informational gatekeepers is necessary to ascertain the journey of texts across bureaucratic caesuras. The interviews carried out for the case studies in this book pointed the way to essential types of documents – such as requests for intelligence reports – and sometimes revealed unexpected reporting pathways.[29] For example, interviews with senior analysts at the US Department of State, with staffers at the US Senate's Foreign Relations Committee, and at the offices of individual senators showed that gaps in reporting pathways arose from practices across bureaucratic caesuras.[30] In the United States, information was delivered in the form of summaries, presentations, informal messages, and other means. To confirm whether the documents I was collecting were drawn upon to inform policymakers, I showed interviewees copies of documents collected at the US National Archives. They explained that policymakers seldom see such originals but that they are cited in summaries, made reference to, and sometimes attached as evidence.[31] The interviews ensure that the textual paper trail follows the pathways of diplomatic knowledge production, allowing the researcher to map and analyse them. When this is not possible, the entire trail must be reconstructed using the texts themselves, which is only possible for historical cases where archival data is plentiful and comprehensive.

The method can, as a consequence of this approach, follow descriptions wherever they go, not only where institutional arrangements suggest they should. This is vital because institutional roles and relevance change over time. The State Department of 2010 was not as influential as that of 1945, which is why the genealogy sections in the Western Sahara and Vietnam case studies deal with it differently: in the Vietnam case study, the pathways diagram links the Department directly to the White House, and documents corroborate that this was the pathway taken by information. In the Western Sahara diplomacy of the 2010s, other institutions such as Congress and the NSC – and their diplomatic knowledge production work – must be accounted for.

Empirically linking the theory and practice of diplomacy to its textual paper trail is a key advance. The next step in this method involves analysing diplomatic text to inductively learn how its descriptions constitute subjects and their contexts.

Reading representation in a single diplomatic text

Representation is not an unproblematic link between sign and signified, for this is a link established in language.[32] This is a philosophical choice to understand the social world as constituted in language, rather than merely described in language. This section discusses applying this poststructuralist concept and its resulting methodology to representations of subjects and their contexts in diplomatic text. A method for the first step of our approach, analysis of a single text's representations, is developed drawing on poststructuralist literary theory and analysis, building on them with further refinements that reflect the nature of diplomatic text.

Drawing on Barthes, early poststructuralists like Shapiro treated political text as literary production rather than straightforward representation.[33] Keeping in mind Nietzschean and Foucauldian warnings to be suspicious of an enunciation's claims of representation, this is a sound strategy.[34] Literary production is free from the claim to truth of scientific texts. The difference is, however, only referential: in literature, language exists 'in an independent form, difficult of access, folded back upon the enigma of its own origin and existing wholly in reference to the pure act of writing' – that is, abstracted from the signified.[35] Considering text as constructed enables analysis to consider how its textual devices create objects, their contexts, and relations among them.[36] Treating diplomatic text as literary production is even more appropriate for diplomatic communication than it was for Shapiro's policy texts because in diplomatic communication, the relationship between its form and its claim to signifying content is essentially deferred. That is, language acts as beginning and end of a discourse of proof, and grounding is essentially postponed – very rarely is proof as blatant as Soviet missiles on ships' decks in 1962. Colin Powell's 2003 UN intervention claiming there American intelligence had evidence of weapons of mass destruction (WMDs) in Iraq exemplifies the deferral of grounding, but also limitations on the possibility of unveiling such proof.[37] Diplomatic text therefore exists in an epistemologically closed loop that posits proof as protected, made secret for security purposes, and yet grounds discourses of action upon it. This is why our analysis must treat diplomatic communications as textual production.

Rather than truth, the analysis here proposed focuses on retrieving subjectivity. Discourse analysis can retrieve how a discourse depoliticises its subjectivity to appear neutral, natural, and ahistorical.[38] To retrieve the subjectivity of depoliticised discourse, one can pervert neutral, ahistorical, and apolitical language by reversing questions and vocabulary.[39] In this way, destabilising the sign demonstrates 'its arbitrariness'. Examining the use of a word in contrast with its root points to the politicisation that placed it there[40] and its derivation.[41] For signs assigned to social and political bodies the reversal reveals violent, repressive and categorising applications of power behind the depoliticised lexicon of bureaucratic technologies of power.[42] Studying derivation involves reaching the limits of signification, achieved by historicising its deployments.[43] We must dig below the current use of the term 'Ministry of Defence', for example, to when 'defence' was only part of the 'Ministry of War'. This uncovers a paradox: either military aggression ('war') was renounced entirely (leaving only 'defence'), or 'defence' replaced 'war' as the sign for the same activity. The representational gap between 'war' and 'defence' is the subjectivity of violence, revealed by the history of the word and its usage in articulation of a discourse.[44] Such tactics destabilise the connection between sign and signified, highlighting linguistic caesuras that, if found or provoked (as poststructuralists are fond of doing at scholarly conferences), lay bare the politicisation of discourse and its subjectivity.[45] This is the archaeology of knowledge, one vocable at a time.

Demonstrating the power of text to create objects and relations among them does not amount to systematic analysis. My task, unlike Shapiro's, is not to demonstrate that diplomatic text politicises, but to understand at a large scale how it does this. This requires systematising analysis of many single diplomatic texts to make them readily comparable. To systematise discourse analysis and the 'thick description' of single texts, this section introduces to IR the methodological logic behind literary commentary. Literary commentary, the bane of first-year literature students, is a formal and systematic analysis of a text designed to understand how its various elements, from form to vocabulary, create a little world out of verse or prose. I specifically draw on the Barthian version, best exemplified in his spectacular *S/Z*, which very specifically focuses on retrieving how meaning is subjectively oriented one way by the text to the exclusion of others. The core objective of this distinctly *post*-structuralist commentary is to show how textual elements operate within different systems of meaning, showing that the plurality of the text is only constrained by the construction of frames that privilege some interpretations over others.[46] In the empirical chapters that follow, only twelve texts are analysed in detail for illustration and demonstration, but this analysis is performed on all texts considered. To make the commentaries representative of the vast body of texts studied, each case study's selection of texts to analyse in detail includes different genres of diplomatic text (reports, démarche reports, scene-setters, analysis). To show the reader how the representations studied are constituted, each detailed textual study focuses on different representations and aspects of representations.

Literary commentary is a good structure to systematise analysis both as methodological ethos when reading many diplomatic texts and for writing up analysis. Commentary organises analysis from the outside in: form (structure), textual context (location within an opus), the stanza (or paragraph), the verse (or articulation), and the word (vocabulary). Form is the expected structure – the structure of cables, for instance, is very old and consistent – but an author has choices within such parameters. For example, placing an issue in the 'summary' at the top of the cable makes it one of its chief contents. Likewise, placing policy recommendations in the main body as opposed to the 'recommendations' section suggests that the suggested action follows existing policy. Outside the text but within

Analysing how diplomatic text describes 71

form lies its immediate (literary) context, which explains some features and links to other texts. We might remark, for instance, that the poem 'The Ritual of my Legs' belongs to Pablo Neruda's collection *Residence on Earth*; we can thus expect lyrical metaphysical imagery and graphic sexual metaphors.[47] Likewise, diplomatic reports are ongoing updates to an existing opus, which explains why they are fragmented and require familiarity with the body of correspondence. Deeper, at the level of the paragraph, literary devices not only create and place objects in situ, but also construct relations among them. Since paragraphs and stanzas are commonly used to organise content, this approach reveals how individual articulations are related to one another, for instance, categorising hierarchy or causality.

For example, if I break a paragraph as I just did, you might expect discussion to move elsewhere – it does not yet, sorry. Further into the text we find sentences where grammar is heavily implicated. Grammatical devices, from subjugate clauses to word order, and orthographical ones like capitalisation or punctuation, construct relations among objects and order hierarchy.[48] Take the Oxford comma for instance: 'subjects, space, time, and motives' and 'subjects, space, time and motives' are not the same. In the second, 'time' and 'motive' are associated as one category, giving us three, whereas in the former, the Oxford comma specifies that there are four. Finally, vocabulary choices are powerful in diplomacy, as standard pieces of diplomatic vocabulary have significant categorisation effects. After all, one person's freedom fighter is another's terrorist.

Systematic discourse analysis, however, only yields answers to the questions asked of the text, for no reading can exhaust all others. In this project, we specifically interrogate how linguistic articulations relate subjects and their contexts to one another, linking or differentiating them, as well as how these are stabilised when challenged. Stabilisation is crucial because the moment linking/differentiation comes under fire is when it needs re-establishment of its representations, which require further linking and differentiation.[49] To account for struggles over frames of representation in diplomatic text, this method examines linking/differentiation at the sites of the diplomatic discursive encounter. Most poststructuralist studies of identity concentrate on the constitution of a single Self – Said's Orientals, for instance. We, however, because diplomacy is constantly re-staging the Self to speak of the Other, must look at multiple Selves, contrasting 'the discourse of the Self with the Other's "counter-construction" of Self and Other' and their encounter in text.[50] This allows analysis to compare the relative effectiveness of competing representations.

To account for the fecundity of representations, it is not sufficient to speak of 'identity'. The term usually refers to the representation of subjects, and theorists like Connolly use the term to mean the constitution of entire groups of subjects. To privilege political identity to the detriment of their contexts is problematic for this research because it does not allow for appreciation of the role of spatial, temporal, and normative constructions and inscriptions. This is vital because international policy analysis and some schools of IR traditionally analyse contexts such as geography to determine interests, limiting agency to rational calculation based on how such contexts drive interest.[51] The relevance of spatialisation is apparent in constructions like the Domino Theory. This is particularly salient for postcolonial subjects, frequently represented as unable to make their own political choices and vulnerable to nefarious influence.[52] Identity construction depends on biographic, normative, racial, temporal, and spatial inscriptions that form a picture of the world subjects inhabit. They are not a corollary of identity as much as creative constructions in their own right that frequently precede the inscription of a subject within them. This research treats representation as a polyptych composed of representations of subjects and the contextual space, time, and norms in which they are inscribed. This level of analytical detail, as shown in both case studies, is vital to understanding why some frames of identity stick and others do not, which entails looking at competing and co-existing representations accounting for the detail of minute referents.

We now have a method to analyse how a single diplomatic text constitutes subjects and their contexts. Its cornerstones are textuality, retrieving politicisation, and identifying and exploring processes of linking and differentiation, with literary commentary systematisation for single-text studies to be repeated for every document. However, to make a truly intertextual approach possible in conjunction with the study of individual texts, we need a textual marker to follow across texts.

Tracing diplomatic descriptions in intertextual space: topoi as textual markers for genealogy

To analyse how representations of subjects and their contexts develop over time, it is necessary to identify textual markers. This section introduces topoi as markers for genealogical analysis. To weave this import from literature into poststructuralist IR methodology, this discussion analyses two examples to demonstrate how to incorporate identification and analysis of topoi into thick description.

Our endeavour needs a textual marker more complex and textually concrete than single representations or positions. Most discourse analysis does not need such markers because they explore either the archaeology or genealogy of a discourse rather than its evolution over the textual constellation of diplomacy.[53] We, however, need a marker located between distinct textual representations and the larger collective social identification of positions. Since this method examines how a single text makes meaning *and* how this meaning evolves across texts, we need a marker to follow representations across the cascade. This marker must help us recognise the pieces from which positions are built while also signposting how each bears significant normative associations.

Following from the many poststructuralist uses of literary philosophy and analysis, I take a step further, importing into IR a literary and rhetorical device: the topoi. Aristotle defined topoi as normative commonplaces (τόπος means 'place') that articulate normative dialectics, of which he listed three hundred in *Topics*, a number reduced to twenty-nine less specifically applicable ones in *Rhetoric*.[54] For most rhetoricians, topoi were 'intellectual themes, suitable for development and modification at the orator's pleasure'.[55] For Cicero, however, topoi could be deployed to construct *and* to analyse and refute arguments. They are devices 'that may trigger an associative process rather than a collection of implicit rules and precepts reducible to rules'.[56] A Ciceronian topos 'is a ready-made argument. It does not guide the construction of an argument, but it can be transferable to several similar cases.'[57] In analysis, topoi 'serve as so many marks or characters for the discovery of arguments, and from which a discourse might be aptly framed on either side of a question'.[58] The 'discovery of arguments' is what interests us: topoi are highly recognisable yet complex and rich signs. This is what Cicero means by 'either side': topoi signpost normative discourses.

References to short hair in Spanish articulations of masculinity are a good example of how topoi signpost normativity. When during my childhood we moved from Italy to Spain, it took me a couple of years to realise that 'decent boys' wore their hair very short. The key basis of that 'decency' was its normative history, a key part of this hairy Spanish topos: short hair is decent, regimented, military, healthy, Franquista, and Falangista.[59] To evoke short hair is to posit a paradigm of right-wing militaristic masculinity. The topos of 'short hair' contains only one representation: orderly man in an orderly body in reference to orderly society. Its antithesis (disorderly) is implied. The topos illustrates and recalls the norm but does not amount to the complete normative discourse. Topoi are helpful because they are part of the articulation of positions, themselves parts of discourses, in this case Spanish masculinity.[60]

Topoi are two- or three-word cubes of super-strength normative historical flavouring. Like soup stock, they are the distillate of a larger history, processes, subjectivities, and representations. Quintilian argues that topoi help audiences relate to the orator through the commonality of the topoi inserted.⁶¹ As textual devices, topoi allow authors to import an entire trope into a text through convenient and short expressions appealing to the audience's shared knowledge. For analysts, their convenience is that they are easily recognisable, short, and consistent articulations. Applying this literary insight, Kristeva reverses the Freudian pathologies of melancholy and depression in *Black Sun*, turning them from textual to analytical devices. These topoi, analysed as literary devices, signpost the presence and composition of discourses and allow Kristeva to map the discursive constitution of depression.⁶²

In the 2010s, Italian conservatives frequently made reference to the 'Years of Lead' (1970–80s, when rival fascist and communist groups committed terrorist attacks) and particularly the 'Brigate Rosse' (BR, communist 'Red Brigades') as a way of deploying history – BR terrorism – to articulate that Berlusconi was the only bulwark against terrorist communism. In the text, this topos appears simply as 'BR'. In this example, the 'seat of arguments' Cicero tells us about recalls history (terrorist attacks), suggests a normative frame (communism contra democracy), and links Italian communists to international communist conspiracies. This example demonstrates the potential of analysing topoi to capture with detail and nuance the representations that differentiate, contextualise, and explain the Other.⁶³

Topoi were never used by any of the grand masters of discourse analysis, from the theorists of Critical Discourse Analysis (CDA) like Fairclough to poststructuralists like Shapiro, Neumann, and Hansen, though they recommend individuating markers. Looking to more historical CDA approaches, Wodak and Reisigl examine textual argumentation through time using topoi, but in my view miss the potential of this ancient literary device. Topoi are not identified as literary devices but 'plausible argumentation schemes'.⁶⁴ This definition is practical but obscures the textuality of the device, essentially leaving us with an Aristotelian *theme*.⁶⁵ While their approach adds chronological mapping of arguments to CDA and topoi are identified, they are not historicised – that is, analytically related to their normative history by identifying its past, like we did for Spanish haircuts or Italy's 'BR'.

Retrieving the historicisation and subjectivity of topoi makes them more precise and nuanced markers. It provides understanding of how they appear in text to help track them, as well as insights about their participation in representation, for they are textual devices in their own right as well as textual markers.⁶⁶ I would conceptually describe them as distillations of the doxa they signal, implicated in subjectivity-governing frames.⁶⁷ Access to the structure of doxa through historicization of the topoi's unwritten but eminently present background allows for recognition of the underlying assumptions and how they sustain representations.⁶⁸ This was the case with the 'BR' example, which illustrated how historicising that topos opened up the normative history of Italian communism and its contemporary use. In our method, this task is allocated to the detailed textual analysis.

Integrating identification and historicisation of topoi, as the above mini-commentaries show, demands historical work. This is because while topoi are recurring, their characters and scripts are renewed – retrieving an older topos under a new name is the challenge, in other words. Taking romantic fiction as an example, topoi surrounding forbidden love dating back to the tenth-century Provençal courtly love tradition recur, be it in the contexts of *Romeo and Juliet*, *Brokeback Mountain*, or the awful *Twilight* variety. In many respects, it would be difficult to build a narrative of forbidden love without the role of the facilitator, a topos present in all the above (apparently unrelated) dramas as, respectively, Juliet's nurse, the mountain, and a friendly vampire sister. They are characterisations of the same norm: loyal and unconditional acceptance of true love. Historicising topoi is key to recognising them across languages, formats, and history, and to intertextually locating their normative construction. Topoi historicisation tells us of the unexplicit histories behind commonplace expressions of political representation. This makes topoi identification and historicisation a sophisticated approach to follow intertextual patterns.[69]

Identifying and historicising topoi in discourse analysis is an essential advance. It provides for the individuation of a unique multi-level, intertextual, trans-historical marker. Historical understanding of key topoi of representation allows for effective recognition beyond a linguistic label that in the third step of this method, elaborated in the next section, helps analysis trace their evolution through the cascade of diplomatic text. Their integration into our detailed textual studies sets the stage for analysis to trace their presence across texts and entire systems of textual knowledge production.

Genealogy and history: mapping the cascade of diplomatic texts

Thanks to the permanence of diplomatic text in the archival afterlife of diplomatic communication, it is possible to map interventions and conflicts over representations. In this method, genealogy finds, maps, and relates the instances, shifts, interventions, and textual and discursive relationships that enable and constitute representation of subjects and their contexts. Genealogy patiently uncovers the history of the ideas diplomacy trades in: the representations that make sense of the world. There are no silver bullets to be found in this investigation, no grand decision by a Kissingerian strategist: only countless cables, summaries, and recommendations, the diplomat at her desk finishing a report.

This method does history backwards. Its approach, both at the archives and in the empirical chapters that follow, backtracks from a policy shift based on a representation of subjects and their contexts, exploring the history of that representation. The text itself, read against a chronology of events, reveals when its representations emerge at the heart of policy shifts. This is the beginning of our chronological frame for data selection: we start from a policy shift marked by representation of subjects, time, space, and norms and trace knowledge production backwards. For example, in the Vietnam 1945–48 case study, we look at the 1948 policy statement that shifted US policy from support of Vietnamese self-determination to support of French colonial reconquest on the basis that rebel alliance Vietminh were Soviet communist proxies, not true nationalists. Having examined the representation that justified the shift, analysis traces the history of that representation, exploring how diplomats and policymakers reading their work went from seeing Vietminh as anticolonial to viewing them as Stalinist stooges. Reversing the chronological order of research, and, unusually, the order of the presentation of the analysis too, is a methodological response to the requirements of diplomatic text. Reverse chronology is tough to conceive, execute, write, and read because it feels so unnatural. So why take an approach to genealogy more radical than Foucault's?

The first reason is a practical application of intertextuality. The argument that texts are made of other texts is important and practical.[70] However, it remains difficult to systematise intertextual exploration without allowing it to stretch to infinity and derail analytical output. The best conceptual and methodological solution is to anchor the limitation of data selection, and thus the entire genealogy, on the text itself.[71] Backtracking to the predecessor of each text is methodologically and empirically transparent. The researcher is set up to find the earlier expressions of the representation of subjects, territory, time, and norms he is documenting, its authors and institutions. This helps account for intertextuality: thanks to diplomatic bureaucratic conventions at the archives, it was clear which text preceded or answered which, and consequently which preceding texts contained the representation whose history I was investigating.

Secondly, this radical execution of genealogy reflects a commitment to reject studying diplomacy 'from power's internal point of view'.[72] That is, rather than researching what a diplomat thinks, I map the world of knowledge she inhabits and contributes to and the mechanics that order it. This choice emerges from the philosophical position that it is not possible to identify effective causality in this research, particularly 'real' motives or interests. This is because identity and policy are not causally related. Rather, identity stands at either side of policy as both its precondition and reproduced in articulation of policy.[73] There is no need for Foucauldian thinking or archival heroics to demonstrate the futility of seeking causality in identity: 'national security' and 'national interest', not to mention 'containment' or the 'War on Terror', directly assume and reproduce separation into differentiated subjects. If policy depends on these definitions to choose whom to befriend or kill, it is of greater interest to find out how subjects are identified and classified. Furthermore, it is impossible to locate effective causality in the intertextual space of diplomatic texts because representations emerge *in*, *through*, and *among them*. Even Kennan's famous Long Telegram was not world-changing on its own: it was its subsequent life in and through myriad texts, including policy, that disseminated its assumptions. The policy-influencing representation that somebody showed the President or the National Security Council was, after all, merely one of the final textual products of knowledge production.

Genealogy in this method reflects, thirdly, a commitment to avoiding historical determinism in establishing the origins and ends of representations. They are in constant creative flux, written over time and time again, inconsistently and discontinuously evolving. The diplomatic text itself sometimes posits reductive historical frames to make sense of temporality and the subjects it inscribes, features that should shame the researcher into not making the same mistake. Arbitrary selection of chronological limits for data selection implicates the researcher in determining subjectivity through assumptions as to the significance of certain dates – the problem of origin. Nietzsche's agonising investigation of mankind's obsession with normative origin urges scholarship to avoid seeking the event or object that explains existence. Rather, we are encouraged to find how an idea came to be normal and universally uncontested, and how its dominance is maintained.[74] In *Daybreak*, Nietzsche proposes a fictional journey through history, first backwards, then forwards, that reveals that there is no grand origin, purpose, or destiny of humanity: only a monkey grinning, and the grave of the last man.[75] Inspired by the transparency of that exercise, I argue that doing history backwards brings this ruthless transparency to empirical analysis, allowing the ape at the beginning of humanity to reveal itself inductively in its banality.

Reverse genealogy is scientifically helpful in empirical analysis: the initial enunciations of a frame of representation are signposted by the first appearance of the topos we have been chasing, independently determining the chronological limit of data selection. As a result, we have two intertwined inductive data selection rationales, one determining the type of documents we read – the diplomatic moment – and another determining how far to go hunting topoi through intertextual space.

'[G]enealogy is grey, meticulous and patiently documentary. It operates on a field of entangled and confused parchments, on documents that have been scratched over and recopied many times.'[76] At the archives, informed by the history of the case studies and my diplomatic text selection criteria, I proceeded to trace topoi backwards. Indeed, it was grey, dusty, meticulous, and patiently documentary work, for no archive indexes or stores files in reverse chronological order. I start with files surrounding the policy event whose representational history I was researching, allowing references in the texts themselves to guide me to their intertextual parents, and so on to establish the genealogy of the representation in the policy event. While reverse chronology is necessitated by philosophical and methodological commitments, it is also driven by empirical commitment to transparent analysis.

Research design: mapping, reading, and tracing diplomatic knowledge production

We can now summarise how the three-step method proposed in this book operates. This section uses detailed versions of the diagram in Figure 3.1 summarising the three-step method, illustrated with archival data and analysis from the First Vietnam War case study. For simplicity of illustration, the diagrams of the first two steps are populated only with French data, while the third includes those of the three key actors to show interactions between them.

The first step of the method maps the pathways taken by diplomatic knowledge production. It is shown in Figure 3.2. This step determines the routes taken by diplomatic information in the first case study, the diplomacy of the First Vietnam War. Its first insight of analytical utility is that the Indochinese colonial establishment was a small government unto itself, including a diplomatic office that did not answer to the MFA but to the High Commissioner for Indochina – its colonial governor. It also shows that a committee called COMINDO was supposed to make policy on Indochina but, as it laid dormant, its staff forwarded communications from the high commissioner directly to the prime minister, which explains why analysis found that the governor exercised huge and unexpected policy implementation latitude and, in some cases, was able to pre-empt and contradict orders from Paris, even when making statements to and communicating with foreign diplomats.

Figure 3.3 shows the second step, exemplified with analysis of a memorandum from the French colonial governor Thierry d'Argenlieu to the defence and colonial minister. It is included because not only does it write on behalf of France, but it also does so *to France* trying to influence policy-making, and its arguments were used widely in French diplomacy up to late 1946. This is an excellent example because it draws lines in the waters of all

Analysing how diplomatic text describes 79

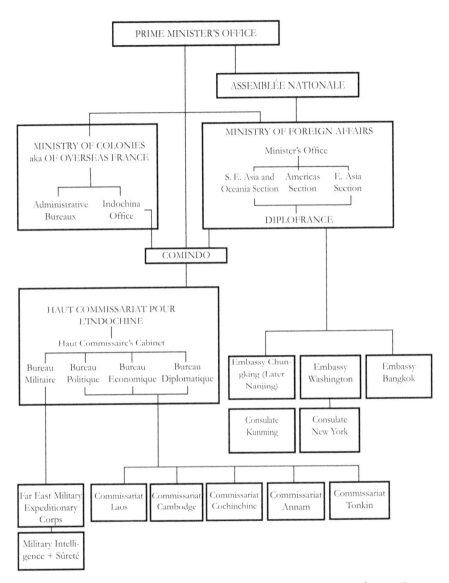

Figure 3.2 Diagram of step 1 of this method: mapping reporting pathways. Boxes indicate institutions in France, in colonial Indochina, and abroad. Straight lines indicate reporting and instruction pathways. Diagram by Tally de Orellana.

80 Hand of the prince

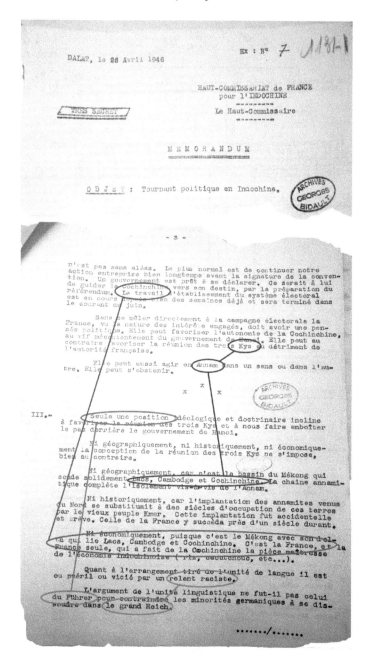

Figure 3.3 Diagram of step 2 of this method: reading how texts represent subjects and their contexts. Text is from Archive Georges Bidault, AN, author's photographs. Composite diagram by Tally de Orellana.

Analysing how diplomatic text describes 81

four dimensions of space, time, norms, and (racialised) subjects. The memorandum argues that the south of Vietnam, the colony of Cochinchine, is not Vietnamese and is distinct. This was more influential than d'Argenlieu could have expected, surviving into the 1980s in American narratives of South Vietnamese national identity. D'Argenlieu separates Cochinchine from Annam and Tonkin temporally, 'recently' taken by the Vietnamese from their righteous Khmer owners, 'just before' the French 'arrived'. Geographical inscription too posits the separation as natural. Cultural inscription is normatively posited: Vietnamese being spoken in Cochinchine does not make it Vietnamese unless one is a Nazi. Normative inscription links the three above to frame Vietminh as immaturely extremist, for Vietnamese reunification can only be animated by an 'ideological and doctrinal position' like 'the Führer's'.[77]

Three topoi, under apparently simple labels, signpost old colonial and new post-WWII discourses. Firstly, *immaturity* ('Kys', etc.) refers to the Orientalist discourse of colonial peoples being too backward and 'immature' for independent politics. The topos contains the demonstration of unpreparedness in the use of the term 'racisme', which in the French Empire denoted the crime of resisting French rule, and its normative framing as 'doctrinaire', 'puerile', and thus irrationally extremist. Secondly, *colonial order* ('Le travail', etc.) is essential – making Cochinchina 'the masterpiece' of the colony, saving it and other Indochinese nations from inevitable Vietnamese tyranny, as 'France and only France' can arbiter among nations in the colony and preserve peace. These nations are delineated and inscribed in history and geography, matching the French administration's division of the Nguyen Dynasty Empire of Vietnam in the 1890s into Annam, Tonkin, and Cochinchine, which they called 'kys' and which were treated as separate nations that French conquest 'liberated' from Vietnamese tyranny. Thirdly, the assertion that *a unified Vietnam is a fascist fantasy* ('Seule une...', etc.), 'racist', comparable to 'the Führer's' 'great Reich', establishes a common post-WWII topos that signposts representation of Vietnamese reunification as a quasi-Nazi evil project. Thanks to these topoi markers, we can now follow these representations of Vietminh across diplomatic knowledge production.

Figure 3.4 illustrates the third step of this method: genealogical mapping of representations as they develop in each actor's cascades of diplomatic text. The constellation of cables arranged into three cascades of diplomatic text highlights the delicate balance to be achieved in analysis. On the one hand, analysis accounts for representations of subjects and their contexts, which are examined against one another to identify developments. We are additionally looking to account for the role of interventions performed by the diplomatic text – indicated by circles around text and lines in the diagram – when a communication crosses from one cascade to the other and its

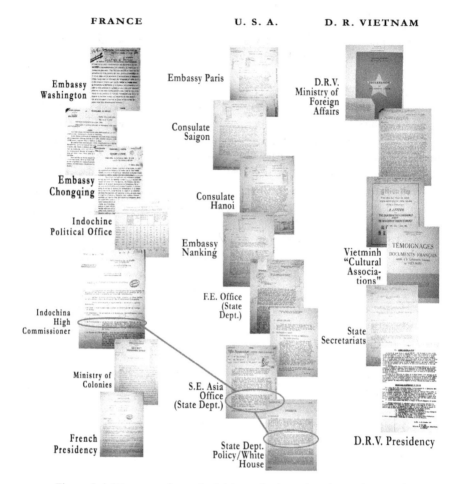

Figure 3.4 Diagram of step 3 of this method: tracing the evolution of representations. Photos of documents from AN, MAE, Archive Sainteny, and NARA, author's photographs. Composite diagram by Tally de Orellana.

representations enter the cascade of another international actor. The circled words and lines highlight how the representation of Vietnam as a fascist project examined in the previous step entered US reporting at the level of the Southeast Asia office and remained present in subsequent US writing about Vietnam.

It is at these instances, when diplomatic knowledge production systems meet, that the text of one can come to be taken up successfully – or not – by another international actor's diplomatic knowledge production. I call this successful intervention a crossover. Crossovers can lay the seeds for its representations to continue to exist and thrive in another country's diplomatic machinery. This is not to say that the representations in interventions are always taken up; on the contrary, it is vital to examine when they do not, and what determines a successful intervention. This analysis is empirical and systematic, resulting in observations of which interventions lead to crossover of representations. The crossover test retrieves whether an *exact* textual formula (not necessarily word by word but with the same mechanisms of representation) has crossed from one cascade into another. These observations lay the empirical groundwork for conceptualisation of the agency of the diplomatic text in transforming representations in the diplomatic text of other actors in Chapter 6. This is how we examine how representations develop and how convincing they are.

Returning to analytical sequencing, one last word is necessary to explain how this is executed in the next two chapters. Each is divided into four parts. The first discusses scholarship about diplomacy in each case, and the second maps diplomatic reporting and instruction pathways, from missions on the ground to policymakers, expounding the primary data used. The third section offers systematic analysis of a selection of six texts (two from each actor studied) to demonstrate analysis of how each describes subjects, their contexts, and their significance to the Self and to identify topoi textual markers, while the fourth, starting in reverse chronology from a major policy shift, traces how representations developed through the three cascades of diplomatic text.

At last, we have the means to understand how representations of subjects, space, time, and norms are constituted in a single text and across the microcosm of diplomatic knowledge production. We are ready. Farewell, Segretario Machiavelli; we are off on mission. Armed with poststructuralist theory of diplomacy, detailed textual studies, topoi, genealogy, bibliography, battered computer, foreign languages, my trusted fountain pen, and a barrel of green ink, we go to the archives. 'Grab a phaser, Ambassador. We're going to get some answers'![78]

Notes

1 Friedrich Wilhelm Nietzsche, *Human, All Too Human: A Book for Free Spirits; Part I*, trans. Alexander Harvey, 2011, I, 11 (Project Gutenberg, EBook No. 38145).
2 Friedrich Wilhelm Nietzsche, *Human, All Too Human: A Book For Free Spirits; Part II: The Wanderer and His Shadow*, trans. Paul Cohn, 2011, II, 11 (Project Gutenberg EBook No. 37841).
3 See Pablo de Orellana chapter in Spence, Yorke, and Masser, *A New Theory and Practice of Diplomacy*; de Orellana, 'When Diplomacy Identifies Terrorists: Subjects, Identity and Agency in the War on Terror in Mali'; de Orellana, '"You

Can Count on Us": When Malian Diplomacy Stratcommed Uncle Sam and the Role of Identity in Communication'; Pablo de Orellana, 'Struggles over Identity in Diplomacy: "Commie Terrorists" Contra "Imperialists" in Western Sahara', *International Relations* 29 (4), 2015, 477–99; Pablo de Orellana, *The Road to Vietnam* (London: I. B. Tauris, 2020).
4 Foucault, *Power/Knowledge*, 96.
5 Hansen, *Security as Practice*, 33.
6 See Jacob Mundy, 'Neutrality or Complicity? The United States and the 1975 Moroccan Takeover of the Spanish Sahara', *The Journal of North African Studies* 11 (3), 2006, 275–306.
7 This literature, and the contributions of this method, are reviewed at the start of each case study chapter.
8 Other possible case studies included diplomatic representations of the East Timor conflict 1975–91, Apartheid 1979–94, and the Northern Mali rebellions 1989–2012.
9 Since Moroccan and French diplomatic communication is primarily written in French, US diplomacy in English, and POLISARIO's in Spanish and English, study of these cases is made possible by my linguistic competence in these languages. Sadly, the only scholarly application of my Italian to this day has been translating Machiavelli.
10 *Nigel Farage vs. Tony Blair, December 2005*, accessed 1 December 2014, https://www.youtube.com/watch?v=DT--RnOYORI&feature=youtube_gdata_player
11 See, for instance, the key documentary collection for this tradition 'Foreign Relations of the United States', accessed 14 May 2015, http://uwdc.library.wisc.edu/collections/FRUS
12 She draws primarily on identity-formation analysis by Walker, Neumann, and Der Derian. Hansen, *Security as Practice*, 58–65.
13 Iver B. Neumann, 'Discourse Analysis', in *Qualitative Methods in International Relations: A Pluralist Guide*, ed. Klotz and Prakash (Basingstoke: Palgrave Macmillan, 2008), 61–77; 'Returning Practice to the Linguistic Turn'.
14 'Pourquoi les sciences sociales doivent se prendre pour objet', in Pierre Bourdieu, *Science de la science et réflexivité. Cours du Collège de France 2000–2001* (Paris: Liber, 2001), 205; my translation.
15 Der Derian examines the genealogy of these concepts in detail, *On Diplomacy*.
16 See last two chapters in Constantinou, *On the Way to Diplomacy*.
17 There is no space here for a discussion on poststructuralist models of sovereignty, but a crucial work for this project is Bartelson, *A Genealogy of Sovereignty*; 'The Concept of Sovereignty Revisited'.
18 Constantinou, *On the Way to Diplomacy*, 69–90.
19 Constantinou, *On the Way to Diplomacy*, 116.
20 David Reynolds, *In Command of History: Churchill Writing and Fighting the Second World War* (London: Allen Lane, 2004), 325.
21 In another example of how focus on practice can reveal ideational commitments in international relations, I would point to recent research on the origins of the

WWII Allied coalition, where analytical focus on shared practice, institutions, and processes reveals a much earlier and deeper Allied commitment to alliance than hitherto imagined. See Th. W. Bottelier, '"Not on a Purely Nationalistic Basis": The Internationalism of Allied Coalition Warfare in the Second World War', *European Review of History: Revue Européenne d'histoire* 27 (1–2), 2020, 152–75; Th. W. Bottelier, 'Of Once and Future Kings: Rethinking the Anglo-American Analogy in the Rising Powers Debate', *The International History Review* 39 (5), 2017, 751–69.

22 Agence France-Presse, 'China Condemns British Inquiry into Progress of Hong Kong Democracy', *The Guardian*, 2014, accessed 3 September 2014, http://www.theguardian.com/world/2014/sep/02/china-condemns-british-inquiry-into-progress-of-hong-kong-democracy

23 See Gareth Porter, ed., *Vietnam: A History in Documents* (New York: New American Library, 1979).

24 MACP, 'Morocco on the Move', accessed 14 July 2014, http://moroccoonthemove.com/policy/western-sahara/#sthash.TZ00fHXC.dpbs

25 The Clinton emails, which I used to apply this method to the diplomacy preceding the 2011 intervention in Libya, are particularly useful because they include entire email chains.

26 See, for example, Copland in Chapter 25 in Andrew F. Cooper, Jorge Heine, and Ramesh Thakur, *The Oxford Handbook of Modern Diplomacy* (Oxford: Oxford University Press, 2013), as well as Pigman in Costas M. Constantinou, Pauline Kerr, and Paul Sharp, *The SAGE Handbook of Diplomacy* (Los Angeles, CA: SAGE, 2016), act 140; Edward Hunt, 'The WikiLeaks Cables: How the United States Exploits the World, in Detail, from an Internal Perspective, 2001–2010', *Diplomacy & Statecraft* 30 (1), 2019, 70–98.

27 Constantinou, 'Between Statecraft and Humanism', 154.

28 The role and development of representations emerging from diplomatic knowledge production in executive government, perhaps continuing the research via archival evidence such as presidential documents, could be the subject of an interesting follow-up project. Allison and Zelikow, *Essence of Decision*.

29 Interviews were carried out under KCL ethical guidelines. Ethical Approval granted 10/5/2013, REC Reference Number: REP (WSG)/12/13–27.

30 They all requested full anonymity, whence I shall not be referring to individual details. Anonymous, Interview with former State Department analyst, 2014; Anonymous, Interview with Senate Member Foreign Relations analyst and advisor, 2014; Anonymous, Interview with a senior Foreign Affairs analyst, Senate Foreign Relations Committee, 2014.

31 A well-known example, a congressional study of the American Vietnam War, included diplomatic documents in a small appendix. Robert M. Blum and United States Congress Senate Committee on Foreign Relations, *The United States and Vietnam, 1944–1947: A Staff Study Based on the Pentagon Papers Prepared for the Use of the United States Senate Committee on Foreign Relations* (U.S. Government Printing Office, 1972).

32 Michel Foucault, *The Order of Things: An Archaeology of the Human Sciences* (London: Routledge, 2002), 74.
33 Michael J. Shapiro, 'Strategic Discourse/Discursive Strategy: The Representation of "Security Policy" in the Video Age', *International Studies Quarterly* 34 (3), 1990, 327–40.
34 Connolly, 'The Politics of Discourse', 218.
35 Foucault, *The Order of Things*, 327.
36 Shapiro, 'Literary Production as a Politicizing Practice', 1984, 218.
37 Colin Powell, *UN Security Council*, 2003, accessed 16 May 2015, https://www.youtube.com/watch?v=Rp6WuTSTyS8
38 Shapiro, *The Politics of Representation*, 88; For discussion on metaphors, see Shapiro, 'Literary Production as a Politicizing Practice', 228; and, for a very interesting 're-politicising' analysis of Joyce's *Ulysses*, see Michael J. Shapiro, *Reading the Postmodern Polity: Political Theory as Textual Practice* (Minneapolis, MN: University of Minnesota Press, 1992), 18.
39 George Orwell's *1984* destabilises representation with oxymorons and lexical perversions Foucault would have adored – slogans such as 'War is Peace' or the 'ministries of Love, Peace, Plenty, and Truth'. Challenging the 'connection between what signifies and what is signified' through contrast between official lexicon and Winston's experience as employee of the Ministry of Truth, 'correcting' history and discussing the reconstruction of 'Oldspeak' into 'Newspeak'. Orwell's perversions highlight caesuras and paradox, which undermine the depoliticisation of words, effectively revealing the subjectivity invested in the use of terms as universally wholesome as 'Love', 'Truth', 'Peace'.
40 Foucault, *The Order of Things*, 115.
41 Foucault, *The Order of Things*, 121.
42 'Two Lectures', in Michel Foucault, *Power/Knowledge: Selected Interviews and Other Writings, 1972–1977* (New York: Random House, 1988), 94.
43 Foucault, *The Order of Things*, 236.
44 Michel Foucault, *The Archaeology of Knowledge* (London: Tavistock Publications, 1972), 38; see also Shapiro, 'Strategic Discourse/Discursive Strategy'.
45 Foucault, *The Order of Things*, 90.
46 R. Barthes, *S/Z* (New York: Hill and Wang, 1974), particularly Appendix 3; Lawrence D. Kritzman, 'Barthesian Free Play', *Yale French Studies* (66), 1984, 189–210.
47 Pablo Neruda, *Residencia En La Tierra* (Madrid: Ediciones Catedra, S.A., 1999).
48 Kristeva, *Desire in Language*, 124.
49 Connolly, *Identity, Difference*, 64.
50 Hansen, *Security as Practice*, 76.
51 This is how 'even Guatemala as a whole unit pales, for the major discursive practice within which we have Guatemala is the geo-political code', in Shapiro, *The Politics of Representation*, 110. This is even more evident in geopolitical approaches to foreign policy à la Kissinger.

52 See Shapiro's Guatemalans in *The Politics of Representation*, 89; and Jabri's postcolonial subjects in *The Postcolonial Subject*.
53 Neumann, 'Discourse Analysis', 62.
54 Aristotle, *The Art of Rhetoric*, trans. Hugh Lawson-Tancred, Reissue edition (London: Penguin Classics, 1991); See also *Topics – Aristotle* (Sioux Falls, SD: NuVision Publications, 2005); Sara Rubinelli, *Ars Topica: The Classical Technique of Constructing Arguments from Aristotle to Cicero* (Berlin: Springer, 2009), 72; and particularly Igor Žagar, 'Topoi in Critical Discourse Analysis', *Lodz Papers in Pragmatics* 6 (1), 2010, 18.
55 Ernst Robert Curtius, *European Literature and the Latin Middle Ages* (Princeton, NJ: Princeton University Press, 1953), 70.
56 Žagar, 'Topoi in Critical Discourse Analysis', 19.
57 Rubinelli, *Ars Topica*, 148.
58 'The Orator' Marcus Tullius Cicero, *Cicero's Brutus or History of Famous Orators; Also His Orator, or Accomplished Speaker*, trans. E. Jones, 2006, §29, (Project Gutenberg, EBook No. 9776).
59 La Falange is Spain's fascist party, 1933–present. 'Falange Española de Las JONS', accessed 19 May 2015, http://falange.es/contenido/
60 See the fascist indoctrination text *ASÍ QUIERO SER (EL NIÑO DEL NUEVO ESTADO) [I Want to Be like This (the Child of the New State)]*, Lecturas Civicas (Burgos: Hijos de Santiago Rodriguez, 1940), accessed 21 April 2015, http://www.fundacionemiliamariatrevisi.com/asiquieroser.htm; and Derrin Pinto, 'Indoctrinating the Youth of Post-War Spain: A Discourse Analysis of a Fascist Civics Textbook', *Discourse & Society* 15 (5), 2004, 649–67; Stacey Guill, 'Pilar and Maria: Hemingway's Feminist Homage to the "New Woman of Spain" in *For Whom the Bell Tolls*', *The Hemingway Review* 30 (2), 2011, 7–20; Tatjana Pavlovic, *Despotic Bodies and Transgressive Bodies: Spanish Culture from Francisco Franco to Jesus Franco* (New York: SUNY Press, 2012).
61 Marcus Fabius Quintilianus, *M. Fabi Quintiliani institutionis oratoriae liber decimus*, ed. William Peterson, 2007, v, 12, (Project Gutenmberg, EBook No. 21827).
62 Her reliance on Freudian psychoanalysis is, however, a matter for another discussion. J. Kristeva, *Black Sun: Depression and Melancholia*, Reprint Edition (New York: Columbia University Press, 1992); see also 'Melancholia Becomes the Subject: Kristeva's Invisible "Thing" and the Making of Culture', *Paragraph* 14 (2), 1991, 144–50.
63 See also Christopher Bush, 'The Other of the Other?: Cultural Studies, Theory, and the Location of the Modernist Signifier', *Comparative Literature Studies* 42 (2), 2005, 169.
64 Reisigl and Wodak, 'The Discourse-Historical Approach (DHA)', in *Methods for Critical Discourse Analysis*, Second Edition, eds Ruth Wodak and Michael Meyer (London: SAGE, 2009), 101.
65 Reisigl and Wodak, 'The Discourse-Historical Approach (DHA)', in Wodak and Meyer, *Methods for Critical Discourse Analysis*, 87.

66 Historicisation of topoi makes use of digital qualitative analysis methods impossible. Software like NVivo can recognise textual markers across digitalised text and apply filters and coding to produce observations (how often an expression is repeated, for instance) in the context of other variables. The limitations are, however, insurmountable for this method. Firstly, most data gathered for this project cannot undergo Optical Character Recognition (OCR, turning images of text into digital text) with available software – 1940s cables are for instance delicate, faded, often almost pulverised and see-through. Such documents successfully undergo OCR at the CIA CREST archive, but I was unable to discover what software achieved this feat. Secondly, NVivo cannot recognise markers as complex as topoi. Since they do not always exhibit the same wording, NVivo would have to be coded with all of the possible aspects and articulations of a topoi, a process that would ironically require thorough traditional reading. A feature of NVivo and other qualitative mapping software like SPAD and FactoMiner (often used in Bourdieusian 'Field' mapping of agents) is their usefulness in creating large-scale annotated digital databases, which due to OCR difficulty and the software's incapacity to account for topoi, makes this approach of limited relevance for this project. See Colm Crowley, Rom Harre, and Clare Tagg, 'Qualitative Research and Computing: Methodological Issues and Practices in Using QSR NVivo and NUD*IST', *International Journal of Social Research Methodology* 5 (3), 2002, 193–97; Asta Sorensen, 'Media Review: NVivo 7', *Journal of Mixed Methods Research* 2 (1), 2008, 106–8.

67 See 'Actif/Passif' in Roland Barthes, *Roland Barthes, par Roland Barthes* (Paris: Points, 2014), 130; Anne Herschberg Pierrot, 'Barthes and Doxa', *Poetics Today* 23 (3), 2002, 438; Paul Julian Smith, 'Barthes, Góngora, and Non-Sense', *PMLA* 101 (1), 1986, 88.

68 Roland Barthes, *Leçon Inaugurale de La Chaire de Semiologie Litteraire Du College de France* (Paris: Seuil, 1978), 34.

69 The topoi-based approach is my literary, historical response to Hansen's tentative but unhistorical and unliterary attempt to evidence 'implicit textual linkages' by linking them to 'quotes' and 'catchphrases' – which returns the problem of the historically variable label of the topos: nurse, mountain, or vampire sister? *Security as Practice*, 57.

70 M. M. Bakhtin, *Dialogic Imagination: Four Essays*, ed. Michael Holquist, trans. Caryl Emerson (Austin, TX: University of Texas Press, 1982); Kristeva, *Desire in Language*, 69.

71 As my undergraduate Italian Medieval Poetry tutor was fond of proclaiming, 'Focus on the text!'. See, for instance, his own exploration of the intertextual constitution of medieval narratives of eschatological torture and punishment in M. Gragnolati, *Experiencing the Afterlife: Soul and Body in Dante and Medieval Culture* (Notre Dame, IN: University of Notre Dame Press, 2005).

72 'Two Lectures', in Foucault, *Power/Knowledge*, 1980, 97.

73 Hansen, *Security as Practice*, 10.

74 This is an approach Nietzsche would fully develop in Friedrich Wilhelm Nietzsche, 'Genealogy of Morals', in *Basic Writings of Nietzsche* (New York: Modern Library, 2000).

75 Uncovering the origin of man and his divine descent, Nietzsche argues, 'has now become a forbidden way, for at its portal stands the ape, together with other gruesome beasts, grinning knowingly as if to say: no further in this direction! One therefore now tries the opposite direction: that mankind is going shall serve as proof of his grandeur and kinship with God. Alas this, too, is vain! At the end of this way stands the funeral urn of the last man and gravedigger'. Friedrich Wilhelm Nietzsche, *Daybreak: Thoughts on the Prejudices of Morality*, eds Maudemarie Clark and Brian Leiter (Cambridge: Cambridge University Press, 1997), §49, 32.

76 Michel Foucault, 'Nietzsche, Genealogy, History', in *The Foucault Reader*, ed. Paul Rabinow (New York: Random House, 1984), 76.

77 Memorandum 26/4/1946 by Haut-Comissaire D'Argenlieu, AN 457 AP127. See Bibliography for details of primary source citation. All translations my own.

78 A phaser is a fictional pistol-like weapon. 'Star Trek, Series 3, Episode 12', *Star Trek, Voyager*, 1996.

4

The diplomacy of the First Vietnam War

[Pyle] was young and ignorant and silly and he got involved. He had no more of a notion than any of you what the whole affair's about, and you gave him money and York Harding's books on the East and said, 'Go ahead. Win the East for democracy.' He never saw anything he hadn't heard in a lecture hall and his writers and his lecturers made a fool of him. When he saw a dead body he couldn't even see the wounds. A Red menace, a soldier of democracy.

Graham Greene, *The Quiet American*[1]

Pyle is a sardonic fictionalisation of a very real American dilemma. In late 1945, Roosevelt's policy for UN trusteeship to replace French sovereignty in Indochina had shifted to acquiescence with French military reconquest. US policymakers initially supported Vietnamese emancipation, but by 1948 they had come to consider Vietminh as unacceptably communist and in July 1948 declared support for French proposals for 'a non-communist solution to the Indochina problem relying on the cooperation of *real* nationalists'.[2] Supporting France's colonial reconquest became part of the solution because US policy had come to accept that France had given voice to 'real' nationalists in a new policy called the Bảo Đại Solution. The new Solution, like the colonial protectorate in place since the 1880s, established former Emperor Bảo Đại as head of a State of Vietnam that chose to remain in the French Empire and asked France to fight Vietminh, the rebel alliance that had declared independence in 1945. Despite the Bảo Đại façade, supporting French imperialism was uncomfortable. As congressman John F. Kennedy noted during a 1951 visit to Vietnam, 'in Indochina we have allied ourselves to the desperate efforts of the French regime to hang on to the remnants of an empire'.[3]

The entire conflict was predicated on who Vietminh were. Scholarship on the diplomacy of the First Vietnam War, as well as US government investigations such as the *Pentagon Papers*, have argued that diplomatic and intelligence assessments of Vietminh communism, read in the context of worsening United States–Soviet relations in 1948, were pivotal to the late 1948 American shift from encouraging negotiated Vietnamese emancipation to assisting France.[4] But assessment of Vietminh as a Stalinist stooge was only one of many representations traded, including how Vietminh represented themselves and their cause, which raises the question of how this policy-defining understanding of the rebels came to be. The method in this book allows us to address firstly how diplomatic descriptions constituted views of Vietminh and, secondly, how this representation and not others emerged as dominant.

The power of diplomatic reporting is, of course, limited and contingent. It does not exist in a vacuum, but rather speaks to concerns that exist within realms of meaning, other texts, power structures, and institutions. Its influence is therefore contingent on how it links with these realms of knowledge. Growing US concern about communism was evidently not created by diplomatic reporting influenced by French diplomacy. Rather, growing anticommunism shaped diplomatic reporting by privileging communist-related reporting, allowing reports of Vietminh communism to prevail over all other descriptions. Dominant policy concerns and diplomatic knowledge production are therefore mutually constitutive, which is why it is vital to determine the specific ways in which policy concerns shape reporting, in essence making it see what it wants to see. Policy concerns emerge in analysis by their presence in the diplomatic text and are triangulated with policy statements, reporting instructions, and contemporary media.[5]

This chapter applies the method advanced in this book to the US turn to assist France in Indochina. It firstly reviews historical efforts to understand how reporting came 'to demonize Hồ Chí Minh and the Viet Minh movement as full-fledged communists',[6] setting the stage to show how this method can contribute to this much-studied case by revealing how this happened in diplomatic knowledge production.[7] The second section maps the institutional paths travelled by diplomatic communications and the archival sources used, while the third determines how representations were inscribed by analysing six texts in detail and identifying topoi textual markers signposting their presence and articulation. The fourth section follows these markers through French, American, and Vietnamese diplomatic knowledge production 1948–45 to trace how representations developed in and through the three cascades and, crucially, how convincing they were, determined by accounting for their presence, longevity, and crossover to another state's diplomatic knowledge production. The final section gathers analytical insights, discussing how representations of Vietminh and France were interdependent and unstable. When their stabilisation in 1947 made French descriptions credible, French representation of Vietminh gradually crossed over to US reporting, while, at the State Department, US diplomatic reporting concerning communist activity gained attention as colonial grievances increasingly fell out of reporting.

Historical debates: the 1945 Vietnamese Revolution, the death of FDR's Trusteeship, and war in 1946

Focus on 'The Character and Power of the Viet Minh', as the *Pentagon Papers* termed it, is justified,[8] as the 1948 decision to back France is broadly recognised as the beginning of the twenty-five-year US commitment to anticommunism in Vietnam.[9] Had Vietminh been seen as nationalist, it would have been difficult for France to obtain US aid to resist Vietnamese emancipation.[10] The problem is that all these representations were possible: Hồ Chí Minh had long been a communist, which does not necessarily belie Vietminh's nationalist and anticolonial cause,[11] and French policymakers, particularly De Gaulle and his entourage, remained fervent colonialists.[12] During 1947–48, the CIA investigated the extent of Soviet control of Vietminh, finding none beyond identifying Vietminh symbols and flags as socialist-looking.[13] It is precisely because the waters of representation were so unclear that descriptions of France, the United States, and particularly 'the key question of the Viet Minh's essential identity' emerge as crucial factors.[14]

The reversal of Roosevelt's Trusteeship policy in Indochina has long been considered a 'lost opportunity' to prevent war.[15] Early scholarship on the conflict argues that in 1943–45, Roosevelt was keen to dispossess France of Indochina,[16] and the reversal of Trusteeship allowed the Truman administration to acquiesce to the French return,[17] while the *Pentagon Papers* conclude that Roosevelt never intended to implement it.[18] Later research nuanced this account, finding that Roosevelt remained committed but implementation became impossible.[19] Truman, it has been argued, half-heartedly implemented it as evidenced by his 1946 refusal to provide military assistance to France and of requests for the liberalisation of the colony.[20] The 'lost opportunity' approach, however, overlooks key international factors.[21] Revisionists added considerable study of mid-1940s diplomacy, particularly Yalta, suggesting that Trusteeship was not abandoned by Roosevelt[22] but sunk due to implementation difficulties and overturned after his death in May 1945,[23] as the need for an anticommunist security compact in Europe made it vital to keep France onside.[24]

This debate assumes that the Truman administration knew whom they were talking to. They clearly did not,[25] as the frantic reporting and briefing on Vietminh analysed in this chapter reveals.[26] Early Vietnamese histories of this question are problematic too, as they are official Communist Party history by Vietminh members, who focused on the 1945 revolution, the role of the party,[27] and how the 9 March 1945 Japanese takeover provided Vietnamese nationalists with respite from French repression. Official Vietminh histories, however, focus on communists to the detriment of other nationalist groups, often incorrectly claiming the entire period and enterprise.[28] More recently, Tuong Vu adds historical nuance to Vietminh communism, finding that the 1945 Revolution was primarily anticolonial, uniting conservatives and Marxist intellectuals, nationalist bourgeois, socialist farmers, and businessmen. This is why the Democratic Republic of Vietnam (DRV) did not reform land ownership, currency, and trade as might have been expected of communists,[29] with ideological 'communistification' beginning only in 1949, with communist economic reforms starting in 1951, encouraged by the prospect of Soviet and Chinese assistance to balance US assistance to France from 1948.[30] Early French approaches reflect colonial and French political debates of the time, from ethnonationalist colonial apologists[31] to Gaullist nationalists proving French grandeur through colonialism[32] and actors in the conflict like Jean Sainteny and Thierry d'Argenlieu.[33]

Philippe Devillers' 'Paris–Saigon–Hanoi' approach, however, established truly transnational studies of the conflict,[34] drawing attention to a multiplicity of actors, including various Indochinese groups, Gaullist nationalists, and their fractured opposition. Stein Tønnesson and David Marr focused on the 1945 revolution and the establishment of the DRV.[35] Marr shows that the terms of Vietnamese independence were heavily contested, with some advocating Indochinese unification, while others could not agree on the name 'Vietnam'.[36] Vietminh's success, he argues, far from staging a socialist revolution in 1945, was to capture anticolonial grievances and articulate Vietnamese aspirations to national liberation.[37]

Building on the 'Paris–Saigon–Hanoi' perspective, Tønnesson challenges the 1980s consensus that Roosevelt diluted Trusteeship, proving that despite French and British pressure, it remained policy until overturned by Truman on 7 June 1945.[38] Tønnesson found no evidence of Vietminh contact with the USSR,[39] concluding that Vietminh subordinated Marxism to national liberation until independence.[40] He concludes that the outbreak of war was the work of a Gaullist colonialist 'Saigon Triumvirate',[41] who set up a 'trap' in December 1946 to begin hostilities.[42] French diplomacy was tasked with keeping the United States neutral, securing continued sales of US and British arms, and avoiding UN intervention.[43] Crucially, Tønnesson found that the conflict's decision-making gravitated around the 'debate among diplomats, politicians and political scientists in every corner of the world as to whether Ho Chi Minh was a communist or a nationalist'.[44] Tønnesson does not explore how French diplomacy achieved its goals but highlights that colonial authorities monopolised communications with Vietminh while managing how, when, and whether Paris received them.[45]

The role in diplomacy of 'perceiving' Vietminh in the context of the Cold War has long been debated[46] but most often results in analysis of whether Vietminh was under Soviet orders. Mark Philip Bradley's research of American and Vietnamese cultural perceptions of one another 1919–50, however, demonstrates the existence of revolutionary and racial ideational contexts preceding and underlying the Cold War. Vietnamese leaders such as Hồ Chí Minh saw America as the most successful anticolonial revolutionary state, but American images of Vietnam were dominated by racial discourses that made a postcolonial Vietnam unimaginable because of 'lingering disdain for Vietnamese capabilities'.[47] American understanding of colonialism was informed by exceptionalism, leading to critiques of French colonialism based on differences with US 'tutelage' of the Philippines rather than emancipation. In a very suggestive conclusion, Bradley identifies the presence of these images in a small selection of diplomatic cables,[48] which brings us back to diplomacy's name-calling.

Mark A. Lawrence was the first to focus on 'perception' of Vietnam, finding that French and British 'diplomatic activism' successfully influenced US policymaking at key turning points in 1945 and 1947–48.[49] The first secured US acquiescence to French reconquest and continued sovereignty over the colony, which killed Trusteeship and ensured the UN would not intervene. In 1947, an embattled France was short of arms, supplies, and finance and unsuccessfully requested US assistance. The problem was not only whether Vietminh was perceived as communist, but also France's own illiberal colonialism. This was addressed in 1947 through a diplomatic campaign highlighting progressive changes, particularly the removal of d'Argenlieu and the 'new' Bảo Đại Solution, while Vietminh's communist credentials were reinforced. The campaign was effective; in late 1948, the 'Bảo Đại Solution' was embraced and discussions started on substantial military assistance.[50] Lawrence identifies the most important representations in US and French diplomatic communication at the policy shift: Vietminh as part of global monolithic communism, French willingness to grant Vietnam some independence under French tutelage, and French anticommunism. Though Lawrence does not explore how they work, or why they were convincing at some times but not others,[51] the method here expounded completes this task.

The historical debates discussed spotlight how much was at stake in diplomatic descriptions of actors in the First Vietnam War, and consequently the potential contribution of this method. We can now move on to analysing the communications involved. The following section maps the institutional context of French, American, and Vietnamese processes of knowledge production as well as the primary sources analysed.

Mapping the diplomatic text: diplomatic knowledge production pathways

The First Vietnam War straddles the ideational, organisational, and military contexts of World War II (WWII) and the Cold War. In the summer of 1945, Britain and America were still fighting Japan in the Far East and Southeast Asian Theatres, and the USSR was about to join the Pacific War. During the war, De Gaulle emerged as president of the Provisional Government of the French Republic, taking sweeping executive powers that would be returned to parliament in October 1946. Gaullism, however, survived in fervent colonialists like Prime Minister Georges Bidault and Indochinese governor Admiral d'Argenlieu.[52] The postwar order negotiated at conferences in Yalta, Potsdam, and San Francisco additionally acknowledged the rights of colonial peoples. Roosevelt died in April but, taking advantage of the Japanese surrender, Vietminh declared independence in September. Yalta partitioned Indochina at the sixteenth parallel into two occupation zones: British in the south, Chinese in the north. British forces disarmed the Japanese, rearmed French forces, and assisted in anti-Vietminh operations, whereas China refused to allow French forces north of the sixteenth parallel, allowing Vietminh to survive in Hanoi. As Stalin claimed Eastern Europe and a communist insurgency begun in Greece in 1946, the rekindling of the Chinese Civil War was initially a rout for communist forces who lost their capital Yan'an in March 1947, though in November 1948, the Lioshen Campaign was highly successful. In June, the Malayan Emergency broke out, a communist insurgency against which Britain launched a ten-year campaign that marked the apparent globalisation of the communist challenge. The June 1948 Tito–Stalin split provided signs that communism was far from monolithic. Crucially, our period of study lies before the test of the first Soviet atom bomb (August 1949), Mao's victory (October 1949), the Korean War (June 1950), and the McCarthy hearings (beginning December 1950).

Mapping of the specific processes of diplomatic knowledge production in France, DRV, and the United States 1945–48 is crucial. Figure 4.1 provides a schematisation of the cascades arranged around institutional reporting and instruction pathways.

French communications were complex due to WWII and the structure of colonial governance. Captain Jean Sainteny established the Mission Militaire Française in Hanoi on 22 August 1945, making first contact on 27 August when he met DRV Interior Minister Võ Nguyên Giáp.[53] Until the Haut-commissariat (governorship) was re-established in Saigon in October 1945, Sainteny reported to Haut-commissaire d'Argenlieu in Calcutta.[54] Sainteny was de Gaulle's envoy with 'power to engage in talks',[55] but was restricted

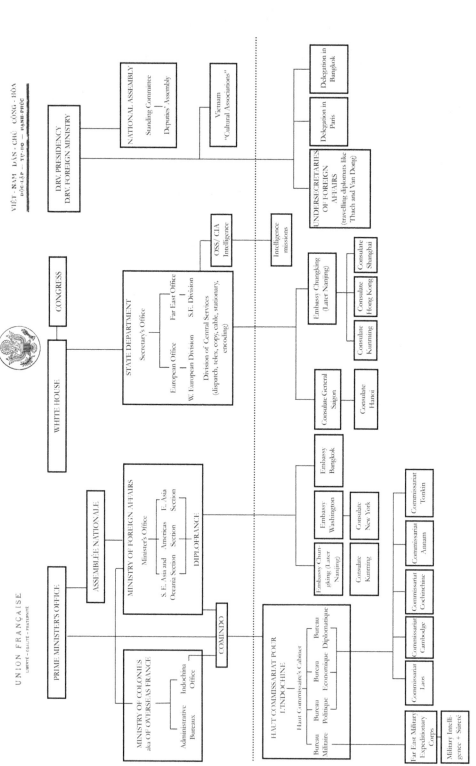

Figure 4.1 Diagram of diplomatic knowledge production pathways by institutions studied. Lines denote channels of reporting and instructions.

by d'Argenlieu to securing intelligence and contacts.[56] On 4 October 1945, d'Argenlieu appointed him Commissaire for Tonkin and North-Annam, authorised to discuss terms with the 'Gouvernement Révolutionnaire Annamite'. Sainteny negotiated the 6 March 1946 accord and remained a key channel of communication until wounded in May 1947. In Saigon, correspondence was processed by one of six offices: the Haut-commissaire's Cabinet and the Political Affairs, Military, Economic, or Diplomatic Sections. The latter forwarded documentation to the Ministry of Foreign Affairs (MFA) in Paris and received updates. Communication with Vietminh was processed through the Political Affairs Section led by Léon Pignon. This office provided analysis, comments, and recommendations that were systematically forwarded to Paris and used in communications with other powers. Political Affairs additionally processed reporting requests from the Interministerial Committee on Indochina (COMINDO), the Quai d'Orsay ('DIPLOFRANCE'), and the Haut-commissaire. The military section made occasional contact with Vietminh via its Supreme Commander.

It is worth briefly noting the structure of colonial Indochina for reference in this chapter. The colony, conquered in the 1880s, was organised as a 'Union', later a 'Federation', governed by a High Commissioner ('Haut-commissaire'). As shown in the colonial map in Figure 4.2, the old Empire of Vietnam had been divided into three 'kys' – two of which, Tonkin and Cochinchine, d'Argenlieu argued, were real countries that had been colonised by the 'Annamese' of the third 'ky', Annam, and which needed French protection. This is relevant because reunification of the three kys was a core issue in the conflict, and indeed continued after partition in 1954. The Haut-commissaire had five Commissaires under him, one for each of the five 'countries' in the colony. At the end of WWII, Vietminh set up its power base in the North, in Hanoi, and with British assistance, the French reconquered the South, re-establishing the Haut-commissariat in Saigon.

The Haut-commissaire reported to COMINDO, chaired by De Gaulle during the Provisional Government and thereafter by the prime and foreign ministers who instructed the MFA on communications with other powers. After De Gaulle left, COMINDO became effectively dormant, and its staff forwarded communications from the high commissioner directly to the prime minister, bypassing the colonial and foreign ministries. Beyond the influence on the prime minister created by this arrangement, the Haut-commissaire had unprecedented diplomatic powers, including representing France to other powers in the Far East for all Indochinese affairs and,[57] crucially, sole representation of France to all 'domestic' Indochinese organisations and 'parties',[58] which is why he monopolised contact with Vietminh.[59] This had significant consequences when d'Argenlieu called the Dalat II conference in August 1946, which, even as Vietminh and the French

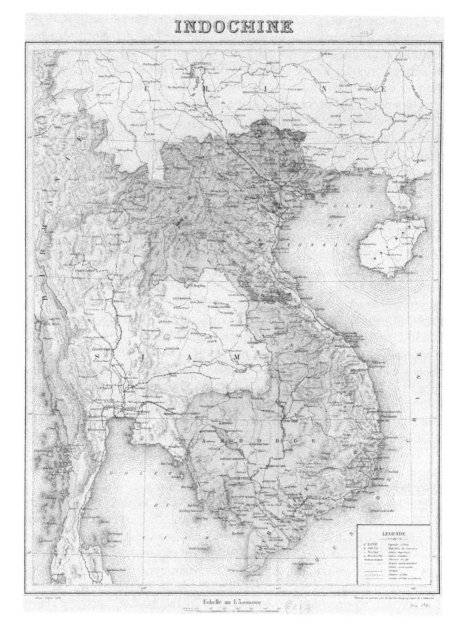

Figure 4.2 Map of colonial Indochina showing subdivisions. Image from Wikimedia Commons.

government negotiated independence and reunification at Fontainebleau, declared the 'République de Cochinchine' and reorganised the colony as a 'Federation' composed of five states, effectively sabotaging the negotiations at Fontainebleau.

Vietnamese diplomacy was not as heavily bureaucratic or extensive. At the bottom we have individuals in Vietnam and abroad, who are increasingly formalised as diplomats. In 1945 and until 1948, communications were sent to US Embassies in Chungking Bangkok, Kunming, and Shanghai, as well as the US consulates in Hanoi and Saigon. Phạm Ngọc Thạch for instance, DRV Undersecretary of Foreign Affairs and diplomat, frequently travelled to Bangkok, where the US Embassy forwarded communications onto State and vice versa. The Foreign Ministry was integrated with the presidency (Hồ held both posts) and dispatched communications to French and US representatives. Hồ and Giáp had leading roles, as did Phạm Văn Đồng, in meeting and negotiating with American Office of Strategic Services (OSS, predecessor to the CIA) officers, the US consul in Kunming, and Moffat, as well as Sainteny, Valluy, Pignon, and d'Argenlieu. Vietnamese foreign policy was clearly directed by this small group.

Vietminh did not benefit from reporting, communication, and analysis from foreign stations – not least because French diplomats and spies were tasked with sabotaging these efforts and assassinating Vietminh messengers.[60] However, 'Vietnam Cultural associations', a network of nationalist front organisations, printed and distributed documents for diplomatic and public distribution. Upon the proclamation of DRV, they produced documentation supporting its diplomacy, including translations, propaganda for foreign consumption, and the 'Letter to the San Francisco Conference' that was dispatched to Western and Chinese missions and handed in person to Conference delegates.

Vietminh communication with France initially depended on dispatches to and from the French Far East mission in Kunming passed on by local Vietnamese residents. Upon his arrival in Hanoi, Sainteny became DRV's main communication channel. Hồ and Giáp negotiated the 6 March accord with him, establishing a ceasefire, providing for the return of French forces to north Vietnam and the Fontainebleau Conference in July 1946. After Fontainebleau, Vietminh left Duong Bach Mai in Paris as chief of the 'Vietnamese delegation in Paris'. He was ignored, however, due to French insistence that all exchanges should proceed via d'Argenlieu.

US diplomatic knowledge production was very extensive, but procedurally clearer than Vietnamese or French diplomacy. Consulates at Kunming, Hong Kong, and Shanghai reported to the Embassy in Chungking (later Nanjing), which forwarded to State. Until the Saigon Consulate-General was re-established in January 1946, OSS officers in Indochina reported via this route from mid-1944 until November 1945. Consulate Hanoi, established in February 1946, effectively acted as an embassy to DRV between 1946 and 1947, forwarding Vietnamese communications and near-daily reports.[61] He reported via the Consulate-General in Saigon, which itself reported on d'Argenlieu's manoeuvres. At the State department's Division of Central Services, communications were copied, translated, and forwarded to relevant offices (stamps on the copy of record determine which received it), including the European, Far Eastern (FE), and the Secretary's Offices, as well as the Southeast Asian (SEA) and Western Europe (WE) sub-divisions. These processed reporting and documentation into briefs, research, analysis, recommendations, and requested further information. With approval and direction from the Secretary, they initiated démarches and met foreign leaders – this is how we find SEA chief Abbot Low Moffat meeting Hồ Chí Minh in 1946.

This research has examined diplomatic communication, including cables, reports, summaries, policy papers, and responses from the US, French, and Vietnamese foreign ministries and executives. They include cables, briefs, summaries, analysis, and policy statements and the feedback loop that sends instructions, parameters, and priorities for reporting and demarches back to missions. Research at the French Archives Diplomatiques of the Ministère d'Affaires Étrangères (MAE) included 1948–3 Fond Fond États Associés (EA) files, devoted to information management and processing to and from Vietnam, Cambodia and Laos until their independence in 1954, as well as all 1948–4 communications to and from the US – some only declassified in 2009. Research also examined files pertaining to the colonial government, especially its Diplomatic and Political sections, at the Archives Nationales d'Autre Mer, the Bidault and d'Argenlieu files at the Archives Nationales, and Sainteny's own archive.[62]

The US National Archives hold diplomatic reporting and subsequent knowledge production, up to and including memos and documents for lawmakers and policymakers. This analysis also examined declassified CIA reports available through CIA Records Search Tool (CREST). The Vietnamese National Archives were a difficult proposition: only Tønnesson and Marr have made substantial use – with significant limitations.[63] Like them, however, we can complete the diplomatic picture thanks to the French sack of archives and interception of Vietminh cables from 1946.[64] A vast amount of Vietnamese diplomatic communication was available in French and US diplomatic archives as well as the Sainteny collection, demonstrating it was received, read, and processed. To account for work carried out by COMINDO, analysis triangulated sources at MAE, Sainteny, Georges Bidault, and d'Argenlieu archives.

How diplomatic texts inscribe actors and their contexts: commie stooges contra libération

This section applies the second step of this method, analysing how individual texts constitute representations of subjects, territory, temporality, and conflict. It is structured as six detailed analyses of individual texts, two for each actor: DRV, France, and the United States. Organised as a literary commentary, analysis of each text firstly locates it within the diplomatic practices from which it issued, and then its structure, articulations of representation, and specific use of words are examined. Analysis additionally identifies topoi textual markers signposting the presence of specific representations. For example, communist conspiracy appears under a variety of labels: 'from Moscow', 'of the Stalin school', and even 'totalitarianism', but in all cases they refer to the topos of monolithic Soviet-directed communism.

In executing this method, it is not always necessary to write up such detailed analyses of individual texts for publication. This would be impractical in, for example, a journal article or report.[65] In this chapter they are written out because, since the method requires researchers to systematically analyse all texts in this way, it is worth evidencing its application transparently and in detail.[66] For this reason, the six texts selected feature the key representations encountered in this research and include different diplomatic genres: a cable, report, brief, petition, letter, and policy statement.

1. Độc Lập: anticolonialism and independence

In 1945, a 'Letter to the San Francisco Conference' from 'the Indochinese Annamese people' begun to circulate among Western and Chinese diplomats.

Vietminh distributed this document to diplomats attending the United Nations Conference on International Organization in April–June 1945. Japanese forces were still in Indochina; in Paris, De Gaulle proclaimed France's love for its colony and its upcoming 'libération'.[67] Signed by 'The National Party of Indochina', it issues an appeal of the 'Annamese' to the San Francisco Conference. Further copies arrived at the State Department and the French MFA from their consulates in Saigon, Hanoi, and Kungming, China. It is a unique one-time communication written in emotional lyrical language proficiently translated into Chinese and English.

The 'Letter' argues for the end of French colonialism in Indochina. 'Undaunted by the fact that we are not entitled to any representation at the conference', the pamphlet expounds Vietnam's 'glorious past': an empire that wrested its independence from China over a millennium ago. The document describes French abuses including discrimination, lack of education and freedom of movement, the promotion and compulsory purchase of opium and liquor, economic exploitation, the division of Vietnam, and French collaboration with Japan. The pamphlet praises the pledges of the Atlantic and Dumbarton Oaks Charters, linking Indochinese self-determination to the promised 'restoration' of those oppressed by fascism.

The language is highly lyrical, differentiating positions with theatrical contrast. The UN, Dumbarton Oaks, and Atlantic conferences are described as the beginning of 'peace, prosperity and the pursuit of happiness without the constant fear of being trampled on'. High-contrast vocabulary and articulations link and differentiate subjects into two diametrically opposed normative identities. Subjects are framed in classical French anticolonial language, such as we might find in a 1930s Parisian intellectual's essay: peaceful, civilised 'Annamese' undeservedly brutalised by greedy colonists, producing an articulation of the 'noble savage' against the perverse conqueror.[68] The letter, interestingly, argues that the 'Annamese' do not deserve or need colonising because of their fiercely independent history, which is expounded in epic normative terms. These representations are bolted together by a poetically expressed passion for independence. Like the title character's passionate filial love in Vietnamese epic poem *The Tale of Kieu*, anticolonial sentiment is inscribed as immanent and righteous.[69]

The appeal emphasises how colonialism contradicts the UN values that Vietminh hopes shall order the postwar world. French names (Annam, Kys, Indochina) are used, rather than Việt Nam, though the quote marks framing 'Annamese' might indicate scepticism of this name, which is not as remarkable as the inordinately prolific use of the words 'nation' and 'peoples', reflecting the language of the aforementioned Charters. 'The National Party of Indo-China (Annam)' is translated into Chinese as 越南國民黨 ('Viet Nam Guo Min Tang'), written with the same *hànzì* (logograms) as Sun Yat-Sen's Guomindang (KMT) party with 'Viet Nam' instead of Zhong Guo (China). Although there existed a KMT-supported Vietnamese Guomindang, which later joined Vietminh, this leaflet was produced by the latter (printed and distributed by the 'Vietnam Cultural Association'), highlighting the significance of the use of 'Guomindang' to frame their position in familiar terms.

Adapting the name of Asia's oldest nationalist party linked Vietminh to a cause that was already legitimate at San Francisco as Guomindang's anticolonialism and China's place among the 'Big Five' were widely accepted by war's end. 'Guomindang' evidences the first topos of this text, signposting representations that refer to Độc Lập (independence) as an immanent international right. Use of the words 'people' and 'nation' denotes a second topos, one that frames the Vietnamese in the normative and linguistic terms of the Atlantic Charter, which used both terms as binding definitions.

2. Việt Nam Độc Lập Đồng Minh Hội: national liberation, not communism

Japan has surrendered. On 2 September 1945, Hồ Chí Minh declares the independence of Vietnam, but France is preparing an expeditionary force commanded by General Leclerc to reconquer Indochina.[70] The 'President of the Provisional Government of the Democratic Republic of Viet-Nam' Hồ Chí Minh wrote to the US Secretary of State, including three attachments that justified the legitimacy of DRV. The first adheres DRV foreign policy to the Atlantic and San Francisco Charters as well as cosmopolitan liberal values of free trade and self-determination of subject peoples. The second draws on these values to demand self-determination, statehood, and reject the prewar status. A further attachment featured a copy of Emperor Bảo Đại's abdication in favour of DRV. Stamps evidence that the State Department's SEA Division and the Secretariat had read it on or by 7 November.

The letter calls for 'immediate interference [intervention] on the part of the United Nations', submitting documents 'to bring some more light on the case of Vietnam'. It expounds the DRV case emphasising '80 years of French oppression and unsuccessful though obstinate Vietnamese resistance' before offering a summary of pro-Allied Vietnamese WWII efforts. After France's 'betrayal of the Allies', the 'Vietnamese, leaving aside all differences in political opinion, united in the Vietminh League and started on a ruthless fight against the Japanese'. The narrative frames desire for independence, Bảo Đại's abdication, and the declaration of independence as 'in keeping with the San Francisco Charter' before returning to the French 'aggressive invasion'. The narrative predicts inevitable violence should anticolonial aspirations continue to be repressed.

The missive is structured as a quick back and forth across binary divides: firstly French imperialism contra Vietnamese efforts, rights, and claims; then French and British manoeuvres to regain the colony against the new expectations of international behaviour. Collaboration with the Allies against Japan inscribes Vietminh in the antifascist side of the wartime binary against Vichy France, inscribing Vietminh an antifascist resistance movement entitled to make claims on the postwar settlement. This is clearly expressed: Vietnam 'only asks for full independence' not through war but through UN intervention. This is reinforced grammatically, where placing the sub-clause 'leaving aside all differences in political opinion, united in the Vietminh League' in the middle of a narrative explaining the demand for independence makes it clear that Vietminh represents the country because this selfsame demand brought various groups together into the League – Vietminh's full name, Việt Nam Độc Lập Đồng Minh Hội, means 'League for the Independence of Vietnam'.

This text marks a break from preceding Vietnamese communications. The language at the beginning and conclusion of the letter is taken directly from the San Francisco Charter, including its 'mission', 'recognition by the UN', and even 'interference' (mistranslated 'intervention' from the French edition of the Charter), which refers to UN provisions for Consultative Commissions and Interventions. The language is procedural and rights-based in its wording choices. This letter's vocabulary linguistically emphasises the rejection of French colonialism, abandoning imperial nomenclature in favour of 'Vietnam', 'Vietminh League', 'the people of Vietnam'. Further emphasising this move to written statehood, all the DRV communications from this point on use the words 'Provisional Government of the Republic of Vietnam', possibly in an effort to achieve some of the internationally accepted legitimacy of de Gaulle's wartime Provisional Government of the French Republic.

This letter contains three crucial representations: UN and US championship of oppressed peoples, proven Vietnamese desire for independence, and Vietminh's role as a legitimate vehicle for these aspirations. While they were present in the previous text studied (signposted by 'peoples', 'nations' and 'Guomindang' topoi markers), this letter reveals a normative and narrative construction behind the short marker 'independence' that binds the legitimacy of anti-Japanese resistance and self-determination, which are treated as immanent and universal, to independence and Vietminh itself.

Representation of Vietminh as existing only to achieve independence reappears often. As it came under pressure for the communist beliefs of figures like Hồ and Giáp, and the 1945 amalgamation of the Communist Party of Indochina (CPI) with five other nationalist parties to form Vietminh, its independentist cause was consistently emphasised until late 1948. If we move to May 1947, for example, we find that American Ambassador in Bangkok E. F. Stanton submitted written questions to DRV Undersecretary for Foreign Affairs Dr. Phạm Ngọc Thạch. The embassy's paraphrase of Thạch's answer to its question 'can a definition be given to Communism as it exists in Vietnam?' offers the same representation of Vietminh: a league of many parties with independence as its goal since 1945. It is updated with the anti-independence position of the French Communist Party, Vietminh's lack of socialist programmes, and the sententia – an unsubstantiated rhetorical argument, like a maxim – that, to Vietnam communism, meant the provision of basic rights and independence.

3. 'Only an ideological and doctrinal position'

The 6 March agreement is holding as DRV and France prepare for negotiations at Fontainebleau. In April 1946, a memorandum was sent by d'Argenlieu to COMINDO and Prime Minister Bidault, part of a series of memoranda prepared with his colonial Political Office concerning Cochinchina.[71] These memoranda were part of his extensive diplomatic duties that extended to acting as sole representative of France to the five 'states' of the Indochinese Federation.

The memorandum makes the case for France to 'continue as we had done before the signing of the [6 March] convention' in respect to Cochinchina. That part of Vietnam was, he explains, conquered by the Vietnamese from the Khmer and should not be reunited. Cochinchina was the first region of Vietnam annexed by France and the heartland of colonisation. Arguing that 'only an ideological and doctrinal position' advocates reuniting the three kys, the memorandum posits that geography, history, and economics separate them. The linguistic unity of Vietnamese speakers is rejected as a 'puerile' or 'racist' argument used 'by the Führer'. D'Argenlieu argues that 'the mission of France was and remains to protect ethnic minorities against the Annamite imperialist tendency', suggesting that 'sooner or later the great Annam would penetrate and absorb Laos and Cambodia'.[72]

In reinventing Cochinchina as geographically, historically, and economically separate from historical Vietnam, the text constitutes spectacular representations of its subjects and the territory, time, and normativity that define them. Annamite imperialist terrorist racists are pitted against helpless Cochinchinese victims. Spatially, Cochinchina's geography 'naturally' separates it from Annam; temporally, the North's smaller economy, lack of progress, and 'racist' 'imperialist tendency' differentiate Annam from France and its more developed Cochinchinese colony. Annamese ambitions are normatively inscribed as cruel, expansionist, ethnically repressive, and comparable to Nazi irredentism.

Involving itself in linguistic battles over representation, the memo avoids using any word evoking Vietnam's existence, even when mentioning the language and the 'Hanoi government', and suggests reinforcing censorship of the word 'Vietnam'.[73] Long sentences with multiple sub-clauses referring to Cochinchina and France contrast with truncated short constructions on Vietminh, reinforcing simple succinct rebuttals. In a formatting and alliteration feat, the short paragraphs each begin with 'not' (in the original French, all seven paragraphs begin with a negative particle). Even grammatical gender and number are implicated: in common with French convention, France and Cochinchina are personified (referred to as 'she'), while Vietminh and 'the government of Hanoi' are referred to as 'them', denying it the grammatical treatment reserved for countries.

Four representations operating in binary pairs emerge from this text. Vietminh's 'doctrinal ideological position' delegitimises the violence, organisation, and ultimately anticolonialism as immature and ideologically extreme. French diplomacy uses terms from 'terrorism' to 'anti-white' and 'racism' to inscribe anticolonial struggle, which stand as useful topoi to mark the representation. It, in turn, depends upon and reinforces the second: Cochinchina as the 'masterpiece' of Indochina thanks to colonisation is consistently found under the topos 'œuvre' (from 'œuvre civilisatrice'). The third representation, reunification as an Annamese imperialist dream, stands in mutually dependent opposition to the fourth, France's mission 'to protect ethnic minorities', signposted by ethnosupremacist topoi from WWII denoted by labels referring to the Third Reich. These binary representations reinforce one another and disestablish Vietminh claims to nineteenth-century Vietnam as imperialist, racist, and divisive, creating normative differentiation that makes French colonialism necessary.

4. The 'so-called "Viet Minh Movement"'

Vietnam declared its independence twenty days ago. The Chinese force that occupied the north to disarm the Japanese is yet to announce a departure date and remains unwilling to assist France repress Vietminh, while the British re-arm and assist French forces in the southern occupation zone. In a late September 1945 cable, US ambassador to France Jefferson Caffery reports his conversation with Philippe Baudet, director of the Asia-Oceania Division at the French MFA. The red stamps denote that this cable was read at the European and SEA offices and was sent up to the Secretary's offices at the State Department.[74]

The conversation concerns the 'so-called "Viet Minh Movement"', which, Baudet tells Caffery, is 'organised somewhat along Communist lines' and 'is in touch with the Soviet Mission at Chungking', since 'the Communist Party in Indochina' 'appears to have been absorbed in the Viet Minh' and a French Communist Party statement 'indicated Moscow's interest in Indo-China'. He explains that 'the status of Indo-China' must be revised, 'taking into consideration the desires of the nationalist groups', but that 'it would be an error to modify the statute until French authority has been restored and the situation studied on the spot'. Baudet's description does not reject nationalist grievances outright (the Trusteeship debacle had only just concluded) but emphasises Vietminh links to the USSR. This, he suggests, is proven by its organisational structure and communication with Moscow. Problematising Vietminh justified the need for re-establishing French rule before granting independence.

The language is descriptive and, as is standard with cables, written almost entirely in the past simple tense. This integrates it into the diplomatic genre of factual description style Nicolson considered so important.[75] Formatting is powerful in this genre; direct citation marks separate facts from Baudet's assertions, affording less credence to French desire to take '"into consideration the desires of the nationalist groups"'. The repetitive insertion of personal pronouns grammatically reinforces that this is reported conversation ('According to Baudet', 'he also said') by bracketing it in subordinate clauses. Baudet's insistence on the 'reestablisment' of French authority emphasises the continuity of French sovereignty over Indochina.

The cable establishes four representations into two opposing pairs: Vietminh-Soviet communism differentiated from French-US postcolonial progressiveness. Representation of international communism is not articulated around socialism but as Soviet expansionism.[76] The topoi signpost the presence of these two linkages: 'Moscow's interest' contra 'French willingness to "take into consideration"' Indochinese nationalism within the 'reestablishment of French authority'.

This representation of Vietminh and France as opponent/ally of the United States in the Cold War is unusual for 1945, and did not reappear with any significant consistency until late 1946. French representations of Vietminh from 1945 to mid 1946 were usually characterised by the inscriptions found in d'Argenlieu's memo (p. 149) and 'Vietminh fascism'.[77] When communism took a significant place in French–US diplomacy in 1946–47, the strategically planned change in emphasis was studied and formalised in the 1948 Claudel Report.

The report was tasked with outlining what strategies might be available for French diplomacy and propaganda in the United States. Its research drew on American public and media sources. It suggests that Franco-American relations would 'thrive' on common enmity with the USSR, described in exactly the same emotive terms common during the American Red Scare that had begun in 1947, and proposes that, to secure consistent support, anticommunist (and Christian Conservative) rhetoric be established as the core motive and dynamic of Franco-American communications.

5. 'Radical Annamese opponents of both France and Japan'

As the United States had not yet established a consulate in Hanoi, a report by Charles S. Millet, an American diplomat passing through Vietnam, was one of the first extensive economic, political, and military reports on Vietnam following Vietminh's takeover.[78] It was written by a US Foreign Service Officer who travelled through Hanoi in October 1945. Consul General Shanghai recommended it to the State Department as 'of interest and value', and it was passed on to the Secretary's and the Economic, Development, SEA, FE, and European Offices at the State Department.

The report assesses various 'factions' operating in northern Vietnam before offering a narrative of events in August–October and an economic, political, and military assessment. A 'markedly pro-Vichy' French colonial government is confronted by small 'deGaullist' groups; Vietminh, 'a vigorous and large body of anti-Japanese and anti-French Annamese very active in guerrilla warfare', is fighting 'a smaller Japanese-sponsored group of Annamese collaborators'.

Vietminh is a 'closely-knit and well organised' 'radical body of Annamites', led by 'an old revolutionary' who 'suffered gravely at the hands of his French political opponents'. 'As might be expected, this party is definitely left-wing and is believed to include many Communist members. Ho himself disclaims the title of Communist', emphasising that Vietminh contains politically different groups and even works with 'the conservatives of Bao-Dai' to achieve independence.

The report differentiates actors, events, and motives along colonial–anticolonial and WWII binaries. Differentiation emphasises those that collaborated with the Japanese (the Vichy French, the 'Annamese collaborateurs' (sic), the Emperor) or the Allies (the 'radical body of Annamese', the 'deGaullist French'). Vietminh is constituted as firmly anti-Japanese and pro-American, having worked and fought with US forces and proven amenable to American suggestions and requests. Vietminh remains 'definitely left-wing', but this is clearly subsumed within a doctrine that 'party denominations and differences must await the success of the revolution'. The use of the vocable 'revolution' is here treated like the American Revolution. Finally, the report discusses the limits of Vietminh's capacity to govern and the anti-French violence it appears unable to control.

Vocabulary like 'radicals' and 'collaborateurs' constitutes a normative inscription that locates subjects in the categories of WWII – down to the French spelling of the hated fascist collaborators. Vocabulary also reveals the realms of knowledge the author was familiar with: terminology like 'overseas Chinese' (海外華人, the Chinese equivalent of 'expats') demonstrates knowledge of Southeast Asia not apparent in the reports of OSS officers also in Vietnam at the time. More obvious are the multiple appearances of 'Vietnam', a politicised – and often illegal – word for French diplomats. In articulations like 'the radical Annamese opponents of both France and Japan', 'radical' is qualified by its specification as targeted against colonialism and fascism. The similarly described linkage between anti-French violence and anti-French grievances compounds these subtle but important qualifications.

The French, when not condemned to the fascist dustbin of WWII representations, are left on the Allied side but similarly qualified. For instance, 'deGaullist French persons (whose most effective activities were those of espionage and the rescue of grounded American aircraft crews)' are qualified by that devastating bracket, which through implied comparison ('most effective' followed by small achievements) suggests they did little. The structure of the report attributes agency to Vietminh, as they constantly take precedence in narrative order. However, this slows down at the Vietminh takeover of Hanoi, at which point the text emphasises that Hồ is having trouble controlling his people and anti-French violence. In this aspect of Vietminh representation, we recognise the incontinence and immaturity attributed to Asian peoples in American interwar racial discourses.[79]

The representations that emerge are faith in the Allied cause, colonial grievances, and Vietminh incapacity to govern. Signposted by topoi like 'collaborateurs' and 'anti-Japanese', WWII references frame this text through the normative, military, and temporal differentiations of the conflict. French colonialism is represented drawing on liberal rejection of colonialism, exploitation, and injustice. The topoi signposting this representation of anticolonialism are adjectives qualifying actions, as opposed to simply the names of principles: 'authoritative government' contra 'vigorous' and 'unyielding' Vietnamese. Representation of colonials unready for government is signposted by terms assuming powerlessness or inability, such as 'disturbances' and Ho's 'inability' to keep order.

6. 'A truly nationalist government in Indochina', or Pyle's Third Force

In late 1948, the United States finally moved to support the French reconquest of Vietnam. This policy shift was first announced in a September 1948 State Department Policy Statement, part of a series regularly updated when new policy is issued. They are distributed to relevant missions and officers to ensure continuity in all diplomatic interaction and reporting.[80]

Representation of the conflict has changed significantly since 1945. The first long-term objective is 'to eliminate as far as possible Communist influence in Indochina' and to establish 'a self-governing nationalist state which will be friendly to the US'. Vietminh is now considered part of a global communist takeover because communists 'captur[ed] control of the nationalist movement' in Vietnam. France appears less negatively than hitherto, even though they 'never understood, or have chosen to underestimate, the enormous strength of the nationalist movement'. Conversely, 'hatred of the Vietnamese people toward the French is keeping alive anti-western feeling among oriental peoples to the advantage of the USSR and the detriment of the US'.

US policy still 'regard[s] with favour the efforts of dependent peoples to attain their legitimate political aspirations', but this is qualified as 'political and economic independence consistent with legitimate French interests'. The statement calls for France 'to accommodate the basic aspiration of the Vietnamese', avoid talks with Vietminh, and establish instead 'a truly nationalist government in Indochina', which the United States is willing to support. It is asserted that there is 'increasing Soviet interest in Indochina'. This is a sententia, since proof – considering the weight given to international communism – consists only of a Soviet 'step-up in radio broadcasts' that criticise US Indochina policy, while '[t]here continues to be no known communication between the USSR and Vietnam'.

Relations of linkage and differentiation in this text appear perverse. Though anticolonial, the US finds itself supporting colonial France because of the communist threat to Indochina. Contradictions only appear because linkages and differentiations operate on three superposed discursive planes, each of which makes more sense on its own.[81] In the first, France and America are differentiated by French colonialism and American support for 'legitimate political aspirations', while America is linked to Vietminh's nationalism. On the second discursive plane, France and the United States are linked by their common anticommunism. Contradiction is further obscured by the 'infiltration' of Vietminh by international communism, leaving this contradictory course of action as the only option, since in Vietminh hands, anticolonialism helps the Soviets. This draws on an older Orientalist qualification of colonial subjects' political capacity inscribed on a plane of differentiation beneath the other two: Vietnamese political immaturity makes anticolonialism liable to hijacking by communism, which ultimately makes Vietminh a Soviet emanation 'capturing' the nationalist cause.

Vocabulary is key to this articulation: 'penetration', 'domination', 'aggression', 'capture', 'totalitarian', 'Moscow' are words of violence, normatively negative adjectives that irremediably inscribe anything they touch as antithetical. Contrast is drawn with US policy: a 'self-governing' Vietnam (otherwise it would be governed from Moscow) against 'US security', US and French 'interests' (reasonable, unlike domination). The extent to which language is implicated in constituting representation is highlighted by this text, where the smallest changes in syntax could make France the seeker of 'domination' or perpetrator of 'aggression', not to mention colonially 'totalitarian'. Vocabulary inserts Cold War binaries in articulations like 'a democratic state as opposed to the totalitarian state which would evolve inevitably from Communist domination'. Similarly, 'capturing control of the nationalist movement' suggests calculated infiltration and American late-1940s communist conspiracy theories.[82]

This statement includes two extremely powerful representations. Global monolithic communism is signposted by the 'Moscow fellow-travellers' topoi. This representation expanded during McCarthysim and remained dominant until the late 1980s. The agency of colonial subjects, signposted by the topos of 'oriental peoples' and conjured by syntax that subordinates Orientals to the verbs of others, supports the 'infiltration' thesis. The last representations in this document are the dynamic (and self-flattering for the United States) pair of greedy European colonialism (apparent under the topos that France 'never understood' anticolonialism) and America ('regarding with favor') such aspirations and helping France realise them. Monolithic international communism holds together the representations in the document by linguistically constructing its existence, subsuming Vietminh under its control, and predicting (sententiae again) that it will 'inevitably' create a 'totalitarian state' 'detrimental to the US'. This linkage reinforces the policy position: it is necessary to help France destroy Vietminh and establish a noncommunist 'Third Force'.

Graham Greene had no need to invent much. This 1947 policy statement describes the 'Third Force' that Pyle creates in *The Quiet American*. In a nod to the American normative absolutism that Greene mocked so cruelly and on which this entire statement is predicated, it concludes that 'effort should be made to explain democratic institutions, especially American institutions and American policy, to the Indochinese, by direct personal contact, by distribution of information about the US'.

Tracing the history of diplomatic descriptions in Vietnam 1948–45

Communists 'capturing control of the nationalist movement' is the explicit basis for the 1948 change in policy analysed above. The new policy – isolating Vietminh, supporting French military efforts against them, and promoting a 'Third Force' – is based on the recognition that, firstly, Vietminh is part of a Soviet conspiracy and, secondly, the French have accepted that progressive concessions must be made to Vietnamese aspirations. Both the 1948 policy-defining descriptions were untrue: Vietminh only established relations with other communists the following year after substantial American assistance to France, while France's 'new' Bảo Đại solution was another rehash of the 1880s formula of using puppet emperors. The impact of these descriptions is, however, undeniable: the 1948 shift to support France was explicitly predicated on Vietminh's participation in the global communist conspiracy and French willingness to allow noncommunist nationalist revindication. How did these vital representations come about?

This section applies the third step of the method, tracing how diplomatic representations of Vietminh and France as communist stooges and progressive colonial reformers that justified the 1948 policy shift developed. It traces their genealogy backwards from a policy instance that is predicated on the representations themselves – in this case, how the representations in the 1948 policy statement came about, following the topoi textual markers that signpost the presence and orientation of each to trace their lineage backwards across the diplomatic knowledge production of the actors involved, finding previous iterations of each in preceding texts, examining the text and context of each rewriting, reassessment, classification, or addition, until reaching the earliest available expression of each. Further, this analysis identifies when representations cross over from the diplomacy of an actor to another's, determining the moment when a description became adopted.

Analysing the representations diplomacy was trading in as we did in the earlier section demonstrates the difference between US understanding of Vietminh and France in 1945 and 1948. In 1945, American views of Vietminh were marked by racialised Orientalism, signposted by references to 'Asian race' and 'unpreparedness'; clear understanding that Vietminh was not a Soviet creation, signposted by references to 'left-wing' and 'nationalist' positions; and support for their goals by references to the legitimacy of their anticolonial struggle. In 1948, however, US diplomacy describes Vietminh as racialised Soviet stooges, signposted by conspiratorial topoi like 'fellow-travellers', expressions of Soviet control of Vietminh, and the qualification of nationalism as 'legitimate' against 'foreign-controlled'. This is the change and development in representations of subjects and their contexts in the First Vietnam War that the following analysis must account for. To help follow what is a complex backward history of representations, it is divided into three periods on the basis of the dominant representation of the conflict in US diplomatic knowledge production. This division is only for ease of exposition to readers and plays no analytical role as the analysis is continuous.

Late 1948–September 1947: Stalinist stooges and the Third Force

The September 1948 Policy Statement inscribed Vietminh as part the global monolithic Cold War enemy, allowing France to reject negotiations altogether.[83] This representation of communism as monolithic, world-conquering, and intractable was partly enabled by the discursive context of 1948. In March, Truman established political loyalty reviews for federal employees and announced the Truman Doctrine.[84] The Berlin Blockade had begun in April 1948 and the Malayan Emergency in June, the Greek Civil War was ongoing, and in August, communist-hunting trials begun. Communism was seen as a conspiracy, a disease that affected 'fellow travellers' for life.[85] American concern about Southeast Asia grew as the June

1948 Malay Emergency fuelled speculation that 'Moscow turns its eye to Southeast Asia'.[86]

As Figure 4.3 exemplifies, Soviet expansionism was represented geo-strategically: the WWII-descended forerunner of the early 1950s Domino Theory.[87] The advances of the Chinese Communist Party (CPC) were not considered a grave concern until December 1948 – after the turnaround in Indochina policy.[88] Though the Berlin blockade reinforced representations of global communist ambitions, the diplomacy of the period suggests that it was far less relevant to Vietnam than the Malayan Emergency.[89] Crucially, throughout this period, French colonial wars in Madagascar and Indochina were heavily criticised in US media.[90]

As policy depended upon it, proving claims of Vietminh–Soviet links was a priority. Between 1945 and 1948, French, US, and British agents made vast but unsuccessful efforts to substantiate it – the CIA, for example, could prove similarity in iconography.[91] Proof was never found.[92] The first representation whose history we trace, the Vietminh–Soviet link, was built of descriptions that purported to demonstrate Soviet–Vietnamese alignment.[93]

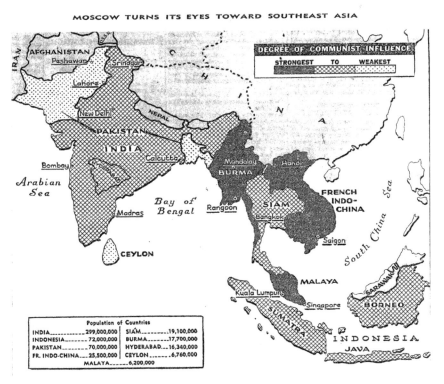

Figure 4.3 Infographic accompanying an article titled 'Comniform is in sight for Southeastern Asia', *New York Times*, July 1948.

The opening of a Soviet embassy in Bangkok, for example, was frequently cited as proof of a 'regional' Soviet offensive, an assessment made possible by the Cold War myth of the monolith: that all communism was controlled from Moscow.[94] This specific articulation 'proving' concerns about Vietminh entered American diplomacy in early 1948.[95] This was clearly a struggle over the representation of Vietminh, not proof.

This specific – and effective – representation of Vietminh as a communist stooge only emerged in late 1947 and depended on two mutually sustaining inscriptions of subjects and their contexts. Firstly, Orientalist inscription of the Vietnamese as a politically indolent race made it possible to argue that Vietminh could never challenge France without Soviet assistance. This assumption was so strong that, in practice, proving Soviet involvement needed little proof. Secondly, the communist plot angle was reinforced by a turnaround in French colonial policy, the "new Bảo Đại solution", which was presented as progressive and eventually leading to some independence that, if not accepted, proved that Vietminh wanted a communist takeover, not independence.[96]

Tracing the history of the Vietminh stooge representation takes us to a 1948 UK Foreign Office report widely circulated in Washington. A response to State Department questions about 'the potential dangers of the situation', it asserted that Vietminh had been taken over by a communist committee.[97] This twist forces our analysis to enter British diplomatic knowledge production, including the three analytical steps here explained, to understand how it constructed this representation.[98] Such assertions were atypical of the British Consulate in Saigon, the first time unsubstantiated information on Vietminh communism was unquestioningly forwarded – *all* previous British descriptions of Vietminh rejected French claims. It absorbed a common mistake in French intelligence that 'proved' Vietminh communism because the name of its policy committee had been mistaken with that of the Standing Committee of the defunct 1920s Communist Party of Indochina.[99] With this unsubstantiated report – supported by the high regard in which US diplomacy held the Foreign Office and British intelligence[100] – the French representation of Vietminh–Soviet links, which made negotiating with Vietminh impossible, entered UK and American diplomacy.

Previous documents reveal that this representation was absorbed from French ones on orders from London. Following the request from State to the Foreign Office for expert opinion, Foreign Secretary Ernest Bevin requested a report from Saigon listing – not substantiating, as was usual in UK diplomacy – 'growing Communist ascendancy in Indochina'. He considered it analogous to the insurgency he feared was brewing in Malaya and, after two drafts that did not include Vietminh–Soviet links, demanded a report in those terms, and his subordinates wrote it.[101] Previously, between 1945 and April 1948, British analysts had consistently discarded links between Vietminh and either the CCP or the Soviets as 'a K.M.T. fabrication, connived or sponsored by the French', finding alleged proof 'rather woolly and insufficiently specific' 'to provide proof of active collaboration'.[102] Proof, it turns out, never existed; it was conjured by a British politician by making diplomats write what he wanted to see.

In hindsight, it seems obvious that US policymakers were sensitive to communist bogeymen. But, as this analysis shows, this representation was the first time that this argument worked for the French – raising the question of what made it work in 1948 and not before. 1948 is marked by vastly increased French analytical awareness that communism is becoming the central US concern. By 1948, French diplomats regularly sent American counterparts reports featuring Vietminh 'Communist activity and propaganda', 'subversion', 'penetration', and 'cells' solidly linked to Moscow's 'long-range plan' to conquer Asia.[103] Contemporarily, France controlled information outflows, granting access only to journalists that affirmed 'Viet Minh is essentially Communist', with American media reports about 'reds' in Indochina greeted exultantly in Paris.[104] Crucially, such diplomatic reports were treated with less scepticism than prevalent until late 1947.[105] This was partly by design; the same French MFA folder on 'communications with the USA' contained copies of a 1948 report advising diplomats to 'sell' (in English in the original) France as America's ally by raising the threat of global communism.[106]

The claim that Soviet conquest targeted French colonies hit a nerve. State requested reports on communist activities in all French colonies as far as French Polynesia, Pontdicherry, and Martinique, many of which were speculative and low quality, including, for example, a ridiculously extensive report from New Caledonia on the socialist leanings of a gasoline seller.[107] In the Martinique report, notes on Aimé Césaire fail to mention that he was a renowned poet, demonstrating that reporting lacked local knowledge and focused on listing 'Communistic' suspects.[108] This frantic reporting on colonial communism marks the earliest appearance of the Domino theory or at least its assumptions. This logic cohabitated with a rival and related thesis at the Department, championed by the SEA Division, that communism was enabled and exacerbated by colonial grievances, which is why their reports consistently advised against any assistance to France if anticolonial claims were not met.[109] This is why US assistance was conditioned on France satisfying demands for a roadmap to independence.

This is why rejecting negotiation with Vietminh and American assistance needed alternative progressive solutions for anticolonial grievances.[110] French diplomats were aware and mooted the 'new' Bảo Đại solution in early 1948. In March 1948, ambassador Washington reported that State was extremely interested in the 'new' Bảo Đại solution,[111] and it dominated US diplomatic reporting in the two weeks after announcements suggesting 'farsweeping independence promises to Bảo Đại'.[112] However, the exclusion of Vietminh raised concerns that Bảo Đại would lack support and be a French puppet.[113] Lawrence argues that US acceptance of the solution was forced by 1948 Cold War events, particularly Malaya in June, placing the initial policy shift in June–September.[114] The above-quoted cable is from March, however, suggesting something else was afoot. A clue as to what made this solution acceptable to US policymakers *before* Malaya came in September 1947 from a French report about US meddling. It found a CIA front company assisting non-French anticommunist forces,[115] which they felt showed Americans have 'come round to a more exact conceptualisation' of Vietminh and were looking for noncommunist nationalists.[116]

Meeting some Vietnamese aspirations was therefore a key condition for US support, as explained to French diplomats in December 1947.[117] By late 1948, US policymakers appeared persuaded of the 'new' Bảo Đại Solution, revamped by newly appointed governor Léon Pignon, which promised autonomy, limited racial equality, and an indefinitely postponed roadmap to independence.[118] Written using American 'progressive colonialism' vocabulary, Léon Pignon has been credited with conceiving it on the basis of the conditions US diplomats expressed in December 1947.[119] Our method, however, led me to follow the topoi signposting its representations far further, revealing that it specifically employed Roosevelt's mid-1940s anticolonial discourse. As Political Officer of the Indochinese administration in 1945–47, Pignon had analysed America's 1946 grant of Philippine independence, US 'enlightened colonialism', and assistance for the suppression of the communist Huk rebellion, which he describes as 'analogous' to Vietminh.[120] These 1946 reports informed Pignon's later work as evidenced by their selfsame representations of 'enlightened colonialism'. These are the missing pieces in understanding the success of Pignon's 1948 'new' Bảo Đại solution.[121]

Backtracking to late 1947, French anticommunism and colonial progressivism appeared unconvincing due to its relentless colonialism, as diplomats worried French intransigence pushed more independentists into Vietminh.[122] Seeking proof of 'French intelligence reports' of a 'group designed reorganise Vietnam military' composed of 'eight Russians now on Indochina border', a Chinese-assisted OSS–CIA manhunt for 'Russian agents' ordered by Secretary of State Marshall only found seven Russian tramps 'leaving a trail of bad debt', which probably did not help French credibility.[123] A key American contact, conservative Catholic monarchist Ngô Đình Diệm, emphasised Vietminh would triumph, as late 1947 French offers (the previous Bảo Đại solution) fell 'far short of real independence' with many 'turning to Communism' in despair.[124] US Consul Saigon agreed they 'show little inclination go much beyond pre-war status',[125] while SEA found it fell short of necessary concessions and contravened previous Franco-Vietnamese agreements.[126]

Before the late 1947 State Department compromise position that anti-communism must be accompanied by progressive colonialism, we find its source in fierce internal debates concerning Vietminh. Paris ambassador Jefferson Caffery and the Western Europe division press the risk of communist takeover, pointing to a speech by 'Soviet Leader Andrei Junnov' listing Vietminh in the 'anti-imperialist camp'.[127] The Southeast Asia divisions and diplomats posted there were sceptical, however. Sceptical of French accusations of communism, Saigon consul Reed advises 'although I believe that perhaps undue emphasis has been given to the matter for propaganda purposes, Indochina is a fertile ground for the spread of Communism'.[128] This report is widely circulated around the Department with the highlight (and frequently just the highlight was circulated) that 'Indochina is fertile ground' and that 'weight must be given to the Communism background of President Ho'.[129] Reed's phrase 'fertile ground' reoccurs frequently, though never again associated to the nationalist grievances that 'fertilise' the ground. This is a case of nuance being lost in knowledge-production processes dominated by anticommunist policy concern.

Backtracking to mid 1947, when the stooge and French progressive representations were still suspicious, we find the last direct United States–Vietminh communications, in which Vietminh had spent the previous year pleading 'for the assistance of the United States'.[130] US embassy Bangkok received a request for US assistance from Dr Phạm Ngọc Thạch, 'who describes himself as Under Secretary of State at the Vietnam Government', requesting US humanitarian and economic assistance and enquiring whether the United States would allow the case of Vietnam to go to the UN or itself mediate. The letter presents the 1945 'Revolution' as the 'expression of the immense majority of the people', a principle espoused by the United States, Thạch notes. Vietnam was fighting against French 'imperialism' against a 'policy of force' carried out using US lend-lease material and 'Nazi troops'.[131] Vietminh's communication in this period shows no shifts in representation of the conflict as an anticolonial struggle.

August 1947–September 1946: colonial greed and commie risks

Backtracking to trace the representation that Vietminh cannot be spoken to, in June 1947 we find the first signs of the Soviet stooge representation we saw in 1948. Bidault tells the US ambassador that French intelligence decoded

Vietminh messages showing 'definite pro-Soviet orientation'.[132] Back in March, Haut-commissaire d'Argenlieu advised COMINDO that Vietminh 'cannot be considered a partner for peace talks' because 'the Indochinese conflict is' 'another battlefield in the struggle between Western democracies and international Marxism'. D'Argenlieu explained this position to an Associated Press journalist before submitting it to Paris – for which he is reprimanded – but in so doing forced COMINDO into an accept-or-reverse predicament.[133] His impatience was due to lack of reply to a Memorandum demanding 'the official announcement that [the French Government] will not deal with the Hồ Chí Minh government'.[134] D'Argenlieu insisted 'that Hồ Chi Minh is in direct contact with Moscow and Mao, is receiving advice and instructions from the Soviets'.[135] D'Argenlieu's 1947 turn to global anti-communism may have been encouraged by analysis predicting that American reactions should be expected if 'Muscovite Hanoi leaders kindle initial links with the USSR'.[136] This reveals that the strategy of diplomatically isolating Vietminh by making it internationally unacceptable was d'Argenlieu's own. Successful entry of these representations of Vietminh into US diplomatic text was prevented, however, by lack of change in the representation of French colonialism.

In mid 1947, we find a period of transition. Some French diplomats and policymakers understand that defending colonialism is hampering relations with the United States. D'Argenlieu was removed in March, and a liberal, Émile Bollaert, was appointed Haut-commissaire and began to try to develop a Bảo Đại solution (1947 version), declaring that France had no intention to resolve Indochina by 'reconquest'.[137] French diplomats insisted 'that we are more than anxious to find a peaceable liberal solution', and that 'the day of colonial empires in the Nineteenth Century sense of the word is a thing of the past'.[138] A circular for worldwide promulgation explained that Bollaert's solution was part of transforming the empire into the French Union: a 'good-will free association of nations' that would 'protect ethnic minorities against Annamite attempts'.[139] Fascinatingly, the origin of this linguistic and representational shift is found in an extensive cable from Embassy Washington advising that, to prevent unfavourable US intervention, it is necessary to emphasise 'caretaking', 'eventual emancipation', 'development', and 'paternal protection' of natives.[140]

As the Bollaert proposal was being mooted, however, February–April 1947 witnessed a concerted media and diplomatic effort to combat 'foul factoids' about French colonialism, funding American publications to 'correct misinformation' created by 'propaganda of an anticolonial tendency'.[141] COMINDO issued data that stupidly revealed itself to be false by concealing practices well known to US diplomats like collective punishment, torture, forced labour, and the use of thousands of Wehrmacht veterans in the

Foreign Legion.[142] It was not a good time to defend colonialism. Hostility to French colonialism was prevalent in US media. For a long time, until late 1947 at least, Vietminh is principally referred to as 'rebels' in the press.[143] There was, however, in both the media and diplomacy, 'doubt as to whether they are capable of running an independent state': 'without Occidental check or control the result would be chaos – and in that chaos either the Soviets or the Chinese would find their opportunity'.[144]

Before June 1947, anti-Vietminh name-calling mixes fascist and communist accusations. When the last report 'demonstrating' Vietminh–Japanese collaboration appears in early 1947, the prevalent representation of Vietminh in French diplomacy was as Axis collaborators with occasional communist references.[145] Fascist-communist inconsistency is purportedly explained by Vietminh's cynical search for military expertise.[146] In an excellent example of text designed to propose a specific representation of actors and their contexts, a report pre-empting a potential Vietminh Human Rights submission to the UN claims that Vietminh is 'a totalitarian regime that reigns by terror', 'distribute[s] death' with 'truly Gestapo-like police', led by 'an old Soviet agent' who had collaborated with the Japanese. Vietminh are 'Hitlerian', 'racist', 'annexationists', Axis 'creature[s]' who rely on 'fanaticising individuals' to perpetrate 'bloodbaths'. Reports argue French actions were marked by 'the strictest pulchritude' as France does not employ ex-Nazis and 'paternally' assists Indochina.[147] Copies of the report in COMINDO archives suggest that it was also aimed at the French government,[148] and its vocabulary and representations are found in an earlier personal letter from d'Argenlieu to Bidault.[149]

The 1947 French name-calling campaign was a failure. American diplomats ignored and were sceptical of French claims about both Vietminh communism and French colonial progressivism. It is helpful to examine this scepticism, as it informed the late 1947 US demands for French concessions. Consul Hanoi reports that 'it remains curious that French discovered no Communist menace in Ho Chi Minh Govt until after September 1946, when it became apparent VN Govt would not bow to French'. Consul Saigon reported 'note-worthy that Communism is nowhere mentioned' in internal French reports, while the 'High Commissioner plays up Communism to cover deficiencies French policy' while Hồ remains 'real representative of people'.[150] Up the chain of reporting, Secretary Marshall agreed and criticised Bollaert's proposals for ignoring Vietminh's widespread support.[151] Following up on French allegations, he enquired 'whether influence Communists in present coalition GOVT' 'would be sufficient put Vietnam in Soviet Camp', whether Hồ had lost Soviet favour, and whether communist advisors assisted Vietminh victories.[152] Replies highlighted the abandonment of Vietminh by the French Communist Party, the 'awkward' 'Soviet

Line on Indochina', and the lack of Soviet aid.[153] In response to French allegations that communism affected the entire 'French empire, where the Communists are busily encouraging the Nationalists',[154] Secretary Marshall speculated whether 'Kremlin prepared sacrifice temporary gains with 40 million French to long range colonial strategy with 600 million dependent people', concluding that France needed to 'be most generous' to find an 'early solution'.[155]

Backtracking to late 1946, American diplomats worry French colonialism fuels communism. They find there was real 'unabated anti-French feeling',[156] estimating that 'given their referendum [Cochinchina] would vote for union with Vietnam'.[157] Their analysis suggests Vietminh's internal divisions substantiate that it is a league composed of various political parties,[158] even including conservative Vietnamese 'drifting toward break with French',[159] and that 'attempts to communize their country are secondary and would await successful operation of a nationalist state'.[160] We also find caustically suspicious analysis of French claims: 'that French should only now become concerned with [communist] development is peculiar'.[161] Crucially, it was thought that French policies 'might open the door for development of strong Communist influence in SEA'.[162] Without Vietminh, Bollaert's Bảo Đại solution would be 'a puppet government'.[163] This is why during this period, State still believes that talks with Vietminh are feasible, and the Secretary and other diplomats regularly offered US mediation, which was rejected.

This scepticism was fuelled by reports of ruthless reconquest. Suspicion is such that consul Hanoi requests intelligence on Sainteny's colonial financial interests and attempts to confirm Vietminh allegations of French chemical weapons use.[164] Back in Washington, Secretary Byrnes is concerned 'puppet GOVT may be set up',[165] and requests reports as to why Vietminh did not meet French Colonies minister Moutet when he visited Indochina. Answers were discouraging: 'VietNamese state messenger bearing letter of invitation for Moutet disappeared'. Vietnamese officials handed the US consul a copy – which offered negotiation terms – as proof.[166] French war conduct was also unimpressive. From Hanoi (being shelled by the French), the consul reports that 'French have made pillaging military policy', with 'burning some villages vicinity' and towns 'MASHED by artillery fire' 'to bring the Vietnamese to accept the French will'.[167] Reporting on Vietminh military action is less critical and highlights that Vietminh protected 'foreigners – one American caught in battle area was even given turkey for Christmas'.[168]

Vietminh worked hard to participate in this conflict over description. Hồ continuously reiterates his availability for peace talks to French officials and the US consul in Hanoi,[169] and grievances are communicated to French ministers but, as they never reply, Vietminh forwards copies to US diplomats.[170] In April 1947, the long-travelling Thạch submits to US embassy Bangkok a folder containing over 70 DRV and French documents to present their view of the conflict. Emphasising that not all French people, only 'imperialists', want war with Vietnam, it presents a struggle of 'imperialism' against 'emancipation'. Vietnam is inscribed within the dependent peoples of the Atlantic Charter signed by the 'missed former President Franklin D. Roosevelt'. Vietminh legitimacy is twice inscribed in universal terms: within an emancipation/imperialist binary and the Axis/Allies binary in which Vietminh 'distinguished itself' fighting the Japanese – unlike the French who 'surrendered the colony without a shot'.[171] Vietminh asks the United States to take the case to the UN or mediate, emphasising that Vietnam desires peace with France and independence with reunification within the French Union.[172] An English-language booklet handed to Consul Hanoi describes a history of Vietnamese thirst for independence from Antiquity to the 1929 rebellion, culminating in the war against the Japanese and the '1945 Revolution'.[173]

Vietminh diplomacy made efforts to disprove allegations of Soviet control. Rather than disprove the communism of leading figures like Hồ, Giáp, or Đồng, the approach posited Vietminh communism as either inexistent or not Soviet. In interviews with US papers, Hồ describes Vietminh as a 'League' of nationalists, Marxists, democrats, and socialists, 'not to mention Catholics and Buddhists'. As to socialist policy, 'France and England have pushed nationalisations further than we have'.[174] Thạch explains to Embassy Bangkok that communism in Vietnam is dedicated to national liberation and embraces capitalism,[175] and expresses frustration that French communists oppose Vietminh.[176] In Paris, Hồ tells the US ambassador that 'he had at one time studied Marxism but that he is not a Moscow fellow-traveller'.[177] In a meeting with SEA Office chief Moffat, Hồ 'claims that the Communist party as such dissolved itself several months ago' and that the Vietnamese constitution guarantees human rights and 'the right to personal property'.[178] In September 1946, Consul Hanoi was handed the 'platform of the Viet-Minh League', which 'promises universal suffrage and democratic liberties' and minority rights.[179] Occasionally, some efforts were less coherent and appeared disingenuous. For example, the above-mentioned booklet about the 1945 Revolution treats Nguyễn Ái Quốc and Hồ Chí Minh (aliases, his real adult name was Nguyễn Tất Thành) as separate people to dissociate Vietminh from communism.

August 1946–April 1945: colonial reconquest or libération

In the immediate postwar, French diplomacy was desperate to prove its grandeur, exasperated by exclusion from the 'Big Three' at Dumbarton Oaks and Yalta and other humiliations, 'slights', and 'betrayals' the US ambassador attributes to 'post-liberation neurosis'.[180] De Gaulle regularly threatens US diplomats that ignoring his demands (which he saw as the needs of France itself) would push France to communism.[181] 'If the public here comes to realize that you are against us in Indochina there will be terrific disappointment and nobody knows to what it will lead. We do not want to become communist; we do not want to fall into the Russian orbit, but I hope that you do not push us into it.'[182] This approach might have been inspired by a report on growing American concerns about communists becoming the second biggest party in the French Parliament in 1946.[183] Indochina was no less than a question of racial pride; as de Gaulle declared to the National Assembly, French greatness, *grandeur*, is proven by its stewardship of inferior races in Asia.[184]

Communism is very inconsistently articulated in this earlier period.[185] Internally, Sainteny's reports appear more concerned about Vietminh's broad-spectrum support than its communism.[186] A detailed 'political physiology' of Vietminh describes it as an alliance of parties on a common independence and reunification platform, with communism a historical factor for some members.[187] Sûreté Genérale Indochinoise (political colonial police) director Humbert thinks Vietminh is a 'hidden Communist party' 'under a nationalist label'.[188] However, these disparate attributions of communism did not make it far in French diplomatic knowledge production 1945–46, revealing that it was considered irrelevant or used as an insult. For example, US diplomats observed that Gaullists had a tendency to accuse opponents – even some Americans – of 'collaborationisme' or 'Communisme'.[189]

French diplomacy portrayed Vietminh as an Axis puppet and defended colonialism, particularly after a report suggested that 'misunderstanding' about French colonialism limited Franco-American relations.[190] Representations of the rebellion were constructed around the Axis/Allies binary. Vietminh was founded under 'Japanese initiative and protection',[191] and 'are but puppets in the hands of the Germans and the Japanese', a 'xenophobic' leftover of Japanese occupation helped by China who 'follows old habit' – presumably Chinese colonisation of Vietnam fourteen centuries earlier.[192] Evidence was fabricated in July–December 1946 to marshal Vietminh atrocities into a defence of French colonialism: without French control, racist 'Annamese' would subjugate the rest of Indochina.[193] Denial of Vietnam's existence was incredibly impactful, developing from d'Argenlieu's office to the MFA and onto diplomacy with other countries.[194] Examined in the third detailed textual study in this chapter, d'Argenlieu misled superiors to escape negotiations at Fontainebleau in 1946 and convened the Dalat II conference, which proclaimed the 'Cochinchinese Republic', scuppering Franco-Vietnamese talks.[195] The Annamite imperialism representation implied that Indochina needs France to survive Vietnamese imperialism.

France presented its goals as the '*libération*' of France from Axis occupation. *Libération* inscribed Indochina as an unliberated part of France while Nationalist groups are 'interference of the Japanese'.[196] In March 1945, Free France, 'remembering the loyal and proud attitude of the Indochinese', promulgated its plan for the future of Indochina.[197] It was to become a federation of the five Indochinese 'countries' and part of the 'French Union'. Diplomats presented it as based on 'liberty of thought, faith, press, association and organisation'.[198] The diplomatic text reveals the origin of this bout of progressivism: a 'diplomatic strategy' 'to manage the positive disposition of the American Government through assurances on French intentions'.[199]

Delving back into French diplomatic knowledge production, discovery of wartime OSS-Vietminh collaboration, and the October 1945 rejection of French requests to assist in the reconquest caused anxiety.[200] Signs of 'Annamite-American contact' were investigated and rumours circulated that American encouragements to negotiate were aimed at wresting Indochina from France.[201] Reporting from the ground was negligible until Sainteny arrived in June to make contacts and report on anti and pro-French feeling.[202] His first report to Paris describes a 'nefarious' alliance between Vietnamese nationalists and 'francophobe' OSS officers, noting that '[i]deally we could obtain that that [Vietminh] be considered by the Allies as a "puppet" force and disarmed' – most likely the beginning of the Japanese puppet argument.[203] An earlier report from Kunming reveals unawareness of Vietminh, but does introduce a familiar acquaintance: Ngô Đình Diệm, who leads Japanese-sponsored nationalist party Dai Viet – the real puppet.[204]

Anticolonial scepticism is constant in US diplomacy 1946–45, and consistently labels Vietminh 'nationalists'.[205] No French representation entered American diplomatic knowledge production without being bracketed by hostility and qualifications. Reports assess that 'the French are hated' as they are 'intolerably opposed giving more than modicum to natives', corroborated by French retaliations including 'wholesale arrests and burning houses'.[206] Earlier reports from OSS officers returning from Indochina suggest Vietminh are well-supported nationalists who 'feel strongly pro-American' and 'should not be labelled full-fledged doctrinaire communist'.[207] The same reports excoriates French administration for purposefully causing the 1945 famine by refusing to release rice reserves.[208] The text demonstrates that the shift away from FDR's hostility towards French rule was reticent, uncomfortable and limited.[209] Though by September 1945 the United States had dropped Trusteeship and was 'not opposed to the reestablishment of French authority in Indo-China', they refused to assist France.[210]

Tracing US knowledge production in this period additionally reveals that newly sworn-in Truman, Secretary Grew, and Assistant Secretary Acheson coordinated US foreign policy together in daily meetings that struggled to replace FDR's personal and secretive management of military and foreign policy. During this period the inexperienced Truman was extremely reliant on Grew and Acheson, requesting daily briefs on Indochinese issues left unresolved by FDR: military (ship French troops to the Far East?), political (continue with FDR's Trusteeship?), and diplomatic (how to prevent further US–French hostility).[211] In the first months of Truman's presidency, State Department knowledge was unusually important in informing policymaking.

Another representation that crossed over to US diplomatic text in this period but which did not become manifest for decades was Cochinchina's national distinctiveness. Although derided by Saigon and Hanoi consuls and not analysed in detail, the national distinctiveness of South Vietnam is recognisable as the key representation in US diplomacy during the American Vietnam War. It is no coincidence South Vietnam existed in the space France disputed from DRV, Cochinchina and Annam South of the sixteenth parallel, and that its first leader was Ngô Đình Diệm, the last prime minister of the 'new' Bảo Đại Solution.[212]

Vietnamese diplomacy in this period works to justify Độc Lập, independence, proclaimed on 2 September 1945. They attempted to engage with French authorities, describing their goals as 'the principles of [17]89 and Free France' and to 'acquire independence'.[213] A memorandum to President Bidault in July 1946 articulates the case for Vietnamese reunification including historical, linguistic, racial, and cultural aspects; rice-farming ties; and French law, which had recognised the extent of the Empire of Vietnam when annexing it in the 1850s.[214] Vietminh also attempted to correspond with French politicians, the President, and foreign and colonial ministers, consistently pleading for peaceful resolution and to grant the Vietnamese the rights the French had given themselves in the French revolution.[215] Hồ wrote an open letter 'to the French National Assembly and Government' deploring violations of agreements but understanding that only 'a number of Frenchmen in Indochina have and continue to act against these accords' and furthermore, since they 'have a monopoly of information, they report falsely' back to France, misleading public and political opinion so as 'to mutilate Vietnam'.[216] He was correct, as we saw above, but this and all other communications went unanswered.

From 1944, Vietminh also engaged with every foreign power it could. It consistently updated US and British diplomats in Kunming, Hanoi, and Bangkok of all progress in Franco-Vietnamese negotiations, though it appears Soviet diplomats refused contact altogether.[217] As Hồ headed to Fontainebleau, Hanoi consul reported that 'Ho Chi Minh probably will call at AMEMBASSY shortly. He has constantly given me impression he would pay great attention to any suggestions made by Dept.'[218] Hồ's October

1945 letter to the State Secretary calling for 'immediate interference' (second detailed textual study in this chapter) represents Vietminh as anti-Japanese and anticolonial, appealing to the Atlantic Charter's provisions for self-determination before arguing that French colonialism is brutal and repressive and betrayed the Allies in WWII. Notably, it legitimises Vietminh representation of Vietnam arguing that it is a multi-party coalition.[219] Hồ appealed to Truman's '12 points' of November 1945 concerning the emancipation and self-determination of dependent peoples, flatteringly implying a comparison with French colonialism and suggesting a way forward in writing 'Vietnam has always followed the enlightened policy of the USA towards the Philippines'.[220]

Vietminh diplomacy worked hard to establish itself as legitimate representative of Vietnam, which is why approaches to China, the United States, Britain, and France in the following two years included copy of former emperor Bảo Đại's abdication in favour of the DRV. Addressing early concerns about communism, Hồ consistently explained that though of communist background, 'he was only as much a Communist as Sun Yat-sen was when he founded the Chinese Republic', as he told a British military intelligence agent.[221] Likewise, he told State Department SEA chief Moffat that independence is Vietminh's priority.[222] While national determination was the main cover for communism, a secondary aspect of this representation highlighted that Vietminh was a League ('Minh') consisting of various parties. A year later, this became Vietminh's primary anticommunist argument.

In an instance of visual reporting, Sainteny took the photo in Figure 4.4 from the balcony of the French colonial offices in Hanoi where Vietminh had billeted him. It shows Hanoi crowds celebrating the declaration of independence on 2 September 1945 and accompanied reports on the unexpectedly large support enjoyed by Vietminh.[223]

Backtracking to the last few weeks of WWII, we find the first the first written international diplomatic move by Vietminh: the July 1945 'Letter to the San Francisco Conference from the Indochinese "Annamese" people', analysed in the first detailed textual study in this chapter, made and distributed by volunteer 'cultural associations' loosely associated to the conservative parties within Vietminh, which articulates an appeal to the values of the French revolution, the US constitution, Dumbarton Oaks, and San Francisco.[224] Crucially, it marks the first appearance of a universal representation of Vietnam and Vietminh's cause that draws on Allied principles, which would remain a constant in Vietminh diplomacy until the late 1950s.

Earlier in 1945, before the revolution, Vietminh draws on anticolonial representations that reference older anticolonial movements such as the Chinese KMT and the Indian National Congress. To OSS Director Donovan, they called themselves 'the Annamite Kuomintang', a 'Free

Figure 4.4 2 September 1945 declaration of Vietnamese independence in Hanoi, photographed by Jean Sainteny. Archive Sainteny.

Annamite organisation, which claims to represent a large revolutionary nationalist movement' who asked him to explain that they do not want the French back and request US assistance or 'a US protectorate'.[225] Like KMT, Vietminh also joined the Allies in WWII, and Hồ even accepted to be an OSS agent and received the codename 'Lucius'.[226] This representation of the conflict explicitly inscribed itself in the tradition of the American, Chinese, and Indian revolutions.

A final question remains: why did US policymakers drop FDR's Trusteeship policy? This method contributes two novel insights to long-running debates as to how this occurred, one usually dominated by the argument that US policymakers were terrified of communism emerging in France and Asia. Firstly, Indochina was the subject of conflict at State between the FE, SEA, and European Offices. SEA was anticolonial, while Europe advocated improving relations with France at any cost.[227] FE and SEA argued that offense caused to France by 'intervention in a problem which they consider strictly French' is 'far less dangerous to the position of France and of all Western powers' than 'a further explosion of Annamese nationalism and French resort to military force'.[228] This option is, however, delayed under advice from the European Office, and an amendment to Trusteeship that applied it only to Axis colonies marked the defeat of SEA.[229]

Secondly, this analysis, by following the links made by the texts themselves, reveals something unexpected: the representation that persuaded Truman's team was not communism in France or Indochina; it was fear that de Gaulle's demands in Europe would provoke another European war or, if refused, lose America French support against the USSR. These demands were very significant, involving annexation of Saarland and Rhineland plus colossal reparations from Germany, Ventimiglia, Breda, parts of Piemonte, and Aosta from Italy.[230] This finding substantiates Walter LaFeber and George Herring in arguing that communist emergency in Europe (rather than in Indochina) was key to the 1945 shift, but adds the key nuance of the danger posed by de Gaulle's extreme demands in Europe, not hitherto considered.[231] In other words, what killed Trusteeship was urgency to appease de Gaulle in May 1945 to prevent another European war and preserve French support against the USSR without giving in to his European demands.

Before FDR's death, US reporting focused on French brutality and Vietnamese subalternity. French demands were being accommodated less obligingly.[232] Roosevelt was unimpressed by French demands in Europe but was willing to understand de Gaulle's lost 'grandeur', ceding on French being a co-official language at San Francisco and the UN, France being a convening power, and France having a permanent seat at the Security Council. Unlike later periods, reporting and analysis focuses on the economic, social, and political effects of colonialism. The largest report, 120 pages, analyses French management, concluding that 'French Indochina in its political, economic, and social development was the least progressive dependency in Southeast Asia'. This text informed Roosevelt's famous memo to Secretary Hull that France ruled Indochina 'for nearly one hundred years, and the people are worse off', concluding '[t]he people of Indochina are entitled to something better'.[233] A memo identifies 'an important and increasingly strong movement for complete independence', predicting that '[u]nless policies ['of democratic self-government'] are followed in Southeast Asia, this government fears that there will be substantial and increasing social and political unrest and possibly armed conflict', recommending supporting negotiated self-rule with eventual independence.[234]

Representation of Vietnam during FDR's tenure was, however, dominated by assumptions of colonial unpreparedness for independence that, as we have seen, shaped the entire history of representations of Vietnamese subjects 1948–45. Finding this Orientalist frame deeply embedded in the first US analyses of Vietminh is important.[235] Rooseveltian goodwill was inseparable from the assumption that undeveloped peoples needed supervision for an independence that was always prefaced by 'future'.[236] This frame worked to support Vietnamese emancipation in 1946–45, but in 1947–48 facilitated the emergence of the 'stooges' thesis.

It is now possible to map the history of representations of subjects and their contexts that we have traced within the diplomacy of the three main actors involved. Figure 4.5 summarises how the conflict, its actors, and its contexts were represented 1945–48. The horizontal rows represent each actor's knowledge production, staggered to highlight that this occurred across multiple texts. The representations traced across texts are marked by textured lines and symbols, one for each representation. Drawn larger in the left is the 1948 Policy Statement linking assistance to France to Vietminh being Soviet stooges and to the 'new' Bảo Đại solution. Lines cross between cascades, showing when these representations entered US diplomatic knowledge in 1948, and how they crossed over from British diplomacy (marked 2), which in turn was imported from French diplomatic reports (1). It shows the moment (3) when the 'new' Bảo Đại solution entered US diplomacy as 'progressive' and its origins in Pignon's 1946 reports (4). The representations that made the crossovers into US diplomacy possible, belief in Oriental backwardness and American anticolonialism, are included, as is the later discarded representation of Vietminh as a non-Soviet socialist ('Asian Tito', as the Pentagon Papers called Hồ), French efforts to frame the reconquest of Indochina as WWII *libération*, and Vietminh attempts to represent their struggle as anticolonial.

Observations

Tracing in detail how representations develop allows analysis to retrieve struggles over descriptions, the role of individuals, and how their influence was exercised *through* textual representations. It accounts for the dynamics governing diplomatic persuasion, such as how Eurocentric racism was vital to 'proving' Vietminh could not possibly challenge France without Soviet direction. Detailed examination of individual texts revealed how texts constitute representations of subjects and their temporal, spatial, and normative contexts, and how they drew on discourses such as Oriental unpreparedness or monolithic communism. These studies identified topoi textual markers signposting representations and their subjectivity, allowing the third step of the method to trace their development in communication between the actors involved and, crucially, determining which representations crossed from the diplomacy of one actor to another's. This section concludes application of this book's method to the case of the diplomacy of the First Vietnam War by summarising its findings in terms of contributions to the literature on that conflict, offering a brief historical account of the evolution of diplomacy's production of knowledge about it, before discussing the factors that conditioned this evolution.

The diplomacy of the First Vietnam War 129

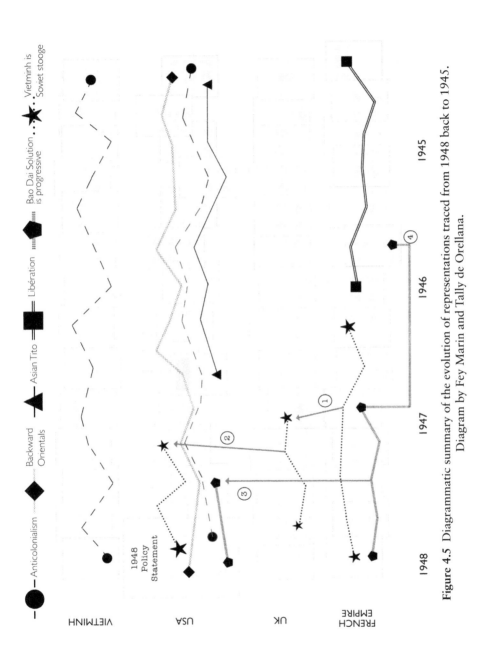

Figure 4.5 Diagrammatic summary of the evolution of representations traced from 1948 back to 1945. Diagram by Fey Marin and Tally de Orellana.

This method identifies hitherto unconsidered diplomatic events, ideas, and individuals. Analysis of the representations that in 1948 led US policymakers to believe Indochina was a communist problem revealed the role of racialised Orientalism, assumptions about monolithic communism, a long-forgotten 1946 French study of American attitudes to colonialism, and how relations among them determined their communication dynamics. This approach lays bare the journeys of specific representations, such as Pignon's 1946 critique of American colonialism inspiring articulation of his 1948 'new' Bảo Đại solution. It substantiates Bradley's thesis that identities were decisive to American choices and Young's argument that the Vietnam Wars were ultimately a delayed decolonisation process.[237] Speaking to the Paris-Saigon-Hanoi school,[238] the method reveals why France's 1948 concessions only became credible when Pignon became governor: French colonialism had hitherto appeared so relentless that only a rewrite of the Bảo Đại solution in American terms could make it look progressive. This approach adds to Lawrence's argument about the decisive diplomatic role of colonial officers, showing how d'Argenlieu and Pignon determined the history of this conflict by promoting representations that shaped the conflict 1948–54 (Vietminh stooge, French progressiveness) and some even 1954–75 (d'Argenlieu's 'Cochinchina is not Vietnam').[239] Turning to the 'missed opportunity' school of Vietnam studies, this method reveals the key role played by de Gaulle's exorbitant demands in Europe, and how Indochina paid the price of postwar Franco-German amity.

Diplomatic knowledge does not shape policy on its own. American views of Vietminh were not solely entirely in diplomatic reporting cunningly influenced by France. Far from it, diplomatic writing evidently draws on the world it inhabits, its dominant views, beliefs, and representations. In this period Washington was clearly shifting its understanding of the world and its threats towards a bipolar structure, told diplomats to focus to reporting communism, and came to view Vietnam as a Cold War conflict. This is partly, of course, because that is what Washington wanted to read, but also because the representation itself became possible. Representations and their ideational contexts are mutually constitutive: searching for communism under every bed made it more likely to see it everywhere, but something had to appear as credibly red. Representation of Vietminh as stooges, for example, was not believable until 1948, suggesting that viable representations, and their promotion, remain subject to conditions that determine whether representations in one country's diplomatic communications convince another's diplomats enough to take them up in their own knowledge production. This means we can now answer a question asked since the 1960s: what made French representations of Vietminh communism persuasive in 1948 and not before?

A novel empirical account of how France persuaded the United States to become involved in Vietnam is now possible. Lawrence argued the turning point was the Malaya Emergency in June 1948, but our analysis finds that the Emergency amplified a change in representation of the conflict that had *already* begun a year before in late 1947.[240] This change was constituted by more stable representations of both the French Self and the Vietnamese communist Other. Until late 1947, representations of French progressivism and Vietminh communism essentially cancelled each other out until French diplomacy was able to stabilise credibility of its 'new' Bảo Đại solution. Representation of French willingness to grant independence obscured the contradiction between stated French willingness to negotiate and refusal to do so with Vietminh. Differentiation was therefore *moved* to differentiating France from communist unreasonableness, rather than over willingness to negotiate. It took two years, because that representation of France, convoluted as it was, took that long to build and stabilise against other representations and discursive conditions.

The most influential representation was racialised Orientalism. Despite protestations of ancient civilisation, Vietminh could not escape being represented as decadent, politically indolent, and incapable of political agency in French, British, and US diplomacy. In US policy, this colonial discourse initially supported Vietnamese emancipation 'under tutelage'. Without changing, it then came to support representation as Soviet stooges too, due to its inscription of postcolonial subjects as vulnerable to influence by powerful advanced states. This made it possible for French diplomats to claim that without Soviet instigation and assistance, Vietminh would never have been able to challenge France. Vietminh's representation as a Soviet stooge (entailing impossibility to negotiate) took nearly two years to cross from French to US text. When it did, it kept its rhetorical speculative alignment of ideological representations of Vietminh and USSR as its only proof. This is remarkable considering that between 1946 and 1947, American diplomats and intelligence thoroughly investigated its veracity, finding no proof. The proof that crossed over was a delicate conceptual balance sustained *only* in language, as opposed to missiles on ships' decks during the 1962 Cuban crisis or evidence of relations between the French Communist Party and the USSR. Racist assumptions about Oriental lack of agency and about global communism as monolithic were the only proof that Vietminh was a Soviet stooge.

Brutal French colonialism was another key representation. Its representation in 1945–46, particularly when combined with Vietminh efforts to help America during WWII, successfully entered US knowledge production, supported by contemporary American media hostility to European imperialism. Vietminh's references to how America peacefully granted independence to Philippines were a helpful factor, as diplomats like SEA Chief Moffat found such a course reasonable and natural to promote it as the most logical and fair, as was Vietminh's inscription of Vietnamese subjects, country, and demands into the normative frames of the postwar charters. But, as seen in our history of this diplomacy, Vietminh had limited influence on US reporting, and it was France's own imperialistic recalcitrance and its explicit defence that entered most visibly into US diplomatic knowledge.

The first condition for representational viability that emerges from this case study is discursive stability. Representation of Vietminh as stooge had been viable for a year, as shown by US officials seeking proof of this for over two years. The problem was that French imperialism destabilised it. Until late 1947, French diplomacy defended its 'œuvre coloniale' in opposition to Vietminh communism. This made it appear that French representations of communism were an instrument to secure US help in reconquering the colony, draining their believability by association to a recalcitrant imperialism keen on preserving Indochina at any cost. When US diplomats considered them side-by-side as in 1947–45, they highlighted Vietminh's well-supported anticolonialism rather than its communism. For differentiation to highlight Vietminh's communism rather than anticolonialism, France had to show willingness to be progressive and grant more, stabilising the freedom-vs.-communism binary. French representation of Vietminh communism crossed into US text in March–September 1948 with the support of British diplomacy, carrying with it exactly the same articulation and flawed 'proof'. Had US diplomatic knowledge retained its suspicion of French assertions and continued to push for substantiation, the US view of Indochina could have been like that of the 1954–62 Algerian War. Occurring after the Korean War, when East–West relations were worse than in 1948, the Algerian Front de Libération Nationale (FLN) was also an independentist coalition including communists, socialists, Arab socialists, and Arab nationalists – not to mention that, unlike Hồ, FLN leader Ben Bella regularly visited Moscow.[241] It was clear to US diplomats that Algeria was an imperial war, not a Cold War struggle, and they treated it with as much hostility as the Anglo-French invasion of Suez.[242]

The second factor conditioning knowledge production is its governance. Reporting is incremental, depending on and adding to previous cables, analyses, and recommendations. Its detail falls out easily, as we saw with representation of Vietminh as a league of various parties, or the often-repeated phrase 'fertile ground', which quickly lost references to the very issues that fertilised it. This suggests that most policymakers never saw powerful representations like 'fertile ground' with the information that qualified it – in this case fertility being provided by French colonial brutality, rather than proficient Soviet gardening. Likewise, Vietminh attempts to negotiate

The diplomacy of the First Vietnam War 133

with France are received at State but never mentioned again, while reporting on policy concerns like communism gains monumental importance. A backward history of diplomacy is difficult but truly pays off in this case. Apparently ridiculous cables like those examining communism in New Caledonia, or the hunt for seven Russian tramps in China, become relevant when they lead us to the 1946 order to report on communism and communist sympathisers and to estimate communist 'penetration' throughout the French empire. By destabilising reporting on communism with their irrelevance, such documents demonstrate how reporting requests can radically curtail and focus knowledge production.

The examples of the Russian tramps or of Césaire, the anticolonial poet who in US diplomacy was defined only by his communist sympathies, demonstrate that centrally mandated focus can entirely reconstitute subjects. In practice, this happens by determining, curtailing, and ordering the salience of future diplomatic knowledge production around dominant policy concerns. The interaction between dominant policy concerns and diplomatic knowledge is addressed in Chapter 6, where it is argued that while in practice this effect is explained by instructions from the Ministry, its ideational power can be explained by conceptualising policy concerns as epistemes that hierarchically order entire representations, dropping many from the text and elevating others like the Russian tramps or the lefty gasoline dealer in New Caledonia. This is how diplomacy forgot what fertilised the ground for communism and saw what it wanted to see.

Notes

1. Graham Greene, *The Quiet American* (London: Heineman, 1955), 32. Greene's own appreciation of US support for a 'Third Force' in Vietnam might well have been less fictional than he claimed. See Kevin Ruane, 'The Hidden History of Graham Greene's Vietnam War: Fact, Fiction and *The Quiet American*', *History* 97 (327), 2012, 431–52. In honour, I sometimes refer to the 'Bảo Đại solution' as 'Third Force'.
2. Bonnet (French ambassador to the USA) triumphantly reporting to the Ministère Affaires Étrangeres (MAE), 17 March 1948; and Bonnet to MAE, 13 July 1948, about the new US policy towards Vietnam, both in film P4715, 91QO.125, MAE (my italics).
3. Gravel, ed., *The Pentagon Papers: The Defense Department History of United States Decisionmaking on Vietnam. Vol. 1* (Boston, MA: Beacon Press, 1971), 72.
4. M. A. Lawrence, *Assuming the Burden: Europe and the American Commitment to War in Vietnam* (Berkeley, CA: University of California Press, 2005), 220.
5. Including the *New York Times*, *The Washington Post*, *Độc Lập*, *Le Monde*, and *Le Figaro* as well as the particularly colonialist and Gaullist *L'Aube*. For

Độc Lập, analysis is guided by Marr's invaluable and incredibly detailed study in David Marr, *Vietnam: State, War, and Revolution* (Berkeley, CA: University of California Press, 2013).

6 Lawrence, *Assuming the Burden*, 9.
7 For a reminder of the three steps of the method, please refer to the diagram summarising the complete method in Chapter 3.
8 S. Tønnesson, 'The Longest Wars: Indochina 1945–75', *Journal of Peace Research* 22 (1), 1985, 9–29.
9 This is the broad explanation of US commitment to fighting communism in SE Asia in the Department of Defence's own study, *The Pentagon Papers*, 42–52; see particularly 1.IV, 'The Character and Power of the Viet Minh', and 1.V, 'Ho Chi Minh: Asian Tito?'; Robert M. Blum and United States Congress Senate Committee on Foreign Relations, *The United States and Vietnam, 1944–1947: A Staff Study Based on the Pentagon Papers Prepared for the Use of the United States Senate Committee on Foreign Relations* (Washington, DC: US Government Printing Office, 1972).
10 See particularly 2.III.A '"Domino Principle" Before Korea', in Gravel, *The Pentagon Papers*, 81–84.
11 William J. Duiker, *Ho Chi Minh: A Life* (London: Hachette Books, 2012).
12 Institut Charles de Gaulle, *Le général De Gaulle et l'Indochine 1940–1946* (Paris: Plon, 1982); Frédéric Turpin, *De Gaulle, Les Gaullistes et l'Indochine: 1940–1956* (Paris: Les Indes savantes, 2005).
13 'Political Information: The Viet Nam Government', 29/7/1947, CIA-RDP82-00457R000700750001–5, CREST.
14 Lawrence, *Assuming the Burden*, 177.
15 Marilyn B. Young and Robert Buzzanco, *A Companion to the Vietnam War* (Oxford: John Wiley & Sons, 2008), 132.
16 John J. Sbrega, '"First Catch Your Hare": Anglo-American Perspectives on Indochina during the Second World War', *Journal of Southeast Asian Studies* 14 (01), 1983, 75.
17 Russell H. Fifield, 'The Thirty Years War in Indochina: A Conceptual Framework', *Asian Survey*, 1977, 857–79; D. Cameron Watt, *Succeeding John Bull: America in Britain's Place 1900–1975*. The Wiles Lectures (Cambridge: Cambridge University Press, 1984); Bernard B. Fall, *The Two Viet-Nams: A Political and Military Analysis* (Westport, CT: Frederick A. Praeger, 1967); Arthur M. Schlesinger, *The Bitter Heritage* (Boston, MA: Houghton Mifflin, 1967).
18 Gravel, *The Pentagon Papers*, 2.
19 Gary R. Hess, 'Franklin Roosevelt and Indochina', *The Journal of American History* 59 (2), 1972, 353–68.
20 Joseph M. Siracusa, 'The United States, Viet-Nam, and the Cold War: A Reappraisal', *Journal of Southeast Asian Studies* 5 (01), 1974, 82–101.
21 See particularly Joseph Siracusa, 'Lessons of Viet-Nam and the Future of American Foreign Policy', *Australian Journal of International Affairs* 30 (2), 1976, 227–37.

The diplomacy of the First Vietnam War   135

22 Spector added considerable nuance through analysis of military and Office of Strategic Services (OSS) missions in China and Indochina, whose actions suggest they believed Trusteeship was still policy. R. Spector, 'Allied Intelligence and Indochina, 1943–1945', *The Pacific Historical Review* 51 (1), 1982, 23–50.
23 An interesting early exception to this consensus is John Sbrega, who, working from FDR's personal papers, argued that Roosevelt never abandoned Trusteeship, and that indeed from 1943 to his death he explored several options to achieve Indochinese independence and discussed them with Stalin, Churchill, and the State Department. '"First Catch Your Hare"'.
24 Walter LaFeber, 'Roosevelt, Churchill, and Indochina: 1942–45', *The American Historical Review* 80 (5), 1975, 1277–95; George C. Herring, 'The Truman Administration and the Restoration of French Sovereignty in Indochina', *Diplomatic History* 1 (2), 1977, 97–117; *America's Longest War : The United States and Vietnam, 1950–1975*, Fourth Edition (Boston, MA: McGraw-Hill, 2001), 6–18.
25 The Southeast Asian and European offices at the State Department had different views as to Vietminh's communist threat, as well as contrasting Eurocentric contra Asian perspectives on postwar priorities. W. Macy Marvel, 'Drift and Intrigue: United States Relations with the Viet-Minh, 1945', *Millennium – Journal of International Studies*, 1975, 10–27.
26 It is worth considering how little Vietnamese history was available to American readers in English in the 1940s and 1950s; see for instance Joseph Buttinger's absolutely dreadful *The Smaller Dragon* (Westport, CT: Praeger, 1958).
27 Trường Chinh, *The August Revolution* (Hanoi: Foreign Languages Publishing House, 1958); Trường Chinh and Bernard B. Fall, *Primer for Revolt: The Communist Takeover in Viet-Nam*, 133 (Cambridge: Cambridge University Press, 1963); Trường Chinh, *The Resistance Will Win* (Hanoi: Foreign Languages Publishing House, 1960).
28 Tran Van Giau, 'The Vietnamese Working Class', 1957.
29 Tuong Vu, '"It's Time for the Indochinese Revolution to Show Its True Colours": The Radical Turn of Vietnamese Politics in 1948', *Journal of Southeast Asian Studies* 40 (03), 2009, 519–42.
30 Tuong Vu, 'Triumphs or Tragedies: A New Perspective on the Vietnamese Revolution', *Journal of Southeast Asian Studies* 45 (02), 2014, 255.
31 They evolved from the École Française d'Extrême Orient, Hanoi. See for instance Philippe Franchini, ed., *Saigon: 1925–1945 : de la Belle Colonie à l'éclosion révolutionnaire, ou, la fin des dieux blancs* (Paris: Autrement, 1992); and the much more interesting Pierre Gourou in *Le Tonkin* (Maçon: Protat, Imprimeurs, 1931); 'Utilisation Du Sol En Indochine Française', 1940, accessed 7 June 2015, http://agris.fao.org/agris-search/search.do?recordID =US201300611003; *L'avenir de l'Indochine* (Paris: P. Hartmann, 1947).
32 Philippe Franchini, *Les Guerres d'Indochine: De La Bataille de Dien Bien Phu à La Chute de Saigon*, vol. 2 (Paris: Pygmalion/G. Watelet, 1988); *Les Mensonges de La Guerre d'Indochine* (Paris: Éd. France loisirs, 2003).

33 Jean Sainteny, *Histoire d'une Paix Manquée* (Paris: Éditions de Saint-Clair, 1967); Thierry d'Argenlieu, *Chronique d'Indochine: 1945–1947* (Paris: A. Michel, 1985); Thomas Vaisset, *L'Amiral d'Argenlieu. Le moine soldat du gaullisme* (Paris: Humensis, 2017).

34 Paul Mus, *Viet-Nam: Sociologie d'une Guerre* (Paris: Seuil, 1952); *Le Destin de l'Union Française de l'Indochine a l'Afrique* (Paris: Éditions du Seuil, 1954); Philippe Devillers, *Histoire Du Viêt-Nam de 1940 à 1952* (Paris: Editions du Seuil, 1952); Philippe Devillers, ed., *Paris-Saigon-Hanoi: les archives de la guerre, 1944–1947* (Paris: Gallimard, 1988).

35 Stein Tønnesson, *The Vietnamese Revolution of 1945: Roosevelt, Ho Chi Minh and de Gaulle in World at War* (London: PRIO Sage, 1991); David G. Marr, *Vietnam 1945: The Quest for Power* (Berkeley, CA: University of California Press, 1995).

36 My own philological exploration of 'Viêt-Nam' (sources ranging from the *Tale of Kieu* to the *Twenty-Four Histories*) revealed that the name means 'Southern Viet', and that the name given to part of the country by the French division, An-Nam, meaning 'Pacified South' (Chinese: 安南), was the same as under the third Chinese colonisation (602–938 AD).

37 Marr, *Vietnam 1945*, 165; see also Chapters 6 and 7.

38 Tønnesson, *The Vietnamese Revolution of 1945*, 269.

39 S. Tønnesson, *Vietnam 1946: How the War Began* (Berkeley, CA: University of California Press, 2010), 237.

40 His minute reading in Chapter 3 of 1941–45 issues of Vietminh newspaper *Doc Lap* ('Independence') is exquisite. Tønnesson, *The Vietnamese Revolution of 1945*, 120.

41 Tønnesson, *Vietnam 1946*, 165; Marr, *Vietnam*, 183.

42 Tønnesson, *Vietnam 1946*, 146.

43 Tønnesson, *Vietnam 1946*, 236.

44 The first thorough Western exploration is that of Alexander Woodside, who explored the intellectual history of Vietnamese Marxism, ultimately linking it not to European modernism but rather to an ethos of intellectualism, leadership, and social structuring long present in Confucian élites. *Community and Revolution in Modern Vietnam* (Boston, MA: Houghton Mifflin, 1976); 'History, Structure, and Revolution in Vietnam', *International Political Science Review* 10 (2), 1989, 143–57.

45 Tønnesson, *Vietnam 1946*, 29–39.

46 See for instance Harrison E. Salisbury, 'Image and Reality in Indochina', *Foreign Affairs* 49, 1970, 381.

47 Mark Philip Bradley, *Imagining Vietnam and America: The Making of Postcolonial Vietnam, 1919–1950* (Chapel Hill, NC: University of North Carolina Press, 2000), 178.

48 Bradley, *Imagining Vietnam and America*, 177.

49 Mark Atwood Lawrence, 'Transnational Coalition-Building and the Making of the Cold War in Indochina, 1947–1949', *Diplomatic History* 26 (3), 2002, 455.

The diplomacy of the First Vietnam War 137

50 Lawrence, *Assuming the Burden*, 221.
51 As Peter Busch concluded in a review of Lawrence's book, '[i]t would have been interesting to see how Lawrence would have seen the utterances of British, French, and American officials in the light of constructivist thought.' Peter Busch, 'Constructing Vietnam', *Diplomatic History* 31 (1), 2007, 155–58.
52 Bidault's colonialism would take him to join the illegal Organisation de l'Armée Secrète to keep Algeria French after the 1962 Evian Agreements granted Algeria independence, after which he fled to Brazil.
53 Hanoi to Kunming, 27 August, 1945, 2, SA.
54 See file EA 20, MAE for Kunming and Chongqing to Algiers 1943–45 correspondence.
55 'Instructions du général de Gaulle', cable Paris to Hanoi via Calcutta, 25 August 1945, 2, SA.
56 Cable Kunming to Hanoi, 1 September 1945, 1, SA.
57 For his diplomatic powers, see 'Organisation Générale du Haut Commissariat' (undated) July 1944, 174Q0.3, Fond EA, MAE.
58 Creation of Haut Commissariat in 'Confidentiel: Indochine', London to Algiers (DIPLOFRANCE headquarters until the liberation of Paris), 13 July 1944, 174Q0.3, Fond EA, MAE. Such powers are unheard of for this post since the nineteenth century.
59 See the ruthless orders that Sainteny 'reassert our interests' and 'not concede on our sovereignty' in dispatch 'Instructions pour M. J. Sainteny', 25 November 1945, 2, SA.
60 See the file 'activités "diplomatiques" extérieures du Viet-Minh', 23 July 1947, which reports with a view to prevent Vietminh foreign communications. 174Q0.96, Fond EA, MAE. Fond EA file 96 is entirely dedicated to French surveillance and countering of Vietminh diplomatic efforts, including attempts to arrest or assassinate Vietminh diplomats and prevent them from obtaining US visas to visit the UN.
61 He was congratulated for 'Excellent political reporting' by Secretary Acheson. State to Saigon 851G.00/8–346, RG59, NARA.
62 While in principle all papers were declassified by 2009, obtaining Fond EA files 113 and 117 (rival depositions to the UN by Vietminh and France concerning human rights abuses, including photographic evidence) necessitated research charm and friendly archivists after several failed requests explained by 'conservation work'. I felt very much like Fowler. A complete list of archives and funds analysed can be found in the Bibliography.
63 See Tønnesson, *The Vietnamese Revolution of 1945*, 21; Marr, *Vietnam 1945*, xii.
64 Found at AP 127, 457, AN.
65 See, for example, publications where I retrieved and expounded the insights from this second step of the method but did not write out the commentaries in full: 'When Diplomacy Identifies Terrorists: Subjects, Identity and Agency in the War on Terror in Mali'; 'Struggles over Identity in Diplomacy'; 'Retrieving How Diplomacy Writes Subjects, Space and Time: A Methodological Contribution', *European Journal of International Relations* 26 (2), 2020, 469–94.

66 Another context where publishing these analyses of individual texts in full is helpful is research where analysing the constructions of identities is itself a contribution; see, for example, my book on the diplomacy of the First Vietnam War, *The Road to Vietnam*.
67 Besides many De Gaulle speeches on the subject (see *Lettres, notes et carnets: Tome 2, 1942–mai 1958* (Paris: R. Laffont, 2010)), plans for a military reconquest of Indochina had been underway since 1943; see policy paper by the Commissary of Colonies, 1 April 1944, 174Q0.3, Fond EA, MAE.
68 See, for instance, the essays (including one by André Malraux) in Andrée Françoise Caroline d' Ardenne de Tizac, Andrée Viollis, and André Malraux, *Indochine S.O.S.* (Paris: Gallimard, 1935). It details French economic and cultural abuses of a romanticised, peaceful, and ultimately powerless Vietnamese population following the 1930 Vietnamese revolt. The collection calls for the 'rescue' of Indochina from exploitation and colonial oppression and is representative of 1930s French socialist and liberal anticolonialism.
69 Nguyen Du, *The Tale of Kieu*, trans. Huynh, New Edition (New Haven, CT: Yale University Press, 1987).
70 The Forces Expéditionnaires Françaises en Extrême-Orient were established a year before to assist the Allies in the Far East (only in Indochina) and to 'liberate' and secure the colony's return to French sovereignty. See De Gaulle – Pleven Memorandum, 1 April 1944, 174Q0.3, Fond EA, MAE.
71 See d'Argenlieu, *Chronique d'Indochine*. He was so concerned by Cochinchina, and pushed so far for this to be explained to British and US diplomats, that French diplomats frequently found themselves explaining that it was 'not only' a fantasy emanating from d'Argenlieu. 'Le cas de la Cochinchine', Federal Information Bureau, 6 September 1946, 4, SA. This series of memoranda is analysed by Gunn, who examined d'Argenlieu's plan to prevent the reunification of Vietnam by proclaiming the puppet Republic of Cochinchina at Dalat II. Geoffrey C. Gunn, 'Prelude to the First Indochina War: New Light on the Fontainebleau Conference of July–September 1946 and Aftermath', *Annual Review of Southeast Asian Studies* 54 2013, 19–51.
72 Imperial Vietnam was considerably larger. Vietminh only claimed its Vietnamese-speaking core, unified by the Tây Sơn dynasty four hundred years before.
73 The Vietnamese name for Cochinchina was 'Nam Bo' ('Southern Province') which not only recalls its history within the Vietnamese Empire, but also includes 'Nam', which means 'south' for the province and in 'Việt Nam'; from the Mandarin 'nan' ('south').
74 I did not note this for the previous three texts because, as dispatches, their very receipt and presence in archive implied reading, whereas (key in enabling Manning's leak to Wikileaks) cables are sent to a central office and distributed. Another key feature of cables is that conversations are reported, not transcribed, which might have endangered our analysis were it not for the crucial factor that, lacking a recording of the conversation, this is the version and exact language that US diplomats and policymakers read.

75 Nicolson, *Diplomacy*, 123.
76 Note this is a full year before Kennan's 'Long Telegram'.
77 See, for instance, 'La mauvaise foi du Président Ho Chi Minh' (undated) December 1946, which accuses Vietminh of being a Japanese stooge; and 'Les relations du Front Viet-Minh', 7 June 1948. Both 174Q0.46, Fond EA, MAE. French communists were in government coalitions in 1946, making it difficult for civil servants to write about communism as a conspiracy. I would posit, however, that Fond EA 1944–47 documents suggest that it was overcome by D'argenlieu's representation of Vietminh as irredentist fascist, Jap-stooges – in his memo analysed above, he does not even mention communism.
78 And the first by a diplomat, the others originating from OSS officers who had worked with Vietminh on anti-Japanese activities.
79 As identified by Bradley, *Imagining Vietnam and America*, 45.
80 Detailed in letter accompanying this document. Airmail State to Hanoi, 711.51G/6–348, RG59, NARA.
81 Foucault calls them 'planes of emergence', discussed in Part II, 3 in *Archaeology of Knowledge*. When considering the formation of objects, surfaces of emergence are where individual differences are accorded status, the discursive as well as practice sites where they emerge and are designated. They 'are not the same for different societies, at different periods and in different forms of discourse'. In other words, they are discursively delimited normative domains like the family as well as debates about family, or in our case, Cold War blocs. Foucault, *Archaeology of Knowledge*, 45.
82 Alistair Cooke, *A Generation on Trial: U.S.A. v. Alger Hiss* (New York: Open Road Media, 2014); Aaron Beim and Gary Alan Fine, 'The Cultural Frameworks of Prejudice: Reputational Images and the Postwar Disjuncture of Jews and Communism', *Sociological Quarterly* 48 (3), 2007, 373–97.
83 Paris to State, 851G.00/5–1548, RG59, NARA.
84 'EXECUTIVE ORDER 9835 | Harry S. Truman', accessed 1 September 2022, https://www.trumanlibrary.gov/library/executive-orders/9835/executive-order-9835
85 'Alger Hiss Denies Ever Turning over Any State Papers: Nixon Wants Tighter Law', *New York Times*, 1948; 'Mere 14 Million Communists Are Altering Globe', *The Washington Post (1923–1954)*, 1948, sec. CURRENT EVENTS National and Foreign EDITORIALS Art Books.
86 'Cominform Is in Sight for Southeastern Asia', *New York Times*, 1948, sec. review of the week's editorials.
87 See also 'Communists Menace South Asia; Unified Blow at Resources Seen', *New York Times*, 1948.
88 The media appeared surprisingly relaxed about the prospects of the Chinese Civil War. See 'U.S. Envoy Urges Chinese Self-Help', *New York Times*, 1948; 'Chinese Reds Shift to New Offensive', *New York Times*, 1947; 'Communists Attack in Area Near Peiping', *New York Times*, 1947.
89 'Grave Peril Seen in Berlin Action', *New York Times*, 1948; 'Malaya Declares Emergency', *New York Times*, 1948; 'Malayan Police Hold 600 in Anti-Red

Raids', *New York Times*, 1948; 'British Official Sees Red Drive in Asia', *New York Times*, 1948; 'Government Takes Stern Steps to Stop Red Disorder in Malaya', 1948.

90 The *New York Times* called it 'the colonial problem' and 'the question of colonies' when referring to the inevitability of 'revolt' against 'old imperialism'. 'Colonial Problem Growing in France', *New York Times*, 1946; 'French Face All-out Colonial War: Indo-China Is Aflame with Many Incidents', *New York Times*, 1946, sec. 'The Week in Review'; 'The Old Era Is Gone in the Far East: The Area Will Never Again Be an Open Field for Political and Economic Imperialists', *New York Times*, 1947, sec. magazine; 'Indo-China Revolt Fateful to France: Other Empire Areas Watching Outcome of Dissidence in Troubled East Asia', *New York Times*, 1946; 'Colonies in Ferment', *New York Times*, 1945, sec. 'The Week in Review'; LANSING WARREN Special to THE NEW YORK TIMES, 'French Combat Wide Revolt on Madagascar; Planes Carry Troops to Threatened Centers', *New York Times*, 1947.

91 See memoranda 10/11/1947, and 'Political Information: The Viet Nam Government', 29/7/1947, CIA-RDP82–00457R000700750001–5, CREST.

92 As Tønnesson and Marr have pointed out, none exists to this day.

93 Vietminh's own 'communistification' and contact with Mao and the USSR only occurred later; see Vu, '"It's Time for the Indochinese Revolution to Show Its True Colours"'.

94 Bangkok to State, 851G.00/2–1048, RG59, NARA'.

95 French and American Southeast Asian Desk chiefs, memorandum of meeting and exchange, 851G.00/2–2448, RG59, NARA.

96 Paris to State, 851G.01/12–2447, RG59, NARA. Translated copies of the speech by governor Bollaert bearing the new policy were provided to the US Ambassador as proof of intention to negotiate.

97 Washington to FO 14/4/48, FO959/18, 11/5/1948, FO959/19, and 'Review of the situation in French Indochina', 11/5/1948, FO959/19, NA.

98 Though not expounded here as this is a case study, this research performed the same mapping of pathways, detailed reading of texts, and genealogy for the British too. See the more detailed version of this research in de Orellana, *The Road to Vietnam*.

99 See Tønneson's discovery of this mistake in Tønnesson, *Vietnam 1946*, 27.

100 As was very evident in both the request and the reception of this document; see the American request in Washington to FO 14/4/48, FO959/18, NA.

101 FO to Saigon, 14/4/48-FO 959/18, NA.

102 Chancery of UK Commissioner-General, Singapore to FO, 2/9/1949-FO371/75975, NA.

103 See State to Saigon, 851G.00B/3–2947, RG59, NARA; 'Report on Chinese Communist Activities in Tonkin', Hanoi to State, 851G.00B/4–1747; 'Communism in Indochina', Saigon to State, 851G.00B/3–747, RG59, NARA; Conversation, 851G.00/4–1448, RG59, NARA; State report, 851G.00/10–1747, RG59, NARA.

The diplomacy of the First Vietnam War 141

104 HAUSSAIRE to COMINDO, 26/9/47; Washington to DIPLOFRANCE, 15/10/47, both Film 4714, 91QO.124, MAE, *New York Times*, 'Totalitarian Character of Ho's Regime Cited as Evidence – Japanese Are Said to Have Installed Viet Minh as "Time Bomb"', *New York Times*, 1947.
105 Hundreds were collected in 1949–47 in a 'subversion in Indochina' file. 'Transmitting Viet Minh documents' (including 'Commie document') Saigon to State, 851G.00B/12–749, RG59, NARA.
106 Henri Claudel report, 26 November 1948, film P4713, 91Q0.123, MAE.
107 Nouméa to State, 851E.5045/8–3045; Delhi to State, 851F.00/7–848; Martinique to State, 851D.00/9–1647, RG59, NARA.
108 Research memorandum 851E.00B/7–748, RG59, NARA.
109 Conversation, 851G.00/2–2448, RG59, NARA.
110 Paris to State, 19/12/1947–851G.00.
111 Washington to DIPLOFRANCE, 17/3/48, Film P4715, 91QO.125, MAE.
112 Paris to State, 851G.00/12–1947, RG59, NARA.
113 Saigon to State, 851G.00/5–1348; Hanoi to State, 851G.00/2–1648; see also Paris to State, 851G.00/5–1548; 851G.00/1–1648, RG59, NARA.
114 Lawrence, *Assuming the Burden*, 216.
115 This is the plot of Joe Tunning in *The Quiet American*!
116 'Étude sur les activités Américaines en Indochine', 11/9/47, HAUSSAIRE, Film 4714, 91QO.124, MAE.
117 Paris to State, 19/12/1947–851G.00, RG59, NARA.
118 'Rapport politique Fevrier-Mars 1949', CP 93/HCI/INDO, ANOM.
119 In Daniel Varga, 'Léon Pignon, l'homme-clé de la solution Bao Dai et de l'implication des États-Unis dans la Guerre d'Indochine', *Outre-Mers. Revue d'histoire* 96 (364), 2009, 277–313.
120 Folders 6–1946, INDO/HCI/CD/2–4, ANOM.
121 1/1946, 6–1946, INDO/HCI/CD/2–4, ANOM.
122 Hanoi to State, 19/7/1947–851G.00, RG59, NARA.
123 Hanoi to State, 851G.00/12–247; 851G.00/9–2447; Saigon to State 851G.00/9–2647; Nanking to State, 851G.00/9–3047, RG59, NARA.
124 State circular 851G.00/7–347; HK to State, 851G.00/12–3047, RG59, NARA.
125 Saigon to State 851G.00/9–1547, RG59, NARA.
126 SEA Memorandum, 851G.01/9–1247, RG59, NARA.
127 Paris to State, 851G.00/10–147; 851G.00/11–347, RG59, NARA.
128 Saigon to State, 851G.00B/3–747, RG59, NARA.
129 Saigon to State, 851G.00B/3–747, RG59, NARA.
130 Dispatch Bangkok to State, 'Approach made by Dr. Pham Ngoc Thach', 851G.00/7–947, RG59, NARA.
131 Attachment to Bangkok to State, 851G.00/7–947, RG59, NARA. It is interesting to note how Vietminh diplomacy learnt from previous Viet–US exchanges, in this case using a questionnaire to establish interlocutor positions. The US embassy in Bangkok had previously submitted one to Thạch in May 1947.
132 Paris to State, 851G.00/6–347, RG59, NARA.

133 HAUSSAIRE to COMINDO and COMIINDO response to HAUSSAIRE, 10/2/47, AP 128, 457, AN. The article was published: 'Statement from D'Argenlieu', *New York Times*, 1947.
134 Letter to MRP deputy and Bidault, 28/1/47, AP 128, 457, AN.
135 Paris to State, 851G.00/11-2946, RG59, NARA; 'Le projet d'union sud asiatique', Presidential Office, 6/11/46, 174Q0.46, Fond EA, MAE.
136 HAUSSAIRE instructions, 28/10/46, AP 127, 457, AN.
137 Paris to State, 851G.00/12-2846, RG59, NARA; 10/3/47, New York to Washington/DIPLOFRANCE, Film 4714, 91QO.124, MAE.
138 Paris to State, 851G.00/2-647, RG59, NARA.
139 DIPLOFRANCE Circulaire, 20/3/47, AP 128, 457, AN.
140 Washington to DIPLOFRANCE 20/10/46, 5/12/46, Film 4714, 91QO.124, MAE.
141 DIPLOFRANCE to Holy See and Washington, 17/3/47, Film P4713, 91QO.123, MAE; 10/3/47, New York to Washington/DIPLOFRANCE, Film 4714, 91QO.124, MAE.
142 COMINDO to DIPLOFRANCE, 4/4/47, Film 4714, 91QO.124, MAE.
143 'The Old Era Is Gone in the Far East'; 'France in Indo-China', *New York Times*, 1947, sec. REVIEW OF THE WEEK EDITORIALS; 'French Combat Wide Revolt on Madagascar; Planes Carry Troops to Threatened Centers'; 'Indo-China Rebels Widen Operations', *New York Times*, 1946; 'French Face All-out Colonial War'; 'Colonial Problem Growing in France'.
144 Saigon to State, summary of Indochinese situation (heartily celebrated by Kennan) 851G.00/6-1447, RG59, NARA.
145 Paris to State, 851G.00/1-1647, RG59, NARA.
146 HAUSSAIRE to COMINDO, 7/6/47, 174Q0.46, Fond EA, MAE.
147 'Réponse Française au mémorandum du Gouvernement Ho Chi Minh', 9/1/47, 174Q0.117, Fond EA, MAE.
148 'Le Viet Minh est un régime totalitaire qui règne par la terreur et par son organisation policière', 17/12/46, 174Q0.113, Fond EA, MAE.
149 7/1/47, AP 128, 457, AN.
150 Hanoi to State, 851G.00/7-1947; Saigon to State, 851G.00/2-2847; Saigon to State, 851G.00/2-1447, RG59, NARA.
151 Washington to DIPLOFRANCE, 5/5/47, Film 4714, 91QO.124, MAE; Saigon to State, 851G.00/2-2847; SEA Memorandum, 851G.00/12-1646, RG59, NARA.
152 State to Saigon, 851G.00/7-1747; Hanoi to State, 851G.00/4-147 and State to Hanoi 851G.00/4-147; Hanoi to State 851G.00/1-2247; State to Hanoi and HK, 851G.00/1-647, RG59, NARA.
153 SEA memorandum, 851G.00/1-247; Circular, 851G.00-2046, RG59, NARA.
154 Paris to State 851G.00/1-947, RG59, NARA.
155 Written like this in the original. The lack of proper grammar and punctuation visible in many of these cables is due to telegraph practice in the 1940s. State circular, 851G.00/5-1347, RG59, NARA.

156 Saigon to State, 851G.00/5–2847 and 851G.00/2–2547. Evidence of Indochinese will to independence isn't solely from Vietnam – which could have worked in favour of French arguments. Navy intelligence obtained a copy of a petition by the 'Free Laos Government' asking Chiang Kai-shek for support. Central intelligence Group to State, 851G.00/11–2246, RG59, NARA.
157 Saigon to State, 851G.00/11–746; 851G.00/11–2746, RG59, NARA.
158 Hanoi to State, 851G.00/12–4446; Saigon for Moffat, 851G.00/12–346, RG59, NARA.
159 Hanoi to State, 851G.00/11–3046, RG59, NARA.
160 'Information circular', 851G.00/12–1746, RG59, NARA.
161 Hanoi to State, 851G.00/12–346, RG59, NARA.
162 London to State, 851G.00/11–2546, RG59, NARA.
163 Paris to State, 851G.00/5–2247; SEA Memorandum, 851G.00/12–1646, RG59, NARA.
164 Hanoi to State, 851G.00/2–1047 and reply Memorandum FW 851G.00/2–1047; Hanoi to State, 851G.00/2–547, RG59, NARA.
165 State Circular 851G.00/1–747, RG59, NARA.
166 Hanoi to State, 851G.00/1–1147, RG59, NARA.
167 Hanoi to State, 851G.00/12–146, RG59, NARA.
168 Hanoi to State, 851G.00/1–947, RG59, NARA.
169 Hanoi to State, 851G.00/1–2047, RG59, NARA.
170 Paris to State, 851G.00/2–2047, RG59, NARA.
171 'Mémorandum concernant l'origine du conflit Franco-Vietnamien', 31/12/46, 174QO.117, Fond EA, MAE.
172 Bangkok to State, 851G.00/4–1747, RG59, NARA.
173 Hanoi to State, 851G.00/12–646, RG59, NARA.
174 Washington to DIPLOFRANCE, 19/2/47, Film 4714, 91QO.124, MAE.
175 Bangkok to State, 851G.00/5–1447, RG59, NARA.
176 Bangkok to State, 851G.00/4–747, RG59, NARA.
177 Paris to State, 851G.00/9–1646, RG59, NARA.
178 Moffat memorandum, Paris, 851G.00/9–1246, RG59, NARA.
179 Hanoi to State, 851G.00/9–1446, RG59, NARA.
180 De Gaulle in *L'Aube*, 18 January and 28 March 1945; Paris to State, 711.51/1–345, RG59, NARA.
181 Paris to State, 711.51/5–545; 711.51/4–1145, RG59, NARA.
182 'FRUS 1945, Vol. IV, Europe' (US State Department, 1945), 300.
183 Washington to DIPLOFRANCE, 9/12/45, Film P4712, 91Q0.122, MAE.
184 Charles de Gaulle, *Lettres, notes et carnets. 1943–1945* (Paris: Plon, 1983).
185 'La prise du pouvoir par le V. M.', 29/8/46, SA4.
186 Sainteny to HAUSSAIRE, 1/46, SA4.
187 'Physionomie politique de l'Indochine du Nord', 10/45, SA3; Rapport B5', 12/45, SA2; Rapport Arnoux, 2/45, SA2.
188 Humbert report, 2/12/45, SA1; HAUSSAIRE, 8/11/45, 174QO.20, Fond EA, MAE.

189 A good example is the Gaullist newspaper *L'Aube*. Gaullist nationalists still use this language. See, for instance, Sarkozy 'Accusé d'«extrémisme», Sarkozy dénonce un «procès stalinien»', leparisien.fr, 2012, accessed 7 July 2015, http://www.leparisien.fr/election-presidentielle-2012/en-direct-hollande-la-limitation-de-l-immigration-economique-necessaire-27-04-2012-1974316.php; 'Sarkozy: "Être Traité de Fasciste Par Un Communiste, c'est Un Honneur !"' Le Lab Europe 1, 2012, accessed 7 July 2015, http://lelab.europe1.fr/sarkozy-etre-traite-de-fasciste-par-un-communiste-c-est-un-honneur-2024.
190 Rapport Brunschwig, July/45, Film P4713, 91QO.123, MAE.
191 Chungking to DIPLOFRANCE, 22/3/45, 174QO.20, Fond EA, MAE.
192 'Circulaire secrete HAUSSAIRE to COMINDO, 8/3/46, 174QO.46; 'L'appui Chinois a l'agitation Annamite anti-Française', 3/46, 174QO.20, Fond EA, MAE.
193 See 'terrorisme' file for COMINDO in 174QO.46, Fond EA, MAE.
194 HAUSSAIRE to COMINDO, 26/7/45, AP 127, 457, AN.
195 DIPLOFRANCE to HAUSSAIRE, 26/7/46, AP 127, 457, AN.
196 15/12/45, SA2; State, Eastern Hemisphere, 851G.00/5–545, RG59, NARA; 22/3/45, Washington to DIPLOFRANCE, Film 4714, 91QO.124, MAE.
197 See January 1944 speech in Gaulle, *Lettres, notes et carnets. 1943–1945*, 136.
198 'Indochine', 24/3/45, MAE, 174QO.5, Fond EA, MAE see also 'Note sur la politique qu'entend suivre le Gouvernement Français en Indochine après sa liberation', 8/45, AP127, 457, AN.
199 'Note pour le Ministre', 4/12/45, AP127, 457, AN.
200 'Activités Américaines', HAUSSAIRE to DIPLOFRANCE (undated)/1/46, Film 4714, 91QO.124, MAE; Hague to DIPLOFRANCE, 31/10/45, Film 4714, 91QO.124, MAE.
201 DIPLOFRANCE to Washington, 27/10/45, Film 4714, 91QO.124, MAE; SEA memorandum, 851G.00/11–2345.
202 One mission report reads like *Heart of Darkness*, with French soldiers fearfully sailing up a 'dark' river with deceitful Annamese and 'hostiles surrounding the mission'. 'Mission a bord du Fegaf' (17)/8/45, SA1.
203 'Puppet' was an official allied term that would have led to the Allied termination of such forces. Renseignements n.2263, 10/9/45, SA1.
204 No.50/Sec., 25/6/45, SA1.
205 France Policy Statement 15 Sept 46 711.51/9–1546, RG59, NARA.
206 Saigon to State, 851G.00/8–3146; Saigon to State, 851G.00/4–3046; Saigon to State, 851G.00/5–446, RG59, NARA.
207 'Voluntary Report', 851G.00/12–145; Patti report, 851G.00/12–545; Gallagher debrief, 851G.00/1–3046, RG59, NARA.
208 Patti report, 851G.00/12–545, Saigon to State, 851G.00/4–2746, RG59, NARA.
209 David B. Woolner, Warren F. Kimball, and David Reynolds, *FDR's World* (Palgrave Macmillan, 2008), 134.
210 European Affairs to Secretary, 851G.00/9–2945, RG59, NARA.
211 Truman, Grew, 711.51/5–1745, RG59, NARA.

212 See 10/3/47, New York to Washington/DIPLOFRANCE, Film 4714, 91QO.124, MAE.
213 Sainteny to HAUSSAIRE, 29/9/45, SA1.
214 'Problèmes du référendum au Nam Bo' ['Southern Region'] 7/46, AP 127, 457, AN.
215 Hanoi to Paris, cited COMINDO to HAUSSAIRE, 12/10/46, also 26/10/46, 174QO.46, Fond EA, MAE; for the many (unanswered) letters Hồ sent to Bidault, see AP127, 457, AN.
216 6/12/46, COMINDO, 174QO.46, Fond EA, MAE. A presidential report confirmed d'Argenlieu purposefully delayed transmission of Vietnamese communications to COMINDO (Rapport 28/11/46, AP 127, 457, AN).
217 Secretary, 851G.00/5–1446, RG59, NARA.
218 Hanoi to State, 851G.00/6–546, RG59, NARA.
219 Kunming to State, 851G.00/10–2445, RG59, NARA.
220 Intelligence report, COMINDO, 1/10/46, 174QO.18, Fond EA, MAE.
221 Undated, unmarked, in file with 851G.00/3–846, RG59, NARA.
222 Moffatt to State, in Porter, *Vietnam: A History in Documents*, 41.
223 Renseignements n.2263, 10/9/45, SA1.
224 Attachment to cable from Consulate Kunming, 851G.00/6–1445, RG59, NARA.
225 OSS memo for State, 851G.00/8–2145, RG59, NARA.
226 His reports to OSS are in Box 1393, file 16, RG226, NARA.
227 The exchange is far too large to examine in detail. It is evident in policy memoranda and analysis from E contra FE and SEA in files 851G.00/5-xx45 (reports on Indochina, May 1945), RG59, NARA.
228 'Memorandum on Indochina' 851G.00/9–2845, RG59, NARA.
229 European Affairs Memo, 851G.00/10–245, RG59, NARA.
230 Conversation, 711.51/5–2145, RG59, NARA. It is worth noting that de Gaulle, as an ethnogeopolitical nationalist, believed that the only way to keep France safe was to literally shrink Germany in people and resources. See also John W. Young, 'The Foreign Office, the French and the Post-War Division of Germany 1945–46', *Review of International Studies* 12 (3), 1986, 223–34.
231 LaFeber, 'Roosevelt, Churchill, and Indochina'; Herring, 'The Truman Administration and the Restoration of French Sovereignty in Indochina'.
232 See, for instance, Paris to State, 711.51/3–1445, RG59, NARA.
233 'The French Regime in Indochina prior to 1940' 751.51G/3–845; (FDR) Memorandum to Cordell Hull, 751.51G/1–2444, RG59, NARA.
234 SEA memorandum, 851G.00/4–2845, RG59, NARA.
235 See, for instance, Chunking to State, 851G.00/1–3045, RG59, NARA.
236 (FDR) Memorandum to Cordell Hull, 751.51G/1–2444, RG59, NARA.
237 Bradley, *Imagining Vietnam and America*; Mark Philip Bradley and Marilyn B. Young, *Making Sense of the Vietnam Wars: Local, National, and Transnational Perspectives* (New York: Oxford University Press USA, 2008); Marilyn Young, *Vietnam Wars 1945–1990* (New York: Harper Perennial, 2020); Young and Buzzanco, *A Companion to the Vietnam War*.

238 Philippe Devillers, *End of a War: Indo-China, 1954* (New York: Praeger, 1969); Devillers, *Paris-Saigon-Hanoi*; Devillers, *Histoire Du Viêt-Nam de 1940 à 1952*; Paul Mus, *Hô Chi Minh, Le Vietnam, l'Asie* (Paris: Éditions du Seuil, 1971); Mus, *Viet-Nam*; Tønnesson, *The Vietnamese Revolution of 1945*.
239 Lawrence, *Assuming the Burden*.
240 This is relevant because the Red Scare was not as dramatic in 1947 when in Greece the US- and British-supported government was successfully containing the insurgency, while in China, the Lioshen Campaign that turned the tables on the Chinese KMT would not conclude until November 1948.
241 Jeffrey James Byrne, 'Our Own Special Brand of Socialism: Algeria and the Contest of Modernities in the 1960s', *Diplomatic History* 33 (3), 2009, 427–47; Hugh Roberts, 'The Politics of Algerian Socialism', *North Africa: Contemporary Politics and Economic Development*, 1984, 5–49; David Ottaway and Marina Ottaway, *Algeria: The Politics of a Socialist Revolution* (Oakland, CA: University of California Press, 1970).
242 Irwin M. Wall, *France, the United States, and the Algerian War* (Oakland, CA: University of California Press, 2001).

5

The diplomacy of the Western Sahara conflict

Son saharauis,	They are Sahrawi,
los saharauis	the Sahrawis
no existen en la crónica de los succesos	they do not exist in chronicles of success
son parte de otro mundo	they belong to another world
el mundo de los ignorados	the world of the unheard
	Ali Salem Iselmu, 'El Mundo de Los Ignorados'[1]

In December 1975, thousands of refugees fled Western Sahara under fire from Moroccan jets dropping napalm and white phosphorous. The Sahrawis struck back.[2] Led by POLISARIO founder El-Ouali Mustapha Sayed, POLISARIO forced Mauritania to withdraw from the south of the territory. On the return journey, in one of the most tangible expressions of the international dimensions of this conflict, French jets attacked the POLISARIO columns with napalm. Sahrawi forces were less successful against Morocco which, with US assistance, managed to gradually force POLISARIO out of the territory. Six months earlier, North Vietnamese troops advanced into Saigon, marking the end of the Vietnam War and the reunification of Vietnam. Though almost entirely unknown, the Western Sahara conflict helps understand modern diplomacy, particularly how it can unlock policy influence for smaller powers like Morocco.

Western Sahara is Africa's only remaining colony and, remarkably, one of only three successful military annexations since WWII.[3] Unlike Tibet, it featured a widely supported independence movement, the Frente Popular de Liberación de Saguía el Hamra y Río de Oro (Popular Front for the Liberation of Saguía el-Hamra and Río de Oro, POLISARIO), which fought Morocco from 1975 until 1991. In 1991, the US ceased supporting Morocco, bringing about a UN-brokered ceasefire and the creation of the UN Mission for the referendum in Western Sahara (MINURSO) to facilitate a final-status plebiscite. Negotiations over voting franchise stretched until 2004, when Morocco rejected the final plebiscite proposal, the Baker II Plan. Upon resigning in 2004 as the UN Secretary-General's envoy for Western Sahara, James Baker declared that any Western Sahara agreement was doomed to failure unless the Security Council supported it with Chapter VII (enforcement) rather than Chapter VI (agreed negotiations).[4] To this day, Morocco benefits from US and French vetoes of Chapter VII resolutions which would enforce agreements onto the parties. Though these sponsors had purportedly supported self-determination since the 1975 ICJ ruling that determined Sahrawi right to self-determination, they heavily supported Morocco's military efforts.

The 2000s, however, witnessed an exceptional change in this US policy position. In 2008, after failed Moroccan–POLISARIO talks at Manhasset, the State Department declared '[a]n independent Sahrawi state is not a realistic option. In our view, some form of autonomy under Moroccan sovereignty is the only realistic way forward.'[5] This constituted a major policy shift: self-determination was altogether abandoned for the first time, accepting and repeating the language of Morocco's own unilateral autonomy proposal.[6]

US acceptance of Morocco's annexation under this plan had seismic consequences. Obama's administration did not reverse the decision 2009–16, and then in 2020, Trump followed on by fully recognising Moroccan annexation – and, again, using the selfsame language.[7] The Biden administration has not reversed this position. In 2020, Morocco invaded the area outside the berm separating Moroccan from POLISARIO-held territory, leading to clashes that by the time of writing in 2023 were gearing up to full-scale war. Spain followed in 2022 with recognition of the annexation, just as younger factions in the Sahrawi refugee camps and within POLISARIO called for a resumption of war. By forever precluding a final-status referendum and the potential for Sahrawi sovereignty, US acceptance of the autonomy plan allowed Morocco to impose its will without negotiation, forcing independentists inside and outside the territory to either accept or fight.

This chapter investigates this policy shift by applying the method expounded in this book to the diplomacy of Western Sahara in the 2000s and the diplomatic text that is evidence of its development. As this conflict is not well known and is in its fifth decade at the time of writing, the first section, below, combines a review of research on the conflict's diplomacy with a summary of events 1975–present. The second section maps Moroccan, US, and POLISARIO diplomatic knowledge-production pathways. Thirdly, two individual diplomatic texts from each actor are examined in detail to determine how they constitute representations and identify topoi textual markers signposting their presence. The fourth section follows these topoi across thousands of texts, analysing how Moroccan diplomacy constituted and communicated these representations, tracing their development and entry into US diplomacy in the runup to the 2008 policy shift, and exploring POLISARIO's own efforts. The final section summarises findings, discussing how despite the more visible threat of terrorism, Morocco did not persuade US policymakers that POLISARIO was an Islamic terrorist group but rather that it was terrorism-enabling due to North Africa's 'ungoverned spaces', a representation that in turn depended on representing Morocco as democratic, stable, and unradicalised, and consequently any Moroccan weakness as dangerous to US security and the War on Terror.

Historical debates: Western Sahara decolonisation, irredentism, and diplomacy 1975–2021

In November 1975, King Hassan II launched the 'Green March': thousands of Moroccan civilians walked from Morocco to al-'Ayun to liberate Spanish Sahara while Morocco's military enveloped the territory and waited for Spanish troops to depart. Franco's Spain was initially determined to decolonise in its own terms, as corroborated by talks on self-determination between Spanish foreign minister Pedro Cortina y Maurí and POLISARIO leader El-Ouali, as well as Prince Juan Carlos' (very public) solo fighter-jet flight to al-'Ayun to support Spanish troops.[8] The International Court of Justice (ICJ), following from a Spanish-Moroccan request, ruled that Morocco had had pre-colonial links to some tribes but that these did not justify 'reattachment' to Morocco without a self-determination referendum as Morocco requested.[9] As Generalísimo Francisco Franco agonised, however, the moribund regime led by Prime Minister Carlos Arias Navarro granted the territory to Morocco and Mauritania on 14 November. By 1975, the most widely supported Sahrawi nationalist group was POLISARIO, founded in 1973 to establish a Sahrawi state in Spanish Sahara, and which has since then fought Moroccan annexation.

The Moroccan crown is deeply invested in annexing Western Sahara. The monarchy's relationship with nationalism has been the engine of its legitimacy since 1945.[10] After independence in 1956, Moroccan nationalism driven by the Istiqlal Party moved for the restoration of 'Greater Morocco', including Western Sahara, Mauritania, western Algeria, and northern Mali.[11] The quest for Greater Morocco led to a failed Moroccan attempt to annex Tindouf province from newly independent Algeria in the 1963–64 Sand War.[12] Failing in its Algerian and Mauritanian claims, annexation of Western Sahara became key to monarchical supremacy as it embraced nationalism (but not the Istiqlal party) to rally loyalty to the King.[13] To this day, annexing the 'Southern Provinces' is the only Royal policy supported by all parties.[14]

Diplomacy played a pivotal role in the 1975 crisis. US diplomats pressured Spain to acquiesce to Moroccan demands following from Secretary of State Kissinger's recommendation to President Ford to 'do it like West Irian where they fuzz the "consulting the wishes of the people", and get out of it'.[15] Of special relevance is how Kissinger described the crisis to Ford: '[o]n the Spanish Sahara, Algerian pressure has caused the Spanish to renege. Algeria wants a port and there are rich phosphate deposits. The Algerians have threatened us'.[16] The 1975 crisis was seen by American policymakers and diplomacy as a superpower proxy conflict that could endanger American ally Morocco.[17] Harassed by Moroccan forces and bombarded by military jets, more than half the Sahrawi population, over one hundred thousand civilians, fled to camps near Tindouf, Algeria. POLISARIO launched a military campaign against Morocco and Mauritania, defeating the latter in 1979, while Morocco kept fighting.[18]

In the 1980s, US military, financial, and diplomatic assistance bolstered Moroccan military efforts.[19] Facing asymmetric warfare by mobile POLISARIO units, Morocco's Royal Armed Forces (Forces Armeés Royales, FAR) built the *berm* (wall) between 1982 and 1987, made of mined sand walls, ramparts, forts, batteries, and sensory equipment more visible on Google Earth than the Great Wall of China. The berm, Moroccan incentives, and forced migration brought hundreds of thousands of Moroccan settlers to the territory.[20] Since 1976, the Sahrawi Arab Democratic Republic (SADR) has operated as a state-in-waiting in the POLISARIO-held parts of Western Sahara and the SADR-governed camps near Tindouf,[21] while the occupied territory has witnessed the emergence of protest and resistance movements for independence,[22] as well as against royal corruption and repression.[23] In 2010, the occupation of al-Zamlah Square in al-'Ayun prefigured Egypt's later Tahrir Square protests and the so-called Arab Spring.[24] Socially, the conflict has focused on ownership of Sahrawi identity. For example, Sahrawi nationalism has found an outlet in a new wave of Sahrawi poetry in their Hassaniya Arabic dialect, recited at traditional *Moussems* poetry festivals, which the Moroccan regime has appropriated.[25] The conflict extends to second languages: under Moroccan rule, children are taught French, whereas SADR teaches Spanish.[26] From clothes to poets writing in Hassaniya and Spanish, never in Darija or French, this is a war to impose sovereignty on identity.[27]

After the 1991 ceasefire, negotiations revolved around who could vote in the referendum. Because of the large number of people Morocco had settled in the territory, negotiations deteriorated into appeals about birth in the territory on or before 1975.[28] On the State Department's initiative, in 2003 the Secretary General's envoy, James Baker, proposed the Peace Plan (Baker II). Adapted to Moroccan rule over the territory and objections to Baker's

2001 Framework Agreement, it proposed the return of refugees, autonomy for four years, and a final-status referendum that, as well as the refugees, enfranchised anyone resident in the territory since 1999, making Moroccan settlers a majority. Despite Baker's requests, the Security Council declined to 'endorse' the Peace Plan, choosing to 'support' both sides in a mutually agreed resolution.[29] Morocco rejected the plan in 2004, arguing that 'the final nature of the autonomy solution is not negotiable'.[30]

That was the last time the United States supported self-determination. In late 2007 and early 2008, the Manhasset negotiations failed as Moroccan negotiators refused to discuss any settlement other than their Autonomy Plan.[31] In May 2008, the policy shift was stated explicitly: a State Department spokesman declared that an 'independent Sahrawi state is not a realistic option. In our view, some form of autonomy under Moroccan sovereignty is the only realistic way forward.'[32] This shift is significant because it completely abandons self-determination. It is significant for our study of representation in diplomacy because it absorbed Morocco's most insisted-upon representations and their language: Moroccan sovereignty is not realistically negotiable, and its plan for autonomy is 'serious and credible'.[33] Though the Trump administration has been criticised for recognising Moroccan annexation in exchange for recognition of Israel, this was itself enabled by recognition in 2008 of Morocco's autonomy plan by Secretary Condoleezza Rice in 2008, and the reiteration of this position by Secretary Clinton in 2009. Ironically, Trump's policy move in fact followed smoothly from the policy shift on Sahrawi self-determination begun by Rice in 2008 and followed by Clinton in 2009 and Trump in 2020. Crucially, each of these statements directly repeats the language and specific wording of the autonomy proposal and Morocco's promotion of it and the only 'realistic' and credible' solution.

Leading research suggests US assistance, as with Vietnam, was predicated on 'perceptions' carefully projected by a Moroccan diplomacy 'constantly obsessed over controlling international perceptions'.[34] During the War on Terror, Morocco appealed to a 'longstanding pillar of US support: Morocco's stability' through insertion of itself, POLISARIO, and the conflict into the global context.[35] Morocco described itself an indispensable ally in the War on Terror and in need of US support to protect its 'democracy' and generously willing to offer 'an advanced autonomy solution' to Western Sahara.[36] This is quite an achievement considering Morocco is constitutionally closer to Kuwait's autocratic monarchy that to Spain, to which it consistently compares itself in the context of autonomy. In Mundy's research, this leads to a series of challenges of perceptions to prove or disprove their veracity.[37] This chapter builds on Mundy's work, treating these 'perceptions' as representations of subjects and their contexts, analysing how they were constituted, developed, and accepted such that they inscribed subjects into frameworks that granted them global significance.

This chapter substantiates research suggesting perceptions of the conflict in terms of the global War on Terror were vital to its diplomacy,[38] adding to understanding of the conflict's diplomacy by exploring how these representations work, providing a history of how they evolved until they were taken up by US diplomats, and revealing the conditions that enabled this event. It is found that it was representation of desert 'ungoverned spaces' and subjects, rather than domestic Moroccan terrorism, that gained most traction in US diplomacy. Representation of POLISARIO in US diplomacy was dominated by POLISARIO's potential role in providing terrorist-enabling space and subjects, not allegations of being terrorist itself. Crucially, US support for the autonomy initiative is found to have additionally hinged on the persuasiveness of Moroccan representations of its social, democratic, and economic progress, which explains why it was not granted until 2008. We are now ready to map the pathways taken by US, Moroccan, and POLISARIO diplomatic knowledge production in the 2000s.

Mapping the diplomatic text: diplomatic knowledge production pathways

This section maps Moroccan, American, and POLISARIO diplomatic knowledge-production pathways. Western Sahara diplomacy is treated as a triangular encounter between Morocco, the United States, and POLISARIO. Though, as with the United Kingdom in the previous chapter, it would be helpful to consider French diplomacy in Western Sahara, this is not done for two reasons. In the period studied, French diplomacy, though very supportive of Morocco, superficially supported some form of self-determination and did not abandon it fully until 2020, unlike the United States, which did so in 2008. French diplomacy is extremely secretive about Franco-Moroccan relations, which means no diplomatic material has been released and probably won't be for nearly another one hundred years. Sadly, application of this method to French efforts to help its Maghrebi ally will have to wait until a leak or greater access are available. Figure 5.1 provides a schematisation of the knowledge-production pathways studied.

These imbrications must be considered in the context of the beginning of the War on Terror and its global campaign to eradicate Islamic terrorism. In North Africa, this meant policing the Western Sahel, a semi-arid region between Algeria, Libya, Chad, Morocco, Western Sahara, Mali, and Mauritania, considered 'ungoverned space' for Islamic militants.[39] In 2001, there was only one major such group, the Salafist Group for Preaching

The diplomacy of the Western Sahara conflict 153

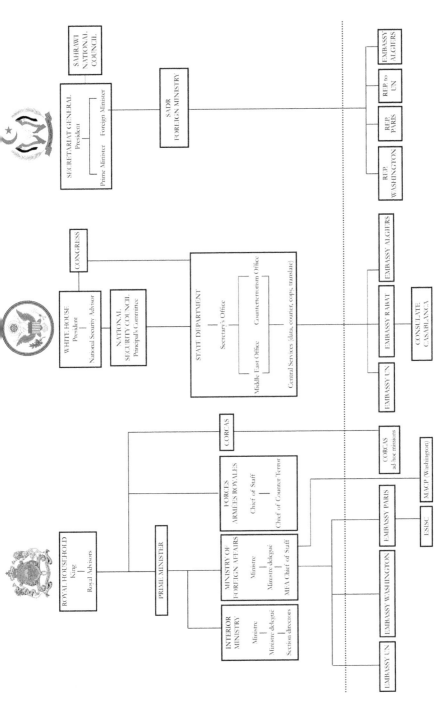

Figure 5.1 Diagram of diplomatic knowledge production pathways by institutions studied. Lines denote channels of reporting and instructions. Vertical lines denote hierarchy. Dotted line divides institutions at home, above, from those abroad, below. Diagram by Tally de Orellana.

and Combat (Groupe Salafiste pour la Predication et le Combat, GSPC), a descendant of Armed Islamist Group (Groupe Islamique Armé, GIA), the main Islamist faction during the Algerian Civil War. It joined Al-Qaeda in 2007, becoming Al-Qaeda in the Islamic Maghreb (AQIM).[40] Morocco suffered no attacks until May 2003, when twelve suicide bombers attacked tourist hotspots in Casablanca. Morocco–US relations thrived, with a Free Trade Agreement and tightening of military, diplomatic and intelligence relations. Moroccan collaboration was crucial in providing bases, aircraft, and interrogation personnel to the Extraordinary Rendition Programme.[41] In this context, previously frosty relations like US–Algeria (not to mention Gadhafi's Libya) warmed to facilitate counterterrorism.

Moroccan diplomacy remained inscrutable until the 2010 leak of State Department cables to Wikileaks revealed the roles played by institutions and individuals outside the MFA.[42] King Mohammed VI and a small circle of advisors alone determine Moroccan foreign policy, announcing it at yearly Royal Speeches that guide ministries and are cited to foreign diplomats. This is because the Moroccan monarch plays three roles. Constitutionally, he can form cabinets, call and dissolve Parliament, and direct foreign, security and military affairs. Economically, he owns much of Morocco's economy through Societé Nationale d'Investissement, Morocco's sovereign wealth fund, which belongs to the crown. Spiritually, he is *Amīr al-Mu'minīn*, 'Commander of the Faithful', derived from his descendance from The Prophet, granting him vast religious influence.

The Foreign Ministry includes high-ranking individuals involved in diplomacy: the Minister, the Minister-Delegate, the Secretary-General, and the Chief of Staff, as well as the military Chief of Staff and counterterrorism. All top-level diplomats are royal appointments or members of the royal family, or come from the King's businesses, like the current ambassador to the United Kingdom. Embassies launch and fund lobbying and information initiatives with partners like the European Strategic Intelligence and Security Center (ESISC), led by former French spy Claude Moniquet.[43] ESISC produced newsletters and reports claiming POLISARIO's destabilising influence, and was the only Western organisation claiming POLISARIO had links to AQIM. Likewise, the Moroccan American Center for Policy (MACP, an 'agent of the Government of Morocco') lobbies and produces documents and websites promoting Moroccan foreign policy in the US, particularly Western Sahara.[44] The Royal Consultative Council for Saharan Affairs (Conseil Royal Consultatif pour les Affaires Sahariennes, CORCAS), appointed by the monarch, claims to represent Sahrawis, sends 'Sahrawi delegations', and promotes the autonomy proposal.

American diplomacy is more formalised. On the ground we find Rabat embassy and consulate Casablanca. Prominent embassy officials include the

Deputy Chief of Mission (DCM) and Chargé d'Affaires (CDA, often the same person), the Political Counsellor, the Military Attaché, and personnel from other agencies including Homeland Security, the military branches, the FBI, and the CIA. These officers meet with Moroccan government agency chiefs, including officials and ministers from the Foreign, Interior, Justice and Defence ministries. To these we should add visiting congressmen and officials, notably Africa Command (AFRICOM) head General Ward and FBI Director Mueller. These visits are organised by diplomats who brief them through 'scenesetter' cables.

Diplomatic reporting is sent to the State Department, which distributes cables to offices including Middle East, North Africa, and Counterterrorism, led by Assistant Deputy Secretaries. Communication with POLISARIO occurs at the UN mission, where the Ambassador, a member of the US cabinet, reports to the Secretary of State and White House advisors. At the very top sits the National Security Council Principal's Committee, which governs the National Security Council (NSC), filters knowledge coming from the State Department (unlike in the 1940s, note), makes policy decisions, and coordinates inter-agency implementation.[45] References in cables demonstrate that it sets policy objectives, timetables, and priorities for diplomats, while the latter summarise reporting and compile half-yearly reports for the Committee's staff to assess progress.[46] The Committee, the highest within NSC, reports only to the President.

The main Sahrawi channels of communication with the US and Morocco are the SADR ambassador in Algiers and the UN representative.[47] SADR's representative in Washington very seldom meets State Department officials, communicating instead via UN and Algiers DCMs – an important point of protocol, since the United States does not recognise SADR. The embassies to Algiers to the AU in Addis Ababa are key points of contact for the fledgling republic. Like Machiavelli five centuries before, POLISARIO demands accurate reporting from its representatives, as demonstrated by what appeared to be the temporary suspension of Representative to the US Mouloud Said, who mistakenly thought 'the U.S. would maintain its express support for self-determination'.[48] The SADR Secretariat-General in effect combines the offices of POLISARIO Secretary-General and SADR President Mohamed Abdelaziz (left post due to death in 2016, currently Brahim Ghali) with those of the Foreign and Prime Ministers. SADR missions report to the Secretary General, the Prime Minister, and the Foreign Minister. They, in turn, report to the Sahrawi National Council, which formulates general foreign policy decisions and is itself accountable to (and elected by) the General Popular Congress, which can hold the Secretariat to account and, on the last two congresses, imposed red lines on negotiating concessions.[49]

This case study brings our investigation to the present day, which means briefly considering the digital evolution in diplomatic knowledge management. As archival declassification is at least thirty years away in the United States and unavailable in Morocco, the bulk of the data collected, nearly two thousand documents, is from Wikileaks' State Department and the 'Wikileaks du Makhzen' leaks of Moroccan Crown diplomatic documents. The US leak exemplifies how knowledge management has changed since our 1940s case study: the files of the State Department's Central Services, which in the 1940s would have been highly classified, were shared with the military in the 2000s, allowing junior army analyst Bradley Manning to download and leak them.[50] The cables are themselves web-based emails, which is what made the leak possible but also facilitates cross-referencing as references are clickable HTML links. The digitalisation of reporting has brought other changes: though the font remains similar, abbreviations are not used as heavily and are standardised.

Following our method's approach to chronology, which allows the diplomatic text to set its own chronological limits by backtracking until the earliest iteration of representations, data selection covers 2010 back to 2003. Triangulation of communications, as with the Vietnam case study, was vital, as many Moroccan communications, when unavailable on the Makhzen leaks or orders from the NSC, were available in copy or in reference or summarised in cables. Data selected according to the diplomatic moment criteria, accounting for when texts enter diplomatic knowledge production, yielded communications by non-MFA individuals who, on select instances, speak for the state, official press releases, analysis, reports, and policy statements by Moroccan government organisations, CORCAS; state press agency Maghreb Arab Presse (MAP); the Moroccan 'Collective of Human Rights Associations in the Sahara' (CHRAS) whose reports are disseminated by Moroccan embassies,;[51] ESISC; as well as POLISARIO declarations; communiqués, press releases, reports, and declarations by SADR officials published by Association pour le Référendum au Sahara Occidental (ARSO); and Sahara Press Service (SPS). Having mapped diplomatic reporting in this conflict and its data selection, we can now move to detailed analysis of how diplomatic text constituted representations.

How diplomatic texts inscribe actors and their contexts: Islamic terrorists contra imperialist invaders

This section analyses six individual diplomatic communications to determine they constitute representations of subjects and their contexts. Analysis is designed to retrieve the practice context that produced them, determine how their textual structure constitutes relations among representations, and reveal how articulations build representations and subjectivity, as well as identify the topoi textual markers signposting their presence. Two texts are analysed from each of the three actors, selected to include the main representations of the diplomacy of the Western Sahara conflict encountered in analysis and identified in scholarship, as well as different types of texts: reports, meeting notes, advice from missions, public policy declarations, and a scenesetter prepared for Secretary of Defense Rumsfeld's visit to Morocco.[52] Morocco's autonomy proposal and its response to the Baker Plan (both in the third analysis below) were studied by Mundy to demonstrate Morocco's unwillingness to negotiate between 2004 and 2007.[53] In contrast, the following analyses determine how they constitute the conflict, its subjects, and the territory.

1. 'The right to self-determination inherent in the decolonisation question'

A report by US deputy ambassador to the UN Jackie Sanders on her March 2007 meeting with POLISARIO Secretary General Mohamed Abdelaziz marks the beginning of UN and US efforts to organise direct talks, which took place at Manhasset 2007–8. Abdelaziz's representations of Morocco and POLISARIO are representative of POLISARIO diplomatic text since 1991. The Sahrawi leader had travelled to the UN to counter Morocco's 'worldwide diplomatic initiative to promote' autonomy by making the case for POLISARIO's core position: any solution, including autonomy, must include a self-determination referendum. Since 1975, the conflict has been 'a decolonisation problem' that according to international law and UN resolutions requires 'implementation of the principle of self-determination', 'inherent in the decolonisation question'. Morocco's autonomy initiative runs against this principle, which 'would complicate regional security'. Responding to encouragement to negotiate with Morocco 'without preconditions', Abdelaziz explains that POLISARIO authorities do not have a mandate to negotiate on a basis that excluded self-determination and 'in which Moroccan sovereignty was a given'. He adds that Morocco 'violated human rights in Western Sahara' and illegally exploits the territory's natural resources. Abdelaziz suggests the precedent of Namibia (UN moratorium on exploitation until self-determination) and that MINURSO be mandated to monitor human rights in Western Sahara.

In this meeting, Abdelaziz articulates three pairs of binary representations. POLISARIO seeks only the self-determination mandated by the ICJ in 1975, numerous UN General and Security councils' resolutions, the 1991

'Settlement Plan, the [1997] Houston Agreements and the [2001 and 2003] Baker Plan'. By linking it to previous agreements, UN resolutions, and rights of colonised peoples, this representation normatively frames self-determination as the only internationally acceptable option against Morocco's 'unilateral' 'occupation'. Morocco's 'diplomatic initiative to promote it' is represented as 'taking everything off the table', including the international norms POLISARIO espouses.[54] The second binary representation is the oldest remaining from the beginning of the conflict: Morocco's colonial treatment of the territory denies Sahrawis human, economic, and political rights and exploits the territory's resources. The third binary representation is legitimate sovereignty over subjects, contrasting Morocco's autocratic governance of Morocco and the Western Sahara territory against POLISARIO's parliamentary democracy. This normative differentiation is reiterated by reference to the 'mandate' of the Sahrawi people to secure self-determination and 'the end of the POLISARIO leadership' should they deviate.

These representations establish normative differentiation between POLISARIO and Morocco. Every issue, including human rights, resource exploitation, precedents (reinforced by reference to Namibia), and the diplomatic process, is articulated in terms of denial or provision of the right to self-determination. Even regional security, Abdelaziz posits, is affected by rejection of that right. The language of his statements emphasises these frames through repeated use of vocables that reinforce their inscription. This is consistent with POLISARIO's descriptions of the conflict in outlets including Sahrawi news agency SPS and even in a journal article authored by Sidi Omar, former POLISARIO representative to the United Kingdom.[55] These words are used with explicit reference to their meaning in international law, and in fact often sound like a law journal article.[56] They include 'inherent' 'right to self-determination', while Morocco 'obstructed the process' of resolution and 'exploits' resources, emphasised again against POLISARIO's 'mandate' 'authorised by the Sahrawi people'. These vocables, particularly 'mandate', 'inherent', and 'right to self-determination', contra Morocco's 'obstruction' and colonial 'exploitation', are the topoi textual markers signposting POLISARIO inscriptions of itself and Morocco in the normative dimension of the conflict.

2. 'POLISARIO ASKS U.S. TO RESPOND TO MOROCCAN PROVOCATIONS'

This section analyses a report of the Deputy Chief of Mission (DCM) and Political Counsellor of the US embassy in Algiers on talks with 'senior Polisario Front leaders'. It is December 2009; a year has passed since the failure of the fourth round of talks at Manhasset due to Moroccan refusal to negotiate on any basis other than its autonomy plan and POLISARIO's refusal to exclude self-determination. Barak Obama had been elected a year before, and POLISARIO was not alone in hoping for change in US support for Morocco's autonomy solution and rejection of self-determination, though there was anguish that recent statements about Morocco's autonomy proposal meant the United States had quietly dropped self-determination – which is exactly what happened in May 2008, when the Department of State quietly adopted the proposal as negotiating basis; and earlier in 2009, when Secretary Clinton visited Rabat. Like the cable in the previous detailed textual study, it shows us what the American diplomatic recipients and transmitters of these declarations think: it is an intertextual site where US reporting bears POLISARIO representations, while comments by the American authors demonstrate Sahrawi awareness of 'strong perceptions' of a US 'tilt in favour of Morocco's autonomy plan'.

Returning to our 'senior Polisario Front leaders', including Prime Minister Abdelkader Taleb Omar, they too believed that representations of the conflict had transformative power. POLISARIO officials argue the Manhasset talks failed due to Moroccan bad faith that 'escalated the dispute' with 'provocations', instead of fostering 'calm and trust'. Morocco was furthermore 'calling for the punishment of traitors', harassing and arresting Sahrawi activists. Conversely, 'since the 1991 ceasefire, the Polisario has put its faith in the UN and has hoped to find a peaceful solution'. POLISARIO prefers a 'democratic solution' which 'would strengthen the credibility of the UN, weaken extremism, and help cultivate a democratic culture in North Africa in accordance, he said, with U.S. goals'. Bachir Mustafa, advisor to the POLISARIO Secretary General, adds an extraordinary counter to the frequent Moroccan description of a referendum as destabilising for Morocco and the region: 'Polisario had an interest in maintaining Moroccan stability. Referring to the Polisario's call for a popular referendum on the territory, Mustafa questioned why Morocco could not reconcile stability with democracy.'

The political identities of Morocco and POLISARIO as regional and international actors are the key representations constituted in this text. They link and differentiate Moroccan and POLISARIO leadership, diplomatic approaches, and their 'interests', at several levels of domestic, regional, and global political concerns. At the level of political leadership, the Moroccan king's recent speech separating all Sahrawis into traitors or loyal subjects, as well as Moroccan human-rights abuses, contrast against POLISARIO's implied lack of repression. POLISARIO diplomacy characteristically emphasises POLISARIO's democratic tradition, practices, and elected leadership to differentiate from Morocco's regime. At the regional level, representations link POLISARIO's desire for 'stability', desire to 'weaken extremism', and 'cultivate a democratic culture in North Africa' with 'U.S. goals' and American democratic values. POLISARIO's opposition to Moroccan human-rights abuses and censorship of free speech in the territory not only links it to American norms of free speech and human rights, but also differentiates Morocco from American values. This link is established at the global level too, with a POLISARIO official pledging 'Polisario's cooperation with regional actors in the area of counterterrorism'.

Language supports this regional and global inscriptions of POLISARIO and Morocco, this time through strategic-sounding articulations and vocabulary reminiscent of RAND reports, inscribing subjects in regional strategic maps marked by American and European concerns about instability in North Africa.[57] This is most apparent in the articulation of POLISARIO's regional role, when one POLISARIO official 'referred to Morocco as a "big brother" in the region' 'with its own interests, which Polisario does not wish to harm', before moving onto POLISARIO's own 'interest in maintaining Moroccan stability'. Topoi textual markers signposting POLISARIO domestic, regional, and global representations of the conflict include 'stability in North Africa', a direct import from frequent US expressions of reliance on Moroccan stability as a regional bulwark, expressed by Secretary Hillary Clinton during a visit to Morocco only twenty-nine days earlier.[58] 'Polisario's cooperation in counterterrorism' signposts representation of POLISARIO as also threatened by extremism and willing to collaborate in counterterrorism.

3. 'Under Moroccan sovereignty': king, autonomy, and modernity

The text of Morocco's autonomy proposal was promulgated in 2007 and has since remained almost entirely unchanged. Ostensibly published in an independent website promoted by two Moroccan journalists, autonomy-plan.org is anonymously hosted on an American domain and hosting service. It shares linguistic, branding, brand positioning ('the kingdom on the move'), design, and aesthetic similarities with MACP's website moroccoonthemove.com. Most diplomacy studied in this chapter revolves around this crucial document. Morocco recognises 'its southern provinces has cultural differences that should be addressed' (sic). Autonomy is a solution successfully applied 'throughout the world', and is 'in keeping with the principle of self-determination'. The proposal is compared to 'constitutional provisions in force in countries that are geographically and culturally close to Morocco', which refers to standard Moroccan comparisons of its proposal with autonomy in the Spanish regions, particularly Catalonia's mini-constitution.[59] Unlike the Catalonian example, however, the proposal reserves 'the constitutional and religious prerogatives of the King' – which, it should be noted, are more similar to Kuwaiti monarchical autocracy and are essentially unlimited.[60] The proposal revolves around the claim that autonomy legally provides for both Moroccan sovereignty and Sahrawi self-determination.

The proposal articulates the core normative representation of the autonomy solution: humanitarian, democratic, includes 'adequate representation of women',[61] fair to all concerned, providing for the return of 'exiles', 'general amnesty' for 'armed elements outside the territory', 'to build a modern, democratic society, based on the rule of law'. This representation is not constituted around such provisions in the proposal itself, which do not exist, but by reference to the 'constitutional provisions' of neighbouring countries (only Spain is both a neighbour and has autonomous regions) and assertion that 'it is based on internationally recognised norms and standards'. This is directly contrasted with the opposite option, 'separation and exile', 'the dispute plaguing the region'. The second representation, the nature of Moroccan sovereignty, is constructed around a linear temporal frame linking the sovereignty of Moroccan Caliphs/Sultans from the tenth century to the present King, positing autonomy as its modern and tolerant twenty-first-century evolution. 'Morocco has a long history of inter-cultural dialogue', the preamble announces, linking successive incarnations of the Moroccan crown to non-Maghrebi subjects.

Analysis of this representation benefits from reference to Morocco's rejection of the Baker II Peace Plan, which proposed a period of autonomy followed by a referendum with autonomy and independence options. It directly posits that 'it is out of the question for Morocco to engage in negotiations with anyone over its sovereignty and territorial integrity' and claims that doubts over Moroccan sovereignty produce 'insecurity and instability for the whole Maghreb'. It explains that Moroccan monarchical sovereignty draws on 'the most sacred principles which have, throughout history, founded its unity and safeguarded its perpetuity'. This principle is far more than the 'Greater Morocco' vision of Moroccan nationalists; it appeals to the sovereignty of the Moroccan Sultan, which was based on religious and political sovereignty over subjects.[62]

This conceptualisation of sovereignty is crucial to the 'reunification' of the 'southern provinces' whose tribes Morocco argues had pledged fealty to the Moroccan Sultan in the nineteenth century (the chief Moroccan representation to the ICJ in 1975) but also within Morocco itself, being the *sole* and vital basis of Alawite right to rule since their rise to power in 1659.[63] This explains Moroccan assertions that departure from this sovereignty brings instability to the region and Moroccan rejection (only shared by Somalia) of the African Union's convention to maintain colonial borders, except when rejected in the exercise of self-determination.[64] Contrast among representations is constituted through articulations that syntactically contrast Morocco's proposal against unattractively written alternatives for a region that 'has suffered for too long' from 'the dispute' causing 'separation and exile'.

The claimed modernity of Morocco's monarchical sovereignty draws on representation of Moroccan democracy, as evidenced by repeated inclusion of vocables like 'constitution', 'rule of law', and 'legality' in articulations representing Morocco's solution. Vocabulary deployment is even more expressive: 'plague', 'dispute', 'conflict', 'exile' contrast with the 'amnesty', 'law', 'integration', 'solidarity', 'internationally-recognised norms' that Morocco offers. Conspicuously absent is any mention of 'POLISARIO', while 'Sahrawi' appears only once and is incorrectly spelled 'sahrwis'. The Spanish inspiration for the proposal is confirmed by the use of the word 'autonomy' to mean the autonomous region rather than its powers, only found in Spanish-language legal and political use of the term 'autonomías'. The key topoi textual marker that emerges from this analysis, 'under Moroccan sovereignty', signposts this specific historical claim to sovereignty over subjects and, crucially, its claimed democratic modern adaptation.

4. 'The key to the Western Sahara conflict lies between Morocco and Algeria'

Sidelining POLISARIO is a key aspect of Morocco's approach to the conflict. It is well exemplified in a US report of an August 2005 meeting in Rabat with King Mohammed VI, Morocco's minister and deputy minister of foreign affairs Fassi Fihri, US Senator Richard Lugar, NATO European Commander General James L. Jones, and ambassador Thomas Riley, who filed the memorandum. It is representative of the Moroccan representation of the conflict as an Algerian creation. The king argues that 'the key to the Western Sahara conflict lies between Morocco and Algeria'. To this day, he argues, Algerian–Moroccan relations are an obstacle to closer Maghreb integration and to EU and US counterterrorism and counter-immigration initiatives – whence Senator Lugar's interest in fostering Moroccan–Algerian rapprochement.[65] When the Senator mentioned a referendum including Moroccan settlers in the territory as proposed in Baker II, 'testily, the King replied he had a suggestion for Bouteflika: Let's try a pilot referendum, he said, with the separatists in the Kabylie region in Algeria and see how that works.' Algeria does this because Western Sahara 'does not mean anything to the people of Algeria', whereas 'I have to be careful' as it 'means a lot to the Moroccan people'. The king is pessimistic about a rapprochement and lists failed efforts to do 'everything he could to move the relationship between the two countries forward. Morocco had received nothing in return. In English, the King said, "I felt like a beggar."' When Senator Lugar mentioned the Islamist Parti de la justice et du développement (Justice and Development Party, PJD), which until 2008 advocated curtailing royal powers, the king retorted that 'Islamists, whether moderates or extremists, they are all anti-American'. The meeting concluded with mutually congratulatory remarks on US–Moroccan military cooperation.

Moroccan–Algerian geostrategic rivalry is posited as the source of the Western Sahara conflict and Maghreb regional cooperation difficulties, articulating both stalemates in terms of Moroccan–Algerian rivalry and reticence to engage meaningfully. This is qualified by the thrice-repeated assertion that the territory matters to Morocco but not to Algeria, stating the conflict is but an Algerian tactic to harm Morocco. This articulation is supported by the absence of any reference to Sahrawi people, nationalism, or POLISARIO. That absence, combined with the articulation of Algerian–Moroccan struggle, completes the differentiations and linkages in the king's exposition, displacing the Western Sahara conflict from nationalist struggle to an Algerian plot in the context of geostrategic rivalry. The three representations erase nationalist normativity (which Moroccan diplomats call 'artificial dispute'), its Sahrawi subjects, and the spatial articulation of Sahrawi territorial claims. The American interlocutors are thrice reminded that the territory is vital to Moroccans, and that 'I have to be careful', for loss of the territory would upset Morocco's stability and monarchy, the interest in which is subtly tied to praise of Moroccan–US cooperation in the same meeting and the desirability of incrementing it.

These articulations are linguistically powerful due to their simplicity. The Algeria–Morocco dichotomy is all-pervasive: on page two, nearly every third sentence features Algerian obstacles to Moroccan efforts. POLISARIO, Sahrawis, nationalism, human rights, and discrimination are entirely subjugated by the claim that Algeria created them, reinforcing this 'Algerian creation' inscription of the spatial and normative dimensions of the conflict by erasing the subjects it concerns. Vocables support this articulation of the conflict's representation not only through the absence of 'Sahrawi' and 'POLISARIO' but also through frequent repetition of 'Algeria' and words qualifying Moroccan efforts at reconciliation being 'rebuffed' so intransigently that the king felt 'like a beggar'. The main topos identified in this text signposts representation of the Algerian nature of the conflict. It is an example of when we do not encounter topoi under labels we expect, but can recognise them by examining the architecture of the concrete articulation of representation it signposts – which is the objective of historicising topoi, as explained in Chapter 3. In this case, we recognise the 'artificial dispute' topos to be the same as 'Algerian conspiracy' because it denotes the same articulation of the conflict.

5. Scenesetter for Secretary Rumsfeld: 'our solid relationship with Morocco'

In 2006, the US embassy in Rabat prepared a scenesetter cable for Defense Secretary Donald Rumsfeld's February 2006 visit to Morocco. Drafted by the Defense Attaché at the Rabat embassy, it includes sentences and two paragraphs from previous scenesetter cables. Such standardisation demonstrates that changes to these representations require another diplomatic text to replace it – and the policy decisions needed for this to happen. Scenesetter cables condense analysis produced the previous year and summarise US policy positions and priorities, providing a wholistic overview rather than the specific communications we usually encounter. They are rare insights into instances when State Department knowledge production directly informs top policymakers, teaching us about the role of diplomats in informing nondiplomats.

The cable concentrates on bilateral military developments. They include vast increases in US nonmilitary (fourfold) and military (twofold) assistance, becoming a 'Major non-NATO ally', signing a Free Trade Agreement, exchanges of high-level visits, counterterrorism training and assistance, Morocco's successful application to the Millennium Challenge Account US development aid, joint military exercises, and the release of the last Moroccan POWs held by POLISARIO, negotiated by Senator Lugar.

The brief 'Algeria and Western Sahara' section is concerned that 'Moroccan resources that could be utilised more productively elsewhere will go to maintaining security in the territory, where roughly two-thirds of the Moroccan army is deployed.' Morocco's involvement in the Middle East Peace process and 'discreet but supportive role' in Iraq are briefly touched upon in the context of US–Moroccan international cooperation. Moroccan 'internal reform on all fronts' is emphasised, as is Mohammed VI's support of a commission to study human rights abuses 1956–99 (from independence until his coronation), a common example in US diplomatic text to show this king being more progressive than his father.

Morocco is normatively linked to the United States by its position on counterterrorism, which is to be pursued through control of borders and subjects,[66] free trade, and economic development.[67] Morocco is progressing in human rights, free speech, women's rights, education, and democracy, important considering Orientalist representations of Middle East and North African social and political stagnation in the 2000s.[68] This temporal linearity is the skeleton of the representations in this cable: Morocco's strives towards American development and international engagement. This is evident in the articulation of Moroccan institutions that 'respond enthusiastically to our invitations to attend counterterrorism seminars and education programs' and the 'much appreciated humanitarian assistance in response to both the Al-Hoceima earthquake and a 2005 locust invasion'. Military assistance is articulated within this linear temporal development frame, with Moroccans responding 'very positively to increased Foreign Military Financing' and 'generous transfers of Excess Defense Articles'.

Representation of political subjects is constructed around the binary of the War on Terror, where Morocco supports control of terrorist subjects. Additionally, its exemplary internal reforms includes 'restructuring mosques and Islamic education to promote tolerance and moderation'. In other words, altering Moroccan subjects differentiates Morocco from the extremist world on the other side of the binary. This cable also articulates a spatial representation of the ungoverned space of the Sahel, where borders need to be controlled through partners like Morocco to deny extremists safe haven.

Different verb tenses structure the cable's temporal frame. In paragraph 2, they set the tempo of 2003–6 as a narrative where the 2003 Casablanca terrorist bombings brought Morocco and the United States to collaborate. In paragraphs 5 and 9, we see how textual structure constitutes agency: extensive lists of Moroccan achievements are followed by sentences highlighting American contribution to these achievements, articulating the relationship as one where a subaltern Morocco benefits from American friendship. These narrative and structural articulations are constant in US text of this period. They do not contrast actors, but rather constitute far subtler differentiation: America is developed and Morocco developing, constituting the United States as paternally assisting a counterterrorism partner. Morocco is appreciated for 'excellent' 'cooperation with the US in countering terrorism' and 'supporting US strategic interests abroad' through 'intelligence-sharing, arrests, border security', 'critical staging, overflight and logistical support for US forces in transit'. Demonstrating 'commitment to our military relationship', '[n]o other country gets that much privilege here, even France'.

Omission of detail again emerges as an important part of articulating representations. Paragraph 14 states that Foreign Military financing 'and continued access to [Excess Defense Articles] play a significant factor in maintaining access to Moroccan bases and training areas and influences Moroccan decision-making in supporting our broader strategic interests.' Military hardware gifts, this suggests, grant the United States agency over Moroccan policy, which appears plausible if the Moroccan drive to gain support over Western Sahara in this period is omitted. Similarly, the cable concentrates heavily on counterterrorism collaboration, but does not mention even once whether Morocco is threatened by terrorism, and if so by whom.

The language is the most militarily technical encountered. '[A]rticle 98 agreement' (immunity for US citizens from the International Criminal Court[69]) is the first of a large series of political-military terms that make sense for the defence brief of the reader. However, they unwittingly constitute the relationship as almost solely based on military collaboration. Morocco's achievements are linguistically emphasised by vocabulary such as 'on all fronts' as well as by their insertion in long (but undetailed) lists that emphasise the comprehensiveness of that progress. US assistance to Morocco is condescendingly emphasised by adjectives like 'instrumental', 'much appreciated', and 'enthusiastically'.

Two topoi textual markers emerge to signpost these temporal and hierarchical representations. Firstly, 'on all fronts' signposts representation of Morocco as exemplarily progressive in all realms, already encountered above. Secondly, US assistance that 'influences Moroccan decision-making' signposts a subaltern representation of Morocco's need for US help that does not, however, include what Moroccan diplomacy desires the most from the United States: support for its Western Sahara policy.

6. 'Western Sahara realities'

Eventually, US diplomacy came to repeat Moroccan descriptions and language. In a four-page cable, Rabat embassy Chargé d'Affaires Robert Jackson expounds the 'reality' of the conflict from the ground. It comes only ten weeks before the 2008 presidential election. The list of recipients suggests policymaking relevance, but also that it was unrequested. They include the National Security Council, embassies in three Security Council permanent member states, and Vienna, where Morocco and POLISARIO were to hold an informal meeting the following month. This document is the most complete and extensive articulation available of the basis of the 'realism' US text attributed to the autonomy solution from 2008.

The cable begins by narrating how, unlike Hassan II, who 'for years at war with the left, used Western Sahara to bolster nationalism and park his army far away in the desert', Mohammed VI is 'maintained in power more by love than fear'. Morocco subsidises the territory so heavily that Moroccan papers complain of the expense – and are not censored, the cable emphasises. It argues, incorrectly, that elections in the territory 'while perhaps not democracy, seems far more open than the Cuba-like Polisario system'. The cable suggests that through democracy, 'development and reduced repression', Morocco is convincing Sahrawis of autonomy, which it finds 'serious, including local police and some independence for the judiciary'.

It questions whether Sahrawi nationalism is real as

> [t]he absence of such larger nationalism [claiming '"Sahrawi" territories in Morocco, Algeria or Mauritania'], along with the Polisario's 1970s war against Mauritania – the world's only Sahrawi state – suggest the conflict is less nationalist than geopolitical, linked to the much older dispute between Algeria and Morocco, and hardly boosts the case for an independent state.

The cable adds a Chagos-like alternative solution: '[g]iven the small population at stake', it might be possible to resettle the refugees in Spain 'but not in the current economic climate'. The UN process is flawed because 'it does not recognize the determinative role of Algiers', which has 'rebuffed' 'GOM overtures', though it acknowledges the king had ordered negotiators at the failed 2007–8 Manhasset talks 'to discuss no solution but autonomy'.

Representations bear the same differentiations we encountered in detailed textual studies 3 and 4 above, but with added nuance. Hassan II was a repressive king whose atrocities are recognised, whereas Mohammed VI is progressive, modernising, democratising, improving human rights, and developing Morocco's economy. This is the core representation of Morocco we find in MACP descriptions of the country and its all-pervading slogan 'The Kingdom on the Move'. These developments contrast negatively with the 'Cuba-like Polisario system', although the cable does nuance that Morocco is not democratic – yet. It is futile for Morocco and POLISARIO to negotiate directly because Algeria is the real problem, a representation reinforced by differentiation between the falsity of Sahrawi nationalism, which is reduced to 'sabre-rattling' by 'youths', against Sahrawi support for autonomy and self-rule. These articulations revolve around the two 'realities' identified in the cable. Firstly, Morocco is unwilling to move from its position on autonomy and will not negotiate otherwise. This, incredibly, is not read as Moroccan intransigence; rather it throws the light back onto the articulation of Algeria as the real 'determinative' of a geopolitical struggle.

In this text we find a succession of binaries, which by now we recognise to be key in articulating powerful textual representations. They are very visibly structured paragraph-by-paragraph, where one makes a representation and the next offers POLISARIO contrast, as is evident between paragraphs 5 and 6 on the right-hand page. The linguistic articulation of 'reality' achieved by contrasting actual and ideal situations in Morocco is the most interesting feature of this cable. It is constituted by nuanced representations (Morocco is not democratic but trying) and radical contrast ('Cuba-like').

This is interesting because they are not a common binary of ideal vs. evil, but rather establish a normative trajectory that is speculative but written authoritatively, which conceals that most are drawn from human-rights announcements the Moroccan government has been making since 2005.[70] In this articulation, common representations known to US diplomats, such as a far-from-ideal situation (Moroccan repression) contra ideal situation (free speech), are replaced by comparative binaries based on dangerous contingencies: far-from-ideal (Moroccan repression) contra potentially worse ('Cuba-like'). Likewise, Morocco's negotiating intransigence is atoned for by Sahrawi nationalism being a lie.

'Reality', it emerges, is framed as a choice between the least bad of two outcomes. Like Pascal's wager, it proves a 'practical' normative duty without substantiating its core assumption, a type of substantiation of belief called fideism. Blaise Pascal, writing in the seventeenth century, posited the contingencies of whether to believe in God in this manner, and in so doing avoided discussing the existence of God while establishing that, in case God does exist, it would be foolish not to have faith.[71] Likewise, this cable's articulation of representation around these contingencies obscures objections to the 'realities' it represents: Algeria's 'geostrategic' ploy and the falseness of Sahrawi nationalism.[72]

This cable is peculiar for its focus on two political lexical genres: governance and geostrategic thinking. Moroccan governance is garnished with governance keywords like 'subsidise', 'social indicators', 'growth' (see paragraph 3). Wording even qualifies royal power: 'by love'. The strategic vocabulary ('asymmetric' diplomacy) explicitly concerns Algeria, particularly when reasoning that Algeria's ideological affinity with a 'fellow liberation movement' is a factor adding to 'historical rivalry'. The first topos marker identified ('power more by love than fear', Moroccan 'real political competition, while perhaps not democracy') signposts the representation of Morocco's admirable development in a frame of temporal progress where democracy is an expected outcome. The 'geopolitical' nature of the conflict signposts the representation of the conflict as a Moroccan–Algerian struggle.

In this text, we recognise two key Moroccan representations, as signposted by the 'artificial conflict' and 'credible proposal' topoi: Algeria's geopolitical designs in relation to the falseness of the Sahrawi cause and the 'realistic' Moroccan proposal. These representations came from earlier Moroccan texts, and, as evident in this cable, had already crossed over to US diplomacy by 2009. Representations of Algeria's geopolitical ploy and of Morocco's generous proposal have the same architecture as that expounded by the king since 2004, analysed in the fourth detailed textual study. The crossover of this representation is further demonstrated by the author's speculation on POLISARIO's limited territorial claims to instantiate the falseness of Sahrawi nationalism, which is original to this cable but is here supporting the selfsame articulation.

It is of interest to compare this cable with the opinion of the US ambassador to Morocco two years before. In a 2007 cable, Ambassador Riley remarked that Morocco consulted on autonomy abroad but not in Western Sahara itself and appears extremely concerned that the United States might endorse 'the Moroccan plan per se' as he felt that Morocco was attempting to impose its unilateral solution by obtaining international recognition for it.[73] In contrast, two years later, representation of 'Western Sahara realities' has deleted the problem of unilateralism and indeed self-determination by writing away actors that need to be consulted: POLISARIO and Sahrawis with grievances, and their entire spatial, temporal, and normative contexts. Unilateralism – and thus the autonomy solution – emerges by default if the history, subjects, and cause of Sahrawi nationalism are written off as Algerian conspiracies.

As well as representations of Western Sahara from Moroccan diplomatic text, the 'Realities' cable also reflects the Bush administration's textualisation of the War on Terror in North Africa, including the need for Morocco as a crucial partner for logistical, military, and torture operations. This suggests that prioritisation of counterterrorism in US policy was key to helping the crossover of Moroccan representations of the conflict, its subjects, and its normative context into US diplomatic knowledge production. Interestingly, this does not take the shape of simply accepting Morocco's shortcomings, as done with other questionable allies of the War on Terror, but rather accepting Morocco's view of itself, the conflict, and the context.

The 2009 'Western Sahara Realities' cable was not only the opinion of a lone diplomat. It is representative of a major shift in US policy and the language in which it occurred. This would become more evident during Secretary Clinton's November 2009 visit to Morocco, when she repeated the cable's language that Morocco's proposal is 'realistic', 'serious', and 'credible', which in turn absorbed the autonomy proposal's own language. This became policy in 2009, complete with the language that Morocco had employed to promote it; was frequently reasserted by the State Department; and went unchanged when John Kerry became Secretary of State.[74]

The crossover of this policy and its language into US diplomatic knowledge and policy raises the question of how this came to pass. Was it policy to disingenuously believe claims of democracy and rule of law that Morocco still lacks, or was this shift in understanding Western Sahara the result of inputs into knowledge production combining with that view being more convenient to implement policy? The next section takes this question to the history of this diplomatic knowledge production across all three actors, tracing the development of this set of representations of Western Sahara, its subjects. and their temporal, spatial. and normative contexts in and among Moroccan, US, and POLISARIO diplomacy.

Tracing the history of diplomatic descriptions in Western Sahara diplomacy 2010 to 2003

The late 2008 shift to supporting Morocco's unilateral proposal was taken on the basis that the proposal was 'realistic' and 'credible', its human rights and democratic progress 'exceptional', and its counterterrorism collaboration essential. These arguments were mutually supporting: the proposal appeared credible to US policymakers because Morocco appeared, unlike other Arab countries, to be on the road to democracy, accountability, and the protection of rights. Moroccan diplomats warned that this progress, and Morocco's role in the War on Terror, were endangered by irresolution of the conflict and POLISARIO. US policymakers concluded that Western Sahara, whether an Algerian plot or a real issue, enabled the 'ungoverned spaces' in which terrorism thrived. US support for autonomy at the expense of self-determination allowed Morocco to reduce negotiations in 2008–9 to either accepting or rejecting the proposal. POLISARIO refused the proposal since it did not include self-determination. As Morocco has since made clear, US recognition of Morocco's sovereignty in 2020 over the territory, granted in exchange for Moroccan recognition of Israel, removed any further need to negotiate with POLISARIO, completing the unilateral imposition of the autonomy solution. Morocco has since renewed political repression in the territory,[75] has not implemented autonomy, and in 2020 sent troops across the neutral zone outside of the Berm, restarting the Western Sahara War.[76]

US acceptance of the autonomy proposal in 2008 is at the heart of these momentous changes, including Trump's subsequent 2020 recognition of Moroccan sovereignty over Western Sahara. This section of our Western Sahara diplomacy case study traces the development of the descriptions upon which this policy shift was predicated. The detailed analyses in the previous sections left us with topoi textual markers signposting these and other key representations, allowing analysis to now trace and examine their history. Going backwards from the aftermath of the representations that supported the decision to support autonomy, examined in the last detailed textual study, this analysis seeks to answer two questions. Firstly, it asks how representations developed in and through diplomatic text, that is, when they changed, appeared, or disappeared; when a specific representation became dominant; and in what context. Secondly, tracing the history of representations determines when and in what manner a representation that determined or justified a policy shift – in this case first and foremost the credibility of the autonomy plan – crossed from one actor's diplomatic knowledge production to another's and was adopted.

Analysing diplomatic texts as we did in the earlier section demonstrates the difference between US understanding of the conflict before and after 2008. After 2008, US text represents Morocco as a quickly developing, exceptionally progressive, like-minded, and indispensable partner in the War on Terror, suffering from agitation that might be partly produced by Algerian designs to destabilise it. Furthermore, we find the powerful representation of the contingency that POLISARIO and the conflict might produce ungoverned borderless safe havens that enable terrorism. Before 2008, US descriptions of the autonomy plan were riven with concern that it was undemocratic, purposefully stalled talks with POLISARIO, expressing concern that it needed improvement in human rights and governance to win Sahrawi 'hearts and minds' and that wide consultation was needed. Backtracking to early 2006–late 2005, we see the beginning of three crucial Moroccan diplomatic representations of the conflict: POLISARIO enables Sahel instability and terrorism, Morocco's human-rights record is improving, and autonomy is 'an advanced form of self-determination'. On the basis of these two chronological clusters of representational shifts in 2008 and 2006–5 and to make exposition more readable for you, long-suffering student of diplomacy, the history of these representations is divided into three periods.

2010–July 2008: 'a long-standing US ally and model'

The diplomacy of this period was impacted by the election of Barack Obama in 2008.[77] He had campaigned on a platform that was generally critical of the Bush-era War on Terror, the Iraq invasion, and extraordinary rendition.[78] This was important to Morocco, which contributed to major counterterrorism initiatives and acted as a subcontractor for extraordinary rendition and torture programmes.[79] Changes in the War on Terror policy could have affected the role and value of this partnership to the United States. Both POLISARIO and Morocco attempted to address the contingency of policy change in this period to their advantage, Morocco by reiterating its strategic value as a reliable ally, POLISARIO by insisting on the need for a self-determination referendum. Policy change concerning Western Sahara did not come.[80] Obama's election marked the end of extraordinary rendition but brought about an expansion of drone warfare and a worldwide drive to locate extremists, which led to intensification of biographic reporting requirements from intelligence and diplomatic sources.[81]

Morocco describes POLISARIO and the conflict as Algerian creations, which justify its position that only unilateral solutions are 'realistic'.[82] This representation has been present in Moroccan diplomacy since the beginning of the conflict in 1975, when it was crucial in persuading Kissinger and Ford, as shown in the historical debates section at the beginning of this chapter. Crucially, almost all issues in Moroccan diplomacy, domestic politics, and even public scandals are blamed on Algerian conspiracies.[83] As explained in 2010 by Moroccan Prime Minister Abbas El Fassi to US Senator Gregg, 'prolonging the conflict benefitted the [Algerian] army and kept it in power'.[84] The claim that the conflict is an Algerian plot is used to attempt to sideline POLISARIO and negotiate directly with Algeria or not at all.[85] It allows for the argument that negotiation is futile and Morocco should be allowed to unilaterally annex the territory with some autonomy as the only 'realistic' solution.[86]

In consequence, the assertion that '[a]utonomy in the Sahara is an advanced form of self-determination in the 21st century'[87] acts as a replacement for self-determination and negotiation with POLISARIO.[88] Even after Clinton had publicly reiterated US support for autonomy in 2009, in a February 2010 meeting with the US Deputy Chief of Mission, Foreign Minister Fihiri 'insisted that only Morocco's proposal is "credible and serious"' and expressed 'continued, deep Moroccan frustration with what [Morocco] perceives as a lack of clear US support', as the US had not followed acceptance of the autonomy solution with recognition of Moroccan sovereignty over Western Sahara.[89]

The autonomy plan could be trusted because Morocco is 'on the move': a progressive, 'reformist' country, an 'oasis of stability amidst a region in turmoil'.[90] Combined with counterterrorist collaboration, this representation is the linchpin of Moroccan representations of Moroccan–US relations and the autonomy plan. They explicitly draw on American concerns about the rapid spread of radicalism in North Africa[91] and promote an exceptionalist view of 'Morocco's role as a model of tolerant Islam', its significant growth, and its development.[92] Progressive achievements include dismantling '130 trafficking networks', and addressing human-rights claims through a reconciliation court – albeit only claims predating the coronation of Mohammed VI.[93] Demonstrating the linguistic standardisation of these representations, phrases like 'the kingdom on the move', 'Morocco's uniqueness in Africa and the Arab world', and Morocco's 'political pluralism' and 'moderation' ('it refuses to deal with HAMAS') as a 'bulwark against extremism' reappear consistently for nearly fifteen years between the mid-2000s and the present.[94]

Conversely, POLISARIO is described as a 'routine' human-rights violator.[95] CORCAS regularly denounces the 'violations of human rights in Tindouf camps', claiming that 'the vast majority of the sequestered population in the camps of Tindouf, south-western Algeria, support Morocco's autonomy initiative for the Sahara'.[96] Reports by the 'Collective of Human Rights Associations in the Sahara' (CHRAS) accuse 'the demons of the polisario' of 'the embezzlement of humanitaren aid [sic]', forced labour, sexual slavery, child exploitation, torture, 'indoctrination lessons', and imprisonment of refugees who are not from 'Moroccan Sahara' but of 'Malian, Algerian or other nationality'.[97] To this day, the contrast between POLISARIO criminality and Moroccan progressiveness is used to oppose a human-rights monitoring role for MINURSO – the only UN peacekeeping mission without such a mandate. Meeting with a US Deputy Assistant Secretary of State, the Moroccan Chief of Intelligence and the MFA Chief of Staff explained monitoring was unnecessary 'since Morocco has willingly become party to all the relevant UN human rights conventions' and is 'open'.[98] This should be seen in the context of Moroccan descriptions of human rights in the territory as equal to the rest of Morocco, attacks on Human Rights Watch,[99] and complaints about State Department human-rights reporting on Western Sahara.[100]

POLISARIO is described as a global threat. Inscribed in the spatial and normative contexts of the War on Terror as both unwitting and wilful enabler, the conflict creates uncontrollable borders which, with POLISARIO criminality, facilitate the activities of terrorists like AQIM and the Movement for Oneness and Jihad in West Africa (MUJAO). Lobbyists MACP regularly publish 'reports' on the Tindouf 'ticking time bomb', refugees that 'fought alongside al-Qaeda' and 'have high-level links with al-Qaeda leaders who operated in Mali; and continue to engage in smuggling drugs and arms in the Sahara/Sahel', while the camps are 'a potential refuge for jihadists'.[101] This thesis was aggressively expounded to Eliot Abrams (of Iran-Contra fame), Assistant National Security Advisor to President Bush until 2009, by a visiting CORCAS delegation in 2009[102] and to US Deputy Assistant Secretary Janet Sanderson in 2010.[103] As corroboration, Moroccan-funded 'intelligence consultants' ESISC assert that POLISARIO is 'blighted by criminality', 'ideological bankruptcy', and 'links between the Polisario and AQIM'.[104] In consequence, 'independence of the Sahara could result in a dependent, inept and chaotic territory failed state dominated by Al Qaida'.[105]

Representation of POLISARIO as a global peril should be read against the Bush administration's concerns about 'ungoverned spaces' as prime enabler of terrorism.[106] As exemplified by the map in Figure 5.2, featured in a MACP article, Moroccan diplomacy places the Sahrawi refugee camps at the meeting point of the 'arc of instability', the 'Cocaine for Arms connection', and terrorism, while identifying Morocco as an indispensable ally.

Moroccan descriptions of the US–Moroccan alliance associate the Saharan issue to Moroccan vulnerability. Frequently stating that if the United States

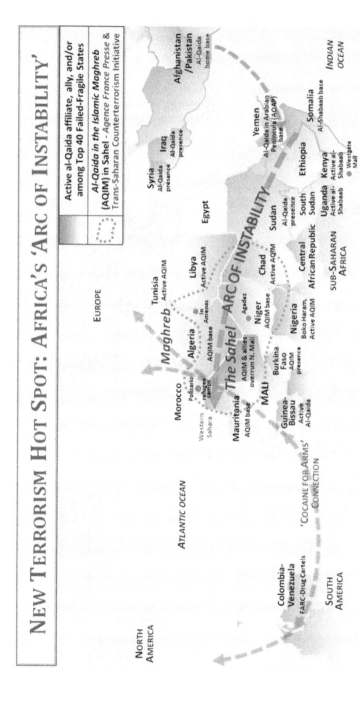

Figure 5.2 Screenshot of map featured on moroccoonthemove.com. 'Morocco on the Move – Terrorism: Two Reports Weigh In after President's State of the Union – Garth Neuffer –', Morocco on the Move, 2014, accessed 6 July 2015, https://moroccoonthemove.com/2014/02/03/terrorism-two-reports-weigh-presidents-state-union-garth-neuffer/

does not help Morocco annex the territory, it might lose a valuable ally, representation of the alliance draws on terrorism, regional instability, and the history of Morocco as the first country to sign a treaty with the United States in 1786.[107] The relationship is represented as founded on shared security, counterterrorism, development, democracy, human rights,[108] the threat emanating from small domestic terrorist groups, desert-based AQIM enabled by crime, and the instability caused by the Saharan conflict.[109] Meeting a five-senator US delegation, Moroccan MFA Secretary General Amrani explained that 'the issue needs to be resolved, he said, because the region cannot afford instability', and concessions to Sahrawis would catastrophically damage Morocco.[110]

Turning to American diplomatic knowledge production, Morocco was seen as an exception among Muslim states. Limits to political reform and unchecked royal power are inscribed within a temporal representation which frames this process as improving towards Western standards. Morocco is described throughout this period as 'a long-standing U.S. ally and model in many respects for other Arab, Muslim and African countries', 'mid-stride in far-reaching transformations, albeit uneven, addressing economic development, political reform, gender equality and religious tolerance.'[111] It draws on a temporal inscription of Moroccan governance where 'gross violations of human rights from 1975 until the end of King Hassan II's regime, and repression intensified after the short-lived Sahrawi uprising of 2005. Since late 2006, Morocco has improved the human rights situation in the territory. Arbitrary arrests have sharply diminished and beatings and physical abuse by security forces have all but disappeared.' This is the core of the oft-cited narrative separating Hassan II, the cruel king, from Mohammed VI, the progressive reformer who should be given time.[112]

The 'bad' and 'good' king narratives and the temporal inscription of development is a crossover from Moroccan representations originating in the 1999 coronation speech of Mohammed VI and promoted to this day. Likewise, MACP's slogan articulation of Morocco's progress ('Morocco on the Move') is absorbed into US diplomatic knowledge and even makes its way verbatim into a scenesetter cable beginning: 'You will find a country that is "on the move" through a range of social, economic and political reforms'.[113] This representation produced significant leniency in analyses of Moroccan repression. For example, the Embassy's analysis of the king's November 2009 speech declaring no quarter for 'traitors' against 'Morocco's territorial integrity'[114] concludes that '[d]espite the harsh rhetoric toward alleged Saharan separatists, there is much good' – a lenient assessment showcasing the influence of temporal and normative inscriptions of Morocco as modernising.[115]

Conversely, US diplomats found that Moroccan allegations of POLISARIO–AQIM collaboration were unfounded. A key report on the issue concludes that '[t]he Mission also agrees with [MINURSO head of mission Harston's] observations that the Polisario and AQIM have very different objectives' and that 'an alliance [...] is unthinkable.'[116] Corroborating, 'Embassy contacts with UNHCR and American NGOs working in the Polisario camps' reported that 'individual Sahrawis have been involved in smuggling activities, but the Polisario "government" severely punishes anyone caught trafficking persons or weapons that could aid terrorists. Polisario also restricts the refugees from accessing extremist websites'. Extremists 'perceive the Sahrawi people as too close to the West and not pious enough'. The same contacts explain that 'if the Polisario were to acquiesce and accept less than a popular referendum with the option of independence, the Polisario would lose the support of the Sahrawi refugees'.[117] The evidence against claims of direct POLISARIO–AQIM collaboration was overwhelming.

From the moment Secretary Clinton adopted it in 2009, the Rabat mission investigated the applicability of the autonomy plan on the ground. Their Sahrawi contacts suggested it 'did not correspond to their desires for and vision of self-determination'.[118] Consul Casablanca notes: [i]f the GOM were serious about the compromise it has proposed under the autonomy, it would do well to begin a more active dialogue with students and other Saharan leaders on the ground rather than try to address the issue only through international diplomacy'.[119] They warn Washington that Morocco's 'whole presentation' is designed 'to lay the groundwork to appeal for US support for the autonomy plan', noting lack of 'any indication that Morocco was willing to reconsider the proposed autonomy plan as the basis for negotiation'.[120] These concerns about the autonomy plan are not, however, carried onto other communications, and never onto policy statements of this period.[121] Scepticism about the autonomy plan simply falls out of US diplomatic knowledge production.

These concerns, like others raised by diplomats in this period – particularly concerning Morocco's 'managed' democracy and corruption involving the Crown;[122] lack of consultation on autonomy; and the arrest, torture, and treatment of activists like Aminatou Haidar,[123] as well as details on POLISARIO itself and its counterterrorist activities – are almost never passed upwards for further reporting and analysis. The scenesetter for Secretary Clinton's 2009 visit, for example, includes this contradiction: Morocco 'is a country in the throes of change and reform. However, the visit follows a crackdown on Shi'a, Christian missionaries, and homosexuals'.[124] That these reports were disregarded in Washington is evidenced in an earlier cable by Secretary Condoleezza Rice commending

Embassy Rabat and ConGen Casablanca for posts' excellent reporting, particularly during the last several months of 2008. As an historic US ally and a robust example of political, economic and social reform to others in the Middle East, events in Morocco impact on our approach to other countries in the region. Your reporting [...] helped to shape decisions regarding the substantial foreign assistance the USG provides Morocco.

Her cable commends specific reports on Western Sahara 'key to shaping USG actions in Washington and New York', none of which contained the significant concerns raised by diplomats, and cables that did rarely reappear in analysis or further reporting.[125]

Tracing the representations contained in the cables that *were* taken into account reveals how this happened. A 2009 cable from State to all missions, an update on previous similar documents, established requirements and frameworks for reporting and assessing its relevance. It was the 'new National [Human Intelligence] Collection Directive (NHCD) on the West Africa Sahel region as well as a request for continued [Department of State] reporting'. In other words, it comprised instructions for diplomats to integrate their reporting into the NSC's National Intelligence Priorities Framework (NIPF).[126] Crucially, it established the assumption that nonstate subjects are potentially linked to terrorist activity. The effect of the NIPF on diplomatic knowledge production is significant: most reporting, even on elections or social initiatives, includes assumed counterterrorism implications, while other information is assumed irrelevant.

As a result of narrowing the relevance of reporting to terrorism, Western Sahara became a variable in regional counterterrorism and Morocco's role therein. This frame appears in diplomatic expressions of support for Morocco's autonomy proposal in this period, which solidly link the two. For instance, the cable analysed in the sixth detailed textual study in this chapter embraces the Moroccan representation of Western Sahara as an Algerian–Moroccan struggle and highlights its threat to regional stability and US counterterrorism objectives. The threat emerging from the Saharan conflict concerns ungoverned borders in the 'vast desert', trafficking, and unsecuritised subjects that assist or join AQIM. The solution was the Trans-Saharan Counterterrorism Initiative, which necessitated the cooperation of Sahelian states.[127] US diplomacy made efforts to jump-start negotiations in the summer of 2008, writing to Security Council members requesting support for a motion calling on Morocco, Algeria, and POLISARIO to negotiate. Tellingly, these démarches were phrased in terms of improving regional relations, particularly Algerian–Moroccan, to facilitate trans-Saharan security.[128] This is how a diplomatic institution sees only what it chooses to see.

POLISARIO focused on emphasising that Western Sahara was never decolonised. This temporal representation posits subjugation to Spain 1884–1975 directly followed by equally unwilling subjugation to Morocco 1975–present.[129] This is why POLISARIO uses the epithet 'Africa's last colony'. All POLISARIO representations analysed describe Moroccan repression, human-rights abuses, and exploitation of the territory's resources as undemocratic and colonial practices. Consequently, description of the conflict focuses on the 'right to self-determination', the referendum mandated by the UN, and the 1975 ICJ ruling,[130] represented as the only 'democratic' solution'.[131] The commitment to democracy is represented as absolute; the Sahrawi people in the camps and representatives of Sahrawis under Moroccan occupation issued a mandate to POLISARIO leaders at successive General Popular Congresses to obtain a referendum to democratically decide their fate. This agonistic approach to democracy has another consequence: POLISARIO would recognise the result of the referendum regardless of whether Sahrawis chose independence, integration, or autonomy.[132]

Morocco is described as aggressively antidemocratic, with Mohammed VI continuing 'the totalitarian traditions of his father'.[133] Moroccan rejections of self-determination in Baker I and II, in which POLISARIO made major concessions, are framed as attempts to avoid any democratic resolution that might not corroborate annexation. Moroccan insistence on negotiating with Algeria is described as a tactic to erase Sahrawi claims, insisting that 'the issue of self-determination only concerned the Polisario and Morocco'.[134] During this period, officials highlight to US diplomats that POLISARIO is having difficulties containing the impatience of Sahrawis, particularly youths born after the 1975–91 war, and that at 'the Polisario Front's last political congress in November 2007, it had taken the Polisario leadership three days to convince the Sahrawi youth that a peaceful solution to the conflict with Morocco was the right solution'. POLISARIO thus presents itself as a moderating influence on Sahrawi demands and expectations which,[135] they insist, reflect fair democratic frustration.[136]

POLISARIO describes Morocco's autonomy plan as a 'tactic' to avoid a vote.[137] Firstly, it is an attempt to fraudulently equate a referendum on autonomy to a self-determination poll. Secondly, Morocco's campaign to persuade the UN Security Council to support autonomy is a move to leverage international support to unilaterally impose its solution,[138] reject international monitoring, and retain powers for the Crown. POLISARIO rejects attempts 'to set the Moroccan autonomy plan as the sole base for discussions', arguing that self-determination requires any referendum to include an independence option, even if autonomy is another option.[139] We scholars are not the only ones to notice the power of the language in describing Morocco's proposal: POLISARIO Ambassador to Algeria Brahim Ghali told US diplomats they objected to 'language such as "realism" and "serious and credible" used to describe' the autonomy proposal because it sidelined self-determination.[140]

Addressing Moroccan accusations of causing instability, POLISARIO blames regional instability on lack of self-determination, which extends the conflict and frustrates hundreds of thousands. To counter accusations of illicit activity, POLISARIO point to their patrols to control smuggling in the Liberated Territories east of the Berm, where they regularly detain drug smugglers, and take any opportunity to demonstrate this to diplomats, NGOs, and journalists visiting Tindouf.[141]

June 2008–early 2006: autonomy 'realism' or 'SHAM'?

Tracing the representations examined above to mid-2008, we find Moroccan diplomacy promoting the autonomy plan. This involved presenting the Crown-appointed CORCAS as a legitimate representative of Sahrawi will, thus as qualified to support the plan on behalf of Sahrawis instead of POLISARIO, and thus to replace self-determination.[142] CORCAS, founded by Hassan II in the 1970s but defunct for twenty years, was re-established in 2006 to promote the autonomy proposal as 'representatives of the Saharan people'.[143] From 2007, Moroccan diplomats sought to obtain that only autonomy should be negotiated at any further talks,[144] a finality we can trace back to a 2007 royal speech stating 'Morocco's intention to negotiate, but solely on the basis of autonomy'.[145] Diplomats claimed that the proposal, analysed in the third detailed textual study in this chapter, fulfilled the UN-mandated exercise of self-determination. Moroccan diplomacy heavily promoted the plan, with three delegations, one led by the king, travelling to Washington to lobby for US adoption.[146]

Backtracking to 2006, we find the logic – and American promise – behind this campaign. Foreign Minister 'Fihri told the Ambassador that he took from consultations with senior U.S. officials that "if we convince you" of the GOM's sincerity in presenting a meaningful autonomy plan, the U.S. would respond in kind by embracing autonomy as the "plan of record" and would work to convince other international actors that this approach is the best way forward'.[147] This is vital, for the autonomy plan, Fihri understood, was explicitly a means to use US influence to bypass self-determination and international law. This is why, for the next three years, Moroccan diplomats and lobbyists worked to allay US doubts,[148] particularly about its democratic and human-rights credibility.[149] When asked about Morocco's 2006 (third) rejection of a UN Human Rights visit, the Moroccan MFA director for UN affairs claimed Morocco 'agreed to the principles of the visit' but was unhappy that the mission did not demand the same scrutiny of Algeria,[150] an argument also used to reject proposals that MINURSO should report on human-rights abuses.[151]

Moroccan diplomacy in the 2008–6 period consistently linked POLISARIO to lawlessness and criminal activities enabling regional terrorism. In a series of comparisons, Interior Minister Benmoussa, in conversation with FBI director Robert Mueller, 'linked the GOM's counterterrorism activities with a need to prevent the Western Sahara from becoming a lawless region ruled by extremists, "like Afghanistan"'.[152] Similarly, CORCAS chairman Khalikhenna Ould Er Rachid compared the status quo in Western Sahara to Somalia.[153] Morocco's head of intelligence stated that 'some members of the POLISARIO have joined AQIM' and that the territory controlled by POLISARIO 'could become a base for terrorist training and operations'.[154] Only Morocco could save the day; at a meeting with the State Department's head of counterterrorism, Morocco's spymaster asserted that 'no Maghreb country, with the possible exception of Morocco, can begin to control its frontiers'.[155] Likewise, emphasising Morocco's alliance with the United States and its reliability, MFA Chief of Staff Amrani told State Department and Embassy officials 'that "Morocco delivers" for its allies, of which he stated the U.S. is the strongest'.[156]

Turning to US diplomacy, in April 2008, we find the policy shift at the heart of our enquiry: Secretary Rice declares that 'to find a way out of the current political impasse through realism', 'the Department of State wishes to publicly announce US support for autonomy under Moroccan sovereignty as the realistic end state for Western Sahara'.[157] US diplomats were instructed to encourage POLISARIO 'to consider engaging realistically in order not to be seen as the cause of a potential breakdown in the negotiations. [... T]he Moroccan autonomy proposal is serious and credible and deserves careful study by the Polisario.'[158]

What made the plan 'credible'? Was it wishful thinking, or disingenuousness to protect an ally? As analysed above, shaping reporting and its relevance through orders from above can have powerful knowledge-production effects, raising some details to unjustified prominence or dropping entire perspectives from diplomatic knowledge. The policy shift was preceded by four months of decreasing frequency and detail in reporting that contradicted the policy. Reporting on Morocco, diplomats still detail police brutality, 'limits to press freedom', the expulsion of Al-Jazeera, and 'authoritarian methods', but in the run up to the policy shift, this was never explicitly linked to Saharan policy.[159]

If we backtrack to 2007–6, American diplomats reported far more critically on the proposal. Indeed, until early 2008, reporting tells a dual story: while autonomy could be realistic and credible, it remains insubstantial in its concessions and lacks democratic consultation.[160] There is substantial explicit questioning of how Morocco's repression of minorities impacts the credibility of autonomy,[161] since in the proposal, 'Rabat would retain full control.'[162] In 2006, Ambassador Riley calls CORCAS a 'SHAM' in the title of a cable, warning that 'CORCAS itself is not a representative institution' and that 'they should not pretend to USG or the rest of the international community that they have the imprimatur of a constituency that has not been consulted'.[163] Diplomats worried that 'any unilaterally-imposed "solution" would prompt retrenchment and hostility',[164] while 'continuing repression and discrimination still constrain their ability to win hearts and minds'.[165] They suggest Morocco 'could take some steps to build confidence that the autonomy proposal is genuine' by legalising human-rights organisations, removing 'known human rights abusers from the territory' and releasing 'some Sahrawi prisoners of conscience', but note this did not occur.[166] US diplomats remained sceptical: 'it remains to be seen, however, if this change in tone is just for our benefit or whether it translates into actual improvement of conditions'.[167]

This comprehensive assessment, too, was the result of instructions. Washington tasked diplomats with reporting on progress linked to the credibility of the plan because US support was explicitly predicated on democracy and rights,[168] resulting in exceptionally energetic reporting in 2007–6.[169] Evaluating the possibility of US support for autonomy, diplomats warn that Moroccan human rights are 'little more than a public relations campaign', highlighting Moroccan refusals to enshrine them in law and institutions.[170] Highlighting why the Ambassador would call this a 'SHAM', American diplomats felt lied to when, canvassing Sahrawi human-rights and activist groups, they found that none, not even government organisations, were 'part of the dialogue that CORCAS claims to seek'.[171] How could Rice, after this, claim that the plan was 'serious and credible'?

Beyond revealing the subtleties of diplomatic descriptions, the cables provide evidence of a conflict between the State Department and the National Security Council on Western Sahara.[172] Earlier, we saw how State reporting came to be directed by the NSC in the 2000s, and how the State Department's previously stated conditions for supporting autonomy were dropped entirely. UN ambassador Bolton corroborated that he and State Department officials sought negotiation, whereas the NSC led by Eliot Abrams prioritised stability for Morocco at any cost. 'They accepted Morocco's line that independence for the Western Sahara – which nearly everyone thought the Sahrawis would choose in a genuinely free and fair referendum – would destabilize Morocco.' The conclusion was that 'stability for king Mohammed VI trumped self-determination'.[173] This conflict sabotaged diplomatic work, suggesting that State had lost considerable influence to the NSC, which was far more concerned with counterterrorism and US-friendly stability.

Analysis of the evolution of representations in diplomatic knowledge production using our method adds substance to the historical account. The NSC trumped the State Department, so presumably Rice either gave in to the NSC's demands, or herself chose to override her approach of conditioning US support for autonomy. This, however, raises a question that only analysis of diplomatic knowledge production can answer: how was this instability presented so successfully, considering the Moroccan monarchy is by far the most successful and long-lasting authoritarian regime in North Africa?

As might be expected, US diplomacy in this period focused on the War on Terror and its requirements. In a scenesetter for Secretary of Defence Donald Rumsfeld, analysed in the fifth detailed textual study, Western Sahara is described as taking up 'roughly two-thirds of the Moroccan army' and resources that 'could be utilized more productively elsewhere'. Most of the missive is, however, concerned with the War on Terror, where Morocco has proven to be an excellent ally in 'intelligence sharing, arrests, border security, and in restricting terrorist financing'.[174] It has since emerged (through leaks and court rulings) that Morocco provided personnel and facilities to detain, torture, and interrogate subjects of extraordinary rendition.[175] The scenesetter explains that US military materiel provision and finance 'play a significant factor in maintaining access to Moroccan bases and training areas and influences Moroccan decision-making in supporting our broader strategic interests'. This, combined with the fear of 'ungoverned spaces' heavily promoted by Moroccan descriptions of the conflict, suggests that Moroccan representations of its place and vulnerability in the War on Terror were more responsible than any other for its capacity to be seen as indispensable to US interests.

POLISARIO, conversely, had little to say about the War on Terror in this period. To a US diplomat attempting to persuade him of the Moroccan autonomy proposal, POLISARIO Ambassador to Algeria retorted he 'could not believe the U.S., with all of its history and values, could confiscate the right of a people to choose their destiny at the ballot box'.[176] With the same consistency and insistence seen in 2010 to 2008, representation of Sahrawi right to self-determination in a referendum is omnipresent, including accepting the result of any referendum that included an independence option.[177] Self-determination and its presence in UN resolutions is so important to POLISARIO that its representative at the UN, Mouloud Said, was dismissed after mistakenly assuring the leadership that the United States still supported a wording including 'self-determination'.[178] Even the autonomy initiative is represented as acceptable should it provide for a self-determination vote – meaning it could not be predicated on Moroccan sovereignty.[179] This draws on the Baker II agreement scuppered by Morocco, which included both an autonomy arrangement and a self-determination vote.

Moroccan diplomacy is represented as seeking to maintain 'the Moroccan status quo' over the territory. They articulate Moroccan rejections of successive negotiated compromises as confirmation of the need for 'the international community to step up pressure and impose sanctions on the Moroccan government to convince it to implement urgently these [UN] resolutions, especially the legitimate right of the Sahrawi people to self-determination through a free, fair and just referendum'.[180] These statements are accompanied by calls to 'ensure that Morocco immediately puts an end to its violations of human rights in the occupied territory'.[181] In contrast, POLISARIO energetically showcases its openness: responding to allegations of a suppressed pro-Moroccan 'uprising' in Tindouf, POLISARIO invited 'the UN High Commission for Human Rights to visit the Tindouf camps to investigate'.[182] This is a constant POLISARIO approach to concretely representing its openness. In contacts with POLISARIO, I too was offered the chance to visit the camps should it be of help for my research – whereas the Moroccan embassy never replied to my requests for interviews. I responded that I was a hunter of diplomatic texts, but I found in the cables that the line was constant with anybody: governments, NGOs, researchers, journalists, and filmmakers. As seen in the analysis of US diplomacy in this period above, these representations did not cross over to US diplomatic knowledge.

2005–mid 2003: Moroccan stability and 'ungoverned spaces'

Backtracking to April 2004, Morocco's response to the Security Council rejecting the Baker II Peace Plan was based on objections to leaving Moroccan sovereignty up to a referendum and a transitional period with a Sahrawi autonomous executive, which would 'usher in an era of insecurity and instability for the whole Maghreb'. Crucially, the document already carries the representation of the conflict we found in US text in 2008: it causes instability; sovereignty is non-negotiable and would destabilise Morocco, and autonomy can 'close the issue of self-determination'.[183] The crossover suggests that what made the 2007 autonomy proposal 'realistic and credible' to US diplomacy, despite being a repetition of the 2004 Moroccan rejection of the Baker Peace Plan, was delivery within Moroccan descriptions that linked it to the utility to the United States of the Moroccan regime and its vulnerability.

The articulation of Morocco's place in the War on Terror is exemplified in Minister of Defence Sbai's statements to US counterparts in 2005 that stressed 'convergence and solidarity in the US–Morocco bilateral relationship' due to Morocco being 'a "laboratory" in which an Arab, Islamic country could make progress promoting democracy', an early iteration of the representation of Moroccan exceptionalism. Since the 2003 Casablanca terrorist bombing, he affirmed, Morocco had worked to fight terror and needed urgent assistance.[184] This representation relates Morocco to the United States through Moroccan fragility and need for a powerful ally with whom to develop counterterrorism. It is in this context that claims that the Saharan conflict was dangerous to Moroccan stability and capacity to collaborate with the United States were most effective, as our analysis found in 2008.

However, why did it take three years to successfully link this representation to its autonomy plan? This analysis suggests this was due to instability in representation of the autonomy initiative from 2003 until early 2008, caused by difficulties in representing Morocco as sufficiently democratic. As demonstrated in the 2008 to 2006 analysis, US diplomats reported Moroccan repression,[185] discrimination, rights abuses, and disregard for law and democracy, and rather crassly discovered that the plan had not been consulted even with handpicked organisations. It did not help that in the early 2000s, Morocco still referred to POLISARIO using Cold War descriptions that had served it well in the 1980s:[186] a 'Cold War orphan beset with decomposition' from 'an independentist extreme left organisation, partly led by adolescents' to 'drifting' towards terrorism and 'the gangrene of organised crime' in line with predecessors 'Stalin' and 'Kim-il Sung', with refugees subject to forced labour, torture, rape, 'forced procreation', malnutrition, murder, and 'systematic diversion of international aid'.[187]

In this period we find the origin of the articulation of empty spaces and Morocco's vulnerability that dominated US reporting until 2010. A 2004 State Department cable relaying the 2003 National Intelligence Priorities Framework (NIPF) re-prioritised focus on ungoverned territory and non-state subjects. Told to assume relations between terrorism and uncontrolled space and subjects,[188] reporting focuses heavily on nonstate actors such as the Tuareg and POLISARIO in Northern Mali, Western Sahara East of the Berm, and Mauritania. This is why pieces of information like Sahrawi grievances and Moroccan repression simply fall out of the diplomatic text: they are not NIPF priorities, while Morocco's need for a solution goes up the chain of reporting stripped of the rest of the issue and its context by the time it reaches policymakers.

We also reach the first articulation of Moroccan vulnerability. Three days after the 16 May 2003 Casablanca attacks, the Embassy reports on the few Moroccan extremist groups they were aware of, concluding that there were a 'few ragtag bands', an assessment that would remain for the next eight years in references to 'small grassroots radical Islamic cells'.[189] This suggests that Moroccan presentation of its vulnerability was not based on danger from domestic terrorism[190] but rather on 'uncontrolled borders'. This is confirmed by a 'top secret' cable from 2005, found thanks to this method's tracing of the 'empty spaces' representation. It reports on the Rabat mission's execution of the decision by the Principals Committee (the central policymaking body of the National Security Council) to improve stability in North Africa by enhancing and intensifying interagency counterterrorism relations with Morocco, 'seeking a solution to the Western Sahara conflict', and 'significantly expanded reporting related to the Western Sahara'.[191] In the representation on which the Principals' decisions are based, terrorist groups pose a threat to the region because they find safe havens in desert 'ungoverned spaces' such as those enabled by POLISARIO's existence, territories in its control, and the refugee camps.

The 'realism' whose story we have been chasing for the first half of this chapter, it turns out, was US need for Morocco's counterterrorism services. Because the NSC's strategy was predicated on Moroccan collaboration, a range of solutions available to the conflict became only one, as no Western Sahara solution could involve deterioration of relations with Morocco or its stability. In 2005, US policymakers had been willing to consider an autonomy solution if it involved human rights, substantial power devolution, and popular consultation,[192] but were sceptical and concerned that Morocco appeared 'determined to have things its way'.[193] There was no explicit decision to let the Western Sahara be annexed. Rather, these concerns fell into irrelevance, out of diplomatic knowledge into State Department cold storage, in the face of more dominant policy concerns. This explains the subsequent persistence of the 'realism' of the autonomy solution in US text, and how self-determination unceremoniously disappears.

Describing Morocco as an essential partner endangered by the Western Sahara conflict was a powerful act. US counterterrorism strategy in the Sahara-Sahel region sought to deny terrorist groups safe haven through counterterrorism partnerships such as the Trans-Saharan Counterterrorism Partnership (TSCT).[194] Moroccan representations of itself and POLISARIO were, over several years, able to carve out agency for Morocco to transform how US diplomacy and policy saw the conflict, its subjects, and its contexts.[195] Morocco was not alone in claiming that US-enhanced security for their state was the only possible bulwark against Islamic terrorism. As application of this method to other diplomatic cases in this period shows, Algeria, Mali and even Gaddafi's Libya also claimed this as they successfully sought US goodwill and assistance in the 2000s.[196] It was self-serving as, to this day, only large deployments (thousands of French troops in northern Mali, 2012–22) and desert-experienced POLISARIO and Tuareg MNLA detachments have succeeded against AQIM and its successors, militarily or in rescuing kidnapped Westerners. For example, in 2011, POLISARIO launched one of few successful armed expeditions across Algeria and Mauritania and into Mali to rescue four kidnapped Spanish volunteers.[197] Morocco, like Algeria, Mali, and Libya, was successful in making actors like the Tuareg or POLISARIO – their long-term enemies – appear part of the problem.

POLISARIO

POLISARIO descriptions of the conflict concentrated on implementing the Baker II Peace Plan and Moroccan bad faith. During an August 2005 visit by Senator Lugar, POLISARIO leader Abdelaziz expounded the post-Baker POLISARIO view: Baker's seven-year negotiation was scuttled by Morocco, who sought to prevent democratic expression of both Sahrawis and Moroccans. Conversely, POLISARIO 'sought a democratic solution and asked that the UN be allowed to organise a referendum'. Abdelaziz differentiated between Morocco and SADR, which was already a democracy where Sahrawis sought the same rights as Americans and 'rejected religious extremism'.[198] They additionally emphasise their frustration that, after the rejection of Baker II by Morocco, the United States expects POLISARIO and not Morocco to make further concessions.[199]

In this period, we find POLISARIO efforts to address terrorism concerns and inscribe themselves on the American side of the binary. Ambassador to Algiers Beissat explained that POLISARIO 'was not a threat to Western interests, but rather sought to be a stabilizing factor in an unstable region' and 'suggested that Polisario was interested in engaging with EUCOM [NATO European Command] in support of efforts to fight GSPC and other terrorist organisations', 'asserting that the only capable, indigenous military forces with a proven desert combat record in the Trans-Sahel were Polisario and the northern Chadians'.[200]

In a counter-name-calling effort demonstrating awareness of the power of descriptions, POLISARIO Foreign Ministry director Sidi Omar responded to the above-analysed 2005 ESISC report accusing POLISARIO of 'decaying' into crime and terror, arguing that POLISARIO has 'clean nationalist objectives'. This nine-page reply demonstrates that POLISARIO was aware that their struggle was playing out partly over representation in diplomacy. Turning to the camps, it explains that not only are there no abuses, but also that POLISARIO's progressive ideological position has brought changes: SADR is a democracy; slavery (a Sahrawi practice still present in Mauritania) was abolished in 1975; women have significantly better rights, education, and prospects than in Morocco; and camp inhabitants are free to move.[201] This letter highlights the nuance of Sahrawi criticism of Moroccan actions since 1975, clarifying, as Abdelaziz did to US diplomats, that 'our enemy is not Morocco but the phenomenon of Moroccan colonization'.[202] None of these representations were observed to have crossed over into US diplomatic text.

It is now possible to map the history of representations of subjects and their contexts that we have traced within the diplomacy of the three main actors involved, with a focus on the most important representations to have crossed over.

Figure 5.3 summarises how the conflict, its actors, and its contexts were represented from 2010 back to 2003. The horizontal rows represent each actor's knowledge production, staggered to highlight how this occurred across multiple texts. The representations traced across texts, the most important observed, are marked by textured lines and symbols, one for each representation. Two key policy moments are highlighted: Condoleezza Rice's 2008 policy shift from self-determination to supporting Morocco's unilateral autonomy proposal, and its reiteration by Hillary Clinton in 2009. Four key representations crossing from Moroccan to US diplomacy are indicated by 1–3.

Observations

Our journey through diplomatic knowledge production on the Western Sahara conflict is almost complete. Detailed textual studies determined how communications constituted representations of subjects and their temporal, spatial, and normative contexts, as well as retrieved their inscription within subjective discourses. Key dynamics were observed of relevance to this case and to diplomatic knowledge production.

Like in the textual studies of the Vietnam case, it was found that representations, such as Morocco's human rights and democracy, necessarily draw on the discursive site at which they surface, in this example well-known precedents such as the Baker II plan, the referendum, and UN standards, against which Moroccan proposals were inevitably benchmarked. The next chapter (Chapter 6) takes this insight forward, arguing that the discursive site at which representations emerge is an important factor in determining their stability, cohesion, and relationality.

In an important addition to the poststructuralist literature and analytics on language and identity, this method was able to retrieve the role played by the exact articulations of a representation, that is, the precise configuration of a description and its framing, such as Morocco's representation of

188 *Hand of the prince*

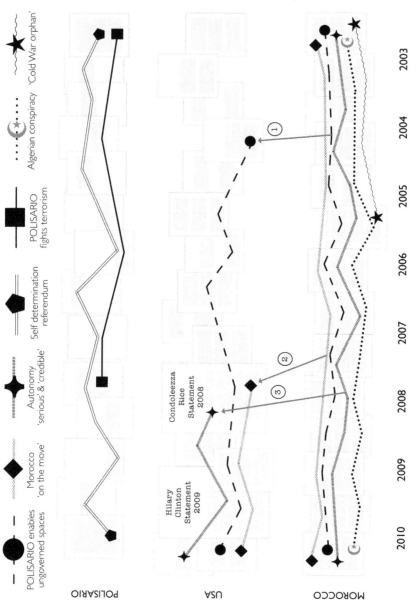

Figure 5.3 Diagrammatic summary of the evolution of key representations traced from 2010 back to 2003.

autonomy as equal to self-determination. Retrieving the precise articulation of this description made it possible to, firstly, determine its diplomatic role (reject questioning of Moroccan sovereignty) and, secondly, determine its conditions of possibility (rejection of an internationally mandated and supervised multilateral process). This, in turn, explains the role of other representations such as descriptions of the conflict as an Algerian creation – which is here revealed to play a key role as it is vital to imposition of a unilateral Moroccan solution.

A detailed empirical understanding of representations made it possible to match them to its topoi textual markers ('credible' and 'serious' for unilateral autonomy, for example). These enabled genealogical analysis to follow their evolution through the diplomatic knowledge production of multiple actors. This determines precisely whether and how diplomacy can transform the representations in the knowledge production of another actor, changing how another country's diplomacy sees a given situation.

This analysis produced one of the first extensive empirical accounts of the diplomacy of the Western Sahara conflict in the 2000s.[203] It substantiates the thesis that representations of dangers to Morocco's alliance with the United States were instrumental in securing US support for unilateral annexation.[204] It was determined that the basis of this diplomatic rapprochement was not domestic terrorism as such but, more specifically, the role of desert 'ungoverned spaces' and subjects in enabling the activities of terrorists, and the need for Moroccan counterterrorism collaboration. While this might appear speculatively logical, this analysis empirically substantiates it and, crucially, accounts in detail for *how* it occurred institutionally and in diplomatic practice.

Analysis identified when specific representations crossed over to the diplomatic knowledge production of another actor, and the conditions of this event. Several representations did not. For example, Moroccan representation of the conflict as an Algerian creation was not believable to US diplomats principally because of discursive instability in its articulation rather than belief in POLISARIO.[205] This instability arose from incoherence in Moroccan articulations of Algerian obstinacy, which varied from Cold War dogmatism to geostrategic rivalry, and from American diplomats corroborating Moroccan unwillingness to negotiate. POLISARIO efforts to represent themselves as counterterrorist and offer assistance in regional counterterrorism initiatives also failed to cross over and were never heard of again.

Six key Moroccan articulations made an impact in US diplomatic text by 2008. The first four are related and mutually supportive: POLISARIO's role in facilitating 'ungoverned spaces', the danger of the terrorist activity thus facilitated, Morocco's domestic terrorism as 'small grassroots', and

Morocco as counterterrorism's most reliable North African ally. The most impactful crossover concerned 'ungoverned spaces' and the role of non-state actors in facilitating and exploiting them. It was convincing because it reflected key aspects of US concerns about Sahel instability as demonstrated by instructions prioritising reporting on securing territory, borders, and subjects. Morocco consistently represented areas of Western Sahara outside its control as safe haven for terrorists, impossible to police due to POLISARIO. While US text did not accept representations of POLISARIO as being directly involved, there were concerns that refugees might be ripe for radicalisation. The last two crossovers observed are Morocco's progressiveness and the autonomy plan as a 'credible' solution. They are mutually dependent: autonomy is not practicable if Morocco is a brutal totalitarian monarchy. This is why the solution, mooted as early as 2004, did not become 'credible' until 2008, when concerns about Moroccan practices in the territory were deprioritised.

A vital representation observed is Morocco's subalternity. Far older than the others, which emerged in the 2000s, it played a crucial role in representation of its progress, framing failure as an inevitable temporal defect, and is accompanied by expressions of will to improve. With deficiencies thus inscribed, representation of Moroccan progressiveness could plausibly mirror American normative political identity in democracy, development, trade, and human rights while 'on the move' towards their fulfilment. This drew on a representation of Morocco as less backward and corrupt than other African countries.[206] An important enabling factor is European and American tourism since the 1920s, particularly to Marrakesh, and – as Egypt in Sharm-el Sheikh, or Thailand in Pattaya – ensuring strict laws on alcohol, drugs, sex work, and homosexuality are not applied to foreigners,[207] though this causes bitter Moroccan public conflicts about profitable clubbing and prostitution havens for drunken Europeans.[208] This representation of exceptionality underwrote other representations and was heavily drawn upon by Morocco's promotion of itself as 'the Kingdom on the move'.

The conditions of possibility enabling these crossovers can now be determined. Moroccan descriptions could comfortably exist within US representations of terrorism and North Africa because representations operate within contextual realms of knowledge that condition their viability. For a popular culture example, a US TV drama about an American soldier lost in the desert depicts the Western Sahara Liberated Territories as a safe haven for criminal Luc, who explains that they were in 'the middle of nowhere, Western Sahara. No sign of life for miles.'[209] This is a common image in relation to Saharan terrorism, featuring heavily in British and American representations of the 2013 Algerian refinery hostage crisis, for example, which through language like 'vast', 'uninhabited', and 'uncontrolled' described a space of 'roaming' criminals, nomads, and terrorists.[210] Representations found can be further linked to and explored with scholarship on cultural and identity discourses. In the Sahara, Western discourses posit that in ancient times, Tuareg and other nomads lived in harmony; however, just as Europeans were arriving, they became decadent, criminal, and dangerous.[211] The image that emerges is a chaotic space of Darwinian struggles, violence, and crime.[212] Evidently, this is not the case: POLISARIO aggressively patrols the territory it controls, and there is no evidence of a 'narco-jihadist' nexus.[213] In the case of the empty desert, like with Moroccan exceptionalism, a representation can itself enable others.

Another vital condition for the crossovers is dominant policy concerns. US counterterrorism policy prescribed controlling space, borders, and subjects, which granted Moroccan diplomacy an opportunity to shape US representations of the conflict. In the radical binary of the War on Terror, POLISARIO became a terrorism-enabling factor and Morocco one facilitating counterterrorism. Simply existing in opposition to Morocco reinforced POLISARIO's terrorism-enabling credentials. The prioritisation of counterterrorism in US diplomatic reporting drew diplomats to report on intelligence-mandated targets and paradigms, particularly the control of subjects and borders. Consequently, contradictory information in reports from the ground, even concerns that Moroccan officials misled American diplomats, was not passed up the chain of reporting nor drawn upon for policymaking. Where in the 1940s, instructions to find communists shaped diplomatic reporting significantly, in the 2000s, State Department reporting became subsumed into the National Intelligence Priorities Framework (NIPF),[214] making diplomatic reporting an appendix of intelligence so that diplomatic cables could be made useful to defence analysis.[215] This had significant effects: as analysed, representation of POLISARIO was hollowed out and came to be dominated by terrorist-enabling 'ungoverned spaces', insecure borders, criminal activity, despairing youth, and a distraction for Moroccan forces that 'could be utilized more productively elsewhere'.[216]

Reporting on conditions in Western Sahara became so obscured that only three months before the start of mass demonstrations and repression in 2010, diplomats reported calm, with Sahrawis increasingly 'convinced' and 'curious' about the autonomy plan. The first demonstration was peaceful, as advocated by Aminatou Haidar, the 'Sahrawi Ghandi'.[217] Protesters established a camp featuring traditional Sahrawi tents and poetry competitions. It was violently dismantled on 8 November 2010 by the Moroccan military (see Figure 5.4), resulting in numerous deaths and further protests.[218]

The reporting feedback loop emerges as a key factor in the constitution of diplomatic knowledge and, as in the above example of events in 2010, can impact its quality. It can also determine the vulnerability of diplomatic

Figure 5.4 8 November 2010: Moroccan police (foreground) and military move to dismantle the protest camp (far background) in al-'Ayun. Note the Moroccan flags and royal portrait. This is one of very few photos of that day's events as the Gendarmerie banned photography, recordings, and journalists. Courtesy of Associazione El Ouali per la libertà del Sahara Occidentale, Italia.

text to other actors' diplomatic textual interventions. By making specific concerns so reportable that any information is passed on with the highest relevance, the door is opened for relevant representations from other actors to be uncritically absorbed. This is how any representations containing terrorism, 'ungoverned spaces', and nonstate subjects are reported with the highest priority, to the extent that sometimes these words alone prove relevance. Enshrining specific concerns, it condemns all others to the dustbin – a tragedy considering that reporting from the ground was at times excellent but disappeared into irrelevance.

These insights allow for a thicker and more substantive account of the diplomacy of the conflict 2003–10. Firstly, identifying key representations on which policies were based, their journeys in and out of an actor's diplomacy and potentially into another's, and the conditions that made this possible adds detail to, specifies, and nuances an otherwise threadbare historical account. We found that, as Bolton claimed, NSC trumped the State Department and Rice either gave in to NSC or agreed to give Western Sahara to Morocco to support the War on Terror. The method here elaborated substantiates precisely *how* this occurred and diplomacy played a role in constructing and delivering them. In Western Sahara, the most powerful argument was based on a specific understanding of 'ungoverned spaces' as enablers of global terrorism, and relatedly, the place of Morocco in these concerns. This representation, it has been shown, thrived in a specific ecosystem of representations, knowledge production, practices, policymaking, and relations between them.

This account analytically relies on text but is not limited to it. While this method relies on examining diplomatic writing, diplomatic textual production is but evidence of many diplomatic practices, and specifically in this approach of diplomatic knowledge production and transmission. These texts do not on their own shape worldviews, belief systems, and policy, but do stand as evidence of the knowledge that does and, crucially, the history of its development. Once again, in this case study, the method did not reveal a Kennan-like text that single-handedly shifted paradigms about Western Sahara. Rather, it accounted for a gradual evolution that consisted of several threads governed, limited, or promoted by diplomatic leaders, which came to absorb views from Morocco's diplomatic descriptions. It might well be the case that nobody was ever convinced of Morocco's autonomy plan and, quietly in a White House dominated by recorder-averse and document-shredding Dick Cheney,[219] a decision was made to give Western Sahara to Morocco in exchange for assistance in torturing suspects and securitising a desert full of ungoverned militants. This could be why from 2008 reports carrying caveats were ignored; I was not able to determine. But this too was based on a specific view of desert terrorism and left marks on diplomatic knowledge production for us to study.

Crucially, the view of the Sahara that justified such choices is itself a representation, one all the more urgent to study because it was very inaccurate. Some of it came from Morocco, amplified beyond proportion by instructions given to diplomats. Whether truth or lie, this was the basis of the disaster of Western Sahara diplomacy. Determining, tracing, and understanding the history of this evolution is warranted because, ultimately, even the realist-sounding priority of controlling 'ungoverned spaces' through Morocco by recognising its 'serious and credible' autonomy solution was based on a diplomatic description.

Representations can even form the basis of and enable the most transactional diplomacy. This might sound counter-intuitive, but if international relations are political, then normative subjectivity is always at play and thus too representation of what alliances cost. This is how even policymakers claiming to exercise realpolitik like Trump or Putin feel the need to perform a remarkable amount of normative arse-covering. For ultimately, a norm is always at play, and subjectivities like norms require normative descriptions.

Returning to representations, transactionalism, and Western Sahara, when in 2020 President Trump's Middle East envoy Jared Kushner signed a deal to recognise Moroccan annexation of Western Sahara in exchange for Moroccan recognition of Israel, it was in exchange for a 'proclamation' wherein

> The United States affirms, as stated by previous Administrations, its support for Morocco's autonomy proposal as the only basis for a just and lasting solution to the dispute over the Western Sahara territory. Therefore, as of today, the United States recognizes Moroccan sovereignty over the entire Western Sahara territory and reaffirms its support for Morocco's serious, credible, and realistic autonomy proposal as the only basis for a just and lasting solution to the dispute over the Western Sahara territory. The United States believes that an independent Sahrawi State is not a realistic option for resolving the conflict and that genuine autonomy under Moroccan sovereignty is the only feasible solution.[220]

Notes

1. Ali Salem Iselmu, 'El Mundo de Los Ignorados', accessed 15 July 2015, http://generaciondelaamistad.blogspot.co.uk/2015/06/poema-de-ali-salem-iselmu-en-apoyo-la.html. My translation.
2. Where possible, I use Sahrawi transliterations of place names and people. Likewise, for Algerian and Moroccan institutions, their preferred official names and abbreviations in French transliterations are used.
3. The other successful annexations are Tibet and Crimea. The other postwar military annexations – East Timor, Eritrea, Namibia, and Kuwait – have all been reversed, while West Irian was UN sanctioned. Munene Macharia, 'Multiple Colonialism in Western Sahara', *Journal of Language, Technology & Entrepreneurship in Africa* 2 (2), 2010, 178–95.
4. S. Zunes and J. Mundy, *Western Sahara: War, Nationalism, and Conflict Irresolution* (Syracuse, NY: Syracuse University Press, 2010), 238.
5. Taken Question, 1/5/2008, Office of the Spokesman, Department of State.
6. 'Reply of the Kingdom of Morocco', enclosure to 'Report of the Secretary-General on the Situation concerning Western Sahara', S/2004/325, UN.
7. 'Proclamation on Recognizing the Sovereignty of the Kingdom O=of Morocco over the Western Sahara – The White House', accessed 21 September 2022, https://trumpwhitehouse.archives.gov/presidential-actions/proclamation-recognizing-sovereignty-kingdom-morocco-western-sahara/
8. Tony Hodges, *Western Sahara: The Roots of a Desert War* (Westport, CT: L. Hill, 1983), 104.
9. International Court of Justice, 'Western Sahara: Advisory Opinion of 16 October 1975', ICJ, accessed 15 July 2015, http://www.icj-cij.org/docket/index.php?sum=323&p1=3&p2=4&case=61&p3=5; George Joffé, 'The International Court of Justice and the Western Sahara Dispute', in *War and Refugees: The Western Sahara Conflict*, eds Richard Lawless and Laila Monahan (New York: Pinter, 1987).

10 E. G. H. Joffé, 'The Moroccan Nationalist Movement: Istiqlal, the Sultan, and the Country', *The Journal of African History* 26 (04), 1985, 289–307; 'Nationalism and the Bled: The Jbala from the Rif War to the Istiqlal', *The Journal of North African Studies* 19 (4), 2014, 475–89.

11 This claim sets Morocco against the 1964 OAU Algiers Convention, which established the principle that colonial frontiers should be maintained to avoid conflict. Douglas E. Ashford, 'The Irredentist Appeal in Morocco and Mauritania', *Political Research Quarterly* 15 (4), 1962, 641–51; George Joffé, 'Self-Determination and Uti Possidetis: The Western Sahara and the "Lost Provinces"', *Morocco: Journal of the Society for Moroccan Studies* (1), 1996, 97–115.

12 A. A. Heggoy, 'Colonial Origins of the Algerian-Moroccan Border Conflict of October 1963', *African Studies Review*, 1970, 17–22; C. Richard Pennell, *Morocco since 1830: A History* (New York: NYU Press, 2000); for contemporary reports of nationalism on the ground, see Attilio Gaudio, *Guerres et Paix Au Maroc: Reportages, 1950–1990* (Paris: Karthala Editions, 1950).

13 G. Joffé, 'Morocco: Monarchy, Legitimacy and Succession', *Third World Quarterly* 10 (1), 1988, 201–28.

14 Khadija Mohsen-Finan, 'Sahara occidental: De la prolongation du Conflit à la nécessité de son règlement', *Politique Étrangère* 61 (3), 1996, 665–75; 'Le règlement du conflit du Sahara occidental', *Politique Africaine* No. 76 (4), 1999, 95–105; 'Maroc : l'émergence de l'islamisme sur la scène politique', *Politique Étrangère* Printemps (1), 2005, 73–84.

15 Mundy, 'Neutrality or Complicity?', 298.

16 Mundy, 'Neutrality or Complicity?', 297.

17 See Cable 'the scene' to CIA, 14/11/1975, CIA-RDP86100608R000300010093-7; State and USIB Bulletin, 31 December 1975, CIA-RDP79T00975A028400010049-3; 'CIA Weekly Summary', 19 December 1975, CIA-RDP86T00608R000300020054-9.

18 This period saw the only direct outside military intervention of the conflict when French jets bombed POLISARIO columns in the 1977 Operation Lamantin. Hodges, *Western Sahara*, 249.

19 Leo Kamil, *Fueling the Fire: U.S. Policy & the Western Sahara Conflict* (Trenton, NJ: Red Sea Press, 1987), 63.

20 Zunes and Mundy, *Western Sahara*, 140–52.

21 Pablo San Martín, 'Nationalism, Identity and Citizenship in the Western Sahara', *The Journal of North African Studies* 10 (3–4), 2005, 565–92; Randa Farah, 'Sovereignty on Borrowed Territory: Sahrawi Identity in Algeria', *Georgetown Journal of International Affairs* 11 (2), 2010, 59–66; Jacob Mundy, 'Performing the Nation, Pre-Figuring the State: The Western Saharan Refugees, Thirty Years Later', *The Journal of Modern African Studies* 45 (02), 2007, 275–97.

22 Zunes and Mundy, *Western Sahara*, 153.

23 M. J. Stephan and J. Mundy, 'A Battlefield Transformed: From Guerilla Resistance to Mass Nonviolent Struggle in the Western Sahara', *Journal of Military and Strategic Studies* 8 (3), 2006, 1–32.

24 Alice Wilson, 'On the Margins Of the Arab Spring', *Social Analysis* 57 (2), 2013, 81–98.
25 Tara Flynn Deubel, 'Poetics of Diaspora: Sahrawi Poets and Postcolonial Transformations of a Trans-Saharan Genre in Northwest Africa', *The Journal of North African Studies* 17 (2), 2012, 300.
26 See Pablo San Martín, '"¡Estos Locos Cubarauis!": The Hispanisation of Saharawi Society (… after Spain)', *Journal of Transatlantic Studies* 7 (3), 2009, 249–63.
27 The poem by Ali Salem Iselmu at the beginning of this chapter was originally written in Spanish. See also Pekka Tarkki, 'El Español En Los Campamentos de Refugiados de La República Arabe Saharaui Democrática', in *Romania Arabica*, ed. Jens Lüdtke (Tübingen: Gunter Narr Verlag, 1996), 83.
28 The most detailed and most extensive treatment of these negotiations and debates over voting lists is by former MINURSO head Erik Jensen, *Western Sahara: Anatomy of a Stalemate* (Boulder, CO: Lynne Rienner Publishers, 2005).
29 Zunes and Mundy, *Western Sahara*, 233; Jensen, *Western Sahara*. See also S/RES/1541 (2004), UN.
30 'Reply of the Kingdom of Morocco', Enclosure to 'Report of the Secretary-General on the Situation Concerning Western Sahara', S/2004/325, UN.
31 Zunes and Mundy, *Western Sahara*, 247.
32 Taken Question, 1/5/2008, Office of the Spokesman, Department of State.
33 Mundy discusses the autonomy plan in some detail, concluding that considering that it consisted primarily of a revival of CORCAS – under Royal authority only – it granted even less democratic rights than those available in Morocco. Zunes and Mundy, *Western Sahara*, 244.
34 Zunes and Mundy, *Western Sahara*, 141.
35 Zunes and Mundy, *Western Sahara*, 144.
36 Press Statement, 11/6/2010, CORCAS.
37 Zunes and Mundy, *Western Sahara*, 219.
38 Irene Fernández-Molina, *Moroccan Foreign Policy under Mohammed VI, 1999–2014* (London: Routledge, 2015); Irene Fernández-Molina, 'Introduction: Towards a Multilevel Analysis of the Western Sahara Conflict and the Effects of Its Protractedness', in *Global, Regional and Local Dimensions of Western Sahara's Protracted Decolonization*, eds Raquel Ojeda-Garcia, Irene Fernández-Molina, and Victoria Veguilla (London: Palgrave Macmillan US, 2017), 1–33.
39 Lawrence Cline, 'Counterterrorism Strategy in the Sahel', *Studies in Conflict & Terrorism* 30 (10), 2007, 889–99.
40 Ricardo René Larémont, 'Al Qaeda in the Islamic Maghreb: Terrorism and Counterterrorism in the Sahel', *African Security* 4 (4), 2011, 242–68.
41 'CIA Tapes Prove Morocco Rendition', *The Australian*, accessed 31 July 2015, http://www.theaustralian.com.au/news/world/cia-tapes-prove-morocco-rendition/story-e6frg6so-1225907071320; 'MI6 and CIA "Sent Student to Morocco to Be Tortured"', *The Guardian*, accessed 31 July 2015, http://www.theguardian.com/world/2005/dec/11/politics.alqaida

42 This is evident in pre-Wikileaks analysis. See Katharina Natter, 'The Formation of Morocco's Policy Towards Irregular Migration (2000–2007): Political Rationale and Policy Processes', *International Migration* 52 (5), 2014, 15–28; Michael Willis and Nizar Messari, 'Analyzing Moroccan Foreign Policy and Relations with Europe', *The Review of International Affairs* 3 (2), 2003, 152–72; John Damis, 'Morocco's 1995 Fisheries Agreement with the European Union: A Crisis Resolved', *Mediterranean Politics* 3 (2), 1998, 61–73.

43 '"Oui, j'étais un agent de renseignement"', *Sud Presse*, 2010, accessed 7 August 2011, http://archives.sudpresse.be/temoignage-l%26%238217-aveu-%26%238220-oui-j%26%238217-etais-un_t-20101108-H2RCPD.html

44 All of its websites contain the slogan 'Morocco on the Move'. See MACP, 'Morocco on the Move'; 'Autonomy Plan – The Kingdom on the Move', 2015, accessed 1 August 2015, http://www.dailymotion.com/widget/jukebox?list[]=/ma/relevance/user/MAPTV_maroc/channel/news/lang/fr/search/sahara&skin=default&autoplay=0&logo=1&no_tabs=1&syndication=145387

45 For more details of its interagency strategic policymaking role see Gabriel Marcella, 'National Security and the Interagency Process', *US Army War College Guide to National Security Policy and Strategy*, 2004, 239–60.

46 Several cables congratulating diplomats on their reporting suggest this. See particularly 7/1/2009, 09STATE1621.

47 In this book I refer to both the state-in-waiting, SADR, and the movement, Frente POLISARIO, as POLISARIO, except when referring to official SADR bodies and government posts.

48 Confided to US DCM Algiers, 8/5/2007, 07ALGIERS637.

49 The 2007 12th Congress almost voted to resume war, a vote that was very narrowly defeated, to the relief of the leadership. 'Polisario 13th Congress Concludes and Confirms "Ignoring Right of Saharawi People, Will Threaten Peace and Stability in the Region" | Sahara Press Service', 2011, accessed 2 August 2015, http://www.spsrasd.info/en/content/polisario-13th-congress-concludes-and-confirms-%E2%80%9Cignoring-right-saharawi-people-will-threaten

50 The complicated research ethics of using leaks are discussed in Chapter 3. All Wikileaks cables cited can be searched using their reference number ('07USUNNEWYORK192' for example) at https://wikileaks.org//plusd/, accessed 16 October 2024.

51 I could not confirm that any of its member associations exist. They do not reply to emails (to Hotmail addresses) and have no websites or contact details besides those on the reports themselves.

52 Screenshots are provided for each detailed textual study.

53 Zunes and Mundy, *Western Sahara*, 221.

54 This is a constant; see Sahara Press Service, 'Polisario Front Intervention before UN Special Committee of Decolonization (C-24) Kingstown, 31 May–June 3, 2011', accessed 4 August 2015, http://www.spsrasd.info/node/841

55 Sidi M. Omar, 'The Right to Self-Determination and the Indigenous People of Western Sahara', *Cambridge Review of International Affairs* 21 (1), 2008, 41–57.

56 Compare with Laurence S. Hanauer, 'Irrelevance of Self-Determination Law to Ethno-National Conflict: A New Look at the Western Sahara Case', *Emory International Law Review* 9 1995, 133.
57 Compare with Comments on Western Sahara in Colin P. Clarke and Christopher Paul, 'From Stalemate to Settlement: Lessons for Afghanistan from Historical Insurgencies' (Washington DC: RAND, 2014), 32, accessed 6 August 2015, http://www.rand.org/content/dam/rand/pubs/research_reports/RR400/RR469/RAND_RR469.pdf
58 Bureau of Public Affairs Department Of State. The Office of Website Management, 'Remarks With Moroccan Foreign Minister Taieb Fassi-Fihri', Remarks|Remarks, U.S. Department of State, 2009, accessed 3 August 2015, http://www.state.gov/secretary/20092013clinton/rm/2009a/11/131229.htm
59 Constitución de España, 'Estatuto de Autonomía de Cataluña', accessed 4 August 2015, http://www.congreso.es/consti/estatutos/ind_estatutos.jsp?com=67
60 'Moroccan Constitution', Maroc.ma, accessed 4 August 2015, http://www.maroc.ma/en/content/constitution; Alfred Stepan, Juan J. Linz, and Juli F. Minoves, 'Democratic Parliamentary Monarchies', *Journal of Democracy* 25 (2), 2014, 41; 'Seven Myths about Democracy in Morocco', openDemocracy, 2015, accessed 4 August 2015, https://www.opendemocracy.net/arab-awakening/till-bruckner/seven-myths-about-democracy-in-morocco
61 This is probably in respect to Western concerns in this respect and particularly a riposte to POLISARIO pride that over a third of the Sahrawi National Council (its parliament) membership are women, the highest proportion in Africa and the Middle East and higher than in the UK Parliament (32 per cent).
62 Joffé, 'Morocco: Monarchy, Legitimacy and Succession'.
63 George Joffé, 'Sovereignty and the Western Sahara', *The Journal of North African Studies* 15 (3), 2010, 375–84. Ironically, if this claim to sovereignty is transferred to spatial conceptualisations, the only time the 'southern provinces' were unified with Morocco was under the eleventh-century Almoravid Dynasty, when Senhaja Tuareg tribes conquered the lands between northern Iberia and Senegal.
64 George Joffé, 'Frontiers in North Africa', in *Boundaries and State Territory in the Middle East and North Africa* (Wisbech: Menas Press, 1987).
65 Yahia H. Zoubir, 'The United States and Maghreb–Sahel Security', *International Affairs* 85 (5), 2009, 977–95; G. Joffé, 'The European Union and the Maghreb', *Mediterranean Politics* 1 1994, 22–46; George Joffé, 'The European Union, Democracy and Counter-Terrorism in the Maghreb', *JCMS: Journal of Common Market Studies* 46 (1), 2008, 147–71.
66 Kenneth Anderson, 'Denial of Territory to Terrorist Groups in US Counterterrorism Strategy', SSRN Paper (Rochester, NY: Social Science Research Network, 2013), accessed 21 January 2015, http://papers.ssrn.com/abstract=2463289
67 The development model uniformly applied in North Africa through this period was distinctly supply-side and neoconservative. In Mali, rapid privatisation

and state disvestment caused the collapse of cotton farming; James Gow, Funmi Olonisakin, and Ernst Dijxhoorn, 'Deep History and International Security: Social Conditions and Competition, Militancy and Violence in West Africa', *Conflict, Security & Development* 13 (2), 2013, 231–58.
68 David Gutelius, 'Islam in Northern Mali and the War on Terror', *Journal of Contemporary African Studies* 25 (1), 2007, 59–76.
69 Crucial for the interrogation of terrorism subjects. See Bureau of Public Affairs Department of State, The Office of Electronic Information, 'Article 98 Agreements and the International Criminal Court', 2006, accessed 5 August 2015, http://2001-2009.state.gov/t/pm/art98/
70 The initiative was, initially, a consultative council very similar to the Sahrawi CORCAS, which then evolved into an interministerial department that reports to the King. All of its reports are translated to English and republished by representatives of Morocco abroad such as embassies and MACP. See 'Délégation interministérielle aux droits de l'homme', DIDH, accessed 21 September 2022, https://didh.gov.ma/en/node
71 Blaise Pascal, *Pensées*, Edition Brunschvicg (Paris: Editions de Cluny, 1934).
72 A representation of which I hope Sahrawi protests and bloody clashes in October 2010 and in 2021–22 disabused the author.
73 5/4/2007, 07RABAT601.
74 'Remarks at the Opening Plenary of the U.S.–Morocco Strategic Dialogue', US Department of State, 2012, accessed 17 December 2022, https://2009-2017.state.gov/secretary/20092013clinton/rm/2012/09/197711.htm
75 Human Rights Watch, 'Morocco and Western Sahara: Events of 2021', in *World Report 2022*, 2021, accessed 22 September 2022, https://www.hrw.org/world-report/2022/country-chapters/morocco/western-sahara
76 'The Failed Diplomacy between Morocco and Polisario', accessed 22 September 2022, https://www.aljazeera.com/news/2020/11/18/the-failed-diplomacy-between-morocco-and-polisario
77 I too wondered, in my very first academic publication, whether the Obama administration might change tack on Western Sahara considering the changes the president sought to bring about to the War on Terror: Pablo de Orellana, 'Remember the Western Sahara? Conflict, Irredentism, Nationalism and International Intervention', E-IR, 2009, accessed 16 October 2024, http://www.e-ir.info/?p=2005
78 'Obama Delivers Bold Speech About War on Terror', ABC News, 2007, accessed 6 August 2015, http://abcnews.go.com/Politics/story?id=3434573&page=1; '2008: Obama on Terrorism', *New York Times*, 2007.
79 'CIA Tapes Prove Morocco Rendition'.
80 23/10/2009, 09RABAT865.
81 Colum Lynch and Elias Groll, 'Obama's Foreign Fighters Campaign Is a Gift to the World's Police States', *Foreign Policy Blogs* (blog), 2014, accessed 30 September 2014, http://thecable.foreignpolicy.com/posts/2014/09/30/obama_s_foreign_fighters_campaign_is_a_gift_to_the_world_s_police_states?utm_content=buffer80246&utm_medium=social&utm_source=facebook.com&utm_campaign=buffer

82 7/10/2010 CORCAS.
83 For example, when one of Morocco's best-known pop stars was detained in Paris for sexual assault, Morocco blamed an Algerian conspiracy. 'Saad Lamjarred: France Detains Moroccan Star over Rape Charge', *BBC News*, 2018, sec. Europe, accessed 22 September 2022, https://www.bbc.com/news/world-europe-45559959; 'Moroccan Star Faces Third Rape Charge', *BBC News*, 2018, sec. Europe, accessed 29 August 2018, https://www.bbc.com/news/world-europe-45319394. Likewise, when the king of Morocco was filmed drunk in Paris, that too was blamed on 'a miserable attempt by separatists and with them Algerians' to discredit the king, see 'The Video of "Mohammed VI Drunk in Paris" Makes the Buzz ... and the "Manager of the Pages of the King of Morocco" Clarifies', Morocco Detail Zero, 2022, accessed 18 December 2022, https://morocco.detailzero.com/news/44745/The-video-of-Mohammed-VI-Drunk-in-Paris-makes-the-buzzand-the-Manager-of-the-Pages-of-the-King-of-Morocco-clarifies.html
84 1/2/2010 10RABAT63.
85 11/2/2010, 10RABAT114; 13/8/2009, 09RABAT693; 10/7/2009, 09RABAT589.
86 25/6/2009, 09RABAT541; 2/3/2010 CORCAS.
87 11/6/2010 CORCAS.
88 29/3/2010 CORCAS.
89 11/2/2010, 10RABAT114.
90 'Moroccan "Exceptionalism" Deserves Support', Morocco on the Move, accessed 7 August 2015, http://moroccoonthemove.com/2015/08/05/moroccan-exceptionalism-deserves-support-american-interest/
91 'North Africa New Test for U.S. as Terror Cells Spread', *New York Times*, 2013.
92 1/2/2010 10RABAT63.
93 16/2/2010, 10CASABLANCA20; 9/2/2006, 06RABAT215.
94 20/10/2009, 09RABAT859.
95 MACP, 'Morocco on the Move – The Truth about the Polisario', Morocco on the Move, accessed 1 August 2015, http://moroccoonthemove.com/policy/the-truth-about-the-polisario/
96 17/9/2010 CORCAS; 5/4/2010 CORCAS. While the language savvy-MACP and MAP use 'kidnapped', CORCAS uses the misleading translation of the French 'séquestrés': 'sequestered'.
97 'The embezzlement of Humanitaren aid by the Polisario'; 'The Polisario detains confined population in the camps of Tindouf, South of Algeria, against their will', CHRAS; 'Stop the breaking up of families: let the children go back to their mothers'; 'The violation of humain rights in the camps of Tindouf' [*sic*], these three CHRAS reports were provided to the author by the Moroccan Embassy in London in July 2015.
98 See cables March–May 2009, particularly 28/4/2009, 09RABAT365; 29/4/2009, 09RABAT363; 7/4/2009, 09RABAT293; 27/3/2009, 09RABAT249; and 16/2/2010, 10RABAT127.

99 See, for example, from this period, Human Rights Watch, 'Human Rights in Western Sahara and in the Tindouf Refugee Camps', 2008, accessed 1 August 2015, https://www.hrw.org/report/2008/12/19/human-rights-western-sahara-and-tindouf-refugee-camps
100 All available at Department of State, 'Human Rights Reports', 2009, accessed 16 October 2024, http://www.state.gov/j/drl/rls/hrrpt/. See Moroccan complaints in 22/7/2008, 08RABAT684.
101 MACP, 'FAQ Western Sahara Conflict' (MAPC, 2012), accessed 1 August 2015, http://moroccoonthemove.com/wp-content/uploads/2014/02/FAQ_WesternSaharaConflict2.pdf; MACP, 'Morocco on the Move –The Truth about the Polisario', accessed 1 August 2015, http://moroccoonthemove.com/policy/the-truth-about-the-polisario/
102 27/12/2010 CORCAS; 16/2/2009 CORCAS.
103 16/2/2010 10RABAT127.
104 'The Polisario Front and the development of terrorism in the Sahel', May 2010, ESISC.
105 19/5/2010 CORCAS.
106 Larémont, 'Al Qaeda in the Islamic Maghreb'; Cline, 'Counterterrorism Strategy in the Sahel'; Zoubir, 'The United States and Maghreb–Sahel Security'.
107 It is never mentioned that the treaty stipulated that the United States pay tribute to the Sultan in exchange for safety for US shipping from Moroccan corsairs. MACP, 'Morocco on t he Move'.
108 MACP, 'Morocco on the Move – US–Morocco Bilateral Relationship', Morocco on the Move, accessed 6 August 2015, http://moroccoonthemove.com/policy/us-morocco-bilateral-relationship/
109 17/3/2009, 09RABAT212.
110 22/2/2010, 10RABAT15; 26/2/2009, 09RABAT172.
111 9/2/2010 10RABAT108.
112 11/12/2009, 09RABAT971.
113 The slogan is omnipresent (see detailed textual study 3); MACP's website is moroccoonthemove.com, 27/10/2008, 08RABAT1031.
114 Royal speech, 6/11/2009, my translation.
115 12/11/2009, 09RABAT908. The same is true of the US Embassy's fieldtrip to the infamous Prisión Negra ('Black Prison', a well-known torture centre) in al-'Ayun.
116 16/12/2008, 09RABAT1154.
117 16/12/2009 09ALGIERS1117; 7/12/2009, 09ALGIERS1082.
118 15/12/2009, 09RABAT977.
119 23/4/2009, 09CASABLANCA79.
120 19/10/2009, 09RABAT854; 13/8/2009, 09RABAT693.
121 See 17/2/2010, 10STATE14132.
122 6/9/2009, 09RABAT752; 14/7/2009, 09RABAT605.
123 18/12/2009, 09RABAT990; see also 16/12/2009, 09PARIS1704; 11/12/2009, 09RABAT971; 15/12/2009, 09RABAT977.
124 7/4/2009, 09RABAT293.

125 7/1/2009, 09STATE1621.
126 16/4/2009, 09STATE37566.
127 17/8/2009, 09RABAT706; similar with Clinton, see 12/11/2009, 09RABAT908.
128 21/8/2008 08SANJOSE684; 20/8/2008, 08JAKARTA1581; 20/8/2008, 08HANOI972; 20/8/2008, 08BEIJING3192 and particularly instructions for these démarches in 19/8/2008, 08STATE88795.
129 See the 'history' sections of POLISARIO websites, 'Sahara Press Service | Sahara Press Service', accessed 9 August 2015, http://www.spsrasd.info/; 'Western Sahara–Sahara Occidental', accessed 9 August 2015, http://www.arso.org/index.htm
130 10/3/2007, 07USUNNEWYORK192.
131 1/12/2009 09ALGIERS1063.
132 4/8/2009, 09ALGIERS729; 1/12/2009, 09ALGIERS1063; 4/5/2009, 09ALGIERS442.
133 22/11/2009, 09ALGIERS1041.
134 27/8/2009, 09ALGIERS781.
135 22/11/2009, 09ALGIERS1041.
136 25/8/2008, 08ALGIERS935.
137 10/3/2007, 07USUNNEWYORK192.
138 1/12/2009 09ALGIERS1063.
139 4/8/2009, 09ALGIERS729.
140 4/5/2009, 09ALGIERS442.
141 1/12/2009, 09ALGIERS1063; see, for example, 'Inside the Cold War in the Desert', VICE News, accessed 7 August 2015, https://news.vice.com/article/inside-the-cold-war-in-the-desert
142 14/2/2008, 08RABAT140; 31/10/2006, 06RABAT2016.
143 See homepage, corcas.com
144 5/12/2007, 07RABAT1814.
145 Royal speech, 30/7/2007. My translation.
146 13/2/2007 MAP.
147 31/10/2006, 06RABAT2016; 28/3/2006, 06RABAT552.
148 1/3/2007, 07RABAT395.
149 26/12/2006, 06RABAT2337.
150 14/4/2006, 14/4/2006, 06RABAT671; 7/4/2006, 06RABAT637.
151 3/7/2006, 06RABAT1280.
152 9/7/2007, 07RABAT1119.
153 6/6/2006, 06RABAT1087.
154 19/2/2008, 08RABAT150.
155 19/2/2008, 08RABAT152.
156 23/8/2007, 07RABAT1340.
157 19/4/2008, 08STATE41408; 31/3/2008, 08STATE33088.
158 3/7/2007, 07USNEWYORK545; 19/4/2008, 08STATE41408; 31/3/2008, 08STATE33088.
159 20/6/2008, 08RABAT570; 9/5/2008, 08RABAT416.
160 28/4/2008, 08ALGIERS483.

161 17/5/2007, 07RABAT880.
162 19/3/2007, 07RABAT494.
163 In capitals in the original. 13/12/2006, 06RRABAT2254; 6/10/2006, 06RABAT1874.
164 5/4/2007, 07RABAT601.
165 30/3/2007, 07RABAT572.
166 29/4/2008, 08RABAT378; 23/1/2008, 08RABAT70.
167 5/12/2007, 07RABAT1814, see also 30/3/2007, 07RABAT573.
168 Instructions cited as STATE200675 in 26/12/2006, 06RABAT2337; the conditionality of the plan on rights and democracy is most evident in 22/9/2006, 06RABAT1775 and 2/3/2006, 06USUNNEWYORK401; see also 26/12/2006, 06RABAT2337.
169 The only exceptions found are 23/10/2006, 06RABAT1984 and 20/12/2007, 07RABAT1873.
170 1/3/2007, 07RABAT395.
171 14/6/2006, 06RABAT1159.
172 14/4/2006, 06USUNNEWYORK794.
173 J. Bolton, *Surrender Is Not an Option: Defending America at the United Nations* (New York: Threshold Editions, 2008), 368.
174 9/2/2006, 06RABAT215.
175 'CIA Tapes Prove Morocco Rendition'; 'Court Sides with C.I.A. on "Extraordinary Rendition"', *New York Times*, 2010; 'MI6 and CIA "Sent Student to Morocco to Be Tortured"'; Nina H. B. Jørgensen, 'Complicity in Torture in a Time of Terror: Interpreting the European Court of Human Rights Extraordinary Rendition Cases', *Chinese Journal of International Law* 16 (1), 2017, 11–40.
176 28/4/2008, 08ALGIERS483.
177 7/1/21, 08ALGIERS21; 30/10/2006, 06RABAT2010; 4/4/2006, 06ALGIERS623; 28/2/2006, 06ALGIERS342. This is consistent in other POLISARIO outlets such as ARSO and SPS.
178 8/5/2007, 07ALGIERS637.
179 20/3/2008, 08ALGIERS335; 10/3/2007, 07USNEWYORK192.
180 2/8/2006, 06ALGIERS1418.
181 7/1/21, 08ALGIERS21.
182 4/6/2006, 06ALGIERS1002.
183 'Reply of the Kingdom of Morocco', Enclosure to 'Report of the Secretary-General on the Situation Concerning Western Sahara', S/2004/325, UN.
184 3/6/2005, 05RABAT1162.
185 See, for example, 13/12/2005, 05RABAT2475.
186 For an excellent account of the 1970s–80s frame of reference, see Mundy, 'Neutrality or Complicity?'.
187 'The Polisario Front: Credible Negotiations Partner or After-Effect of the Cold War and Obstacle to a Political Solution in Western Sahara?' November 2005, ESISC.
188 Cited as 04STATE179667 in cables that cite and reference it; updated in 2009 in cable 16/4/2009, 09STATE37566.

189 9/2/2010, 10RABAT108.
190 As argued by Mundy, Zunes and Mundy, *Western Sahara*, 144.
191 3/3/2005, 05RABAT458.
192 23/9/2005, 05RABAT2008.
193 16/8/2005, 05RABAT1721.
194 Larémont, 'Al Qaeda in the Islamic Maghreb', 262.
195 Lianne K. Boudali, 'The Trans-Sahara Counterterrorism Partnership', 2007; Anderson, 'Denial of Territory to Terrorist Groups in US Counterterrorism Strategy'.
196 Pablo de Orellana, 'The Power of Describing Identity in Diplomacy: Writing Subjects, Territory, Time and Evil at the End of Gaddafi's Libya', in *A New Theory and Practice of Diplomacy: New Perspectives on Diplomacy*, eds Jack Spence, Claire Yorke, and Alastair Masser (London: I. B. Tauris, 2021); de Orellana, 'When Diplomacy Identifies Terrorists: Subjects, Identity and Agency in the War on Terror in Mali'; de Orellana, '"You Can Count on Us": When Malian Diplomacy Stratcommed Uncle Sam and the Role of Identity in Communication'.
197 The Spanish media found this thrilling and extensively reported on the chase and the rescue: 'Los Secuestradores Trasladan a Malí a Los Cooperantes de Tinduf', El Periódico, accessed 1 August 2015, http://www.elperiodico.com/es/noticias/internacional/gobierno-evita-atribuir-qaeda-secuestro-los-dos-cooperantes-espanoles-tinduf-1194712; *El Polisario Saca a Los Cooperantes No Imprescindibles de Los Campamentos de Tinduf*, 2013, accessed 1 August 2015, http://www.abc.es/internacional/20130123/abci-polisario-saca-cooperantes-tinduf-201301231059.html; 'Secuestran a Dos Españoles En El Sáhara', *El Mundo*, 2011, accessed 1 August 2015, http://www.elmundo.es/elmundo/2011/10/23/solidaridad/1319358758.html
198 22/8/2005, 05ALGIERS1768.
199 20/5/2005, 05ALGIERS1011.
200 11/9/2005, 05ALGIERS1910.
201 Reply of the SADR Ministry of Foreign Affairs to the ESISC, 29/9/2005, retrieved August 2010 at arso.org as ESISC never published the reply.
202 13/6/2005, 05ALGIERS1199.
203 First published, in far briefer form, as de Orellana, 'Struggles over Identity in Diplomacy'.
204 Zunes and Mundy, *Western Sahara*, 214.
205 As analysed in detailed textual study 6, POLISARIO nationalism was in doubt.
206 This representation of Morocco was most recently visible in the 2022 Qatar Football World Cup.
207 A fantastic example of this representation is this fun-weekend-out piece 'Instant Weekend … Marrakech', *The Guardian*, 2008, sec. Travel, accessed 15 August 2015, http://www.theguardian.com/travel/2008/dec/21/marrakech-morocco-weekend-break where 'there's even a branch of the famous Ibiza club Pacha'.
208 'Immersion dans le monde des hommes prostitués', Afrik.com, accessed 15 August 2015, http://www.afrik.com/article26130.html; 'Maroc : L'homo

sexualité est encore taboue', *Le Point*, 2015, accessed 15 August 2015, http://www.lepoint.fr/editos-du-point/mireille-duteil/maroc-l-homosexualite-est-encore-taboue-19-06-2015-1938079_239.php; Agence France-Presse, 'Moroccan Teenage Girls to Face Trial on Homosexuality Charges', *The Guardian*, 2016, sec. World News, accessed 3 November 2016, https://www.theguardian.com/world/2016/nov/02/moroccan-teenage-girls-to-face-trial-on-homosexuality-charges; *Marrakesh Medina: Neocolonial Paradise of Lifestyle Migrants? Contested Spatialities, Lifestyle Migration and Residential Tourism* (London: Routledge, 2013).

209 'American Odyssey', 2015, episode 3.

210 'Hardline Mali Rebel Demands Stall Hopes for Peace', *New York Times*, 2015; 'Algeria Hostage Crisis: Desert Siege Ends in Bloodshed', *The Telegraph*, 2013, accessed 15 August 2015, http://www.telegraph.co.uk/news/worldnews/africaandindianocean/algeria/9813195/Algeria-hostage-crisis-desert-siege-ends-in-bloodshed.html.

211 Jean-Claude Vatin, 'Désert construit et inventé, Sahara perdu ou retrouvé: Le jeu des imaginaires', *Revue de l'Occident Musulman et de La Méditerranée* 37 (1), 1984, 107–31.

212 A representative example of this European representation of the dangerous desert is *Tintin: Le Crabe aux Pinces d'Or* (Tournai: Egmont, 2011).

213 Wolfram Lacher, 'Challenging the Myth of the Drug–Terror Nexus in the Sahel', WACD Background Paper (West Africa Commission on Drugs – Kofi Annan Foundation, 2013), accessed 7 August 2015, http://www.wacommissionondrugs.org/wp-content/uploads/2013/08/Challenging-the-Myth-of-the-Drug-Terror-Nexus-in-the-Sahel-2013-08-19.pdf

214 16/4/2009, 09STATE37566.

215 Which is, notably, what permitted Chelsea Manning to access and leak them.

216 17/8/2009, 09RABAT706

217 'Western Sahara Activist on Hunger Strike', *The Guardian*, 2009, sec. World News, accessed 17 August 2015, http://www.theguardian.com/world/2009/nov/17/western-sahara-hunger-strike

218 Wilson, 'On the Margins Of the Arab Spring'; Inmaculada Szmolka, 'Western Sahara and the Arab Spring', in *Global, Regional and Local Dimensions of Western Sahara's Protracted Decolonization* (New York: Springer, 2017), 101–19.

219 Clint Hendler, 'What We Didn't Know Has Hurt Us: The Bush Administration Was Pathological about Secrecy. Here's What Needs to Be Undone after Eight Dark Years – and Why It Won't Be Easy', *Columbia Journalism Review* 47 (5), 2009, 28–33; Marcy Lynn Karin, 'Out of Sight, but Not Out of Mind: How Executive Order 13,233 Expands Executive Privilege While Simultaneously Preventing Access to Presidential Records Note', *Stanford Law Review* 55 (2), 2002, 529–70.

220 'Proclamation on Recognizing the Sovereignty of the Kingdom of Morocco over the Western Sahara – The White House'.

6

The confessions of the diplomatic text: writing, representation, and the reflection of will

'Charley Fortnum's no good to you as a hostage.'
'He is a member of the diplomatic corps', Aquino said.
'No, he isn't. An Honorary Consul is not a proper Consul.'
[...] 'But he is a British *Consul*.'
Doctor Plarr began to despair of ever convincing them of how unimportant Charley Fortnum was. He said, 'He had not even the right to put CC on his car.'

Graham Greene, *The Honorary Consul*[1]

Our journey through the diplomatic archives is nearing its end. We are reaching the embankment by the Lungarno degli Acciaiuoli to make fall in Florence. Segretario della Repubblica Machiavelli is waiting for us on the quayside. It is time to report the findings of our mission. We walk past the Republic's administration at the Uffizi, where the missives from my mission were received and processed, and up to his office at the Palazzo Vecchio (Figure 6.1). Pigliamo un caffè strada facendo.[2]

The last two chapters have interrogated the empirical evidence of two case studies to determine how diplomatic text constitutes representations of subjects and their temporal, spatial, and normative contexts; how these evolve across diplomatic knowledge production; and how they might enter another actor's knowledge. The empirical studies, powered by the method developed in this book, yielded observations on how diplomacy wrote about, evaluated, and interpreted these conflicts, their subjects, and their contexts. This chapter takes these findings back to international political thought.

Detailed textual studies showed how language establishes descriptions and relations among them. We encountered gardening metaphors (Indochinese 'fertile ground' for communism, Sahrawis 'ripe' for radicalisation) that established the political horizon of subjects, their agency, and how they were linked to discourses of colonial and postcolonial subjects. Descriptions and their interpretations could suffer from instability and

Figure 6.1 Left: the author about to report to the Segretario di Stato. Right: the offices of the Florentine Republic, including Machiavelli's diplomacy-focused Second Secretariat of State, both at the Palazzo Vecchio. Photographs by Fey Marin, 2023.

become unbelievable due to contradictory descriptions (Vietminh as both fascist *and* communist, POLISARIO communist *and* Islamist) as well as from contradictions in writing about oneself (French colonialism and the abuses of the Moroccan regime). The discursive context within which subjects and their contexts are described was a vital factor in creating hierarchies of knowledge where Moroccan human rights abuses in the 2000s became domestic details in the frame of the War on Terror.

Analysing how diplomatic descriptions evolved, we found some were dropped, while others, like 'Morocco on the Move', were reproduced, their representations copied into further texts travelling up knowledge production to policymakers. Demonstrating how in practice power is invested in diplomatic knowledge and its production, we saw Secretary Rice and Foreign Secretary Bevin shape its production, sometimes disingenuously. This was shown to have significant effects, overemphasising some factors, or leading to inaccurate knowledge, as found with Vietnamese–Soviet conspiracy theses or Sahrawis enabling terrorism. Otherwise, obvious information, like Vietminh being a diverse alliance united to achieve independence, or POLISARIO's own fight against extremism, dropped entirely from diplomatic knowledge as it developed from text to text. In some key cases, descriptions entered and gained prominence in the diplomatic knowledge production of other actors, empirically revealing the circumstances of their articulation and successful crossover.

What determines the domestic and foreign impact of a representation? Five dynamics were observed that condition, firstly, the domestic impact of a specific understanding of subjects, territory, time, and norms; and, secondly, their capacity to impact the diplomatic knowledge practices of another actor. These are not policy conditions and factors, but rather conditions that determine the viability of diplomatic descriptions in the context of policy and diplomatic practice. They are determined by language and its functioning as a machinery that communicates subjective positions, which is why we need to take them back to concepts of language and politics to understand how they work. For example, deciding to fight communism worldwide is not one of these five conditions. They are, however, closely related and draw upon it. They include: how the policy is described (looking for 'fifth columnists' for example), the management of knowledge production that emerges from policy (prioritising search for any sign of communism), the stability of a representation linked to it (Vietminh 'fellow-traveller'), the context in which a representation emerges (claiming Vietminh were fascists in the context of the Cold War), and how a representation is articulated (Vietminh taken over by communists *because* oriental). Representations depend on these conditions to emerge and be inscribed in a discursive context that grants them agency to convince.

These conditions are related and mutually constitutive. They can be understood drawing on Foucauldian conceptualisations of knowledge producing practices that enable and condition the emergence of objects of discourse within discursive formations. This perspective is why I have forced my reader to bear the aesthetic atrocity of calling our object of study 'diplomatic knowledge production'. The five conditions of representation are discussed, conceptualised, and related to one another in the first section across five subsections. The final part of this chapter discusses the agency and power of diplomatic descriptions. This conceptual discussion is the last move in this project exploring how diplomacy constitutes representations of subjects and their contexts and what makes them persuasive to interlocutors. The ultimate consequence of this very real power cannot be understated: persuading policymakers, or even those of another country, of your view of certain subjects and their contexts grants you unprecedented influence over their policymaking.

The conditions of diplomatic description

This project has followed an inductive research model to understand the emergence and evolution of representations in diplomatic communication. This approach inductively demonstrated under what circumstances representations impacted knowledge production within the diplomatic and policy establishment that made them, as well as when other actors found them persuasive. To assure empirical certainty, representations that crossed from one actor's cascade of knowledge production to another's while retaining the same structure – sometimes the same wording like Morocco 'on the move' – empirically demonstrated when representations achieved this act of persuasion. The five conditions advanced over the following pages are a conceptual effort to make sense of the dynamics observed in this empirical analysis.

To represent subjects, space, time, and norms is to constitute Foucauldian objects of discourse, the currency of the knowledge production we have studied. The homogeneity, coherence, and grounding of discourses are not immanent to the objects they classify and enunciate, but rather emerge from how practices like description establish relations among objects. In sum, there are 'conditions necessary for the appearance of an object of discourse'. Foucault considers the utility of studying objects of discourse in relation to where their coherence is most apparent: 'the first surfaces of their emergence' (discursive sites where objects emerge), 'the authorities of delimitation' (who classifies them), and 'the grids of specification' (the rationale for classification). These categories do not form objects on their own – they are only three of many potential constitutive factors. They are expressions of 'the historical conditions necessary for the appearance of an object', which is 'but discourse as a practice': the expression of 'a group of *rules* that are immanent in a practice and define its specificity'.[3]

Establishing rules conditioning knowledge production is what we witnessed when Secretary Rice issued reporting targets. We can therefore consider diplomatic knowledge production as a practice that determines the constitution of its objects of study through rules that restrict where objects surface, their classification, and their classification rationale. Foucault was correct in arguing that these three conditions were never alone but only the most common.[4] This project identified a further two: the internal mechanics of the articulation of representation, and the piece of knowledge that governs knowledge production: dominant policy concerns. The five conditions shape the practices where power (of Segretario Machiavelli or the NSC) is invested in ordering, creating, highlighting, obscuring, and destroying knowledge.[5] The production of representations is therefore determined by the conditions of practice found at these sites. The next five sub-sections discuss them in relation to observations in the empirical chapters.

1. The architecture of articulation

The architecture of links and differentiations within an articulation of representation determines its shape. Articulation of Vietminh as a Soviet stooge is more complex than simply shouting 'Commie': it requires claiming Soviet–Vietminh links. Articulations, small constructions, greater than vocables but smaller than discourses, exhibit regularity in 'types of statement, concepts or thematic choices', exhibiting specific 'order, correlations, positions and functionings'.[6] As the textual studies showed, articulations organise links and differentiations between referents within a representation. An example is linking Morocco's fragility and counterterrorism efforts to POLISARIO enabling ungoverned space. This is a structure whose architecture furthermore determines its relations with other representations.

Representational architecture is constrained by the specific referents present in its articulation, textualised by vocables and linguistic devices. I do not use an architectural metaphor lightly: I draw on the philosophy of architecture as the government of spatial existence, determining what space, light, emptiness, and the material signify for the soul through the aesthetic language of stone, brick, and mortar.[7] The architecture of articulation determines representation by ordering the deployment of linguistic means and referents. This is how we can conceptualise what happens between single words and representations in diplomatic text.

An architectural conceptualisation of articulations reflects and draws attention to the multiple levels and objects of analysis we have found to be part of each representation. These are the articulation, its component 'thematic choices',[8] and the referents inside each thematic grouping. Analysing the architecture of articulations grounds our understanding of representations as a descriptive practice on the linguistic mechanisms found on the page. This forces analysis to consider how articulations of representation draw on presence as well as on absence. In representations, the presence or omission of referents is crucial to the form of the articulation and its interaction with others.

Figure 6.2 schematises the architectural conceptualisation of articulation. It shows the representation of Vietminh articulated in French diplomatic text and absorbed by US diplomatic text in 1948. The diagram shows how the architecture articulates relations among its components. The representation is built of three thematic groups (the circles), each of which includes various referents, lines representing specific subjective linkages. As textual studies showed, representations do not include every possible theme or referent. In the articulation in the diagram, to omit representation of Vietminh as a *league* including nationalists and monarchists as well as communists is one such crucial choice. Articulations may include referents that inscribe subjects, space, time, or norms, but most frequently they include some from all four. This shows that it was worthwhile deconstructing political identity in this way, as there are key details to retrieve when the four do not move in tandem.

The confessions of the diplomatic text

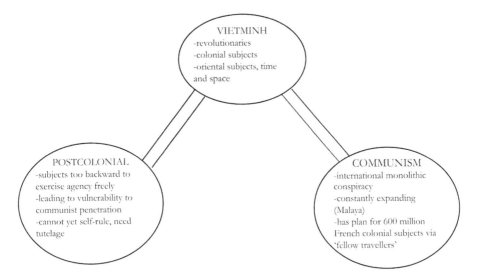

Figure 6.2 Architecture of a representation of Vietminh as analysed in Chapter 4.

Articulations are the most basic form of representation observed. Conceptualising the discursive formations of representation in diplomatic text as articulations inserts them into the Foucauldian processes of discursive formation, delimitation, and construction.[9] The architectural perspective, meanwhile, highlights the need to account for the details of their internal construction. This allows us to relate them to other representations and analyse how they relate to the other conditions that determine their future.

2. Planes of emergence

Once articulated, when to bring up representations? This issue appeared unexpectedly in application of the detailed textual studies.[10] The United States represented its policy as contemporarily hostile to and supportive of colonialism, both supportive and suspicious of Vietnamese emancipation. This only appeared coherent when these discrete acts of differentiation surfaced at three superposed yet separate discursive sites: civilisational development, colonial sovereignty, and Cold War blocs. Emergence into these separate discursive sites, which I call planes of emergence, explains how it is possible for multiple representations to coexist without incoherent contradiction.

Representation of US sympathy to colonial emancipation could coexist with supporting French colonial war only when support for French anticommunism was differentiated from Vietminh communism at a separate plane. This allows for the coexistence of multiple and contradicting aspects of representation that make sense when hierarchically ordered. Planes of emergence are choices as to the discursive contexts in which representations surface. Political instability might have local or global repercussions, which is indicated by the plane where the author chooses to inscribe the articulation. Diplomatic texts usually feature similar planes of emergence for a length of time. Planes of emergence vary; for example, British diplomacy in the 1940s featured a distinct 'imperial' plane of emergence centred on India even after its independence.

Separation into generic planes of domestic, regional, and global significance is constant between the 1940s and the present, making it the most permanent and significant hierarchical order of inscription observed. US articulations of Morocco's democratic record, progress, and improvement were found in opposition to the articulation of POLISARIO human-rights abuses and trafficking. The site where both articulations emerge is that of domestic politics and crime, which the text always subjugates to the regional instability POLISARIO enables and Morocco fights, in turn less salient than the global War on Terror, which is strikingly delocalised. Figure 6.3 schematises how referents emerged at different planes in the Western Sahara case.

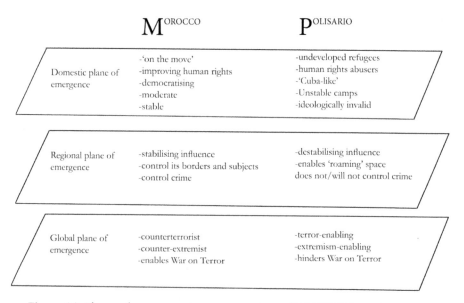

Figure 6.3 Planes of emergence in representations of POLISARIO and Morocco studied in Chapter 5.

The confessions of the diplomatic text 213

In the representation of the Western Sahara conflict analysed in Chapter 5, the emergence of representations into separate planes was betrayed by the different linguistic and discursive mechanics at work in each. 'Destabilising' is relevant at the domestic and regional levels, but at the global level, the discursive effect of 'destabilisation' is enabling terrorism. The global-level plane is remarkable, for since WWII it draws on geostrategic vocabulary – in the Vietnam case, very much ethnogeostrategic.[11] Referents of representation at different planes draw on one another: terror-enabling at the global level depends on instability at domestic and regional levels.

This conceptualisation draws on Foucault's 'surfaces of emergence': sites of practice and discourse (the family as a discursive site, where representation of a rude relative emerges). They are implicated in the constitution of the object and its inscription in relation to others, and are different in each social context. Planes are normative, their subjectivity alive and fluid, but 'have a margin of tolerance' 'beyond which exclusion is demanded'.[12] Separation into planes is not absolute: objects have mutually constitutive relations across the divides, as shown by the diplomatic representations exhibiting links within, above, and below the plane where they appeared. Adding planes of emergence to theory and analysis of diplomatic knowledge helps account for the multi-level complexity of diplomatic representations.

Separation of objects into planes demonstrates a hierarchy of discourses of salience, raising the question of who and what established it. Why are human rights in Western Sahara a question of domestic and not regional consequence?[13] This question is addressed in the fourth condition of representation, which addresses how knowledge production is governed.

3. Discursive stability

We can now discuss how representations behave across many texts. While the variety of architectures of articulation observed and the discursive relations among them is almost infinite, only some were truly stable. Discursive stability in articulations of representation and relations among them emerged as a vital condition for diplomatic representations to cross onto another actor's diplomatic text. This was evident in 1946, when early French attempts to describe Vietminh as communist failed to convince American diplomats due to instabilities deriving from suggestions Vietminh were simultaneously racist Japanese stooges. Linking these two articulations contradicted US dominant policy concerns, existing US diplomatic representations of Vietminh, and related contextual realms of knowledge. Not all what was written was unbelievable; rather, the unbelievable parts sunk the rest.

Contradictions in relations among articulations cause instability when similarity and differentiation at specific planes of emergence highlight the wrong representation. Returning to the case of France's 1948 representation of the conflict that successfully crossed over to US diplomacy, we should first look at the previous version of French representation.

Figure 6.4 shows how subtle details in the arrangement and selection of referents cause contradictions even when the rest of the representation works coherently. In this description of the entire conflict, colonial/anticolonial Franco-American differentiation was unwittingly inscribed and emphasised (*). A second, less expected, effect was linking Vietminh to US representation of itself as anticolonial (line connecting POSTCOLONIAL to ANTICOLONIAL). This produced the severe American 'scepticism' of French representations observed 1945–47.

France did not gain US support until late 1948, when its representation changed to include claims of progress towards decolonisation. The new description inscribed Vietminh and France into the communism–democracy binary of US dominant policy concerns. Obscuring French colonialism neutralised Vietminh anticolonialism, resulting in more radical differentiation between Vietminh and the United States and closer Franco-American linking. This representation of the conflict that could exist in US diplomatic text, enabling it to cross over, additionally making the policy change feel

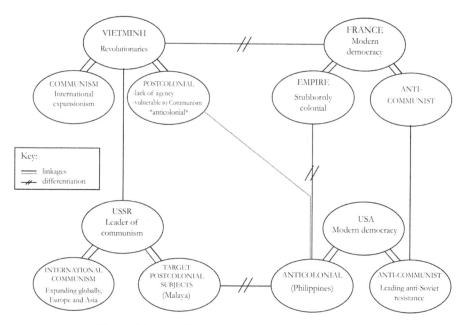

Figure 6.4 Unstable French representations 1945–47.

The confessions of the diplomatic text 215

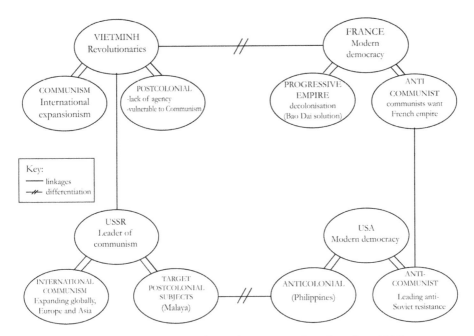

Figure 6.5 Stabilisation of French representations from late 1947.

more acceptable. The stabilising change is shown by modifying the above diagram to reflect the change operated in French description of the conflict in 1948.

When representing France as progressive and decolonising, colonialism ceased to be a point of contrast between US and French representations. It ceased to draw attention to Vietminh anticolonialism, obscuring it enough for the more radical communist/anticommunist binary to dominate its representation, stabilising it around the Cold War divide. Discursive stability determines believability through the final balance of similarity and differentiation in relation to what already exists in the diplomatic knowledge of the interlocutor. As with planes of emergence, discursive stability depends on dominant policy concerns too.

4. How dominant policy concerns govern knowledge production

What determines the relevance of each representation? What happens to a representation once our diplomat submits her report determines whether it comes to be included in other texts. If some or all its representations make it onto other texts, it is surviving in and impacting diplomatic knowledge production. It might be considered of such salience, as occurred with Kennan's

'Long Telegram', or Rabat Charge d'affaires Robert Jackson's 'Western Sahara realities' cable (Chapter 5, sixth detailed textual study), that its representations are reproduced in myriad other texts and repeated as the basis for policy in statements like Rice's 2008 policy turnaround. Texts can also disappear with their representations, filed and never seen again, until researchers find them in the archival underworld and wonder why they were ignored.

This salience-defining phenomenon also concerns representations coming from other international actors. In the aftermath of WWII, French descriptions of Vietminh as Japanese stooges sent to American diplomats went nowhere. Conversely, Morocco's representations of POLISARIO as an enabler of 'ungoverned spaces' and terror crossed from Moroccan to US texts and thrived there, reproduced up to policymakers where we found them at the NSC. This suggests that salience-defining also impacts how representations coming from other actors' diplomacy are treated.

Additionally, observations suggest there is a cyclical dynamic at work. Instructions from the Secretary of State and the NSC focused reporting onto specific issues, leading missions to increase reporting on those. At the MFA, instructions condition which reports from missions are analysed, copied, summarised, and briefed. Some are fast-tracked and studied intensely, frequently attributed unreasonable salience, explaining the absurd 1940s speculations on the socialist tendencies of a gasoline merchant in French New Caledonia and the hunt for seven Russian tramps in China. Conversely, much reporting is never dealt with again, not followed up with further requests nor analysed in subsequent briefs, even when carried by the same texts. As we go up the hierarchy of diplomacy, more and more texts, with their representations, simply fall out, never to inform policymaking.

This is a question of both theory and praxis, as this conceptual hierarchy is constituted in assessment and processing practices. Allison briefly considered this in the context of policymaking, arguing that 'groupthink' in policymaking elites reflects dominant assumptions.[14] Examining speechwriting at the MFA, Neumann enquired 'why diplomats never produce anything new', concluding that textual processing and revisions are the means by which discursive homogeneity is achieved.[15] Drawing on our observations on the prioritisation or disappearance of texts, it is now possible to determine what governs diplomatic knowledge.

The diplomatic text holds the answer in documents that explicitly and implicitly direct knowledge production. In Vietnam, d'Argenlieu ordered the compilation, analysis, and fabrication of dossiers on Vietminh atrocities; Byrnes and Marshall requested information concerning communism in Indochina and the French Empire; Bevin compelled UK diplomats to acknowledge Vietminh communism out of French speculations; and in the

2000s, the NSC instructed diplomats to prioritise reporting pertinent to the National Intelligence Priorities Framework. Cables congratulating diplomats on their reporting further corroborates which knowledge production was prioritised and, indirectly, which information was less welcome. In sum, this documentary evidence shows political investment into determining what knowledge should be produced and managing how it should be treated.

We could conceptualise these governing principles as 'authorities of delimitation' (what to report) and 'grids of specification' (which are priority).[16] These and the practices that implement them are demonstrated by the National Security Council Principals' Committee decisions uncovered in the Western Sahara case study, which established policy priorities and the means to pursue them. The subsequent shift in reporting proves how and the substantial extent to which these priorities shaped knowledge production. This is a very real application of executive power that imposes an observable hierarchy of knowledge, explaining how, in theory and practice, diplomacy sees what it wants to see and ignores the rest.

Philosophy defines the power governing knowledge as epistemes. Foucault conceptualised epistemes in three evolutions. In the first, practices and intellectual enquiry 'rest upon one and the same fundamental ground of knowledge', 'an obscure knowledge that does not manifest itself for its own sake in a discourse' that 'defines the conditions of possibility of all knowledge, whether expressed in theory or silently invested in a practice'. In this version, there is only one episteme at work.[17] In the second evolution, epistemes constrain and limit knowledge production, while also driving and governing its creation. Relating power to practice, the episteme is 'the total set of relations that unite, at a given period, the discursive practices that give rise to epistemological figures, sciences and [as we found in diplomacy] formalized systems'.[18] The episteme is alive, 'constantly moving', which is why this book investigated transitions in dominant policy concerns from WWII to the Cold War, from the Cold War to the War on Terror, allowing this conceptualisation to draw on the effects of different dominant policy concerns.

Epistemes do not only constrain, but also prompt the creation of subjects, categories, and discursive dimensions.[19] This helps makes sense of the double effect of policy concerns: determining which knowledge should be produced and then which is relevant. Foucault's third conceptualisation arose in a 1977 colloquium and drew on his work on the mechanisms that constrain the acceptable or deviant.[20] In this latter conceptualisation, the episteme is a 'specifically discursive' 'apparatus'. It grounds practices of knowledge production, which 'allows, among all possible enunciations, for the triage of those acceptable within a field of scientificity and about which it then possible to say: this is true or false'. In this final development, epistemes no longer reign in splendid isolation: they compete and coexist, helping make sense of the concurrent fall of antifascism and rise of anticommunism as dominant policy concerns in 1945–46. The analytical benefit is that 'the episteme makes it possible to grasp the set of constraints and limitations which, at any given moment, are imposed on discourse', allowing us to examine how dominant policy concerns govern diplomatic knowledge production.[21]

Analysis of diplomacy benefits from conceptualisation of policy concerns as epistemes. NSC instructions to the State Department determined that the priority in North Africa was degradation of terror groups, to be achieved by denying them 'ungoverned spaces' and human subjects without which, it was assumed, they would disappear. Reflecting how Foucauldian epistemes govern knowledge, the NSC not only decided what mattered, it also prescribed how information about terror-enabling spaces and subjects was to be garnered. This resulted in reporting from missions from Libya to Ghana focusing on controlling borders and biographical data.

Figure 6.6 illustrates how diplomacy produces and assesses knowledge. The episteme's government of diplomatic textual production determines what information should be produced (left) and what information is priority reading and which is irrelevant (right), and then continues to issue

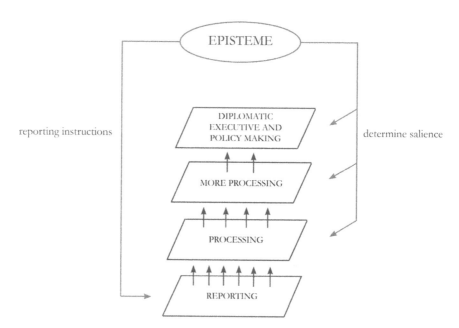

Figure 6.6 Epistemological constitution of subjectivity in diplomatic text.

further instructions for both writing and reading (the knowledge production textual acts, arrows rising).

Conceptualising dominant policy concerns as epistemes is analytically helpful. The episteme governs referents of representation by defining the salience of each. This is how vital details of representation (Moroccan abuses, Sahrawi antiextremism, Vietminh being an anticolonial league of different parties) come to be obscured into irrelevance. By deletion, representations filled by referents privileged by the dominant policy concern of the time, communism and terrorism, become the dominant referents in representation of subjects and their contexts. While it might seem instinctive that big concerns subsume others, this explains and makes sense of how this occurs in practice, allowing for analysis of its impact on diplomatic knowledge production.

5. *Representation of dominant policy concerns*

Deeply embedded in knowledge production, dominant policy concerns rarely appear explicitly. Few attend the secret meetings where they emerge, like those of the NSC. When documentary evidence of their emergence is available, they mostly appear as assumptions within policy directives. I write 'assumptions' because they are not enunciative acts creating objects ('we will hunt terrorists') but rather 'the total set of relations that unite, at a given period, the discursive practices' that produce the representations we are studying.[22] Empirically, their traces – disciplinary, hierarchical, normative – are observable in the diplomatic text.

Less directly, we can observe the reflections of these epistemes in diplomatic text when it betrays the outlines of dominant policy concerns. In the 1940s, for example, after meeting the President, Secretary Byrne issued priorities and parameters that would be fragmentally reflected in hundreds of cables. Piecing them together, reflections of epistemological dominant policy concerns can tell us what they looked like. Importantly, they are also but limited representations: imperfect, partial, relying on narrative and other representational devices, possibly out of date, but which stand in for the will and needs of the country.

Outside diplomacy we find refractions of dominant policy concerns in the chatter of the Westminster village, inside the Washington beltway, in the waiting room at the Makhzen in Rabat, as well as in the media. These are less direct than reflections due to varying degrees of diplomatic confidentiality that, depending on classification and distance from the MFA and policy practice, can cause substantial distortion. So much detail is missing, and that detail frequently so procedurally banal or complex, that the gaps end up being filled with speculation, conspiracies, or endless theorising as to what policymakers really are, want, or seek.[23] Refractions encounter contextual realms of knowledge where the media, opinion, and other actors, public and private, produce and distribute their own representations of the subjects and contexts diplomatic practice is tackling, as well as of policy concerns.

Reflected and refracted representations of dominant policy concerns in contextual realms of knowledge are vastly powerful. In Britain, we currently live with the consequences of such representations about the effect of EU membership. Crucially, in Brexit negotiations and their aftermath, British diplomats had to deal with the substantial impact of representations in contextual realms of knowledge. I am not referring to the power of public opinion but, rather, to the impact on diplomatic knowledge production of what policymakers believe it to mean. It is vital to empirically and conceptually account for how reflections and refractions of policy concerns impact the epistemes governing diplomatic knowledge.

Policy concerns in contextual and diplomatic realms are mutually constitutive. We have encountered the twice-reflected-and-refracted representation of dominant policy concerns on several occasions – media refraction of policy reflected back into to diplomatic text, impacting the original policy concern. In the 1940s, promoting French colonialism was rendered difficult by American public and media hostility to Old World imperialism, Roosevelt's sharing of this position making some of it policy, and what diplomats thought this to mean. In turn, a French report based on study of US press reports advised that representing France and its policies as part of an anticommunist struggle, rather than colonial, would help secure US collaboration.

Even more clearly demonstrating this epistemological meta-cyclicality, Washington-based Moroccan agent MACP employs former Western parliamentarians, policymakers, civil servants, and journalists to publicly praise the autonomy plan. It then publishes press articles containing this praise – as well as the policy shifts by Clinton, Rice, and Trump – on its websites and press releases. These often describe it as 'serious and credible' and Morocco as 'on the move'. MACP then redeploys this commentary to prove to Washington that Morocco's autonomy plan is the only 'credible and realistic' solution. In this example, we can see the full loop in action: Morocco's persuasive transformation of US representations of Western Sahara and the autonomy plan; enunciation of America's new representation of the plan as 'credible and realistic' by Clinton in 2009; further re-praising of the plan by actors in contextual realms of knowledge; this enunciation cited in Moroccan representations of the conflict and its solution; and finally, in 2020, the self-same formula used by the Trump administration to justify recognising annexation by Morocco.

This cycle is a key condition for a representation to fit in diplomatic knowledge, within a diplomatic institution and in conditioning its crossover to the diplomacy of another actor. This conditioning is determined by compatibility and incompatibility of articulations. The discursive stability of representations was discussed above with reference to the encounter with another actor's cascade. An encounter also occurs between representations in diplomatic text and those borne in contextual realms of knowledge. At this encounter, discursive instability is similarly manifested, negatively impacting the capacity of a description to cross over and remain viable. This is because these realms of knowledge are the context of the practitioners whose textual production we have been examining and impact the epistemes that govern their knowledge production.

Contextual realms of knowledge condition the capacity of one actor's descriptions to persuade. This complex mechanism is the conceptual and real-life diplomatic practice that explains how the adage of 'lots of people seem to think so', Neumann's observation of homogeneity, and Allison's 'groupthink' come to be a diplomatic reality. The capacity of a representation to be convincing is affected because diplomatic knowledge production is not abstracted from contextual realms of knowledge. Not only do diplomats read newspapers but, worst of all, their policymaking masters do too, and they abide by them far more. Diplomatic knowledge carries and is impacted by the reflection of the epistemes of dominant policy concerns, in turn partly constituted by refractions in the public of what they are thought to be.

The episteme in the diplomatic mirror and the emergence of agency

Diplomatic text is revealed as the immutable witness to how diplomacy represents what it sees, communicates it, and elaborates this knowledge. In it are invested the powers, opportunities, ideas, work, and opinions of all its authors. The diplomatic authors effectively die after submitting their work, and in their texts and their subsequent iterations live their descriptions, ambitions, ideas, and points of view. Text on its own does not have the power – and, really, we specifically mean the agency – to persuade policymakers of a description. However, this agency is enacted and practiced *in* and *through* text, the vessel and site of diplomatic knowledge and its creation.

In and through diplomatic text, agency is enacted to constitute representations, promote them, and persuade of their veracity. Our findings demonstrate that under the five conditions discussed above, a representation can be persuasive to one's own diplomatic masters and even those of another actor. Additionally, observing their crossover to the knowledge production of other actors empirically denotes when they have been absorbed and made part of their own knowledge. Conducting genealogy backwards adds accuracy to this analysis, pinpointing which representation precedes which, when one thrives and others fall out, and instances of crossover (sometimes the exact document) or rejection. This, in turn, makes it possible to identify the circumstances of these events. The persuasiveness of a description is conditioned by the representational and epistemological effect of practices, effects that I have called conditions of diplomatic description, themselves constituted by smaller instances of agency by myriad practitioners often not working in syntony.

Taking some distance from the diplomatic text, the five conditions help conceptualise relations between diplomatic knowledge, its production, and dominant policy concerns. To use a realist term, the five conditions determine 'alignment' between representations and policy concerns. I say 'alignment' because the conceptualisation of the agency invested into diplomatic text I am here elaborating explains the phenomenon that Walt conceptualises as the alignment of interests and threats and its persuasive power, which he articulates as a rational calculation.[24] Contrary to realists, however, while my conceptualisation can be simplified into the constitution of 'alignment', what lays underneath it, the five conditions expounded in this chapter, speak of a world where there is no material grounding to the objects considered when deciding whom to ally to.

Descriptions are a world like architecture, where the immaterial (light, space) participates in constituting the material – a world made entirely of language, where descriptions constitute the very discourses of interest and threat that realists consider objective, material, and measurable realities. I am not saying that the diplomatic text invents fantasies. Whether diplomatic descriptions are complete fabrications or exceedingly accurate (we have encountered spectacular examples of both), their agency to persuade is not related to their material grounding, but rather to the mechanisms of their subjectivity. Their persuasiveness is therefore more like what critical security scholarship call 'stickiness': the properties that make name-calling persuasive and enable securitisation.[25] This is diplomacy's greatest power: to persuade – that is, make dominant knowledge – of the subjects, territories, time, and space it describes in its dispatches.

It seems obvious that international actors seek to befriend great powers by fitting into what they seek and their worldview. This would make this book a great deal of work for rather little novel insight. While it appears evident that actors do so, what this project has set out to understand is *how* they do so through analysis of what this looks like in the empirical evidence of the diplomatic text – more specifically, what about their communications makes the pandering effective. Identifying crossovers empirically determined the precise instance representations were able to persuade.

But what type of agency are we looking at? The impact of diplomatic descriptions resists traditional analysis of their agency, and its resulting causality, through the lens of independent efficient causality – that is, the extent to which representations themselves and on their own affect policymaking. Beyond establishing that they had *an* impact as proven by their presence in policy decisions, how can we be certain that representations of Vietminh as communist menace and France as like-minded democracy persuaded the State Department and Truman? There might be entirely unexpected contextual factors. Analysing identity-making in US policymaking during the Balkan conflicts, Hansen analysed *Balkan Ghosts* by Robert Kaplan as an account that helped change Bill Clinton's Balkan policy.[26] What if in 1948, Truman was reading a novel depicting a communist coup? Unless some form of extremely invasive neurological historical psychiatry emerges,[27] enabling analysis to enter the minds of policymakers such as Truman or Rice, we might never find a debate-ending answer. This is why our methodology sets the test for agency at the level of the evidence available in diplomatic text. Similarly, Connolly accounted for causality by identifying representations that work in 'resonance' with pre-existing discourses of fear,[28] a co-constitutive causal model that, however, obscures when representing similarity is at least as important.[29] In an evolution of this idea, I gather contextual knowledges into the fifth condition, policy concerns as represented in contextual realms of knowledge.

I suggest that the agency of diplomatic descriptions is constitutive and 'structurationist'.[30] The five conditions discussed in this chapter, from word choice to the broadest contextual realms of knowledge, together determine the form and emergence of the agency of the descriptions made in and through diplomatic text. Dominant policy concerns emerge as the most powerful variable. They determine the salience of communications bearing representations and that of different referents, hierarchically ordering them. This conditions all diplomatic knowledge production practices, representations of policy concerns in the diplomatic text, and their reflections in contextual realms of knowledge such as the media or presidential bedtime reading, as well as their feedback into diplomacy. The crossover test empirically supports these conclusions about diplomatic agency being structured by a matrix of constitutive factors. The 1948 and 2008 shifts in policy studied were preceded by crossovers of French and Moroccan representations, which then came to be present in policy statements and impacted how their assumptions were structured, as most evident in the Vietminh–Soviet conspiracy thesis absorbed from French diplomacy. At the level of narrative causal explanation (such as Suganami's), this establishes that changes in representation are very significant in determining and indeed shaping policy changes.[31]

The five conditions of diplomatic description *are* the factors that constitute and structure the agency to persuade of a specific representation. Focus on these five interlocked factors can even account, in subsequent analyses, for factors apparently hitherto unexplored. To return to the case studies in this book, a factor I left unexplored is the careerism of individual diplomats. Does it not stand to reason that diplomats too pander to dominant policy concerns to raise their profile? For example, Robert Jackson, the author of the cable analysed in the sixth Western Sahara detailed textual study, analysed every possible counterterrorism angle and linked it to POLISARIO. I could not find evidence of whether this helped his subsequent promotion to Principal Deputy Assistant Secretary for African Affairs.[32] Conversely, we also encountered, more often in fact, instances of diplomats subtly criticising or offering evidence against dominant policy concerns and their practical implications, such as the US Consuls in Hanoi and Casablanca. The impact of careerism or contrarianism were, however, accounted for because, while diplomats have the agency to reach for one of several (finite) descriptive choices, their agency over those descriptions ends the instance they submit their reports. Their descriptions now live only in text and their impact is empirically accounted for in analysis of their presence and influence in subsequent texts. Whether the result of careerism, conviction, or an opium hangover, the description itself and its later impact on diplomatic knowledge is empirically accounted for.

Though atypical for poststructuralists to make causal claims of such stricture, this is necessary because diplomatic practice itself carries and implements discourses of causality that must be analysed, not abided by or uncritically accepted. In the Western Sahara case study, for example, we charted how NSC instructions explicitly embedded the causal assumption that 'ungoverned' Muslim subjects and spaces enable terrorism. It is, furthermore, necessary to consider agency and the assessment of resulting causality because this project has sought to free this history of representations from the prejudices that emerge from the subjective choices of selecting an 'origin' for an effect. This involved a backward genealogical approach that aggressively avoided pre-categorising cause and effect, instead allowing the history of representations to reveal its own conditions of possibility and impact. These in turn informed conceptualisation of the five conditions of representation and how they shape causal conditions. I do not claim that they are the final exhaustive explanation of the agency of diplomatic text and the causality of its impact. Rather, they are its vital condition, their sine qua non, and help situate the power of diplomatic descriptions in relation to the conditions upon which it is contingent.

In broader IR terms, the five conditions and the conceptualisation of agency offered in this chapter serve as a guide to understanding what shapes the power of descriptions. They additionally explain how a description can persuade one's own policymakers and even those of another country and navigate their respective complexities of knowledge production and hierarchies. The agency enabled by convincing descriptions does not end there, however. The textual crossovers we traced creatively inserted subjects, territories, time, and norms into these representations. For instance, while there is not much new in saying that Morocco sang the antiterrorism tune the Bush administration wanted to hear, it was a feat of an entirely different order to embed POLISARIO into terror-enabling factors, and an even greater one to reinvent a discredited decade-old Moroccan autonomy proposal as the sole 'realistic' and 'credible' resolution. In these examples, we see how diplomatic descriptions, and the act of representing that constitutes them, are also an event of creative agency.

The consequences of diplomatic descriptions are vast. A dominant piece of knowledge, once embedded in state bureaucratic practices, expresses itself firstly in the policy shifts it informs. These in turn drive very real material, symbolic, and subjective changes to state practices and everything they touch. In the Vietnam case study, the emergence of a new understanding of Vietminh materially involved the United States through vast funding of the French war effort, and the interpretive understanding of what this meant in the Cold War, which kept them involved until 1975. The aftermath of that war – and the misunderstandings of why it occurred – subjectively devastated American understanding of itself and, one might argue, the very meaning of an American war. The consequences of descriptions, or 'perceptions' as realists like to call them, are very real. The causal impact of diplomatic descriptions widens in a cascade of consequences, which are ultimately shaped by the political subjectivity introduced by a description.

Diplomatic descriptions do not usually impact grand policy like anticommunism or grand strategy like containment. In North Africa, US policy continued to focus on controlling subjects and space to counterterrorism. Descriptions can, however, significantly shape the execution of policy and strategy. In American counterterrorism in North Africa, the choice of which subjects and borders were of concern was significantly shaped by Moroccan diplomatic descriptions. This is how counterterrorism came to involve finding a solution where Morocco annexes Western Sahara in its own terms. Ultimately, diplomatic descriptions granted Morocco the agency to transform application of US policymaking to its favour. Such is the power of reporting who you and the Other are.

Segretario Machiavelli demanded much of his diplomats' reporting, as did Byrne, MacArthur, Bidault, Abdelaziz, Rice, and Clinton. Inevitably, understanding situations through detailed knowledge production is essential to achieving policy goals. Practices of knowledge production, however, because of the equally inevitable subjectivity inherent in any description, afford the opportunity for mistakes, overstatement, and misinterpretation, and for other actors' diplomats to intervene proposing their own view of the situation. This does not mark a return to an instrumental view of diplomacy; far from it.

Those seeking support for policy goals through diplomatic means often have highly instrumental views of diplomatic communication, as our French and Moroccan policymakers clearly did. Manipulating representations in diplomatic text, however, proved a hard task, and the fate of representations in diplomatic knowledge productions was not what their authors expected. As we saw, only after years of diplomatic descriptive efforts did France and Morocco obtain support for their policy goals. This analysis of representations demonstrated that they are the ever-changing, complex, and evolving fruit of thousands of diplomatic hands and applications of agency. Very few of the five representational conditions can be instrumentally deployed or manipulated – and then only in limited circumstances, such as articulations. The best instrumentalist diplomats might attempt to pander to the representations and reflections of these concerns, attempting to align themselves to the 'right' side of the categories and hierarchies they impose. This is possible, as we have found, but extremely difficult and unpredictable, since crossovers require the alignment of an entire constellation of factors, few of which yield to manipulation.

Diplomatic text often fails to convince anyone. It evidently sometimes fails even in adequately informing the prince. It can be blinded by allowing priority policy concerns to gain such dominance that the entire process of diplomatic knowledge production is rendered outright deficient, producing dreadful reporting. Excessive ascendancy of dominant policy concerns also makes diplomatic knowledge vulnerable to absorbing descriptions that persuade because they inscribe additional objects within these already-dominant concerns. Let us remember the US consul in New Caledonia reporting on a lefty gasoline seller, or Sainteny and Hô trying to talk peace while sabotaged by the fiercely racist determination of a colonial governor. There was no glory, no Ferrero Rocher, only fear, loathing, violence, and foreignness negotiated by those who practise the art of diplomatic writing.

Notes

1 Graham Greene, *The Honorary Consul* (London: Vintage Classics, 2004), 27.
2 'We get a coffee on the way there.' I suggest you do the same.

3 Foucault, *Archaeology of Knowledge*, 41–51.
4 Foucault, *Archaeology of Knowledge*, 46.
5 Foucault, *The Order of Discourse*.
6 Foucault, *Archaeology of Knowledge*, 41.
7 Leon Battista Alberti, *On the Art of Building in Ten Books* (Cambridge, MA: MIT Press, 1991) The aesthetic language of spatiality remains a powerful artistic endeavour. See, for instance, the work of Lucio Fontana, who spent most of his life exploring aesthetic 'spazialismo', spatiality; or Jorge Oteiza.
8 Foucault, *Archaeology of Knowledge*, 41.
9 Foucault, 'The Order of Discourse'.
10 See detailed studies 6 for Vietnam and 2 for Western Sahara in particular. They are a good example of the inductive methodology here employed, where empirical observations drive analysis and inform conceptual responses.
11 Compare with the language in the American geopolitical theory classic by Alfred Thayer Mahan, *The Interest of America in International Conditions* (New Brunswick, NJ: Transaction Publishers, 2007).
12 Foucault, *Archaeology of Knowledge*, 47–49.
13 The so-called Arab Spring showed, in Morocco and across North Africa, that this was a terrible oversight.
14 Allison and Zelikow, *Essence of Decision*, Chapter 5, 'Groupthink'.
15 Neumann, '"A Speech That the Entire Ministry May Stand For"'.
16 Foucault, *Archaeology of Knowledge*, 46.
17 Foucault, *The Order of Things*, 183.
18 Foucault, *Archaeology of Knowledge*, 211.
19 Foucault, *Archaeology of Knowledge*, 212.
20 Foucault, *Power/Knowledge*, 197.
21 My translation of the original discussion with D. Colas, A. Grosrichard, G. Le Gaufey, J. Livi, G. Miller, J. Miller, J.-A. Miller, C, Millot, and G. Wajeman, 'Le Jeu de Michel Foucault', *Bulletin Périodique Du Champ Freudien* (10), 1977, 62–93. The colloquium is clearer in the original French than in the above-cited English edition, emphasising the co-existence of epistemes as a struggle for supremacy over knowledge.
22 Foucault, *Archaeology of Knowledge*, 211.
23 One only needs to think of the scandals caused by the leak of hundreds of thousands of diplomatic cables by Chelsea Manning in 2010 to gauge the distance between reflections and refractions of the epistemes of dominant policy concerns.
24 See particularly Walt, 'Alliance Formation and the Balance of World Power'; *The Origins of Alliances*; 'Why Alliances Endure or Collapse'.
25 See particularly Chapter 2 in K. M. Fierke, *Political Self-Sacrifice Agency, Body and Emotion in International Relations* (New York: Cambridge University Press, 2013), 55.
26 Hansen, *Security as Practice*, 150.
27 Such as that found in the videogame *Assassin's Creed*, where the player enters the memories of people in the past.

28 William E. Connolly, 'The Evangelical-Capitalist Resonance Machine', *Political Theory* 33 (6), 2005, 869–86.
29 See particularly Chapter 3, Connolly, *Identity, Difference*, 64.
30 Anthony Giddens, *The Constitution of Society: Outline of the Theory of Structuration*, New Edition (Cambridge: Polity, 1986).
31 In this causality framework, narrative 'is a means of comprehension'. Hidemi Suganami, 'Agents, Structures, Narratives', *European Journal of International Relations* 5 (3), 1999, 381.
32 'Jackson, Robert P.', US Department of State, accessed 10 January 2023, https://2009-2017.state.gov/r/pa/ei/biog/218230.htm

7

Epilogue

What does this mean for diplomacy? Our démarche is not complete. I stroll to the library to draft my last report: a synthesis, a recommendation of efforts made in the previous pages. We have analysed how diplomacy represents subjects and their spatial, temporal, and normative contexts in language; how these descriptions develop in their textual existence; and how they are categorised, prioritised, ignored, or absorbed into the diplomacy of other actors. The question remains, however, of what these analytics add to the study and practice of diplomacy as well as international relations more broadly. After a brief summary of the conceptual, methodological, and empirical advances offered in this book, this chapter locates their contributions to the conceptual and analytical study of diplomacy and its practice.

Travel log

It has been an arduous journey. This project set out to investigate diplomatic descriptions by examining their constitution at the site where they occur and through which they are communicated, the diplomatic text. The text acted as the immutable empirical evidence of the construction and development of representations. Its interrogation forced it to confess its workings, how in and through its pages subjects and their contexts were represented, and analysis compelled it to betray the power invested in the descriptions it carried.

The first leg of our journey determined what a diplomat is from the perspective of the practice of representing and writing on behalf of the state. This review of theories of diplomatic practice, executed in Chapter 2, helped overcome institutionalist perspectives that include irrelevant knowledge production like embassy telegraph bills, or broad constitutive ones that include all knowledge of the international, from videogames to Tomahawk missile footage. Drawing on Constantinou, diplomatic practice was narrowed to the mutually constitutive cycle where diplomatic enunciation of its knowledge of self and the world reifies the state, which is in turn diplomacy's raison d'être.

The second turned this conceptualisation into a data selection rationale. In Chapter 3, it resulted in a praxis-based empirical understanding of who diplomats are, which included non-ministry individuals performing speaking on behalf of the state as well as MFA officials. Conceptualisation of 'the diplomatic moment' helped empirically nail down the contribution of these individuals by capturing the moment their reports enter the bureaucracy of diplomatic knowledge production.

In its third leg, this endeavour developed an analytical method adapted to the specific challenges of the diplomatic text. Expounded in Chapter 3, it consists of an integrated method divided into three steps. The first draws on the data selection rationale and its conceptualisation of the diplomatic moment – empirically denoted when diplomats submit their descriptions into processes of diplomatic knowledge production – to map the pathways taken by diplomatic knowledge production. This reveals who, where, and when diplomatic knowledge production is produced, moved, edited, and governed. The second step determines how single texts represent subjects and their contexts by analysing their language in its various layers, from words to complete articulations. This additionally identifies topoi textual markers signposting the presence of specific representations. The third step traces how descriptions develop across texts by following the textual markers signposting their presence, analysing how descriptions change as they move from diplomats on the ground up to policymakers in capitals. It determines how they are governed, leading to descriptions being emphasised, repeated, or dropped, and the instances when they cross over to the diplomatic knowledge of other international actors. Following this trail, it is then possible to determine the impact of these descriptions, whether they were believed and absorbed or noted and rejected.

The fourth leg took us to the archives to apply the method to two case studies. Documentary evidence, over eight thousand documents in total, was collected from archives in Paris, Aix-en-Provence, London, and Washington DC; media sources from several countries; declassified material; and the vast trove of cables in Wikileaks. In US–French–UK–Vietnamese diplomacy 1945–48, it was found that initial communist name-calling was unprovable and persuaded nobody. Its later believability to US diplomats was determined not on the basis of evidence, but on UK corroboration of a Stalinist plot and apparent French willingness to relinquish the colony. Both depended on a racist understanding of non-Western subjects, shared by US and French diplomats and policymakers, which regarded the Vietnamese as unable to mount a successful rebellion without Soviet help and direction. In US–Moroccan–POLISARIO diplomacy 2003–10, it was determined that American diplomats and policymakers never believed POLISARIO was terrorist. Rather, US support for Moroccan annexation was predicated on Moroccan descriptions of itself as a reliable ally, and of POLISARIO and Sahrawi self-determination as themselves enablers of the empty spaces that engendered terrorism. Unilateral annexation became supportable due to successful Moroccan self-description as 'on the move', progressive, and democratic. Crucially, analysis determined the exact instances, context, and conditions of convincing descriptions within MFAs and crossing over from the diplomacy of others.

In the fifth and final leg of this journey, I did some theorising of my own. In Chapter 6, empirical observations inductively informed a theoretical account of the dynamics of representation of subjects and their contexts in diplomatic knowledge. Conceptualised as five conditions for a description to emerge, survive, and thrive in diplomatic knowledge in and through text, they determine whether and how this occurs. They are the architecture of articulations of representation, the specific discursive planes where they emerge, their stability in discursive contexts, the impact of policy concerns governing knowledge production, and the representation of these concerns in contextual realms of knowledge. These five factors are crucial to understanding how, when, and why descriptions articulated and communicated in text are convincing.

The diplomatic text revealed itself to be so much more than a vehicle. Through it, diplomats and policymakers exercised agency, power in practice, and it was deeply implicated in what might be called great power politics. This is not to claim that the text does anything on its own but, rather, that power is invested into it. We located and examined instances where the power to describe and to govern descriptions was invested into diplomatic texts, and along their journeys these in turn carried and exercised this power to tell what is and isn't. We saw the traces of these applications of agency: little ones when late at night a diplomat represented in words what they saw and thought, larger ones to decide which of these descriptions were relevant and should be passed on, and greater ones to choose what policymakers should or should not know. Such is the importance of diplomatic text beyond its role as instrumental vehicle of subjectivity that we witnessed policymakers like UK Foreign Secretary Bevin investing their authority in forcing it to tell unlikely stories or even lie. They invested their authority in forcing the diplomatic text to tell their view of subjects and their contexts because, ultimately, it stands as the record of the view of the state, informing its will.

Refining empirical analyses of diplomacy

This project contributes to a wide array of analytical perspectives on diplomacy. The contributions expounded in this volume, particularly the inductive method to empirically analyse how diplomacy produces knowledge about subjects and their contexts, provide key insights. Speaking to analysis and practice of how the state produces and manages knowledge, the method determines how descriptions are produced and developed and their subsequent journeys within and across MFAs. Speaking to events where a subjective view becomes persuasive, the crossover test pinpoints when and in which circumstances this takes place. This makes it of relevance to several schools of thought on diplomacy, from the most realist to critical. This section locates how, despite but also thanks to its critical lineage, the empirical approach here developed contributes to realist, English School, and constructivist approaches to the empirical analysis of diplomatic practice and its conceptualisation before, in the following section, locating its contributions to my critical and poststructuralist predecessors.

The diplomatic text is not an objective instrument of observation and communication. Kissinger too remarked that in diplomacy 'exalted' words 'used to justify the various demands obscured rather than illuminated fundamental positions'.[1] To realists, this project empirically reveals how exactly this occurs. This is relevant to realism because, as Walt argued, the ultimate utility of diplomacy lies in its 'recognition' of factors that inform the establishment of international relationships such as alliances or opposition.[2] A very great deal is therefore at stake in critically engaging with the 'exalted' words of descriptions. Whether one believes, or not, that it is possible to discern the reality of a state's needs and intentions, the method advanced in this book can empirically determine how diplomatic communications construct subjective descriptions that concern almost any aspect and level of representation. As we saw with Moroccan–American alignment predicated on terrorism, state interests are negotiated in the awkward medium of descriptions. This is why it is worth examining how they come about and might prove convincing.

In realist analytics, my five conditions of representation can be treated as factors determining alignment between representations and policy concerns. This conceptualisation explains the very same phenomenon that Walt conceptualises as the alignment of interests and threats.[3] Even where these alignments had long been identified as key to major policy events, my method can substantiate in minute detail *how* this occurred, accomplishing what a reviewer of my research on Vietnam called 'a truly remarkable feat: saying something truly fresh and important about the U.S. embroilment in Vietnam'.[4] If one is inclined to an instrumentalist approach, with descriptions ruthlessly deployed to co-opt or even deceive another actor into a specific relationship, this approach is perhaps even more useful. While critical and poststructuralist approaches to International Relations reject assumptions of instrumentalisation in analysing international practices, part of me admires such unrelenting cynicism. Our case studies provide examples where diplomacy was indeed used to achieve policy ends by cheating US diplomacy and policy into believing French and Moroccan problems were American problems. While this does not mean that all diplomacy is as horrifically deceitful, or that this is its purpose, empirically analysing if and how this happens remains a substantial contribution.

For the English School, this project can bring a substantial empirical dimension. The method could contribute to empirically substantiating work that, not unlike my above comment on realist 'alignment', conceptualises a crossover of meanings, identity, and views of international contexts that, crucially, takes place in diplomacy.[5] Bull emphasised three essential aspects of diplomacy that share much with the work in this book: the agency of diplomats in choosing words, diplomacy's rarefied conceptual existence, and its role in producing and transmitting information.[6] Watson and Reus-Smit emphasise that understanding diplomacy necessitates approaches that can retrieve the development of their role in international society,[7] while Wight warned of problems in international relations research arising from 'the intellectual prejudice of the sovereign state' that obscure the role of practices.[8]

This analytical compatibility has long been coming and, as Neumann emphasised, needed.[9] In research with English Schooler Filippo Costa-Buranelli and critical theorist Nicholas Michelsen, I put this long-awaited collaboration to work. It applies my method to empirically analyse the discursive, normative, and diplomatic international collaboration of New Right movements like Trump's America First, British Brexiters, Meloni's in Italy, and Le Pen's in France, which we argue amounts to the emergence of a Reactionary Internationale.[10] Watson's 'art of the possible' was, in the constitutive role of descriptions, more art than he could have imagined.[11]

To our interest in diplomacy's descriptions, the most interesting broadly constructivist contribution remains Jonathan Fisher's, who argued that diplomacy 'manages perception'.[12] To this perspective, this project can contribute further substantiation, explaining how this was possible and retrieving further nuances. In particular, the 'management' of representation is extremely difficult and contingent, and I would add that representing similarity is in practice far more challenging than difference. To Fisher's Uganda case study, my methodology would add that it was not only management of the perception of Uganda's 'helpfulness' that secured donor support, but also, as with our Moroccan case study, description as a democracy articulated in opposition to a common terrorist threat.[13]

Whether instrument, international institution, or constitutive practice, diplomacy is a key part of the making and interaction of the international. From Walt to Adler-Nissen via Bull, Watson, or Wendt, diplomacy bridges a space that is full of shaky subjectivities. Even if they were truly knowable and objectively real, diplomacy is always caught mediating their perception. This mediation rests on descriptions that, produced by practices ranging from espionage to reporting and briefing, rely on text to exist, develop, and be communicated. This method demonstrates that diplomatic knowledge production practices are a creative site, not an objective instrument of communication. Text is their instrument, yes, but also their core site of practice, where power is invested, and this method can determine how.

Diplomatic practice, identity, and violence

This project is the first critical analysis dedicated entirely to the manner and content of the textual evidence of diplomatic knowledge and its communication – official cables, reports, and analysis. This proposition, and its ambition of doing so on a large scale, systematically analysing thousands of documents, was a major challenge never addressed before in such a way. This section re-engages with the study and practice of diplomacy and international relations, acknowledging some key intellectual debts before outlining how this project contributes to their development.

I am particularly indebted to the pioneers of critical diplomacy. This project drew on Der Derian's conceptualisation of diplomacy's essential conditions: the constitution of the Other, and the fiction I call 'hand of the prince': the state as a single-will individual wielding diplomatic instruments.[14] Constantinou conceptualised diplomacy as mutually constitutive theory and praxis.[15] This project employed this insight to define diplomacy's empirical evidence through the instance of practice I call the 'diplomatic moment', facilitating mapping of diplomacy's paper trail. This development was spurred by Neumann's convincing warning that without regard to praxis, discourse analysis cannot provide empirical accounts of practical relevance.[16] In resolving this, Adler-Nissen's rigorous tracing of practices and their evidence inspired the praxis-based rigour of the data selection and mapping steps of my method.[17]

The analytical concepts and methods developed here contribute an empirical basis that links the archive, a key source of evidence of diplomatic events and praxis, to the exceptional work on diplomatic practices by the practice turn, particularly as pioneered by Adler-Nissen, Pouliot, and Neumann, enabling another layer of empirical rigour. My approach adds detail, substantiation, and in-depth understanding of the descriptions that are the currency and subject of the negotiations that enable the 'power in practice' they research. Likewise, it can provide an empirical bridge between subjective politics in representation and emerging analyses of the materiality of diplomatic practices such as Dittmer's.

Firstly, the method with its attendant concepts and three analytical steps is useful to produce detailed and empirically convincing histories of diplomacy, as demonstrated in the case studies. It can also be used to analyse narrower, shorter, and more concise diplomatic events predicated on a specific understanding of subjects and their contexts.

Secondly, aspects of the method and its concepts can also be of use on their own. The 'diplomatic moment' serves as an analytical concept that solidly links the theory and praxis of diplomacy to the empirical paper trail of practices and the knowledge they produce. It could also be used to link the same evidence to other practices, from negotiations to the delivery of démarches, and could be combined with other methods such as anthropological observation, sociological interviews, or practice tracing to build a solid documentary empirical basis for different analyses of diplomacy. The different pieces of the method, besides being usable on their own, can also be used to research aspects of knowledge production other than, or single aspects of, subjects and their contexts. The first step of the method, the detailed mapping of diplomatic knowledge production pathways, is a useful addition to practice-tracing Bourdieusian approaches and discourse analyses of diplomacy alike. The second step, detailed textual studies, thanks to their systematic Barthian-inspired format, can systematise discourse analyses, particularly if they need to remain comparable to one another. The third step, tracing development, would be difficult to employ on its own as it requires the previous two to have a pathway and textual markers to follow.

Thirdly, the conceptualisation of the five conditions can help both in theorising and analysing diplomacy. As an analytical principle, they can help detailed discourse analysis and assessment. As a concept, they contribute to practice-based poststructuralist understanding of diplomatic practices of knowledge production. In these three ways, the volume in your hands might add to a distinctly poststructuralist understanding of diplomacy.

To debates on identity and violence, this project reveals diplomacy's role in inscribing subjects and their contexts in discourses of violence, danger, agency, and security. Years ago, in Vivienne Jabri's *Discourses on Violence*, I found the relevance and raison d'être of the IR poststructuralist project as I see it: violence is predicated on an object, the dangerous Other, a representation of political identity that is the sine qua non of violence. The Other can be killed because political power is invested in the constitution of representations that explain, justify, and ultimately structure the conditions for violence against its identity. This raises crucial questions on empathy and diplomacy that this method can help answer.[18] We found these violence-enabling discourses in the representations we explored, witnessing document by document how representation in diplomacy too is the vital enabler of violence, war, death, and exile.

Inscriptions made in diplomacy can dissociate a subject from its own claim to agency, as occurred to Vietminh and POLISARIO, 'denying the insurgent as the subject of its own history', 'and representing them as instruments of some other will.'[19] Subjects become a construction whose 'very presence is both "overlooked" and at the same time overdetermined, psychically projected, made stereotypical and symptomatic.'[20] This is the effect we retrieved in representations of Vietminh and POLISARIO after the successful crossover of French and Moroccan representations that facilitated 'invocation of the global' against communism and terrorism.[21] In a testament to the value of researching diplomatic descriptions, we also witnessed the success of Morocco's inscription of itself as the exception to North African dangerous subjects, temporality, norms, and spaces. Diplomacy's representation can therefore act as the first move in processes that banalise and systematise violence against certain subjects.[22]

Analysing representations of subalternity helps understanding the postcolonial dimensions of diplomacy. Racist subalternity, supported by assumptions that Vietnamese rebels could never achieve such success against the French Empire, deleted Vietnamese will and success from descriptions and replaced them with Soviet conspiracies, supporting the case for US support of France. More subtly, we also witnessed the impact of framing oneself as subaltern. Temporal inscription is a key aspect. Where reality falls short, as with Moroccan democracy or French progressivism, subalternity in temporal frames of progress supports claims they are catching up to the interlocutor, who is flattered in their role model. This helped Morocco influence US counterterrorism in the Sahel to the extent that maintaining Moroccan stability and facilitating Morocco's annexation of Western Sahara became key parts of US North African counterterrorism policy.

Turning to outcomes in practice, diplomatic descriptions contribute to securitisation, stigmatisation, or diplomatic protection. Securitisation helps understand what happened to the subjects and spaces of the Saharan 'ungoverned spaces' we encountered in the 2000s.[23] The language of the unknowable desert and the inscription of Oriental subjects as constantly on the verge of extremism launched processes that resulted in the securitisation of subjects and spaces.[24] Another outcome is stigmatisation. Its first act, 'labelling', is an outcome of the representation of actors produced in and through diplomatic text,[25] crucial to 'coalition building' against the stigmatised that we saw when Vietnamese rebels were inserted into the stigma of communism, helping the emergence of a Franco-American coalition. Another possible outcome is diplomatic sponsorship. US sponsorship in the form of UN vetoes is why Morocco (and similarly sponsored Israel) cannot be forced, unlike Indonesia in 1991, to hold a final-status referendum. This is how Morocco joins the extremely select club of successful invasions and annexations of the postwar era.

Quae bene valeant: diplomatic knowledge in diplomatic practice

Segretario Machiavelli's letters of instructions to Florentine diplomats concluded with the phrase *Quae bene valeant*: 'for what it's worth'. In this spirit, we now take just a few more lines to discuss what this project might contribute to diplomatic practice. Drawing on the analyses offered in this book, this section concludes that a critical approach to its production and government is vital to avoiding real-life mistakes and, crucially, making better use of the work of diplomats.

In practice, this means critically engaging with knowledge produced and its management.

The method and approach in this book are a possible beginning to better understanding diplomatic knowledge production, its practices and key events, and its relationship with the diplomacy of other actors. It should be applied, I contend, to known policy mistakes to provide critical learning lessons. Using my method, studies such as the two analysed in this book can provide thorough chronology-sensitive guides to the history of present diplomatic communication and the practices invested into it, as well as reveal the interventions of specific officials into knowledge production and its impact.

In the case of Vietnam, we answered an old question that haunted Vietnam policymakers: how did they miss the opportunity to see that 'Hồ Chí Minh was an "Asian Tito"' and not necessarily aligned with the Soviets? We can now determine that this was a disaster facilitated by French accusations of Vietminh communism, which was initially much less successful than might be expected, and only impacted US policy when trusted British allies lied to support the claim, and, even less well-known, when racisms aligned and France pretended to adopt US-style colonial progressivism. Crucially, we also revealed how exactly the pressure of anti-Soviet policy turned US knowledge production into a single-minded blunt tool, producing endless reports on communist phantoms and missing key factors. To avoid future misidentification, all the signs are there right now, waiting to be analysed in the diplomatic text.

There is a clear case for analysing policy mistakes using this method. One close to my interests is Libya in 2011. Analysed in a contribution to a book about new approaches to diplomacy, the method revealed useful insights. Firstly, it was evident that Hillary Clinton's knowledge production circle was extremely narrow and relied heavily on old loyal political hands rather than

State Department work. This made her vulnerable to the outsize influence of journalists she trusted as well as characters like Tony Blair, who praised her for doing 'God's work'. Secondly, it was shown that the policy turn against Gaddafi, from ally of the War on Terror to global enemy, depended heavily on two claims that turned out to be false: that Gaddafi was going to engage in genocide, and that there was a substantial liberal constituency expecting to establish a democracy after his fall. These and other mistakes were completely avoidable. The diplomatic record shows exactly what advice Clinton rejected, when, how she explained this, and more broadly how these mistakes, which led to a multi-sided civil war still ongoing at the time of writing, were made in practice.[26] As with Vietnam and Western Sahara, better use and management of existing diplomatic reporting would have led to better policy decisions, and this method can pinpoint exactly how such mistakes happen.

How about instrumental uses of descriptions? Our analysis found that descriptions are not easily manipulated, and instrumentality is far more easily described than put into effect. While feasible, it is extremely difficult and unpredictable, since crossovers require the alignment of an entire constellation of factors, few of which yield to manipulation and might have unexpected conditions of possibility, like shared hierarchical racism in Vietnam. No analysis can reveal intentions as such, but this method can reveal poor reporting, how it emerged, who and what actions are responsible, and its role in policy. In a case I'd be keen on applying this method to because of its multiple layers of assumed instrumentality, when Bashar Al-Assad of Syria declared in 2012 that Syria was fighting against Islamic 'terrorism', he was not believed – newspapers even put his use of the word 'terror' in scare quotes to emphasise this suspicion.[27] Descriptions delivered by his diplomats were not believed but, worse, as former British Prime Minister David Cameron declared in the House of Commons, the UK government apparently believed the rebels were formed of democratic liberals. We now know Assad was not lying: the rebels were Islamist extremists and ISIS arose as the most extreme. This method could determine how exactly policymakers either ignored reporting or prioritised what fitted their view, revealing how *all* Syrian descriptions were framed as instrumental lies. It could also reveal when poor use of knowledge is being made, even where policymakers are ignoring institutions or making them see the world how they see it. In sum, it is useful to empirically chart how diplomacy and other institutions can see only what they want to see. Such is the power of descriptions, the will to know, the will to refuse to know, and their tragic consequences.

It's all about interests; 'rhetoric cannot substitute for interest', you might say.[28] As we have seen, however, focus on dominant policy concerns produces disastrous mistakes in knowledge production and policy application, and make states vulnerable to the abuse of their concerns we witnessed in the two case studies. Interests as framed in policy are also composed of descriptions of dominant policy concerns, which act as an episteme in governing all knowledge production. In conjunction with the method, this insight holds the key to understanding how power invested into diplomatic knowledge production shapes reporting, analysis, and ultimately information reaching policymakers. The relevance is highly practical: when focus on the tree does not let you see the forest, it is necessary to step aside. The policy of securing subjects and spaces in North Africa was disastrous: it resulted in support of states at the expense of minorities whose repression was facilitated by US assistance, which provoked anti-American responses.[29] After a spate of Malian military and paramilitary abuses facilitated by US assistance, Tuareg autonomy movement MNLA joined forces with Islamist Ansar Dine and took over the north of Mali. Only weeks later, Ansar Dine betrayed its Tuareg allies and took over the region. My research on the diplomacy preceding the Malian crisis revealed that US diplomats reported extensively on Northern Malian grievances. They repeatedly warned that ignoring Tuareg grievances and only shoring up the Malian state was a recipe for disaster.[30]

In sum, this method can help make better use of reporting and prevent mistakes, such as unwittingly helping create Islamic terrorism in North Africa, by revealing the unwanted effects of dominant policy concerns. In Western Sahara, we now know that policy concerns concentrated reporting on 'ungoverned spaces' and subjects, while other concerns fell out of knowledge production. This is a missed opportunity considering excellent work was done and sent to State. Awareness of the power of excessive policy fixation, and particularly of its literally blinding effects, suggests a clear pathway to better utilisation of diplomatic resources. Critically approaching policy priorities and its practical impacts is necessary to ensure that diplomatic knowledge production practices do not make the mistakes we witnessed in Western Sahara and Vietnam, where the terrorist and communist trees meant policymakers never saw the forests behind.

Representations of subjects and their temporal, spatial, and normative contexts are how a state understands whom it is dealing with. Though not done by text itself, representative practices and the descriptions they produce are invested into the diplomatic text, which stands as both their formative site and witness for analysis. These descriptions are the currency of diplomacy's longstanding duty to inform. As this book has shown, they can be so incredibly influential, unleashing military, economic, and diplomatic might, that it is urgent to consider their making, transmission, and development as key to exercising power in international relations. Having discovered how such power can be practiced in and through diplomatic writing, let us now take care in our reporting and analysis. Machiavelli was correct in being so cautious and warning that reporting requires 'prudence' 'rather than punditry', for power lies in the very words that make, categorise, and carry knowledge in the diplomatic pouch.

Notes

1. Kissinger, *White House Years*, Chapter X.
2. Walt, *The Origins of Alliances*, 81.
3. See particularly Walt, 'Alliance Formation and the Balance of World Power'; *The Origins of Alliances*; 'Why Alliances Endure or Collapse'.
4. Vietnam War historian Mark Atwood Lawrence in bloomsbury.com, 'The Road to Vietnam', Bloomsbury, accessed 13 January 2023, https://www.bloomsbury.com/us/road-to-vietnam-9780755637126/
5. Costa Buranelli, 'Authoritarianism as an Institution?'; Costa-Buranelli, '"Do You Know What I Mean?"'.
6. Bull, *The Anarchical Society*, 176.
7. Watson, *Diplomacy*; Reus-Smit, *The Moral Purpose of the State*.
8. H. Butterfield and M. Wight, *Diplomatic Investigations: Essays in the Theory of International Politics* (London: George Allen & Unwin, 1969), 20.
9. Neumann, 'The English School on Diplomacy'.
10. Michelsen, De Orellana, and Costa Buranelli, 'The Reactionary Internationale'.
11. As textualised by China (see the entry for Tibet in the Chinese equivalent of Wikipedia (baike.baidu.com, accessed 16 October 2024) and Morocco (corcas.com, accessed 16 October 2024).
12. Fisher, 'International Perceptions and African Agency'; 'Managing Donor Perceptions'.
13. Fisher, '"Some More Reliable Than Others"'.
14. Der Derian, *On Diplomacy*; Der Derian, *Antidiplomacy*.
15. Constantinou, *On the Way to Diplomacy*.
16. Neumann, 'Returning Practice to the Linguistic Turn'.
17. Adler-Nissen, 'The Diplomacy of Opting Out'; Adler-Nissen, 'Stigma Management in International Relations'.
18. Keys and Yorke, 'Personal and Political Emotions in the Mind of the Diplomat'; Yorke, 'The Significance and Limitations of Empathy in Strategic Communications'; Yorke, 'Is Empathy a Strategic Imperative?'.
19. Ranajit Guha, 'The Prose of Counter-Insurgency', in *Subaltern Studies II* (Delhi: Oxford University Press, 1983), 338.
20. Homi K. Bhabha, *The Location of Culture* (London: Psychology Press, 1994), 339.
21. Vivienne Jabri, *War and the Transformation of Global Politics* (Basingstoke: Palgrave Macmillan, 2007), 62.
22. Jabri, *Discourses on Violence*; Chapter 5 in *The Postcolonial Subject*, 108.

23 Williams, 'Identity and the Politics of Security'; Williams, 'Words, Images, Enemies'.
24 Caron E. Gentry, 'Anxiety and the Creation of the Scapegoated Other', *Critical Studies on Security* 0 (0), 2015, 1–14.
25 Adler-Nissen, 'Stigma Management in International Relations'; *Opting Out of the European Union*.
26 de Orellana, 'The Power of Describing Identity in Diplomacy: Writing Subjects, Territory, Time and Evil at the End of Gaddafi's Libya'.
27 'Bashar Al-Assad Vows to Stamp out "Terror" with Iron Fist', *The Telegraph*, 2013, accessed 4 September 2015, http://www.telegraph.co.uk/news/world-news/middleeast/syria/10222325/Syria-Bashar-al-Assad-vows-to-stamp-out-terror-with-iron-fist.html
28 Stephen M. Walt, 'The Ties That Fray: Why Europe and America Are Drifting Apart', *The National Interest* (54), 1998, 3–11.
29 Gutelius, 'Islam in Northern Mali and the War on Terror'; Larémont, 'Al Qaeda in the Islamic Maghreb'.
30 de Orellana, 'When Diplomacy Identifies Terrorists: Subjects, Identity and Agency in the War on Terror in Mali'.

Bibliography

Primary sources

Archival, digital, and Wikileaks documents are cited by original reference number so that future research can retrace my steps. Citations of archival documents begin with a brief descriptive name ('Memorandum from D'Argenlieu to COMINDO'), followed by the date (British format, day/month/year) and its original archive reference. All translations from French, Spanish, Italian, and Portuguese are my own. The below breakdown of sources includes primarily archival as well as open-source data.

Archives

Archives Diplomatiques du Ministère des Affaires Étrangeres (MAE), Rue de La Courneuve, Paris

Fonds États Associés The collection was in process of migration with a temporary system in place for computer-based requests and recalls when I visited in June 2014. The old system (as found in Tonnesson, Marr and Lawrence) was classified according to Fond/Theme/Date range, like so: Fonds EA /II/A. Fonds EA I refers to the Vichy Forces in Indochina during WWII; II refers to Free French and French Republic affairs 44–48; III is 48 to 54. Within each theme and chronological section, there are divisions by date ranges: A: January 1944 – 6 March 1946, B: 6 March 1946 – 19 December 1946, C: 20 December 1946 – 30 June 1948.

Documents are cited with currently usable MAE box numbers under 'Fond EA' following the new classification and box number like so: '174QO.18, Fond EA, MAE'. The archive has produced a table of equivalences between the coexisting old and new systems so as to be able to correspond old and new references.

Communication avec les États-Unis This is principally on microfilm, so in addition to the MAE reference number I add the film number, as they do not correspond in the least to shelf or recall numbers, in the format: 'Film 4714, 91QO.124, MAE'.

Archives Nationales, Pierrefitte-sur-Seine, Paris

Bidault Presidential papers collection (AN fond 457AP)

Documents cited as: 'Detail of document'+author title_author surname+ ref. For instance: Memorandum 26/4/1946 by Haut-Comissaire D'Argenlieu, AP127, fond 457AN'.

D'Argenlieu private collection (AN fond 517AP)

This is seldom cited as most papers found of relevance were replicated in the Sainteny and Bidault collections, which were made available to me months earlier, since the D'Argenlieu collection, though deposited at the Archives Nationales, is still privately curated and permission must be individually requested and explained. Cited as per Bidault fund.

Archives d'Autre-Mer, Aix en Provence

Ranges consulted include **Collections Indochine et Hanoi.**
For diplomatic papers, since many were copied in the MAE, I preferentially cite the latter version.

Archive Historique Fondation Nationale des Sciences Politiques, Paris

Fond Sainteny (aka Archive Sainteny).
Cited as 'document name'+date+SAbox number, photos as 'Archive Sainteny'.
I must thank the archive of our Parisian sister institute, better known as Sciences-Po, for the absolute trust and availability of Madame Parcollet, the archivist, who simply gave me all the boxes at once and let me have free rein over them for over a week, including photos featured in this book.

National Archives and Records Administration (NARA)

State Department Diplomatic communication and telegrams in Record Group 59 (State Department), particularly file ranges under G51 (France) and subsequent series under G51 and a letter, each of which refers to a French colony.
Cited as per original NARA reference: '"Memorandum XXX", 851G.00/7–2646, RG59, NARA'. Document dates are included in original NARA reference – in the example here (7–2646) it's the 26th July 1946, so they are omitted from my citations. 'Conversation' refers to 'Memorandum of Conversation'; 'Memorandum' refers to office-produced analysis, summary, and abridged communications memoranda; and 'Mission name to State' or vice versa denote cables and airmail and diplomatic pouch dispatches.
Posters and maps archive at NARA

CIA Declassified Records: CIA Records Search Tool (CREST)

https://www.cia.gov/readingroom/collection/crest-25-year-program-archive, accessed 16 October 2024.
Ranges include **1945–54** on SEA and FE affairs/ **1975–89** on North and West African records.
The entire archive is digital but cannot be browsed; it is only searchable by keyword and date. Performed using searches for Vietminh, Vietnam, Cochinchine, Tonkin, Annam, Bao Dai, Ho Chi Minh/POLISARIO, El Ouali, Western Sahara, Morocco, Sahara Occidental, Sahara Marocain, to guide file identification. Methodological

backtracking developed in this book was applied. Cited using original CIA declassification number (a condition of using this archive is to cite using these long declassification document ID numbers), as: 'short description of document', date/date/date, CIA-RDP 00-L00000NGDECLASSIF1CATI000NNUMBER-00, CREST.

Other primary sources

Conseil Royal Consultatif pour les affaires Sahariennes (CORCAS)

Reports, press releases, press highlights, policy papers and declarations cited by date. Available at http://www.corcas.com.
Cited as '11/6/2010, CORCAS'.
Speeches of the King of Morocco.
All available at http://www.maroc.ma/fr/discours-du-roi. Cited by date in the format: 'Royal Speech', x/x/xxxx. Originals in French, all translations my own.

Moroccan-American Centre for Policy (MACP)

Documents available online at http://moroccoonthemove.com.
Policy statements, as well as republished material from other sources, including scholarly, legal, commercial, and policy statements.

Maghreb Arab Press (MAP)

Government press releases and highlights, analysis, and policy statements available at http://www.map.ma/. Cited by date.

Association pour le Référendum au Sahara Occidental (ARSO)

Often used by SADR ministers and high-raking officials and diplomatic officers as a mouthpiece for policy positions, statements; see for instance letter response to ESISC. Cited by date and original document reference since they hail from a number of sources. Cited as 'Reply of the SADR Ministry of Foreign Affairs to the ESISC', 29/9/2005, retrieved August 2010.

European Strategic Intelligence and Security Center, ESISC

Reports available at http://www.esisc.org/.
'The Polisario Front and the development of terrorism in the Sahel', May 2010.
'Unlikely bedfellows: Are some Saharan Marxists joining al Qaeda operations in North Africa?' 3 January 2011.
'The Polisario Front: Credible negotiations partner or after-effect of the Cold War and obstacle to a political solution in Western Sahara?' November 2005.

Collective of Human Rights Associations in the Sahara, CHRAS

It does not have a website. Its reports, all undated, were available and retrieved by the researcher in 2010 at the website of the Moroccan Embassy in London after friendly advice by an embassy employee.

'The embezzlement of Humanitaren aid by the Polisario' [sic].
'The Polisario detains confined population in the camps of Tindouf, South of Algeria, against their will'.
'Stop the breaking up of families: Let the children go back to their mothers'.
'The violation of humain rights in the camps of Tindouf' [sic].

Sahara Press Service, SPS

Official press agency of the Sahrawi Arab Democratic Republic and POLISARIO Front. Available online at http://spsrasd.info/.

United Nations

Security Council and General Assembly resolutions.
UN Secretariat, Special Envoy and Research reports.
All available permanently at http://www.un.org/documents.
Cited by original reference number in the format: 'Reply of the Kingdom of Morocco', Enclosure to 'Report of the Secretary-General on the situation concerning Western Sahara', S/2004/325, UN.

US Department of State

Public communications, documents, press releases, declarations, and documents released under Freedom of Information Act requests 2001–9 available as a permanent archive at http://2001-2009.state.gov. Cited by original document title and date in the format: Taken Question, 1/5/2008, Office of the Spokesman, Department of State.

Wikileaks 'Cablegate' Department of State diplomatic cables

Available at http://www.wikileaks.org (not a reliable website, I had my own copy of the entire collection of cables), and also as fully searchable texts at https://cablegatesearch.wikileaks.org/search.php. All the Wikileaks cables cited can be found on that website using the original State department reference (e.g. 05RABAT458). Cited by date (day and month in British format) and original State Department reference number (which includes year and station of origin) in the format: '3/12, 05RABAT458'. In this example, 'RABAT' indicates a cable from Rabat Embassy to State Department. For State department cables to stations, destination is indicated.

Published document collections

Blum, Robert M., and United States Congress Senate Committee on Foreign Relations. *The United States and Vietnam, 1944–1947: A Staff Study Based on the Pentagon Papers Prepared for the Use of the United States Senate Committee on Foreign Relations*. Washington, DC: U.S. Government Printing Office, 1972.
de Gaulle, Charles. *Le salut 1944–1946*. Paris: Pocket, 2010.

de Gaulle, Charles. *Le salut 1944–1946*. Paris: Pocket, 2010.
de Gaulle, Charles. *Lettres, notes et carnets. [5], [5]*, Paris: Plon, 1983.
de Gaulle, Charles. *Lettres, notes et carnets 8 Mai 1945 – 18 Juin 1951*. Paris: Plon, 1983.
de Gaulle, Charles. *Lettres, notes et carnets. 1943–1945*. Paris: Plon, 1983.
de Gaulle, Charles. *Lettres, notes et carnets: Tome 2, 1942 – mai 1958*. Paris: R. Laffont, 2010.
Devillers, Philippe, ed. *Paris-Saigon-Hanoi: les archives de la guerre, 1944–1947*. [Paris]: Gallimard: Julliard, 1988.
'Foreign Relations of the United States'. Accessed May 14, 2015. http://uwdc.library.wisc.edu/collections/FRUS.
Porter, Gareth, ed. *Vietnam: A History in Documents*. New York: New American Library, 1979.
Gravel, ed. *The Pentagon Papers: The Defense Department History of United States Decisionmaking on Vietnam. Vol. 1*. Boston, MA: Beacon Press, 1971.
Herring, George C. *The Secret Diplomacy of the Vietnam War: The Negotiating Volumes of the Pentagon Papers*. Austin, TX: University of Texas Press, 1983.
Williams, William Appleman, Thomas McCormick, Lloyd C. Gardner, and Walter LaFeber, eds. *America in Vietnam: A Documentary History*. Reissue edition. New York: W. W. Norton & Company, 1989.

Newspapers

L'aube
L'aurore
El País
Le Figaro
L'Humanité
Le Monde
The New York Times
The Washington Post

Secondary sources

Adler, E. 'The Spread of Security Communities: Communities of Practice, Self-Restraint, and NATO's Post-Cold War Transformation'. *European Journal of International Relations* 14, no. 2 (2008): 195–230.
Adler, Emanuel, and Vincent Pouliot, eds. *International Practices*. Cambridge: Cambridge University Press, 2011.
Adler-Nissen, Rebecca. 'The Diplomacy of Opting Out: A Bourdieudian Approach to National Integration Strategies'. *JCMS: Journal of Common Market Studies* 46, no. 3 (2008): 663–84.

Adler-Nissen, Rebecca. 'Diplomatic Agency'. In *SAGE Handbook of Diplomacy*, 92–103. London: SAGE Publications, 2016.
Adler-Nissen, Rebecca. *Opting Out of the European Union: Diplomacy, Sovereignty and European Integration*. Cambridge: Cambridge University Press, 2014.
Adler-Nissen, Rebecca. 'Stigma Management in International Relations: Transgressive Identities, Norms, and Order in International Society'. *International Organization* 68, no. 01 (2014): 143–76.
Adler-Nissen, Rebecca, and Alena Drieschova. 'Track-Change Diplomacy: Technology, Affordances, and the Practice of International Negotiations'. *International Studies Quarterly* 63, no. 3 (2019): 531–45.
Adler-Nissen, Rebecca, and Vincent Pouliot. 'Power in Practice: Negotiating the International Intervention in Libya'. *European Journal of International Relations* 20, no. 4 (2014): 889–911.
Alberti, Leon Battista. *On the Art of Building in Ten Books*. New Edition. Cambridge, MA: MIT Press, 1991.
Ali Salem Iselmu. 'El Mundo de Los Ignorados', http://generaciondelaamistad.blogspot.co.uk/2015/06/poema-de-ali-salem-iselmu-en-apoyo-la.html, accessed 16 October 2024.
Allison, Graham T., and Philip Zelikow. *Essence of Decision: Explaining the Cuban Missile Crisis*. Second Edition. New York: Pearson, 1999.
Alloul, Houssine, and Darina Martykánová. 'Introduction: Charting New Ground in the Study of Ottoman Foreign Relations'. *The International History Review* 43, no. 5 (2021): 1018–40.
American Odyssey. Dune Films, Fabrik Entertainment, Pico Creek Productions, 2015.
Anderson, Kenneth. 'Denial of Territory to Terrorist Groups in US Counterterrorism Strategy'. SSRN Paper. Rochester, NY: Social Science Research Network, 2013.
Anonymous. Interview with a senior Foreign Affairs analyst, Senate Foreign Relations Committee, 2014.
Anonymous. Interview with former State Department analyst, 2014.
Anonymous. Interview with Senate Member Foreign Relations analyst and advisor, 2014.
Arangio Ruiz, Vladimiro, ed. *Niccolo Machiavelli, Scritti Scelti*. Verona: Mondadori, 1941.
Argenlieu, Thierry d'. *Chronique d'Indochine: 1945–1947*. Paris: A. Michel, 1985.
Aristotle. *The Art of Rhetoric*. Translated by Hugh Lawson-Tancred. Reissue Edition. London: Penguin Classics, 1991.
Aristotle. *Topics – Aristotle*. S.l.: NuVision Publications. Sioux Falls, SD: 2005.
Ashford, Douglas E. 'The Irredentist Appeal in Morocco and Mauritania'. *Political Research Quarterly* 15, no. 4 (1962): 641–51.
Ashley, Richard K. 'Living on Border Lines: Man, Poststructuralism, and War'. In *International/Intertextual Relations: Postmodern Readings of World Politics*, edited by James Der Derian and Michael J. Shapiro, 259–321. Lexington, MA: Lexington Books, 1989.
ASÍ QUIERO SER (EL NIÑO DEL NUEVO ESTADO) [I Want to Be Like This (the Child of the New State)]. Lecturas Civicas. Burgos: Hijos de Santiago Rodriguez, 1940.

Association de soutien à un référendum libre et régulier au Sahara Occidental, https://www.arso.org/index.htm, accessed 9 August 2015.
Austin, John Langshaw. *Quand dire, c'est faire*. Translated by Gilles Lane. Paris: Seuil, 1970.
Austin, John Langshaw. *How to Do Things with Words*. Oxford: Clarendon Press, 1975.
'Autonomy Plan – The Kingdom on the Move'. 2015.
Bakhtin, M. M. *Dialogic Imagination: Four Essays*. Edited by Michael Holquist. Translated by Caryl Emerson. Austin, TX: University of Texas Press, 1982.
Banai, Hussein. 'Diplomatic Imaginations: Mediating Estrangement in World Society'. *Cambridge Review of International Affairs* 27, no. 3 (2014): 459–74.
Bartelson, J. *A Genealogy of Sovereignty*. Cambridge: Cambridge University Press, 1995.
Bartelson, J. 'The Concept of Sovereignty Revisited'. *European Journal of International Law* 17, no. 2 (2006): 463.
Barthes, R. *S/Z*. New York: Hill and Wang, 1974.
Barthes, Roland. *Leçon Inaugurale de La Chaire de Semiologie Litteraire Du College de France*. Paris: Seuil, 1978.
Barthes, Roland. *Roland Barthes, par Roland Barthes*. Paris: Points, 2014.
'Bashar Al-Assad Vows to Stamp out "Terror" with Iron Fist'. *The Telegraph*, 2013.
Beim, Aaron, and Gary Alan Fine. 'The Cultural Frameworks of Prejudice: Reputational Images and the Postwar Disjuncture of Jews and Communism'. *Sociological Quarterly* 48, no. 3 (2007): 373–97.
Berridge, G. *Diplomacy: Theory and Practice*. London: Palgrave Macmillan, 2002.
Berridge, G. R. 'Machiavelli: Human Nature, Good Faith, and Diplomacy'. *Review of International Studies* 27, no. 04 (2001): 539–56.
Berridge, G. R., Maurice Keens-Soper, and Thomas Otte. *Diplomatic Theory from Machiavelli to Kissinger*. London: Palgrave Macmillan, 2001.
Bhabha, Homi K. *The Location of Culture*. London: Psychology Press, 1994.
Blum, Robert M., and United States Congress Senate Committee on Foreign Relations. *The United States and Vietnam, 1944–1947: A Staff Study Based on the Pentagon Papers Prepared for the Use of the United States Senate Committee on Foreign Relations*. Washington, DC: U.S. Government Printing Office, 1972.
Bolton, J. *Surrender Is Not an Option: Defending America at the United Nations*. New York: Threshold Editions, 2008.
Botero, Giovanni. *Della ragion di Stato e delle cause della grandezza della città*. Venice: Forni Editori, 1598.
Botero, Giovanni. *Relations of the Most Famous Kingdoms and Common-Weales Thorough the World*. Iohn Iaggard, 1611.
Bottelier, Th. W. '"Not on a Purely Nationalistic Basis": The Internationalism of Allied Coalition Warfare in the Second World War'. *European Review of History: Revue Européenne d'histoire* 27, no. 1–2 (2020): 152–75.
Bottelier, Th. W. 'Of Once and Future Kings: Rethinking the Anglo-American Analogy in the Rising Powers Debate'. *The International History Review* 39, no. 5 (2017): 751–69.
Boudali, Lianne K. 'The Trans-Sahara Counterterrorism Partnership'. 2007.

Bourdieu, Pierre. *Science de la science et réflexivité. Cours du Collège de France 2000–2001*. Paris: Liber, 2001.
Bradley, Mark Philip. *Imagining Vietnam and America: The Making of Postcolonial Vietnam, 1919–1950*. Chapel Hill, NC: University of North Carolina Press, 2000.
Bradley, Mark Philip, and Marilyn B. Young. *Making Sense of the Vietnam Wars: Local, National, and Transnational Perspectives*. New York: OUP USA, 2008.
'British Official Sees Red Drive in Asia'. *New York Times*, 1948.
Bull, Hedley. *The Anarchical Society: A Study of Order in World Politics*. New York: Columbia University Press, 2002.
Bull, Hedley. 'Society and Anarchy in International Relations'. In *Diplomatic Investigations: Essays in the Theory of International Politics*, edited by H. Butterfield and M. Wight. London: George Allen & Unwin, 1969.
Busch, Peter. 'Constructing Vietnam …' *Diplomatic History* 31, no. 1 (2007): 155–58.
Bush, Christopher. 'The Other of the Other?: Cultural Studies, Theory, and the Location of the Modernist Signifier'. *Comparative Literature Studies* 42, no. 2 (2005): 162–80.
Butterfield, H., and M. Wight. *Diplomatic Investigations: Essays in the Theory of International Politics*. London: George Allen & Unwin, 1969.
Buttinger, Joseph. *The Smaller Dragon*. Westport, CT: Praeger, 1958.
Buzan, Barry, and Lene Hansen. *The Evolution of International Security Studies*. Cambridge: Cambridge University Press, 2009.
Buzan, Barry, and Laust Schouenborg. *Global International Society: A New Framework for Analysis*. Cambridge: Cambridge University Press, 2018.
Buzan, Barry, Ole Wæver, and Jaap De Wilde. *Security: A New Framework for Analysis*. Boulder, CO: Lynne Rienner Publishers, 1998.
Byrne, Jeffrey James. 'Our Own Special Brand of Socialism: Algeria and the Contest of Modernities in the 1960s'. *Diplomatic History* 33, no. 3 (2009): 427–47.
Callières, François de. *De la manière de négocier avec les souverains*. Paris: Michel Brunet, 1716.
Campbell, David. *National Deconstruction: Violence, Identity and Justice in Bosnia*. Minneapolis, MN: University of Minnesota Press, 1998.
Campbell, David. *Writing Security: United States Foreign Policy and the Politics of Identity*. Second Revised Edition 1998. Manchester: Manchester University Press, 1992.
Chan, Stephen. *Exporting Apartheid*. London: Macmillan Education, 1990.
'China Week: Xinjiang'. BBC, 2015, sec. China.
Chingambo, Lloyd John, and Stephen Chan. 'Sanctions and South Africa: Strategies, Strangleholds, and Self-Consciousness'. *Global Society: Journal of Interdisciplinary International Relations* 2, no. 2 (1988): 112–32.
Chinh, Trường. *The August Revolution*. Hanoi: Foreign Languages Publishing House, 1958.
Chinh, Trường. *The Resistance Will Win*. Hanoi: Foreign Languages Publishing House, 1960.

Chinh, Trường, and Bernard B. Fall. *Primer for Revolt: The Communist Takeover in Viet-Nam*. Cambridge: Cambridge University Press, 1963.

'CIA Tapes Prove Morocco Rendition'. *The Australian*, 9 August 2010.

Cicero, Marcus Tullius. *Cicero's Brutus or History of Famous Orators; Also His Orator, or Accomplished Speaker*. Translated by E. Jones, 2006. Project Gutenberg: EBook-No. 9776, http://www.gutenberg.org/ebooks/9776, accessed 21 April 2015.

Cizek, Judith. 'The "Définition Du Néo-Traditionnisme" of Maurice Denis: Contributing Factors Leading to Its Content, Its Premises, and Later Influences'. MA, Northern Illinois University, 1975, https://huskiecommons.lib.niu.edu/allgraduate-thesesdissertations/5273/, accessed 16 October 2024.

Cline, Lawrence. 'Counterterrorism Strategy in the Sahel'. *Studies in Conflict & Terrorism* 30, no. 10 (2007): 889–99.

Colin P. Clarke and Christopher Paul. 'From Stalemate to Settlement: Lessons for Afghanistan from Historical Insurgencies'. Washington DC: RAND, 2014.

Colin Powell, UN Security Council, 2003.

'Colonies in Ferment'. *New York Times*, 1945, sec. The Week in Review.

'Communists Attack in Area Near Peiping'. *New York Times*, 1947.

Connolly, William E. 'The Evangelical-Capitalist Resonance Machine'. *Political Theory* 33, no. 6 (2005): 869–86.

Connolly, William E. 'Identity and Difference in Global Politics'. In *International/Intertextual Relations*. Lexington, MA: Lexington Books, 1989.

Connolly, William E. *Identity/Difference: Democratic Negotiations of Political Paradox*. Minneapolis, MN: University of Minnesota Press, 2002.

Connolly, William E. 'The Politics of Discourse'. In *Language and Politics*, edited by Michael Shapiro, 139–67. Oxford: Blackwell, 1984.

Constantinou, C. M. *On the Way to Diplomacy*. Minneapolis, MN: University of Minnesota Press, 1996.

Constantinou, C. M., O. P. Richmond, and A. Watson. *Cultures and Politics of Global Communication: Volume 34, Review of International Studies*. Cambridge: Cambridge University Press, 2008.

Constantinou, Costas M. 'Between Statecraft and Humanism: Diplomacy and Its Forms of Knowledge'. *International Studies Review* 15, no. 2 (2013): 141–62.

Constantinou, Costas M., and James Der Derian. 'Introduction: Sustaining Global Hope: Sovereignty, Power and the Transformation of Diplomacy'. In *Sustainable Diplomacies*, edited by Costas M. Constantinou and James Der Derian, 1–22. London: Palgrave Macmillan UK, 2010.

Constantinou, Costas M., Pauline Kerr, and Paul Sharp. *The SAGE Handbook of Diplomacy*. First Edition. Los Angeles, CA: SAGE Publications Ltd, 2016.

Constantinou, Costas M., and Sam Okoth Opondo. 'On Biodiplomacy: Negotiating Life and Plural Modes of Existence'. *Journal of International Political Theory*, 2019, 1755088219877423.

Constitución de España. 'Estatuto de Autonomía de Cataluña'.

Cooke, Alistair. *A Generation on Trial: U.S.A. v. Alger Hiss*. New York: Open Road Media, 2014.

Cooper, Andrew F., Jorge Heine, and Ramesh Thakur. *The Oxford Handbook of Modern Diplomacy*. Oxford: Oxford University Press, 2013.
Costa Buranelli, Filippo. 'Authoritarianism as an Institution? The Case of Central Asia'. *International Studies Quarterly* 64, no. 4 (2020): 1005–16.
Costa-Buranelli, Filippo. '"Do You Know What I Mean?" "Not Exactly": English School, Global International Society and the Polysemy of Institutions'. *Global Discourse* 5, no. 3 (2015): 499–514.
Crean, Jeffrey. 'War on the Line: Telephone Diplomacy in the Making and Maintenance of the Desert Storm Coalition'. *Diplomacy & Statecraft* 26, no. 1 (2015): 124–38.
Crowley, Colm, Rom Harre, and Clare Tagg. 'Qualitative Research and Computing: Methodological Issues and Practices in Using QSR NVivo and NUD*IST'. *International Journal of Social Research Methodology* 5, no. 3 (2002): 193–97.
Curtius, Ernst Robert. *European Literature and the Latin Middle Ages*. Princeton, NJ: Princeton University Press, 1953.
Damis, John. 'Morocco's 1995 Fisheries Agreement with the European Union: A Crisis Resolved'. *Mediterranean Politics* 3, no. 2 (1998): 61–73.
Department of State. 'Human Rights Reports', 2009.
Department of State. The Office of Electronic Information, Bureau of Public Affairs. 'Article 98 Agreements and the International Criminal Court', 2006.
Department of State. The Office of Website Management, Bureau of Public Affairs. 'Remarks with Moroccan Foreign Minister Taieb Fassi-Fihri'. Remarks|Remarks. U.S. Department of State, 2009.
Der Derian, J. *Antidiplomacy: Spies, Terror, Speed, and War*. Cambridge, MA: Blackwell, 1992.
Der Derian, J. *On Diplomacy: A Genealogy of Western Estrangement*. Oxford: Oxford University Press, 1987.
Der Derian, James. 'Great Men, Monumental History, and Not-So-Grand Theory: A Meta-Review of Henry Kissinger's Diplomacy'. *Mershon International Studies Review* 39, no. 1 (1995): 173.
Derrida, J. *The Post Card: From Socrates to Freud and Beyond*. Chicago, IL: University of Chicago Press, 1987.
Derrida, J. *Writing and Difference*. London: Routledge, 2001.
Derrida, Jacques, Peter Caws, and Mary Ann Caws. 'Sending: On Representation'. *Social Research*, 1982, 294–326.
Deubel, Tara Flynn. 'Poetics of Diaspora: Sahrawi Poets and Postcolonial Transformations of a Trans-Saharan Genre in Northwest Africa'. *The Journal of North African Studies* 17, no. 2 (2012): 295–314.
Deutsch, Karl W. 'On Communication Models in the Social Sciences'. *Public Opinion Quarterly* 16, no. 3 (1952): 356–80.
Deutsch, Karl Wolfgang. *Nationalism and Social Communication: An Inquiry into the Foundations of Nationality*. Cambridge, MA: MIT Press, 1953.
Deutsch, Karl Wolfgang, and Karl W. Deutsch. *The Nerves of Government: Models of Political Communication and Control*. New York: Free Press of Glencoe, 1963.
Devillers, Philippe. *End of a War: Indo-China, 1954*. New York: Praeger, 1969.

Devillers, Philippe. *Histoire du Viêt-Nam de 1940 à 1952*. Paris: Editions du Seuil, 1952.
Devillers, Philippe, ed. *Paris-Saigon-Hanoi: les archives de la guerre, 1944–1947*. Paris: Gallimard, 1988.
DIDH. 'Délégation Interministérielle Aux Droits de l'Homme'. https://didh.gov.ma/wp-content/uploads/2024/06/la-note-conceptuelle.pdf, accessed 16 October 2024.
Discussion with D. Colas, A. Grosrichard, G. Le Gaufey, J. Livi, G. Miller, J. Miller, J.-A. Miller, C, Millot, G. Wajeman. 'Le Jeu de Michel Foucault'. *Bulletin Périodique Du Champ Freudien*, no. 10 (1977): 62–93.
Dittmer, Jason. *Diplomatic Material: Affect, Assemblage, and Foreign Policy*. Durham, NC: Duke University Press Books, 2017.
Dittmer, Jason, and Fiona McConnell, eds. *Diplomatic Cultures and International Politics: Translations, Spaces and Alternatives*. First Edition. London: Routledge, 2015.
Drinkwater, Derek. *Sir Harold Nicolson and International Relations: The Practitioner as Theorist*. Oxford: Oxford University Press, 2005.
Duiker, William J. *Ho Chi Minh: A Life*. London: Hachette Books, 2012.
Edkins, Jenny. *Poststructuralism & International Relations: Bringing the Political Back In*. Boulder, CO: Lynne Rienner Publishers, 1999.
Edwards, Jill. *Anglo-American Relations and the Franco Question, 1945–1955*. Oxford: Oxford University Press, 1999.
Eliot, T. S. *Four Quartets*. London: Faber & Faber, 2001.
Enloe, Cynthia. *Bananas, Beaches and Bases: Making Feminist Sense of International Politics*. Berkeley, CA: University of California Press, 2014.
Epstein, Charlotte. 'Who Speaks? Discourse, the Subject and the Study of Identity in International Politics'. *European Journal of International Relations* 17, no. 2 (2011): 327–50.
Erlandsson, Susanna. *Personal Politics in the Postwar World: Western Diplomacy Behind the Scenes*. London: Bloomsbury Academic, 2022.
'EXECUTIVE ORDER 9835 | Harry S. Truman'. https://www.trumanlibrary.gov/library/executive-orders/9835/executive-order-9835, accessed 16 October 2024.
'Falange Española de Las JONS'. https://falange.es/, accessed 16 October 2024.
Falcone, Michael. '2008: Obama on Terrorism'. *New York Times*, 2007.
Fall, Bernard B. *The Two Viet-Nams: A Political and Military Analysis*. Westport, CT: Praeger, 1967.
Fan, Ying. 'Branding the Nation: Towards a Better Understanding'. *Place Branding and Public Diplomacy* 6, no. 2 (2010): 97–103.
Farah, Randa. 'Sovereignty on Borrowed Territory: Sahrawi Identity in Algeria'. *Georgetown Journal of International Affairs* 11, no. 2 (2010): 59–66.
Farwell, James P. *Persuasion and Power: The Art of Strategic Communication*. Washington, DC: Georgetown University Press, 2012.
Fassi, Enoch El. 'Immersion dans le monde des hommes prostitués'. Afrik.com. Accessed 15 August 2015.

Feinberg, Alexander. 'Alger Hiss Denies Ever Turning over Any State Papers: Nixon Wants Tighter Law'. *New York Times*, 1948.

Fernández-Molina, Irene. 'Introduction: Towards a Multilevel Analysis of the Western Sahara Conflict and the Effects of Its Protractedness'. In *Global, Regional and Local Dimensions of Western Sahara's Protracted Decolonization*, edited by Raquel Ojeda-Garcia, Irene Fernández-Molina, and Victoria Veguilla, 1–33. London: Palgrave Macmillan US, 2017.

Fernandez-Molina, Irene. *Moroccan Foreign Policy under Mohammed VI, 1999–2014*. London: Routledge, 2015.

Fierke, K. M. *Diplomatic Interventions: Conflict and Change in a Globalizing World*. Basingstoke: Palgrave, 2005.

Fierke, K. M. *Political Self-Sacrifice Agency, Body and Emotion in International Relations*. New York: Cambridge University Press, 2013.

Fifield, Russell H. 'The Thirty Years War in Indochina: A Conceptual Framework'. *Asian Survey*, 1977, 857–79.

Figliuolo, Bruno, and Francesco Senatore. 'Per un ritratto del buon ambasciatore: regole di comportamento e profilo dell'inviato negli scritti di Diomede Carafa, Niccolò Machiavelli e Francesco Guicciardini'. In *De l'ambassadeur : Les écrits relatifs à l'ambassadeur et à l'art de négocier du Moyen Âge au début du xixe siècle*, edited by Stefano Andretta, Stéphane Péquignot, and Jean-Claude Waquet. Collection de l'École française de Rome. Rome: Publications de l'École française de Rome, 2016.

Finnemore, M., and K. Sikkink. 'Taking Stock: The Constructivist Research Program in International Relations and Comparative Politics'. *Annual Review of Political Science* 4, no. 1 (2001): 391–416.

Finnemore, Martha, and Kathryn Sikkink. 'International Norm Dynamics and Political Change'. *International Organization* 52, no. 4 (1998): 887–917.

Fish, Stanley E. 'How to Do Things with Austin and Searle: Speech Act Theory and Literary Criticism'. *Modern Language Notes* 91, no. 5 (1976): 983–1025.

Fisher, Jonathan. 'International Perceptions and African Agency : Uganda and Its Donors 1986–2010'. D. Phil, University of Oxford, 2011.

Fisher, Jonathan. 'Managing Donor Perceptions: Contextualizing Uganda's 2007 Intervention in Somalia'. *African Affairs* 111, no. 444 (2012): 404–23.

Fisher, Jonathan. '"Some More Reliable Than Others": Image Management, Donor Perceptions and the Global War on Terror in East African Diplomacy'. *The Journal of Modern African Studies* 51, no. 01 (2013): 1–31.

Fisher, Jonathan. 'Structure, Agency and Africa in the International System: Donor Diplomacy and Regional Security Policy in East Africa since the 1990s'. *Conflict, Security & Development* 13, no. 5 (2013): 537–67.

'Foreign Relations of the United States'. https://www.archives.gov/research/alic/reference/foreign-relations/about-frus.html, accessed 16 October 2024.

Foucault, M. *Power/Knowledge*. Edited by C. Gordon. New York: Pantheon Books, 1980.

Foucault, Michel. *The Archaeology of Knowledge*. London: Tavistock Publications, 1972.

Foucault, Michel. *Archaeology of Knowledge*. Routledge, 2002.
Foucault, Michel. 'Nietzsche, Genealogy, History'. In *The Foucault Reader*, edited by Paul Rabinow. New York: Random House, 1984.
Foucault, Michel. 'The Order of Discourse'. In *Language and Politics*, edited by Michael Shapiro. Oxford: Blackwell, 1984.
Foucault, Michel. *The Order of Things: An Archaeology of the Human Sciences*. London: Routledge, 2002.
Foucault, Michel. *Power/Knowledge: Selected Interviews and Other Writings, 1972–1977*. New York: Random House USA Inc, 1988.
'France in Indo-China'. *New York Times*, 1947, sec. Review of the week's editorials.
France-Presse, Agence. 'China Condemns British Inquiry into Progress of Hong Kong Democracy'. *The Guardian*, 2014.
France-Presse, Agenc. 'Moroccan Teenage Girls to Face Trial on Homosexuality Charges'. *The Guardian*, 2016, sec. World news.
Franchini, Philippe. *Les Guerres d'Indochine: de la Bataille de Dien Bien Phu à La Chute de Saigon*. Vol. 2. Paris: Pygmalion/G. Watelet, 1988.
Franchini, Philippe. *Les Mensonges de La Guerre d'Indochine*. Paris: Éd. France loisirs, 2003.
Franchini, Philippe, ed. *Saigon: 1925–1945: de la Belle Colonie à léclosion révolutionnaire, ou, la fin des dieux blancs*. Paris: Autrement, 1992.
Freeman, Damien. *Art's Emotions: Ethics, Expression and Aesthetic Experience*. London: Routledge, 2014.
Friedner Parrat, Charlotta. 'Change in International Society: How Not to Recreate the "First Debate" of International Relations'. *International Studies Review* 22, no. 4 (2020): 758–78.
'FRUS 1945, Vol. IV, Europe'. US State Department, 1945.
Gaudio, Attilio. *Guerres et Paix Au Maroc: Reportages, 1950–1990*. Paris: Karthala Editions, 1950.
Gaulle, Charles de. *Lettres, notes et carnets. 1943–1945*. Paris: Plon, 1983.
Gaulle, Charles de. *Lettres, notes et carnets: Tome 2, 1942–mai 1958*. Paris: R. Laffont, 2010.
Gentry, Caron E. 'Anxiety and the Creation of the Scapegoated Other'. *Critical Studies on Security* 0, no. 0 (2015): 1–14.
'George Kennan "The Sources of Soviet Conduct" (1946)'.
Giddens, Anthony. *The Constitution of Society: Outline of the Theory of Structuration*. New Edition. Cambridge: Polity Press, 1986.
Gilpin, Robert. *War and Change in World Politics*. Cambridge: Cambridge University Press, 1983.
Gkoutzioulis, Athanasios. 'With Great Power Comes Great Responsibility: On Foucault's Notions of Power, Subjectivity, Freedom and Their (Mis)Understanding in IR'. *Global Society* 32, no. 1 (2018): 88–110.
Gordon, Michael R. 'North Africa New Test for U.S. as Terror Cells Spread'. *New York Times*, 2013.
Gourou, Pierre. *L'avenir de l'Indochine*. Paris: P. Hartmann, 1947.
Gourou, Pierre. *Le Tonkin*. Mâcon: Protat Imprimeurs, 1931.

Gourou, Pierre. *Utilisation du sol en Indochine Française*. Paris: Hartmann, 1940.
Gow, James, 'Funmi Olonisakin, and Ernst Dijxhoorn. 'Deep History and International Security: Social Conditions and Competition, Militancy and Violence in West Africa'. *Conflict, Security & Development* 13, no. 2 (2013): 231–58.
Gragnolati, M. *Experiencing the Afterlife: Soul and Body in Dante and Medieval Culture*. Notre Dame, IN: University of Notre Dame Press, 2005.
'Grave Peril Seen in Berlin Action'. *New York Times*, 1948.
Gravel, Mike, ed. *The Pentagon Papers: The Defense Department History of United States Decisionmaking on Vietnam*. Vol. 1. Boston, MA: Beacon Press, 1971.
Greene, Graham. *The Honorary Consul*. London: Vintage Classics, 2004.
Greene, Graham. *The Quiet American*. London: Heineman, 1955.
Grosser, Pierre. *Traiter avec le diable ? Les vrais enjeux de la diplomatie au XXIe siècle*. Paris: Odile Jacob, 2013.
Guha, Ranajit. 'The Prose of Counter-Insurgency'. In *Subaltern Studies II*. Delhi: Oxford University Press, 1983.
Guill, Stacey. 'Pilar and Maria: Hemingway's Feminist Homage to the "New Woman of Spain" in *For Whom the Bell Tolls*'. *The Hemingway Review* 30, no. 2 (2011): 7–20.
Gunn, Geoffrey C. 'Prelude to the First Indochina War: New Light on the Fontainebleau Conference of July–September 1946 and Aftermath'. *Annual Review of Southeast Asian Studies* 54 (2013): 19–51.
Gurman, Hannah. '"Learn to Write Well": The China Hands and the Communistification of Diplomatic Reporting'. *Journal of Contemporary History* 45, no. 2 (2010): 430–53.
Gutelius, David. 'Islam in Northern Mali and the War on Terror'. *Journal of Contemporary African Studies* 25, no. 1 (2007): 59–76.
Hailey, Foster. 'The Old Era Is Gone in the Far East: The Area Will Never Again Be an Open Field for Political and Economic Imperialists.' *New York Times*, 1947, sec. Magazine.
Hanauer, Laurence S. 'Irrelevance of Self-Determination Law to Ethno-National Conflict: A New Look at the Western Sahara Case'. *Emory International Law Review* 9 (1995): 133.
Hansen, L. *Security as Practice: Discourse Analysis and the Bosnian War*. London: Routledge, 2006.
Hansen, Lene. 'A Case for Seduction? Evaluating the Poststructuralist Conceptualization of Security'. *Cooperation and Conflict* 32, no. 4 (1997): 369–97.
Haslam, Jonathan. *No Virtue Like Necessity*. New Haven, CT: Yale University Press, 2002.
Heggoy, A. A. 'Colonial Origins of the Algerian–Moroccan Border Conflict of October 1963'. *African Studies Review*, 1970, 17–22.
Hendler, Clint. 'What We Didn't Know Has Hurt Us: The Bush Administration Was Pathological about Secrecy. Here's What Needs to Be Undone after Eight

Dark Years – and Why It Won't Be Easy'. *Columbia Journalism Review* 47, no. 5 (2009): 28–33.

Hergé. *Tintin: Le Crabe aux Pinces d'Or*. Tournai: Egmont, 2011.

Herring, George C. *America's Longest War: The United States and Vietnam, 1950–1975*. Fourth Edition. Boston, MA: McGraw-Hill, 2001.

Herring, George C. 'The Truman Administration and the Restoration of French Sovereignty in Indochina'. *Diplomatic History* 1, no. 2 (1977): 97–117.

Hess, Gary R. 'Franklin Roosevelt and Indochina'. *The Journal of American History* 59, no. 2 (1972): 353–68.

Hodges, Tony. *Western Sahara: The Roots of a Desert War*. Westport, CT: L. Hill, 1983.

Human Rights Watch. 'Human Rights in Western Sahara and in the Tindouf Refugee Camps', 2008, https://www.hrw.org/report/2008/12/19/human-rights-western-sahara-and-tindouf-refugee-camps, accessed 1 August 2015.

Human Rights Watch. 'Morocco and Western Sahara: Events of 2021'. In *World Report 2022*, 2021.

Hunt, Edward. 'The WikiLeaks Cables: How the United States Exploits the World, in Detail, from an Internal Perspective, 2001–2010'. *Diplomacy & Statecraft* 30, no. 1 (2019): 70–98.

Huysmans, Jef. 'The European Union and the Securitization of Migration'. *JCMS: Journal of Common Market Studies* 38, no. 5 (2000): 751–77.

'Indo-China Rebels Widen Operations'. *New York Times*, 1946.

'Inside the Cold War in the Desert'. *VICE News*.

Institut Charles de Gaulle. *Le général De Gaulle et l'Indochine 1940–1946*. Paris: Plon, 1982.

International Court of Justice. 'Western Sahara: Advisory Opinion of 16 October 1975'. ICJ.

Interview with Doña Amparo Calles Zamora, widow of Captain Adolfo Calles, 2013.

Ivins, William M. 'Geoffroy Tory'. *Bulletin of the Metropolitan Museum of Art*, 1920, 79–86.

Jabri, Vivienne. *Discourses on Violence: Conflict Analysis Reconsidered*. Manchester: Manchester University Press, 1996.

Jabri, Vivienne. *Mediating Conflict: Decision-Making and Western Intervention in Namibia*. Manchester: Manchester University Press, 1990.

Jabri, Vivienne. *The Postcolonial Subject: Claiming Politics/Governing Others in Late Modernity*. Abingdon: Routledge, 2012.

Jabri, Vivienne. *War and the Transformation of Global Politics*. Basingstoke: Palgrave Macmillan, 2007.

Jabri, Vivienne, and S. Chan. 'European Involvement in the Western Contact Group: The Stress and Convenience of Coalition Mediation'. In *Mediation in Southern Africa*. London: Macmillan, 1993.

Jackson, Patrick Thaddeus. 'Whose Identity?: Rhetorical Commonplaces in "American" Wartime Foreign Policy'. In *Identity and Global Politics: Empirical and Theoretical Elaborations*, edited by Patricia M. Goff and Kevin C. Dunn,

169–89. Culture and Religion in International Relations. New York: Palgrave Macmillan US, 2004.
'Jackson, Robert P.' U.S. Department of State, https://2009-2017.state.gov/r/pa/ei/biog/218230.htm, accessed 10 January 2023.
Jacobs, Daniel. 'Instant Weekend ... Marrakech'. *The Guardian*, 2008, sec. Travel.
Jensen, De Lamar. *Diplomacy and Dogmatism, Bernardino de Mendoza and the French Catholic League*. Cambridge, MA: Harvard University Press, 1964.
Jensen, Erik. *Western Sahara: Anatomy of a Stalemate*. Boulder, CO: Lynne Rienner Publishers, 2005.
Joffé, E. G. H. 'The Moroccan Nationalist Movement: Istiqlal, the Sultan, and the Country'. *The Journal of African History* 26, no. 04 (1985): 289–307.
Joffé, G. 'Morocco: Monarchy, Legitimacy and Succession'. *Third World Quarterly* 10, no. 1 (1988): 201–28.
Joffé, G. 'The European Union and the Maghreb'. *Mediterranean Politics* 1 (1994): 22–46.
Joffé, George. 'The European Union, Democracy and Counter-Terrorism in the Maghreb'. *JCMS: Journal of Common Market Studies* 46, no. 1 (2008): 147–71.
Joffé, George. 'Frontiers in North Africa'. In *Boundaries and State Territory in the Middle East and North Africa*. Wisbech: Menas Press, 1987.
Joffé, George. 'The International Court of Justice and the Western Sahara Dispute'. In *War and Refugees: The Western Sahara Conflict*, edited by Richard Lawless and Laila Monahan. New York: Pinter, 1987.
Joffé, George. 'Nationalism and the Bled: The Jbala from the Rif War to the Istiqlal'. *The Journal of North African Studies* 19, no. 4 (2014): 475–89.
Joffé, George. 'Self-Determination and Uti Possidetis: The Western Sahara and the "Lost Provinces"'. *Morocco: Journal of the Society for Moroccan Studies*, no. 1 (1996): 97–115.
Joffé, George. 'Sovereignty and the Western Sahara'. *The Journal of North African Studies* 15, no. 3 (2010): 375–84.
Jönsson, C., and M. Hall. *Essence of Diplomacy*. London: Palgrave Macmillan, 2005.
Jørgensen, Nina H. B. 'Complicity in Torture in a Time of Terror: Interpreting the European Court of Human Rights Extraordinary Rendition Cases'. *Chinese Journal of International Law* 16, no. 1 (2017): 11–40.
Kamil, Leo. *Fueling the Fire: U.S. Policy & the Western Sahara Conflict*. Trenton, NJ: Red Sea Press, 1987.
Karin, Marcy Lynn. 'Out of Sight, But Not Out of Mind: How Executive Order 13,233 Expands Executive Privilege While Simultaneously Preventing Access to Presidential Records Note'. *Stanford Law Review* 55, no. 2 (2002): 529–70.
Katzenstein, P. 'Alternative Perspectives on National Security'. In *The Culture of National Security: Norms and Identity in World Politics*. New York: Columbia University Press, 1996.
Katzenstein, Peter Joachim. *The Culture of National Security: Norms and Identity in World Politics*. New York: Columbia University Press, 1996.

Keys, Barbara, and Claire Yorke. 'Personal and Political Emotions in the Mind of the Diplomat'. *Political Psychology* 40, no. 6 (2019): 1235–49.
Kissinger, H. *Diplomacy*. New York: Simon and Schuster, 1994.
Kissinger, H. *White House Years*. New York: Simon & Schuster, 1979.
Kissinger, Henry A. 'The White Revolutionary: Reflections on Bismarck'. *Daedalus* 97, no. 3 (1968): 888–924.
Kowert, V. Kubálková, Nicholas Greenwood, Onuf Paul. *International Relations in a Constructed World*. New York: M. E. Sharpe, 1998.
Krebs, Ronald R., and Patrick Thaddeus Jackson. 'Twisting Tongues and Twisting Arms: The Power of Political Rhetoric'. *European Journal of International Relations* 13, no. 1 (2007): 35–66.
Kristeva, J. *Black Sun: Depression and Melancholia*. Reprint edition. New York: Columbia University Press, 1992.
Kristeva, Julia. *Desire in Language: A Semiotic Approach to Literature and Art*. Edited by Leon S. Roudiez and Alice Jardine. Translated by Thomas Gora. New York: Columbia University Press, 1980.
Kritzman, Lawrence D. 'Barthesian Free Play'. *Yale French Studies*, no. 66 (1984): 189–210.
Kütt, Moritz, and Jens Steffek. 'Comprehensive Prohibition of Nuclear Weapons: An Emerging International Norm?' *The Nonproliferation Review* 22, no. 3–4 (2015): 401–20.
Laclau, Ernesto. *New Reflections on the Revolution of Our Time*. London: Verso, 1997.
LaFeber, Walter. 'Roosevelt, Churchill, and Indochina: 1942–45'. *The American Historical Review* 80, no. 5 (1975): 1277–95.
Laffey, M., and J. Weldes. 'Decolonizing the Cuban Missile Crisis'. *International Studies Quarterly* 52, no. 3 (2008): 555–77.
Lapid, Yosef, and Friedrich Kratochwil. *The Return of Culture and Identity in International Relations Theory*. London: Lynne Rienner, 1996.
Larémont, Ricardo René. 'Al Qaeda in the Islamic Maghreb: Terrorism and Counterterrorism in the Sahel'. *African Security* 4, no. 4 (2011): 242–68.
Lawrence, M. A. *Assuming the Burden: Europe and the American Commitment to War in Vietnam*. Berkeley, CA: University of California Press, 2005.
Lawrence, M. A., quoted in bloomsbury.com page for 'The Road to Vietnam'. Bloomsbury. Accessed 13 January 2023.
Lawrence, Mark Atwood. 'Transnational Coalition-Building and the Making of the Cold War in Indochina, 1947–1949'. *Diplomatic History* 26, no. 3 (2002): 453–80.
leparisien.fr. 'Accusé d'«extrémisme», Sarkozy dénonce un «procès stalinien»', 2012.
Logevall, Frederik. *Embers of War: The Fall of an Empire and the Making of America's Vietnam*. New York: Random House, 2012.
'Los Secuestradores Trasladan a Malí a Los Cooperantes de Tinduf'. El Periódico..
Lynch, Colum, and Elias Groll. 'Obama's Foreign Fighters Campaign Is a Gift to the World's Police States'. *Foreign Policy Blogs* (blog), 2014.
Macharia, Munene. 'Multiple Colonialism in Western Sahara'. *Journal of Language, Technology & Entrepreneurship in Africa* 2, no. 2 (2010): 178–95.

Machiavelli, Niccolò. *Le opere di Niccolò Machiavelli*. Rome: Tipografia Cenniniana, 1877.
Machiavelli, Niccolò. *Tutte Le Opere Storiche, Politiche e Letterarie*. Edited by A. Capata. Rome: Newton Compton, 2011.
MACP. 'FAQ Western Sahara Conflict'. MAPC, 2012.
MACP. 'Morocco on the Move'.
MACP. 'Morocco on the Move – The Truth About the Polisario'. Morocco on the Move.
MACP. 'Morocco on the Move – US–Morocco Bilateral Relationship'. Morocco on the Move.
Madrid, Luis De Vega. 'El Polisario Saca a Los Cooperantes No Imprescindibles de Los Campamentos de Tinduf'. 2013.
Mahan, Alfred Thayer. *The Interest of America in International Conditions*. New Brunswick, NJ: Transaction Publishers, 2007.
'Malaya Declares Emergency'. *New York Times*, 1948.
'Malayan Police Hold 600 in Anti-Red Raids'. *New York Times*, 1948.
Marcella, Gabriel. 'National Security and the Interagency Process'. In *US Army War College Guide to National Security Policy and Strategy*, First Edition. West Point, CA: US Army War College Press, 2004.
'Maroc : L'homosexualité Est Encore Taboue'. *Le Point*, 2015.
Marr, David. *Vietnam: State, War, and Revolution*. Berkeley, CA: University of California Press, 2013.
Marr, David G. *Vietnam 1945: The Quest for Power*. Berkeley, CA: University of California Press, 1995.
Marrakesh Medina: Neocolonial Paradise of Lifestyle Migrants? Contested Spatialities, Lifestyle Migration and Residential Tourism. London: Routledge, 2013.
Marvel, W. Macy. 'Drift and Intrigue: United States Relations with the Viet-Minh, 1945'. *Millennium–Journal of International Studies*, 1975, 10–27.
'Melancholia Becomes the Subject: Kristeva's Invisible "Thing" and the Making of Culture'. *Paragraph* 14, no. 2 (1991): 144–50.
Meyer, Christopher. *DC Confidential*. New Edition. London: W&N, 2006.
'MI6 and CIA "Sent Student to Morocco to Be Tortured"'. *The Guardian*.
Michelsen, Nicholas, Pablo De Orellana, and Filippo Costa Buranelli. 'The Reactionary Internationale: The Rise of the New Right and the Reconstruction of International Society'. *International Relations* (2023), https://doi.org/10.1177/00471178231186392.
Minter, William. *King Solomon's Mines Revisited: Western Interests and the Burdened History of Southern Africa*. New York: Basic Books, 1988.
Mohsen-Finan, Khadija. 'Le règlement du conflit du Sahara occidental'. *Politique africaine* 76, no. 4 (1999): 95–105.
Mohsen-Finan, Khadija. 'Maroc: l'émergence de l'islamisme sur la scène politique'. *Politique étrangère* Printemps, no. 1 (2005): 73–84.
Mohsen-Finan, Khadija. 'Sahara Occidental: de la prolongation du conflit à la nécessité de son règlement'. *Politique Étrangère* 61, no. 3 (1996): 665–75.

Morgenthau, Hans. *Politics among Nations: The Struggle for Power and Peace*. New York: Knopf, 1966.
'Moroccan Constitution'. Maroc.ma. Accessed 4 August 2015.
'Moroccan "Exceptionalism" Deserves Support'. Morocco on the Move.
'Moroccan Star Faces Third Rape Charge'. *BBC News*, 2018, sec. Europe.
'Morocco on the Move – Terrorism: Two Reports Weigh In After President's State of the Union – Garth Neuffer'. Morocco on the Move, 2014.
Mundy, Jacob. 'Neutrality or Complicity? The United States and the 1975 Moroccan Takeover of the Spanish Sahara'. *The Journal of North African Studies* 11, no. 3 (2006): 275–306.
Mundy, Jacob. 'Performing the Nation, Pre-Figuring the State: The Western Saharan Refugees, Thirty Years Later'. *The Journal of Modern African Studies* 45, no. 02 (2007): 275–97.
Murty, Bhagevatula Satyanarayana. *The International Law of Diplomacy: The Diplomatic Instrument and World Public Order*. Leiden: Martinus Nijhoff Publishers, 1989.
Mus, Paul. *Hô Chi Minh, Le Vietnam, l'Asie*. Paris: Éditions du Seuil, 1971.
Mus, Paul. *Le Destin de l'Union Française de l'Indochine a l'Afrique*. Paris: Éditions du Seuil, 1954.
Mus, Paul. *Viet-Nam: Sociologie d'une Guerre*. Paris: Seuil, 1952.
Natter, Katharina. 'The Formation of Morocco's Policy Towards Irregular Migration (2000–2007): Political Rationale and Policy Processes'. *International Migration* 52, no. 5 (2014): 15–28.
Navari, Cornelia. 'The Concept of Practice in the English School'. *European Journal of International Relations* 17, no. 4 (2011): 611–30.
Neruda, Pablo. *Residencia En La Tierra*. Madrid: Ediciones Catedra, S.A., 1999.
Neumann, I. B. 'Returning Practice to the Linguistic Turn: The Case of Diplomacy'. *Millenium: Journal of International Studies* 31, no. 3 (2002): 627.
Neumann, I. B., and J. M. Welsh. 'The Other in European Self-Definition: An Addendum to the Literature on International Society'. *Review of International Studies* 17, no. 4 (1991): 327–48.
Neumann, Iver B. '"A Speech That the Entire Ministry May Stand For", or: Why Diplomats Never Produce Anything New'. *International Political Sociology* 1, no. 2 (2007): 183–200.
Neumann, Iver B. *At Home with the Diplomats: Inside a European Foreign Ministry*. Ithaca, NY: Cornell University Press, 2012.
Neumann, Iver B. 'The Body of the Diplomat'. *European Journal of International Relations* 14, no. 4 (2008): 671–95.
Neumann, Iver B. *Diplomatic Sites: A Critical Enquiry*. New York: Columbia University Press, 2013.
Neumann, Iver B. 'Discourse Analysis'. In *Qualitative Methods in International Relations: A Pluralist Guide*, edited by Klotz and Prakash, 61–77. Basingstoke: Palgrave Macmillan, 2008.
Neumann, Iver B. 'The English School on Diplomacy: Scholarly Promise Unfulfilled'. *International Relations* 17, no. 3 (2003): 341–69.

Neumann, Iver B. *Russia and the Idea of Europe: A Study in Identity and International Relations*. Vol. 3. London: Psychology Press, 1996.
Neumann, Iver B. 'Self and Other in International Relations'. *European Journal of International Relations* 2, no. 2 (1996): 139–74.
Neumann, Iver B. 'Sublime Diplomacy: Byzantine, Early Modern, Contemporary'. *Millennium – Journal of International Studies* 34, no. 3 (2006): 865–88.
Neumann, Iver B. *Uses of the Other: 'The East' in European Identity Formation*. Manchester: Manchester University Press, 1999.
Nguyen Du. *The Tale of Kieu*. Translated by Huynh. New Edition. New Haven, CT: Yale University Press, 1987.
Nicolson, Harold. *Curzon: The Last Phase – 1919–1925: A Study in Post-War Diplomacy*. London: Constable, 1934.
Nicolson, Harold George. *Diplomacy*. Institute for the Study of Diplomacy Ed. Washington, DC: Georgetown University Press, 1998.
Nietzsche, Friedrich Wilhelm. *Daybreak Thoughts on the Prejudices of Morality*. Edited by Maudemarie Clark and Brian Leiter. Cambridge: Cambridge University Press, 1997.
Nietzsche, Friedrich Wilhelm. 'Genealogy of Morals'. In *Basic Writings of Nietzsche*. New York: Modern Library, 2000.
Nietzsche, Friedrich Wilhelm. *Human, All Too Human: A Book for Free Spirits; Part I*. Translated by Alexander Harvey. New York: Modern Library, 2011.
Nietzsche, Friedrich Wilhelm. *Human, All-Too-Human: A Book For Free Spirits; Part II: The Wanderer and His Shadow*. Translated by Paul Cohn. New York: Modern Library, 2011.
Nigel Farage vs. Tony Blair, December 2005. https://www.youtube.com/watch?v=DT--RnOYORI&feature=youtube_gdata_player, accessed 1 December 2014.
Nightingale, Andrea Wilson. *Spectacles of Truth in Classical Greek Philosophy: Theoria in Its Cultural Context*. Cambridge: Cambridge University Press, 2004.
Omar, Sidi M. 'The Right to Self-Determination and the Indigenous People of Western Sahara'. *Cambridge Review of International Affairs* 21, no. 1 (2008): 41–57.
Orellana, Pablo de. 'The Power of Describing Identity in Diplomacy: Writing Subjects, Territory, Time and Evil at the End of Gaddafi's Libya'. In *A New Theory and Practice of Diplomacy: New Perspectives on Diplomacy*, edited by Jack Spence, Claire Yorke, and Alastair Masser. London: I. B. Tauris, 2021.
Orellana, Pablo de. 'Remember the Western Sahara? Conflict, Irredentism, Nationalism and International Intervention'. E-IR, 2009, http://www.e-ir.info/?p=2005, accessed 16 October 2024.
Orellana, Pablo de. 'Retrieving How Diplomacy Writes Subjects, Space and Time: A Methodological Contribution'. *European Journal of International Relations* 26, no. 2 (2020): 469–94.
Orellana, Pablo de. *The Road to Vietnam*. London: I. B.Tauris, 2020.
Orellana, Pablo de. 'Struggles over Identity in Diplomacy: "Commie Terrorists" Contra "Imperialists" in Western Sahara'. *International Relations* 29, no. 4 (2015): 477–99.

Orellana, Pablo de. 'When Diplomacy Identifies Terrorists: Subjects, Identity and Agency in the War on Terror in Mali'. In *The Palgrave Handbook of Global Counterterrorism Policy*, edited by Scott Romaniuk, Francis Grice, and Stewart Webb. London: Palgrave Macmillan, 2016.

Orellana, Pablo de. '"You Can Count on Us": When Malian Diplomacy Stratcommed Uncle Sam and the Role of Identity in Communication'. *Defence Strategic Communications* 3, no. 1 (2017): 99–170.

Ottaway, David, and Marina Ottaway. *Algeria: The Politics of a Socialist Revolution*. Oakland, CA: University of California Press, 1970.

Pascal, Blaise. *Pensées*. Edition Brunschvicg. Paris: Editions de Cluny, 1934.

Pavlovic, Tatjana. *Despotic Bodies and Transgressive Bodies: Spanish Culture from Francisco Franco to Jesus Franco*. New York: SUNY Press, 2012.

Pennell, C. Richard. *Morocco since 1830: A History*. New York: NYU Press, 2000.

Pierrot, Anne Herschberg. 'Barthes and Doxa'. *Poetics Today* 23, no. 3 (2002): 427–42.

Pinto, Derrin. 'Indoctrinating the Youth of Post-War Spain: A Discourse Analysis of a Fascist Civics Textbook'. *Discourse & Society* 15, no. 5 (2004): 649–67.

'Polisario 13th Congress Concludes and Confirms "Ignoring Right of Saharawi People, Will Threaten Peace and Stability in the Region" | Sahara Press Service', 2011.

Porter, Gareth, ed. *Vietnam: A History in Documents*. New York: New American Library, 1979.

Pouliot, Vincent. 'Diplomats as Permanent Representatives: The Practical Logics of the Multilateral Pecking Order'. *International Journal* 66, no. 3 (2011): 543–61.

Pouliot, Vincent. *International Pecking Orders: The Politics and Practice of Multilateral Diplomacy*. Cambridge: Cambridge University Press, 2016.

Pouliot, Vincent. *International Security in Practice: The Politics of NATO-Russia Diplomacy*. First Edition. Cambridge: Cambridge University Press, 2010.

Pouliot, Vincent. 'The Logic of Practicality: A Theory of Practice of Security Communities'. *International Organization* 62, no. 2 (2008): 257–88.

Press, The Associated. 'Communists Menace South Asia; Unified Blow at Resources Seen'. *New York Times*, 1948.

'Proclamation on Recognizing the Sovereignty of the Kingdom of Morocco over the Western Sahara – The White House'.

Quintilianus, Marcus Fabius. *M. Fabi Quintiliani institutionis oratoriae liber decimus*. Edited by William Peterson, 2007. http://www.gutenberg.org/ebooks/21827, accessed 21 April 2014.

Ranke, Leopold von. *The Theory and Practice of History: Edited with an Introduction by Georg G. Iggers*. Edited by Georg G. Iggers. London: Routledge, 2010.

'Remarks at the Opening Plenary of the U.S.-Morocco Strategic Dialogue'. US Department of State., 2012.

Reus-Smit, Christian. *The Moral Purpose of the State: Culture, Social Identity, and Institutional Rationality in International Relations*. Princeton, NJ: Princeton University Press, 2009.

Reuters. 'Hardline Mali Rebel Demands Stall Hopes for Peace'. *New York Times*, 2015.
Reynolds, David. *In Command of History: Churchill Writing and Fighting the Second World War*. London: Allen Lane, 2004.
Rice, Xan. 'Western Sahara Activist on Hunger Strike'. *The Guardian*, 2009, sec. World News.
Robert Trumbull. 'Cominform Is in Sight for Southeastern Asia'. *New York Times*, 1948, sec. Review of the Week's Editorials.
Roberts, Hugh. 'The Politics of Algerian Socialism'. *North Africa: Contemporary Politics and Economic Development*, 1984, 5–49.
Roberts, Sean. 'Imaginary Terrorism? The Global War on Terror and the Narrative of the Uyghur Terrorist Threat'. PONARS Eurasia Working Paper. Washington, DC: George Washington University, 2012.
Ruane, Kevin. 'The Hidden History of Graham Greene's Vietnam War: Fact, Fiction and *The Quiet American*'. *History* 97, no. 327 (2012): 431–52.
Rubinelli, Sara. *Ars Topica: The Classical Technique of Constructing Arguments from Aristotle to Cicero*. Berlin: Springer, 2009.
Rumelili, Bahar. 'Constructing Identity and Relating to Difference: Understanding the EU's Mode of Differentiation'. *Review of International Studies* 30, no. 01 (2004): 27–47.
Russell, Greg. 'Machiavelli's Science of Statecraft: The Diplomacy and Politics of Disorder'. *Diplomacy & Statecraft* 16, no. 2 (2005): 227–50.
'Saad Lamjarred: France Detains Moroccan Star over Rape Charge'. *BBC News*, 2018, sec. Europe.
Sahara Press Service. 'Polisario Front Intervention before UN Special Committee of Decolonization (C-24) Kingstown, 31 May–June 3, 2011'.
'Sahara Press Service | Sahara Press Service'.
Said, Edward W. *Orientalism*. London: Penguin, 2003.
Said, Edward W. 'The Problem of Textuality: Two Exemplary Positions'. *Critical Inquiry*, 1978, 673–714.
Sainteny, Jean. *Histoire d'une Paix Manquée*. Paris: Éditions de Saint-Clair, 1967.
Salisbury, Harrison E. 'Image and Reality in Indochina'. *Foreign Affairs* 49 (1970): 381.
Salter, Mark B., ed. *Making Things International 1: Circuits and Motion*. Minneapolis, MN: University of Minnesota Press, 2015.
San Martín, Pablo. '"¡Estos Locos Cubarauis!": The Hispanisation of Saharawi Society (… after Spain)'. *Journal of Transatlantic Studies* 7, no. 3 (2009): 249–63.
San Martín, Pablo. 'Nationalism, Identity and Citizenship in the Western Sahara'. *The Journal of North African Studies* 10, no. 3–4 (2005): 565–92.
'Sarkozy: "Être Traité de Fasciste Par Un Communiste, c'est Un Honneur !"'. *Le Lab Europe 1*, 2012.
Satow, Ernest Mason. *A Guide to Diplomatic Practice*. Neully Sur Seine: Ulan Press, 1917.
Savage, Charlie. 'Court Sides with C.I.A. on "Extraordinary Rendition"'. *New York Times*, 2010.

Sawer, Patrick. 'Algeria Hostage Crisis: Desert Siege Ends in Bloodshed'. *The Telegraph*, 2013.
Sbrega, John J. '"First Catch Your Hare": Anglo-American Perspectives on Indochina during the Second World War'. *Journal of Southeast Asian Studies* 14, no. 01 (1983): 63–78.
Schlesinger, Arthur M. *The Bitter Heritage*. Boston, MA: Houghton Mifflin, 1967.
Searle, John R. *Expression and Meaning: Studies in the Theory of Speech Acts*. Cambridge: Cambridge University Press, 1985.
Searle, John R. 'Meaning and Speech Acts'. *The Philosophical Review* 71, no. 4 (1962): 423–32.
Searle, John R. *Speech Acts: An Essay in the Philosophy of Language*. Cambridge: Cambridge University Press, 1969.
'Secuestran a Dos Españoles En El Sáhara'. *El Mundo*, 2011.
Sending, Ole Jacob, Vincent Pouliot, and I. B. Neumann, eds. *Diplomacy and the Making of World Politics*. Cambridge: Cambridge University Press, 2015.
Sending, Ole Jacob, Vincent Pouliot, and Iver B. Neumann. 'The Future of Diplomacy: Changing Practices, Evolving Relationships'. *International Journal* 66, no. 3 (2011): 527–42.
'Seven Myths about Democracy in Morocco'. openDemocracy, 2015.
Shapiro, M. J. 'Textualising Global Politics'. In *International/Intertextual Relations*, edited by James Der Derian and M. J. Shapiro. Lexington, MA: Lexington Books, 1989.
Shapiro, M. J. *The Politics of Representation: Writing Practices in Biography, Photography, and Policy Analysis*. Madison, WI: University of Wisconsin Press, 1988.
Shapiro, Michael J. 'Literary Production as a Politicizing Practice'. *Political Theory*, 1984, 387–422.
Shapiro, Michael J. 'Literary Production as a Politicizing Practice'. In *Language and Politics*. Oxford: Blackwell, 1984.
Shapiro, Michael J. *Reading the Postmodern Polity: Political Theory as Textual Practice*. Minneapolis, MN: University of Minnesota Press, 1992.
Shapiro, Michael J. 'Strategic Discourse/Discursive Strategy: The Representation of "Security Policy" in the Video Age'. *International Studies Quarterly* 34, no. 3 (1990): 327–40.
Sharp, Paul. *Diplomatic Theory of International Relations*. Vol. 111. Cambridge: Cambridge University Press, 2009.
Siracusa, Joseph. 'Lessons of Viet-Nam and the Future of American Foreign Policy'. *Australian Journal of International Affairs* 30, no. 2 (1976): 227–37.
Siracusa, Joseph M. 'The United States, Viet-Nam, and the Cold War: A Reappraisal'. *Journal of Southeast Asian Studies* 5, no. 01 (1974): 82–101.
Smith, Paul Julian. 'Barthes, Góngora, and Non-Sense'. *PMLA* 101, no. 1 (1986): 82–94.
Smith, Tony. 'New Bottles for New Wine: A Pericentric Framework for the Study of the Cold War'. *Diplomatic History* 24, no. 4 (2000): 567–91.

Sorensen, Asta. 'Media Review: NVivo 7.' *Journal of Mixed Methods Research* 2, no. 1 (2008): 106–8.
Spargo, Mary. 'Mere 14 Million Communists Are Altering Globe'. *The Washington Post (1923–1954)*, 1948, sec. Current Events National and Foreign Editorials Art Books.
Spector, R. 'Allied Intelligence and Indochina, 1943–1945'. *The Pacific Historical Review* 51, no. 1 (1982): 23–50.
Spence, Jack, Claire Yorke, and Alastair Masser. *A New Theory and Practice of Diplomacy: New Perspectives on Diplomacy*. Edited by Claire Yorke and Alastair Masser. London: I. B. Tauris, 2021.
'Star Trek, Series 3, Episode 12'. *Star Trek, Voyager*, 1996.
'Statement from D'Argenlieu'. *New York Times*, 1947.
Stepan, Alfred, Juan J. Linz, and Juli F. Minoves. 'Democratic Parliamentary Monarchies'. *Journal of Democracy* 25, no. 2 (2014): 35–51.
Stephan, M. J, and J. Mundy. 'A Battlefield Transformed: From Guerilla Resistance to Mass Nonviolent Struggle in the Western Sahara'. *Journal of Military and Strategic Studies* 8, no. 3 (2006): 1–32.
Sud Presse. '"Oui, j'étais un agent de renseignement"'. 2010.
Suganami, Hidemi. 'Agents, Structures, Narratives'. *European Journal of International Relations* 5, no. 3 (1999): 365–86.
Suganami, Hidemi. 'On Wendt's Philosophy: A Critique'. *Review of International Studies* 28, no. 01 (2002): 23–37.
Szmolka, Inmaculada. 'Western Sahara and the Arab Spring'. In *Global, Regional and Local Dimensions of Western Sahara's Protracted Decolonization*, 101–19. New York: Springer, 2017.
Szondi, Gyorgy. 'From Image Management to Relationship Building: A Public Relations Approach to Nation Branding'. *Place Branding and Public Diplomacy* 6, no. 4 (2010): 333–43.
Szondi, Gyorgy. *Public Diplomacy and Nation Branding: Conceptual Similarities and Differences*. Netherlands Institute of International Relations' Clingendael', 2008.
Tapper, Jake. 'Obama Delivers Bold Speech About War on Terror'. *ABC News*, 2007.
Tarkki, Pekka. 'El Español En Los Campamentos de Refugiados de La República Arabe Saharaui Democrática'. In *Romania Arabica*, edited by Jens Lüdtke, 83. Tübingen: Gunter Narr Verlag, 1996.
'The Failed Diplomacy between Morocco and Polisario'. *Al Jazeera*, 18 November 2020.
'Totalitarian Character of Ho's Regime Cited as Evidence – Japanese Are Said to Have Installed Viet Minh as "Time Bomb"'. *New York Times*, 1947.
'The Video of "Mohammed VI Drunk in Paris" Makes the Buzz ... and the "Manager of the Pages of the King of Morocco" Clarifies'. *Morocco Detail Zero*, 2022.
Times, Benjamin Welles Special to The New York. 'Chinese Reds Shift to New Offensive'. *New York Times*, 1947.

Times, C. L. Sulzberger Special to The New York. 'Indo-China Revolt Fateful to France: Other Empire Areas Watching Outcome of Dissidence in Troubled East Asia'. *New York Times*, 1946.

Times, Harold Callender Special to The New York. 'Colonial Problem Growing in France'. *New York Times*, 1946.

Times, Henry R. Lieberman Special to The New York. 'U.S. Envoy Urges Chinese Self-Help'. *New York Times*, 1948.

Times, Lansing Warren Special to The New York. 'French Combat Wide Revolt on Madagascar; Planes Carry Troops to Threatened Centers'. *New York Times*, 1947.

Times, Robert Trumbull Special to The New York. 'French Face All-out Colonial War: Indo-China Is Aflame With Many Incidents'. *New York Times*, 1946, sec. The Week In Review.

Times, Special to The New York. 'Government Takes Stern Steps To Stop Red Disorder in Malaya', 1948.

Tizac, Andrée Françoise Caroline d'Ardenne de, Andrée Viollis, and André Malraux. *Indochine S.O.S.* Paris: Gallimard, 1935.

Tønnesson, S. 'The Longest Wars: Indochina 1945–75'. *Journal of Peace Research* 22, no. 1 (1985): 9–29.

Tønnesson, S. *Vietnam 1946: How the War Began*. Berkeley, CA: University of California Press, 2010.

Tønnesson, Stein. *The Vietnamese Revolution of 1945: Roosevelt, Ho Chi Minh and de Gaulle in World at War*. London: PRIO Sage, 1991.

Turpin, Frédéric. *De Gaulle, Les Gaullistes et l'Indochine: 1940–1956*. Paris: Les Indes savantes, 2005.

Vaisset, Thomas. *L'Amiral d'Argenlieu. Le moine soldat du gaullisme*. Paris: Humensis, 2017.

Van Giau, Tran. *The Vietnamese Working Class. Vol. I, 1930–1935*. Hanoi: Nha Xuat Ban Su Hoc, 1962.

Varga, Daniel. 'Léon Pignon, l'homme-clé de la solution Bao Dai et de l'implication des États-Unis dans la Guerre d'Indochine'. *Outre-Mers. Revue d'histoire* 96, no. 364 (2009): 277–313.

Vatin, Jean-Claude. 'Désert construit et inventé, Sahara perdu ou retrouvé: Le jeu des imaginaires'. *Revue de l'Occident Musulman et de La Méditerranée* 37, no. 1 (1984): 107–31.

Vu, Tuong. '"It's Time for the Indochinese Revolution to Show Its True Colours": The Radical Turn of Vietnamese Politics in 1948'. *Journal of Southeast Asian Studies* 40, no. 03 (2009): 519–42.

Vu, Tuong. 'Triumphs or Tragedies: A New Perspective on the Vietnamese Revolution'. *Journal of Southeast Asian Studies* 45, no. 02 (2014): 236–57.

Wæver, Ole. 'European Security Identities'. *JCMS: Journal of Common Market Studies* 34, no. 1 (1996): 103–32.

Wall, Irwin M. *France, the United States, and the Algerian War*. Oakland, CA: University of California Press, 2001.

Walt, S. M. 'Alliance Formation and the Balance of World Power'. *International Security* 9, no. 4 (1985): 3–43.
Walt, S. M. *The Origins of Alliances*. Ithaca, NY: Cornell University Press, 1987.
Walt, S. M. 'Testing Theories of Alliance Formation: The Case of Southwest Asia'. *International Organization*, 1988, 275–316.
Walt, S. M. 'Why Alliances Endure or Collapse'. *Survival* 39, no. 1 (1997): 156–79.
Walt, Stephen M. 'Alliance Formation and the Balance of World Power'. *International Security* 9, no. 4 (1985): 3.
Walt, Stephen M. 'The Ties That Fray: Why Europe and America Are Drifting Apart'. *The National Interest*, no. 54 (1998): 3–11.
Wang, Jian. 'Managing National Reputation and International Relations in the Global Era: Public Diplomacy Revisited'. *Public Relations Review* 32, no. 2 (2006): 91–96.
Watson, Adam. *Diplomacy: The Dialogue Between States*. London: Routledge, 1984.
Watt, Donald Cameron. *Succeeding John Bull: America in Britain's Place 1900–1975*. Cambridge: Cambridge University Press, 1984.
Weber, C. *Simulating Sovereignty: Intervention, the State, and Symbolic Exchange*. 37. Cambridge: Cambridge University Press, 1995.
Wendt, Alexander. 'Anarchy Is What States Make of It: The Social Construction of Power Politics'. *International Organization* 46, no. 02 (1992): 391–425.
Wendt, Alexander. 'Collective Identity Formation and the International State'. *The American Political Science Review* 88, no. 2 (1994): 384–96.
Wendt, Alexander. *Social Theory of International Politics*. Cambridge: Cambridge University Press, 1999.
Wight, Martin. 'Why Is There No International Relations Theory?' In *International Theory: Critical Investigations*, edited by James Der Derian. London: Macmillan, 1995.
Wille, Tobias. 'Diplomatic Cable'. In *Making Things International 2*, edited by Mark B. Salter. Minneapolis, MN: Minnesota University Press, 2016.
Wille, Tobias. 'Representation and Agency in Diplomacy: How Kosovo Came to Agree to the Rambouillet Accords'. *Journal of International Relations and Development* 22, no. 4 (2019): 808–31.
Williams, Michael C. 'Identity and the Politics of Security'. *European Journal of International Relations* 4, no. 2 (1998): 204–25.
Williams, Michael C. 'Words, Images, Enemies: Securitization and International Politics'. *International Studies Quarterly* 47, no. 4 (2003): 511–31.
Williams, Michael C., and Iver B. Neumann. 'From Alliance to Security Community: NATO, Russia, and the Power of Identity'. *Millennium – Journal of International Studies* 29, no. 2 (2000): 357–87.
Willis, Michael, and Nizar Messari. 'Analyzing Moroccan Foreign Policy and Relations with Europe'. *The Review of International Affairs* 3, no. 2 (2003): 152–72.
Wilson, Alice. 'On the Margins of the Arab Spring'. *Social Analysis* 57, no. 2 (2013): 81–98.

Wodak, Ruth, and Michael Meyer, eds. *Methods for Critical Discourse Analysis*. Second Edition. London: SAGE, 2009.

Wolfram Lacher. 'Challenging the Myth of the Drug–Terror Nexus in the Sahel'. WACD Background Paper. West Africa Commission on Drugs – Kofi Annan Foundation, 2013.

Woodside, Alexander. *Community and Revolution in Modern Vietnam*. Boston, MA: Houghton Mifflin, 1976.

Woodside, Alexander. 'History, Structure, and Revolution in Vietnam'. *International Political Science Review* 10, no. 2 (1989): 143–57.

Woolner, David B., Warren F. Kimball, and David Reynolds. *FDR's World*. London: Palgrave Macmillan, 2008.

Yorke, Claire. 'Is Empathy a Strategic Imperative? A Review Essay'. *Journal of Strategic Studies* 0, no. 0 (2022): 1–21.

Yorke, Claire. 'The Significance and Limitations of Empathy in Strategic Communications'. *Defence Strategic Communications* 2, no. 2 (2017): 137–60.

Young, John W. 'The Foreign Office, the French and the Post-War Division of Germany 1945–46'. *Review of International Studies* 12, no. 3 (1986): 223–34.

Young, Marilyn. *Vietnam Wars 1945–1990*. New York: Harper Perennial, 2020.

Young, Marilyn B., and Robert Buzzanco. *A Companion to the Vietnam War*. New York: John Wiley & Sons, 2008.

Žagar, Igor. 'Topoi in Critical Discourse Analysis'. *Lodz Papers in Pragmatics* 6, no. 1 (2010): 3–27.

Zehfuss, Maja. 'Constructivism and Identity: A Dangerous Liaison'. *European Journal of International Relations* 7, no. 3 (2001): 315–48.

Zoubir, Yahia H. 'The United States and Maghreb – Sahel Security'. *International Affairs* 85, no. 5 (2009): 977–95.

Zunes, S., and J. Mundy. *Western Sahara: War, Nationalism, and Conflict Irresolution*. Syracuse, NY: Syracuse University Press, 2010.

Index

Notes: Page numbers in italic refer to illustrations. 'n.' after a page reference indicates the number of a note on that page.

Abdelaziz, Mohamed 157–58, 186
Adler-Nissen, Rebecca 41, 234
agency
　of diplomatic texts 48, 221–26, 231
　in diplomatic texts 236
　of diplomats 31, 47
Al-Assad, Bashar 238
Algeria and the Western Sahara conflict
　annexation by Morocco 149
　blamed by Morocco for the conflict 150, 171–72, 189
　Morocco and 162–64, 167, 168
Algerian War (1954–62) 132
Allison, Graham T. 216
Al-Qaeda in the Islamic Maghreb (AQIM) 152, 154
alterity, degrees of 17, 40, 42
　see also Other
archives 66, 100
Argenlieu, Thierry d'
　on communism 118
　memorandum to COMINDO (April 1946) 78, *80*, 81, 104–6, 122
Aristotle 73
articulations 37, 209–11, *211*
Ashley, Richard K. 40

backwardness 38, 39
　see also Orientalism
Baker, James 148, 150
Baker II Plan 150–51, 161, 183
Bảo Đại Solution 90, 94, 114–16, 128, *129*
Baudet, Philippe 106–7
Bevin, Ernest 114
Bidault, Georges 117–18

Blair, Tony 62–63
Bollaert, Émile 118
Bosnian war 39–40
Bourdieu, Pierre 63
Bradley, Mark Philip 94
Brexit 220
'Brigate Rosse' 74
Bull, Hedley 33, 34, 233
Byrnes, James 120

cables 106, 138n.74
Caffery, Jefferson 106–7, 117
Calles, Adolfo 12, *13*
Callières, François de 9, 10
Cameron, David 238
Campbell, David 39–40
Canning, George 29
case studies 15–16, 19–20, 60–62
　see also Vietnam War (1945–48); Western Sahara conflict (1975–present)
categories 5, 6, 12–14
　see also identity; name-calling
causality 76–77, 223, 224
Chan, Stephen 33
Chile 12
China 5, 45
Churchill, Winston 64
Cicero 73
Clinton, Hillary 66, 151, 160, 169, 176, 187, 237–38
Cochinchina 81, 105–6, 124, 138n.71, 138n.73
Cold War 32, 94, 112, 114, 130
colonialism in Vietnam 94, 101–2, 104, 109–11, 116, 118–19, 122, 214

communism
  category of 5
  and colonialism in Vietnam 110–11
  and diplomatic knowledge
    production 45, 132–33
  in Vietnam 112–17, *113*, 119–22
Connolly, William E. 37, 223
Constantinou, Costas 42–43, 63, 234
constructivist conceptualisations of
  diplomacy 34–35, 233
CORCAS (Royal Consultative Council
  for Saharan Affairs) 154, 171–72,
  179–81
Critical Discourse Analysis (CDA) 74
crossover of representations 82–83,
  222, 223, 225, 232
  Vietnam War (1945–48) case study
    128, *129*
  Western Sahara conflict (1975–
    present) case study 168–69, 175,
    183, 189–91

Der Derian, James 42, 234
descriptions
  analysis of 9–14
  instrumental use of 238
  introduction 1–5
  and representations 6–8
  see also diplomatic descriptions;
    diplomatic knowledge production
Devillers, Philippe 93
digital knowledge management 156
digital qualitative analysis methods 74,
  88n.66
diplomacy
  conceptualisation of 15, 17–18,
    31–34, 42, 43, 234
  introduction 1–5
  philology of 29
  towards a poststructuralist theory of
    41–46
diplomatic agents 12
  see also diplomats
diplomatic descriptions
  changes in 16
  consequences of 225–26
  and diplomatic text 6–8
  genealogy of 67, 75–78
  language and 11, 36–37
  outcomes of 41, 236–37
  reading of, in diplomatic texts 68–72
  research method 15
  successes and failures 62, 226
  see also diplomatic knowledge
    production; research method
diplomatic descriptions, conditions of
  208–21, 223–24, 231, 235
  architecture of articulation 209–11,
    211
  discursive stability 213–15, *214–15*
  dominant policy concerns 219–21,
    223
  planes of emergence 139n.81,
    211–13, *212*
  policy concerns and knowledge
    production 215–19, *218*
diplomatic descriptions in the Western
  Sahara conflict (1975–present)
  case study 170–87
  autonomy 'realism' or 'SHAM' (June
    2008–Early 2006) 179–83, 190
  Moroccan stability and 'ungoverned
    spaces' (2005–mid 2003) 183–86,
    189–90, 192–93
  Morocco as US ally and model
    (2010–July 2008) 171–79, 189
diplomatic descriptions in Vietnam War
  (1945–48) case study 111–28
  colonial greed and commie risks
    (August 1947–September 1946)
    117–21
  colonial reconquest or *libération*
    (August 1946–April 1945) 121–28
  communism and Vietminh–Soviet
    links (Late 1948–September 1947)
    112–17, *113*
diplomatic history 18, 19
diplomatic knowledge production
  62–68
  access to documentary evidence
    66–67
  cascade of diplomatic knowledge
    production 67
  case study selection 60–62
  categories of evidence 65–66
  diplomatic authorship and 63–64
  diplomats, role of 31
  genealogy of 67, 75–78
  homogenisation in 45
  interviews 67–68
  introduction 1–5
  stages of 11–12
diplomatic moment 11, 15, 63–65, 235
diplomatic practice 6
  application of research to 237–40
  conceptualisation of 57

guides to 30–31
toolkit for 18–19
variety of 46
diplomatic protection or sponsorship 41, 236–37
diplomatic text
 conceptualisation of 7–8, 46–48
 and political identity 48–49
 topoi, analysis of 72–75
 see also research method
diplomats 11–12
 agency of 31, 47
 careerism of 224
 conceptualisation of 43–44
discourse analysis 36, 37, 40, 74–78

English School conceptualisations of diplomacy 33–34, 233
epistemes 217–19, *218*, 221–26
exceptionalism of Morocco 184, 190, 236

Farage, Nigel 62–63
fascism 5, 81, 82, 108, 119
'fascist' name-calling 4
Fassi, Abbas El 172
Fihri, Fassi 179
First Vietnam War *see* Vietnam War (1945–48)
Fisher, Jonathan 35, 233
forbidden love 75
Foucauldian concepts and methods 36–37, 139n.81, 209, 213, 217–19, *218*
France 4–5
 colonial Indochina 97, *98*
 diplomacy in the Western Sahara 151
 diplomatic knowledge production in Vietnam 95, *96*, 97, 99, 115–19, 122–23, *129*, 130–32
 histories of the Vietnam War 93
 policy on Vietnam 92, 94

Gaddafi, Muammar 5, 238
Gaulle, Charles de 92, 122, 127
genealogy, as discourse analysis method 36, 37, 67, 75–78
Ghali, Brahim 178–79
Gilpin, Robert 32
Gulf Wars 40

hair length 73
Hall, M. 33

Hansen, Lene 39, 40, 63, 223
Hassan II (King of Morocco) 149, 167
Herring, George C. 127
Hồ Chí Minh 92, 93, 103, 118, 124–25, 237
human rights 172–73, 179–81

identity 4–5, 37
 construction of 34–35
 diplomatic outcomes 41
 and diplomatic texts 48–49, 71–72
 and policy, relationship of 76–77
 poststructuralist approaches 36–39, 44
 readings of the Bosnian War 39–40, 223
 Sahrawi identity, war on 150
 Vietnam War (1945–48) 81, 90–92
 see also categories
image management 5, 35
instrumentalist approaches to diplomacy 18, 232–33, 238
international relations 6, 19, 33
intertextuality 76
interviews 67–68
Iraq 40
Islamic terrorism 5, 185
 see also War on Terror
Italy 74

Jabri, Vivienne 235
Jackson, Robert P. 166, 224
Jönsson, C. 33

Kennan, George 3, 38
Kennedy, John F. 90
Kissinger, Henry 32, 150, 232
knowledge management *see* archives; digital knowledge management
knowledge *see* diplomatic knowledge production
Kristeva, Julia 73
Kushner, Jared 193–94

Laclau, Ernesto 47
LaFeber, Walter 127
language 2, 5
 and representations 11, 36–37, 57, 68–69, 206–7
 words, importance of 9–10, 71, 110
Lawrence, Mark A. 94
leaks 66–67, 154
 see also Wikileaks
Libya 4, 47

literary commentary 70–71
Lugar, Richard 162, 163

McCarthy, Joseph 45
Machiavelli, Niccolò 2, 5, 9, 17, 21n.2
Malaya Emergency (1948) 131
Mali 239
Marr, David 93
Marshall, George 119, 120
masculinity 73
Mendoza, Bernadino de 4, 5
method of research *see* research method
Millet, Charles S. 107–9
Mohammed VI (King of Morocco) 154, 162–63, 166, 167, 175
monarchs, roles of 154
Morgenthau, Hans 32
Moroccan-American Center for Policy (MACP) 154, 167, 173, 175, 220
Morocco 41
  Algeria and the Western Sahara conflict 162–64
  autonomy proposal (2007) 160–62, 170, 179–82
  diplomatic knowledge production 152, *153*, 154
  monarch, roles of 154
  nationalism in 149
  perceptions of 151–52
  representation as US ally and model (2010–July 2008) 171–79
  representations of stability and vulnerability (2005–mid 2003) 183–86
  subalternity and exceptionalism of 172, 184, 190, 236
  US scenesetter for Secretary Rumsfeld (February 2006) 164–66, 182
  and the War on Terror 151, 154, 169, 183–84
  Western Sahara conflict background 147–50
'Morocco on the Move' 167, 172, *174*, 175, 190, 220
Mundy, Jacob 151

name-calling
  consequences of 4–5, 14, 186, 222
  failure of 14, 119, 230
National Intelligence Priorities Framework (NIPF) 177, 184, 191
Neumann, Iver B. 44–45, 63, 216, 233, 234

New Right movements 233
Nicolson, Harold 9, 10, 31
Nietzsche, Friedrich 67, 77, 89n.75

Obama, Barack 171
Omar, Sidi 186
Orientalism 81, 111, 112, 114, 127, 128, 130, 131
  see also backwardness
Orwell, George, *1984* 86n.39
O'Sullivan, James 49–50
Other 39, 40, 42, 235
  see also alterity, degrees of; identity

Phạm, Ngọc Thạch 99, 104, 117, 120–21
Philip II (King of Spain) 4
Pignon, Léon 116
policy
  dominant policy concerns 219–21, 223, 238
  and identity, relationship of 76–77
  representations, condition of 215–19, *218*
policy mistakes 237–38
policy shifts 76, 223–24
  in US policy on Vietnam 109, 111, 115–16
  in US policy on the Western Sahara 148, 151, 169, 180
POLISARIO
  diplomatic knowledge production 152, *153*, 155
  foundation of 149
  representations of 151, 171–73, 176, 180, 186–87, 189
  representations of Morocco 178–79
  role of 147, 150
  self-determination and 157–58, 170, 172, 178, 182
  US report on meeting with POLISARIO Secretary General (March 2007) 157–58
  US report on talks with Polisario front leaders (December 2009) 158–60
  War on Terror and 171, 182, 191
the political 36, 47
postcolonial studies 38–39
  see also colonialism in Vietnam
poststructuralist approaches
  to diplomacy 41–46, 235
  to identity 36–39, 44
  to political text 69

power 36
  see also agency
punctuation 71

qualitative mapping software 74, 88n.66
Quintilian 73

realist conceptualisations of diplomacy 18, 31–32, 232
'Red Brigades' 74
Reisigl, Martin 74
reporting, introduction 1–5
research method 2
  case study selection 60–62
  example of process 78, 79–80, 81–83, 82
  genealogy of a representation 67, 75–78
  mapping knowledge production 58, 59, 62–68
  questions addressed 8
  reading representation in diplomatic texts 68–72
  research strategy 14–16
  summary 230
  topoi, analysis of 72–75, 88n.66
  value of 17–20, 231–36
Reus-Smit, Christian 35, 233
Rice, Condoleezza 151, 176–77, 180, 187
Riley, Thomas 162
romantic fiction 75
Roosevelt, Franklin D. 92, 93, 126–27
Royal Consultative Council for Saharan Affairs (CORCAS) see CORCAS

Sahrawi Arab Democratic Republic (SADR) 150, 153, 155, 186
Sainteny, Jean 95, 97, 99, 122, 123
Sanders, Jackie 157–58
Satow, Ernest Mason 9, 10, 10, 30–31
scenesetters 164–66, 176, 182
secrecy 67
securitisation of subjects 41, 236
Shapiro, Michael 37, 69
Sharp, Paul 33–34
Smith, Tony 32
South Africa 33
sovereign theory 43, 63–64
sovereignty, Moroccan 151, 161–62

Spain 4–5, 12, 149
Spanish masculinity 73
Stalin, Joseph 64
Stanton, E. F. 104
stigmatisation 41, 236
subalternity 19–20, 172, 184, 190, 236
subjectivity 69–70, 86n.39
Syria 238

textual markers see topoi
Tønnesson, Stein 93
topoi as textual markers 72–75, 88n.66
  in Vietnam War (1945–48) case study 81, 102, 106, 107, 109–12
  in the Western Sahara conflict (1975–present) case study 158, 160, 162–64, 166, 168
Truman administration 92
Truman, Harry S. 92, 112, 123–24
Trump administration (2020) 151, 193–94
Trusteeship policy of Roosevelt 92, 93, 126–27
typefaces 5, 22n.11

United Kingdom
  Brexit 220
  diplomatic knowledge production in Vietnam 114–15, 129
United States of America
  diplomatic knowledge production in the Western Sahara 152, 153, 154–55, 175–77
  diplomatic knowledge production in Vietnam 96, 99–100, 115–17, 119–20, 123–24, 127, 129, 130–32
  National Intelligence Priorities Framework (NIPF) 177
  perceptions of Vietnam 94
  policy on the Western Sahara 147–48, 150–51, 169, 180–82
  policy on Vietnam 90–91, 93, 94, 131
  Vietnam War (1945–48) case study texts 106–7, 109–11
  Western Sahara conflict (1975–present) case study texts 157–60, 162–70
Uyghurs 5

Vietnam/Vietminh
  colonial greed and commie risks 117–21
  communism and Vietminh–Soviet links 112–17, *113*
  diplomatic knowledge production 96, 99, *129*, 131–32
  histories of the Vietnam War 92–93
  independence, calls for 124–26
  perceptions of the US 94
  request for US assistance 117
Vietnam War (1945–48) case study 90–133
  case study selection 61–62
  diplomatic descriptions (1948–45) 111–28, 130–31, 210–11, *211*, 213–15, *214–15*
  historical background 90–91
  historical debates 92–94
  mapping knowledge production 95, 96, 97, *98*, 99–100, 132–33
  policy shifts 76
  sources used 100
  structure of colonial Indochina 97, *98*
  summary and conclusions 128, 130–33, 230
  textual analyses 101–11
Vietnam War (1945–48) case study texts
  cable from US ambassador on conversation with Baudet (September 1945) 106–7
  letter from Hồ Chí Minh to US Secretary of State (1945) 102–4
  letter from 'the Indochinese Annamese people' to the San Francisco Conference (1945) 101–2
  memorandum from d'Argenlieu to COMINDO (April 1946) 78, *80*, 81, 104–6
  report by American diplomat Charles S. Millet (October 1945) 107–9
  US State Department Policy Statement (September 1948) 109–11

violence 19, 235–36
vocabulary 9–10, 71, 110

Walt, Stephen 32, 222, 232
War on Terror
  Morocco, position of 151, 154, 169, 183–84
  in North Africa 152, 154, 169, 185–86
  POLISARIO and 173, 182
  US policy on 171, 182, 191
Watson, Adam 33, 233
Weber, Cynthia 40
Wendt, Alexander 34
Western Sahara conflict (1975–present) case study 147–94
  case study selection 61–62, 156
  diplomatic descriptions (1948–45) 152, 170–87, *188*, 189–92, 212–13, *212*
  historical background 147–49
  historical debates 149–52
  mapping knowledge production 152, *153*, 154–56
  perceptions of the area in the West 190–91
  summary and conclusions 187, *188*, 189–94, 230–31
Western Sahara conflict (1975–present) case study texts
  Morocco's autonomy proposal (2007) 160–62
  US cable on 'Western Sahara realities' (2008) 166–70
  US report on meeting in Rabat (August 2005) 162–64
  US report on meeting with POLISARIO Secretary General (March 2007) 157–58
  US report on talks with Polisario front leaders (December 2009) 158–60
  US scenesetter for Secretary Rumsfeld (February 2006) 164–66, 182
Wight, Martin 33, 233
Wikileaks 154, 156
Wodak, Ruth 74
words, importance of 9–10, 71, 110

EU authorised representative for GPSR:
Easy Access System Europe, Mustamäe tee 50,
10621 Tallinn, Estonia
gpsr.requests@easproject.com